90.1 - 6
ADK0764

10651245

WITHDRAWN
SMU LIBRARIES

LIBRARIES
Southern Methodist University
Dallas, Texas 75275

RELIGION AND SOCIETY IN THE AMERICAN WEST

Historical Essays

Edited by
Carl Guarneri
David Alvarez
Saint Mary's College of California

UNIVERSITY
PRESS OF
AMERICA

Lanham • New York • London

Copyright © 1987 by

University Press of America,® Inc.

4720 Boston Way
Lanham, MD 20706

3 Henrietta Street
London WC2E 8LU England

All rights reserved

Printed in the United States of America

British Cataloging in Publication Information Available

Library of Congress Cataloging-in-Publication Data

Religion and society in the American West.

   ''All but one of the essays ... presented in earlier
versions at a conference on religion in the American
West in June 1984 at Saint Mary's College of
California''—Acknowledgments.
   Includes bibliographies and index.
   1. West (U.S.)—Religion—Congresses. 2. Religion
and sociology—West (U.S.)—Congresses. I. Guarneri,
Carl, 1950   II. Alvarez, David J.
BL2527.W47R44 1987   291'.0978   87-10591
ISBN 0-8191-6431-3 (alk. paper)
ISBN 0-8191-6432-1 (pbk. : alk. paper)

"Reluctant Polygamists" © 1987 by Lawrence Foster
"Church Life Among Filipinos in Central California"
© 1987 by Edwin B. Almirol

All University Press of America books are produced on acid-free
paper which exceeds the minimum standards set by the National
Historical Publication and Records Commission.

Acknowledgments

All but one of the essays which appear in this volume were presented in earlier versions at a conference on Religion in the American West in June 1984 at Saint Mary's College of California. Both the conference and this book owe their existence to many persons, some of whom the editors would like to acknowledge directly. Brother William Beatie, FSC, Academic Vice President at Saint Mary's College of California, encouraged the development of a symposium on western religion and supported it generously. Mary Lou Rudd and Janna Brown assisted us in organizing and publicizing the event. The following persons served generously as moderators and commentators, in many cases providing insights and suggestions that greatly improved the essays: Lynn Dumenil, Philip Gleason, Harland Hogue, Gerald E. Jones, Rudolph Lapp, Charles LeWarne, Leo Lyman, Henry F. May, Irena Narell, John C. Scott, Lawrence Scrivani, and James P. Walsh. After the conference, Gerald Eisman expedited the editorial process with his computer skills. Finally, the entire manuscript was read by Catherine Albanese, Mario DePillis, and Stephen J. Stein; the editors and contributors benefited from their comments and criticism, but of course claim sole responsibility for the results.

C.G. and D.A.

Contents

Contents

VI Social Christianity in the City

VII Communal Sects and New Religions

Introduction

Carl Guarneri

In the hills behind Salt Lake City, at the western end of Emigration Canyon, a monument to Brigham Young stands at the spot where he halted the great westward trek of the Mormons. "This is the place," Young reportedly declared when he looked down upon the site where the Mormon vanguard had begun plowing. Today the statue points toward the regular, clean streets of modern Salt Lake City, with the Temple at their center, the mecca for Mormons throughout the West and indeed the world. But a hundred miles to the west, across a sheet of baked white salt, there stands another kind of mecca. Behind a rise and a pile of rocks on the border between Utah and Nevada lies tiny Wendover, a collection of gas stations, housing for the nearby Air Force Base--and glittering gambling casinos. On the main street a sixty-foot neon cowboy beckons the traveler from dry and virtuous Utah, his mechanical arm pointing to the gambling house below. As if in response to Brigham Young, the blinking message at his feet declares: "*This* is the place."

From the earliest settlement by American whites there have been divergent definitions of the West. Though not always gaining the upper hand, religious programs and images have coexisted and competed with secular ones. Yet the saga of the gold rush migrants and other pioneers, of gamblers, ranchers, cowboys and Indians has dominated historical treatment of the West. Popular magazines, movies and television have turned the adventure and violence of the West's early days into a multi-million dollar industry. Professional historians and amateur buffs draw a more comprehensive and realistic picture of western history, but they too have fixed upon the familiar frontier themes of conflict, settlement and development. There are signs that things are changing. Local and denominational historians have all along been chronicling the growth and influence of religious institutions, and recently the theme of religion was the subject of a special issue of *Journal of the West*.[1] Still, with the exception of the Mormons and the Spanish missions--the latter often romanticized beyond recognition--general attention has not been paid to the role of religion in shaping this distinctive and colorful region. Even the latest "state-of-the-field" anthology on western history includes (apart from an essay on Mormonism) only two paragraphs on religion in the West, one of which bemoans scholars' neglect of "the extensive impact of churches and ministers on western culture."[2]

Given this neglect, it is not surprising that western developments have not entered the larger story of religion in America. A search through the most respected scholarly histories of American religion--by William Warren Sweet, Winthrop Hudson, Sidney Mead, Martin Marty and Sydney Ahlstrom--yields a few remarks on the California missions and extensive sections on the Mormons, but almost nothing further on the West. In most cases the description of home misssions ends in the 1830's at the Mississippi River.[3] As Eldon Ernst has written, "It is as if the western two-thirds of the nation, beyond Chicago, did not exist."[4]

This book is an attempt to redress the balance. Defining the West as the present-day Pacific, Rocky Mountain and Southwestern states, the essays collected here explore areas where religion influenced western social life and public policy or was influenced by them--a field which scholars call the social history of religion. Some essays offer thematic or topical overviews of the region, others present detailed case histories. While most are framed in conventional narratives, some explore new approaches, such as Mary Lyons's rhetorical analysis of Father Yorke's sermons or Lawrence Foster's anthropological look at Mormon polygamy. A few authors make explicit comparisons with other sections of the United States, though most bridge the question of comparison only by implication or inference. Nevertheless, from the variety of subjects and approaches common themes emerge.

One of these themes is what Eldon Ernst calls secularity. The image of a "godless" frontier is surely an exaggeration, but with the exception of Utah the Far West still has the highest percentage of "unchurched" persons in America. As Robert Baird recognized in the 1840s, distance from older settled regions has meant distance from their churches as well. In some cases western migrants left religion entirely behind amid what Baird called the "engrossing cares and manifold temptations" of the frontier; but in others they evolved new, less austere creeds. Evidence that more secularized versions of religion have taken root in the West is rife in contemporary California. But Tony Fels's essay suggests that even in the nineteenth century the beliefs and rituals of Freemasonry acted as a watered-down substitute for evangelical piety, providing all the religion many western males required.

Of course, established denominations were not about to surrender without a fight. The atmosphere of secularity called out an internal missionary effort to "tame the West," a process of building churches and schools which would instill discipline and moral restraint among Anglo pioneers seduced by the lawless isolation of the frontier. Here western women played a conspicuously large role. In addition to the quiet heroism of missionary wives in isolated outposts or on railroad churches, a more public and autonomous role for women emerged from the special conditions of pioneer life, as the career of Eliza R. Snow of the Mormons demonstrated, and the lives of several "gentile" counterparts further attested.

In the minds of many new settlers the beliefs of indigenous Indians and Hispanic colonists were further evidence that the West meant moral degeneration. These occasioned yet another missionary effort, a huge and complex enterprise that drew upon the energies of pioneer churchmen. The names of Archbishop Lamy, Fathers Serra and De Smet, Marcus Whitman and Sheldon Jackson are enshrined in western regional history. Less well known are the careers of Methodist John Beeson in Oregon, indigenous converts of the Southwest like José Ynes Perea, or twentieth-century Baptist missionaries along the rails. Beeson's surprising openness to Indian religion and culture was the exception; Protestant and Catholic clergy most often brought not simply a religious message but a set of values and codes of behavior which, as Frances Campbell notes, they expected indigenous peoples to adopt. On both counts they met resistance.

Ethnic minorities cling to distinctive versions of traditional faiths because they often lend dignity to a disparaged group and provide stability in a changing world, Edwin Almirol's essay on the California Filipinos argues. And to this day, according to Jeffrey Burns's account, the popular religious traditions and practices of the huge Hispanic minority of California especially remain a "problem" for the Catholic church to which most nominally belong.

In the vast spaces of the West this drama of religious diversity has played itself out in especially interesting ways because no one group dominated the others. On the West Coast mainline Protestants did not enjoy the hegemony of back East; Catholics, Mormons and other groups were large enough to be a major force. Inside the Catholic Church the huge Hispanic contingent struggled with the Irish hierarchy to have its own clergy and saints. While such diversity frequently bred conflict and competition it also fostered a greater degree of mutual toleration. William Toll's essay on Jews in the West, for example, shows how on the frontier Jews were accepted, even admired, because of their stable community life and capitalist values. The legends and rituals of Freemasonry, according to Tony Fels, served as common platform for a wide range of non-evangelical believers, including many Jews. And in the career of José Ynes Perea, as presented by Mark Banker, we get a fascinating glimpse of the Southwestern mosaic: the wary but tolerant coexistence of Protestant and Catholic missionaries, and the native convert acting as cultural broker between Anglos and Hispanics.

For others who were victims of intolerance in the East, or perhaps carriers of exotic religious visions, the West has offered a place of refuge. The group involved could be as small and modest as William Keil's German pietists, whose transplantation to Oregon is analyzed by Patrick Harris. Or it could be as large and spectacularly successful as the Mormons. The important and unusual history of the Latter-Day Saints is the subject of essays by Lawrence Foster, Maureen Beecher and Guy Bishop, each confronting differently the characteristic problem of harmonizing individual freedom with religious community on the frontier.

Thanks to this atmosphere of relative tolerance and diversity the history of religion in the West is, at least in part, a story of innovation. Sometimes innovation has taken the form of new religions; at other times it has meant the transformation of older American religious traditions by the West. The great historian of the American frontier, Frederick Jackson Turner, never analyzed the role of religion in the West or its transformation on western soil. But a generation after Turner the Methodist historian William Warren Sweet developed a kind of religious "frontier thesis." In *The Story of Religions in America* (1930), Sweet argued that continuous contact with the frontier was the most significant influence upon American religion, breeding a more liberal attitude toward doctrine, multiplying small sects, and fostering greater acceptance of revivalist methods. The essays in this volume do not address Sweet's argument, which has by now been carried beyond the West into a debate on international versus indigenous American religion.[5] They provide colorful evidence, however, of the varied impact the West has had upon American religion. Salvatore Mondello's appreciative description of railroad churches demonstrates how, faced with a widely scattered population, Baptist missionaries in the West used the railroads to revive their commitment to itinerant evangelization after the Civil War. Ronald Isetti's sensitive and ironic portrayal of Catholic higher education in California suggests that conditions in the West--and perhaps in America as a whole--caused the rival Jesuits and Christian Brothers to converge upon a blend of classical and vocational education. Eldon Ernst's discussion of John Muir implies that in the Far West the Protestant idea of wilderness metamorphosed from a negative symbol of isolation and sinfulness into an inspiring image of God's handiwork and humanity's revitalization. Finally, if Mormon Utah shows the success of religious colonization in the West, the histories of Aurora and San Bernardino make it clear that the frontier's cheap land and its isolation from churchly authority could also destroy attempts to achieve organic religious community.

All these examples fit within the conventional notion that American religion, like the nation itself, began in the East and moved westward across the continent. From an eastern perspective the West has been the place "out there" toward which people and ideas move from their original home. Increasingly, however, the West has itself become the seedbed of new religions. At the edge of the continent, it is the port of entry for variants of Asian Buddhism and Hinduism. And at the "cutting edge" of America's future it has seen new religious movements, from late nineteenth century "New Thought" to contemporary California's cornucopia of sects and "cults," prosper and then spread throughout the nation. This "eastward movement" of new American religions is represented in this collection by James McBride's history of Reverend Moon's Unification Church.

We must be careful not to exaggerate the distinctiveness of western religion. Many aspects of its history are similar to the dominant American patterns, perhaps more so as the trends of urbanization and secularization become nationwide. As long ago as 1955, Earl Pomeroy called for a reorientation of western history away from Turner's emphasis on distinctiveness, stressing instead the continuities between East and West Coast experiences.[6] Several essays in this collection present evidence that western religion replicated eastern trends and conflicts. Catherine Curry's narrative of the origins of San Francisco's school systems recalls the public-private school conflict in New York City just a decade earlier. Tony Fels's careful examination of Masonic religion and membership in San Francisco needs to be compared with other local studies, but its findings complement several national patterns portrayed in a recent overview of modern American freemasonry.[7] The Black churches in Civil War era California, as described by Larry Murphy, appear to have played a role similar to those in other Northern cities. Perhaps most strikingly, a trio of essays on the western Social Gospel--Douglas Anderson's on the Christian Socialist J. Stitt Wilson, Dale Soden's on Seattle's fundamentalist Mark Matthews, and Mary Lyons's on the Catholic activist Peter C. Yorke--describe a range of Christian social thought that could be found, with minor variations, in other American cities of the Progressive era.

One need not argue that religion in the American West was unique in order to justify giving it more attention. Disproving western "exceptionalism" may be as important as demonstrating it. It is enough to say that the West has been the scene of religious events and movements which have profoundly influenced millions of Americans in that section and in the nation as a whole. Whatever the generalizations that may emerge after many case studies are undertaken, religious developments in the West deserve to be included in the history of American religion--and by implication, the history of American society. This collection begins that task.

Inevitably in such a sampling important individuals, groups and movements are neglected. Besides Frederick Norwood's glimpse at white missionary attitudes toward Indians, this book includes no study of Native American religion and its interaction with Anglo-Christianity.[8] Other subjects which deserve more than passing mention may readily come to the reader's mind: religious beliefs among Chinese and Japanese Americans, religious questions in politics, the impact of non-Christian religions from Asia. In some cases these omissions reflect the availability of particular studies for this volume. In others they suggest where good scholarship has been lacking. The editors hope that such gaps will serve as challenges to researchers rather than affronts to the groups or interests involved. For the present, Eldon Ernst's sweeping overview and the fine bibliography in the notes accompanying it ably summarize the work that has been done; while his eloquent interpretations suggest what may emerge from future scholarship.

Notes

1. *Journal of the West*, 23 (January 1984). See also the special issue of *Listening: Journal of Religion and Culture*, 19 (Fall 1984), on "Religion in the American West."

2. Michael P. Malone, ed., *Historians and the American West* (Lincoln: University of Nebraska Press, 1983). The quotation is from Richard W. Etulain's essay, "Shifting Interpretations of Western American Cultural History," 423.

3. William Warren Sweet, *The Story of Religion in America*, revised and enlarged ed. (New York: Harper & Row, 1950); Winthrop S. Hudson, *Religion in America* (New York: Charles Scribner's Sons, 1965); Sidney E. Mead, *The Lively Experiment: The Shaping of Christianity in America* (New York: Harper & Row, 1963); Martin E. Marty, *Righteous Empire: The Protestant Experience in America* (New York: Dial Press, 1970); and Sydney E. Ahlstrom, *A Religious History of the American People* (New Haven: Yale University Press, 1972). Marty's most recent synthesis, however, contains much more material on the Far West. See Martin E. Marty, *Pilgrims in Their Own Land: 500 Years of Religion in America* (Boston: Little, Brown, 1984).

4. Eldon G. Ernst, "Winthrop S. Hudson and the Great Tradition of American Religious Historiography," *Foundations* 23 (April-June 1980): 113.

5. See, for example, Winthrop S. Hudson, "How American is Religion in America?" in Jerald C. Brauer, ed., *Reinterpretations in American Church History* (Chicago: University of Chicago Press, 1968), 153-167.

6. Pomeroy, "Toward a Reorientation of Western History: Continuity and Environment," *Mississippi Valley Historical Review* 41 (March 1955): 579-600.

7. Lynn Dumenil, *Freemasonry and American Culture, 1880-1930* (Princeton: Princeton University Press, 1984).

8. For a summary and bibliography of the literature, see Ake Hultkrantz, *The Religions of the American Indians* (Berkeley: University of California Press, 1979). A recent critique of American religious historiography along these lines is Robert S. Michaelson, "Red Man's Religion/White Man's History," *Journal of the American Academy of Religion* 51 (1983): 667-684.

I

An Overview

1.
American Religious History From a Pacific Coast Perspective

Eldon G. Ernst

In 1492 some European adventurers and some native peoples of the Americas discovered one another. The Europeans, thinking at first that they successfully had reached Asia by sailing westward across the Atlantic Ocean, named their new aquaintances Indians who inhabited these West Indies. As Christian Europeans continued to come to this New World they began to conquer and evangelize the Indians, whom they regarded as savages with souls to be saved and cultures to be civilized. The American Indians, of great variety, had lived religiously for thousands of years before being confronted by European Christians. Some had developed highly sophisticated cultures. Originally they had migrated to the Americas through the North Pacific Coast, and indeed they were of Asian ancestry. They had come from Siberia and other Pacific locations, though probably not from India.[1] But only the Europeans kept historical records; and they concentrated on their Old World culture engaging those of the New World, each being transformed in the process of this trans-Atlantic westward movement.

This dramatic historic encounter a half-millennium ago introduced certain permanent themes in the subsequent religious history of the American people: the mixing of diverse migrating peoples who settle in a vast untamed wilderness; the transforming of parts of the wilderness into societies of heterogeneous populace; the transplanting and experimenting with cultural-religious expressions in which innovation and tradition enter into unresolved dialectic. When viewed from the Pacific side of the northern continent, with focus on the land eventually nationalized as the United States of America, these themes assume distinctive qualities. The international, interracial, intercultural engagements predominate; the wilderness environment obsesses; secularity surrounds a relatively balanced plurality of new religious movements and old religious traditions.

The Spanish and Russian Connections

From a Pacific Coast perspective, North American religious history began to take shape in the seventeenth century, when Spain became concerned about colonial competitors for the New World and moved defensively into its New Mexican frontier along the southwestern border of North America.[2] There the Spanish related to native Pueblo Indians through military and Christian mission institutions. Meanwhile Northern Europeans began moving into the Atlantic Coast of North America, where in the New England colonies Protestant Christianity began to make indelible impressions. When by the eighteenth century French, Dutch, British, and finally Russian explorers probed the Pacific Coast, Spain extended its mission and *presidio* system up the California Coast.

In July 1769, on the eve of the American Revolution, the Spanish Catholic mission of San Diego de Alcala was founded along with a nearby *presidio*. For the next fifteen years Father Junipero Serra led the remarkable extension of California Franciscan missions--a process that would reach a total of twenty-one outposts planted as far north as Sonoma, just beyond San Francisco Bay.[3] Around these missions many thousands of native Indians came into close enough contact with Spanish Franciscans to become baptized Christians. At best some Indians benefitted from Franciscan spirituality and European technology; at worst many Indians died from imported diseases; overall, much of the Indians' cultural heritage was emasculated. By the turn of the century this Spanish religious (mission) and secular (*presidio*) enterprise reached its maximum strength and prosperity. Then, as Mexico sought independence from Spain, the missions' life-line became diverted and threatened; and this happened just as another social-religious enterprise from the North was challenging Spain's brief hegemony in California.

At the northernmost point of Western New Spain, around the San Francisco Bay, the Spanish confronted Russian explorers and settlers plus the Aleut Indians who accompanied them. The Russians had crossed the Bering Straits in 1740; by the end of the century, about the time the United States ratified its Federal Constitution, they began moving South from their Alaskan colonial settlements. With this Russian connection, where Latin Catholic Orthodoxy met Greek Orthodoxy in frontier California, an old era ended and a new one began in far western American religious history.[4]

In the year 1812, as the United States battled the British on the Atlantic side of the Continent, the Russian American Company established Fort Ross three thousand miles to the West near Bodega Bay on the Pacific Coast. There they built an Orthodox chapel. For the next twenty-nine years the settlement thrived. During those years Mexico won its independence from Spain, the California Franciscan Missions declined, the United States declared its Monroe Doctrine in 1823 and began moving westward. The Russians continuously negotiated with Spain, then Mexico, England, the United States, and the Californios for possession of North American land.

But these negotiations failed. In 1841 the Russians left Fort Ross, and in 1867 they left Alaska. But an Orthodox diocese had taken root from these early plantings. Eventually the Russian Bishop moved his seat from Sitka to San Francisco. The Orthodox presence persevered, and Fort Ross became a time and a place to be recalled by later Orthodox immigrants to the United States. The historic parameters of this North American tradition became clarified in 1963 when a Russian Orthodox deputation from the Soviet Union celebrated worship in the chapel at Fort Ross, bringing to memory the great Russian priest, Ivan Veniaminov, Bishop of Alaska and Metropolitan of Moscow, who had visited the same chapel in the 1830's.[5]

By the time the Russians departed from Fort Ross in 1841, the United States' occupation and ultimate conquest of far western territories had become apparent. Boundaries had yet to be determined, but the Americans' vision was grandiose. The Lewis and Clark expedition in 1804, followed by Christian missionaries in the 1830's, opened the Oregon Territory to American settlements. After Mexican Independence in 1821, United States citizens began migrating into Texas--Christian missionaries among them. Meanwhile California had become the focus of American interests not only for continental expansion but as an access to Asian ports as well. The Russian activity helped catalyze international contentions for control of the Pacific Coast. In 1841, as the Russians pulled out, the United States Navy increased its Pacific Squadron. By the end of the decade, through battles and negotiations America had annexed the Southwest from Mexico, the Northwest from England, and brought California into Statehood--all in the religiously colored ideology and emotion of "manifest destiny." Then "the world rushed in," spurred at first by gold but soon by other opportunities as well. With these migrations came the religious transformation of the now United States Far West.[6]

The New Tradition of American Religious Historiography

In the year 1844, America's "year of decision" for manifest destiny conquest, an original narrative analysis of *Religion In America* by Presbyterian Robert Baird was printed in the United States.[7] The book gained a wide American reading and was reprinted in a revised edition in 1856. If not in the literary class of such contemporary works as Hawthorne's *The Scarlet Letter* (1850), Melville's *Moby Dick* (1851), Stowe's *Uncle Tom's Cabin* (1852), or Thoreau's *Walden* (1854), Baird's book became a classic in its field. The story it told contained the immediate background and substance of the next stage of the American religious experience in the Far West.

Religion in the westward-expanding nation of the 1840s and 1850s expressed the dynamic fervor of the times. Immigration had multiplied religious traditions. Freedom and space for innovation expanded further the range of religious variety. Revivalism swept Eastern cities and frontier alike. Millennialism, prophecy, spiritualism, holiness perfectionism, utopianism, and new revelations to charismatic leaders swept through society. In 1844 the new Mormon religious community underwent crisis with the murder of Joseph Smith in Nauvoo, Illinois, after which the newly appointed leader, Brigham Young, led them en masse on their epic trek to Utah. Meanwhile in Western New York William Miller and his followers waited intensely but in vain for the coming of Christ. The Oneida Community flourished, as did the Shakers. In New England Henry David Thoreau went to jail briefly for his civil disobedient stand in protest of a war he believed would extend slavery into the Southwest. Frederick Douglass railed eloquently against the barbarism of a nation that would condone human slavery. At Seneca Falls, New York, a convention met in a Methodist Church to formulate a Woman's Rights declaration in 1848; and five years later Antoinette Brown Blackwell became the first American woman to be fully ordained to Christian ministry. Churches divided as Civil War approached. They divided also over the reductionism of popular evangelicalism, as Old School Presbyterians, Confessional Lutherans, High Church Episcopalians, and Old Landmark Baptists labored to recover their distinctive traditions. Yet evangelical fervor predominated in North and South, even as the growing immigrant Roman Catholic Church became organized on a national scale. All the while, mission societies and religious orders organized to carry these messages and activities into the settlements of the West, and to the world beyond.

With remarkable skill and range of insight, Robert Baird described and interpreted much of this religious life in ante-bellum America. He traced its historic roots and major developing traditions. He mapped its geographical context, noting in some detail that the Far West beyond the Rocky Mountains remained largely untamed wilderness but surely would become settled and part of American Christian civilization. He analyzed the religion and tragic cultural experience of American Indians, whom he expected to be squeezed into western reservations and there perhaps Christianized. He evaluated the challenges and opportunities confronting Christian traditions in a land of enormous space, continual new immigration, religious plurality and religious freedom. As for "natives of the Atlantic slope" and immigrants from abroad who moved to the American Far West, Baird described their "peculiar exposure to evil":

7

Their removal almost always withdraws them from the powerful influence of neighborhoods where true religion more or less flourishes. Such of them as are not decidedly religious in heart and life, greatly risk losing any good impressions they may have brought with them, amid the engrossing cares and manifold temptations of their new circumstances; circumstances in which even the established Christians will find much need of redoubled vigilance and prayer.[8]

Robert Baird originated a tradition of American religious historiography that in some ways has moved far beyond the limits of his Protestant imperial interpretation but that in geographical orientation has not maintained his largest vision. Most historians of American religion have ignored the Far West, and historians of the Far West have neglected religion.[9]

The early frontier years have received most of the attention--the period of Baird's own lifetime and the religious activity of his day. Missionaries sent by Eastern churches to labor, mostly in vain, among the Nez Perces, Flathead, and Cayuse Indians of the Oregon Country in the 1830s and 1840s, for example, often are recalled as paving the way for pioneer migrations along the Oregon trail. Methodists Jason and Daniel Lee, Presbyterians Marcus and Narcissa Prentice Whitman along with Henry H. and Eliza Spalding, Baptists Ezra Fisher and Hezekiah Johnson, Belgium Catholic Pierre Jean De Smet and French Catholics Francois Norbert Blanchet and Modeste Demers are names em-bedded in the memory of subsequent Pacific Northwest culture.[10]

Similar frontier names appear in the annals of other far western territories, such as Presbyterian Sheldon Jackson in the Rocky Mountain region and Catholics Joseph Machebeuf and Archbishop John Lamy in the Southwest. They represent a momentous transitional stage between the colonial Spanish Catholic mission heritage of the Southwest and the next period of Anglo-American dominated culture.[11] But the far western religious history of the United States during the later nineteenth century, and especially the twentieth century, remains largely untold.

Geography and Demography

From a Pacific Coast perspective, Hawaii and Asia being across the Pacific Ocean to the West, the Rocky Mountains bordering the East, British Columbia and Alaska to the North, and Mexico to the South, the story of American religious history since 1850 takes form and meaning in several regional versions.[12]

Catholic New Spain had permeated the mountains, canyons, and deserts of the Southwest--a legacy apparent in such cities as Santa Fe, Albuquerque, Tucson, and Phoenix. The Spanish-Mexican-Indian heritage represents a diverse fusion of religious cultures whose historical memory reaches to ancient America as well as to Europe. Its Christian festivals, sacraments, art and symbols persevered in the unique mosaic of regional Catholicism that developed in New Mexico when integrated with the slow but dominating cultural impact of Anglo-American missionaries and settlers. Its presence remained a factor in American manifest destiny ideology and emotion through the nation's war with Mexico and later with Spain. Today this religious culture has been reinvigorated as Hispanic immigrants from Mexico and other Latin American countries comprise a rapidly increasing proportion of the far western United States population.

In contrast to New Mexico, the Pacific Northwest became a United States Territory in the primarily British colonial context of the Hudson's Bay Company, which linked the region to the religious orientations of New England and British Columbia. Here no solid fusion of native American and European cultures occurred, though Protestant and Catholic missionaries met Indians before settlers arrived. Indians and white settlers then co-existed, with little lasting rapport. British and Northern European-rooted Christians, especially Methodists, Scottish Presbyterians, Baptists, Dutch Reformed and Scandinavian Lutherans, along with solid Roman Catholic and Jewish minorities contributed to the religious influence in such cities as Seattle and Tacoma, Portland and Salem, Spokane and Boise. Religious institutions did not have a strong impact on this regional society, however, where the large majority of people never affiliated with churches.

Often portrayed as pioneers of the last frontier, thereafter rather isolated from the rest of the nation geographically and in their independent social spirit, people of the Northwest have lived conscientiously close to the mountaineous forests, the valley fields, and along the waterways of nature. In their work and play most have maintained a committed secularity. A remarkably diverse people seeking the good life on their own terms, among whom organized religion has struggled creatively but met with dogged resistance, Northwesterners have defined a major strand of the far western ethos.

Between the Northwest and the Southwest at the inland center, spreading outward in all directions from an urban hub surrounded by great mountains, a great lake, and great desert-like flats, as if symbolizing a wilderness people's drive to be salt of the earth, looms a religious empire of Latter Day Saints both uniquely American and unique in America. Here at Deseret, the new wilderness zion at the crossroads of the West in Utah Territory, the Mormons brought their newly discovered ancient history to bear on their sense of prophetic mission. Whereas in Hispanic Christianity, Spanish Catholic orthodoxy was brought from the Old World to the New World where it mixed with native American cultures, *The Book Of Mormon* revealed a heterodox Christian theology that identified American Indians as descendents of peoples from the ancient House of Israel who had migrated to the New World. Yet few Indians became Saints in the Latter Day. Among the Utah population at large, however, in contrast with the largely unchurched Northwest, Mormons gained a religious dominance in numbers and social influence unsurpassed elsewhere in American history. With evangelistic zeal and a disciplined, structured life style Mormons became a major religious force in the twentieth century American Far West.

Finally, California represents a distinctive region while relating to all other parts of the American Far West. Its stark geographical contrasts between waterways and deserts, mountains and valley farmlands, urban centers and vast areas of sparse population have been matched by its dramatic cultural-religious diversity. Religious traditions and religious innovations have flourished alongside celebrated secularity. From San Francisco and the Sonoma-Napa Valley southward through San Jose, Santa Clara, Monterey, Santa Barbara, Los Angeles, and San Diego, California touches the Hispanic Southwest heritage. From San Francisco and Stockton northward through Sacramento, Chico, Redding, Eureka, and Crescent City, California reaches toward the more Anglo-Protestant heritage. Eastward beyond the Sierra Nevadas beckons the Rocky Mountain country, symbolized perhaps by the golden Mormon Church steeple reaching to the sky in the Oakland Hills. If California Indians received one kind of mixed blessing from the Franciscan missions, they experienced little blessing at all from the subsequent onslaught of white settlers. The Californios represented a connecting link between the Hispanic South and the Anglo-European North, but they too became swallowed up in the flow of new migrations. Among the newcomers were Black pioneers, as California entered the Union a Free State. But the most distinctive California contribution to far western cultural-religious history was the flow of Asian immigrants, whose presence after the mid-nineteenth century greatly expanded the dimensions of the story.

California has brought a certain integrative unity to the entire far western experience even as it has affected the nation as a whole. Americans with a California dream could wander and settle almost anywhere west of the Rockies and feel pretty much at home, if not always at ease, in Zion.[13]

Clearly these four regions of the American Far West find religious definition in their demography as well as their geography.[14] By 1912 the Territories of New Mexico, Utah, Oregon, and California had become eleven States in the Union, joined in 1959 by Alaska and Hawaii. Within this far western third of the nation arose several major urban centers and hundreds of small towns separated and surrounded by a vast wilderness of mountain chains, deserts and canyons, plains and farmlands, rivers and lakes, bays and the ocean. Two-thirds of the Nation's public lands are contained in this one-third of the Continent. From crude overland trails and primitive coastal docks to modern railroads, highways, seaports and airports the land opened to the peoples of the world. Their religious life, usually undergoing upheaval and adjustments, has developed into unusual flux and diffusion, innovation and plurality.

All of United States history is a story of immigration. What distinguishes the Far West is the degree to which a wide variety of peoples came from many places to build new societies in relatively free competition and cooperation. Unlike the long-developing New England colonial societies, no cultural-religious hegemony had laid a social foundation of the Far West before the great migrations began.[15] Even the descendents of the Spanish-Mexican frontier quickly became an American frontier minority. Each region presented distinctive circumstances for this mixing of peoples, and overall, most religious groups came to know both majority and minority experiences as well as general equality.

A frequently disdained minority in most places, for example, Mormons finally enjoyed advantage in Utah. There Protestants and Catholics have struggled to maintain influence as minorities.[16] If the more Catholic Southwest historically provided an interesting context for Presbyterian missions, so did the more Protestant Northwest produce noteworthy Jesuit and Jewish histories.[17] Moreover, as we observe the impact of Anglo-Christians in the Southwest, so we might trace the migrations of Hispanic Christians into the Northwest.[18] In California the religious *potpourri* has presented peculiar opportunities and obstacles. The distinctive Irish, Italian, French, and German San Francisco Catholic communities could enjoy some of the religious mainstream advantages that accrued nationally to the major Protestant denominations, while at the Golden Gate Protestants became the major minority alongside smaller Jewish and Buddhist communities.[19] Los Angeles offers a variation on this theme, with late-nineteenth-century Protestant strength followed by cosmopolitan Catholic growth and one of the largest Jewish communities in the Nation.[20] California also attracted the religiously health-minded, as diverse as Seventh Day Adventists, Christian Scientists, and varieties of New Thought advocates who found the natural and social climate conducive to their free expression.[21]

Not all enjoyed equal status or opportunity, however. Black citizens and other racial minorities struggled to survive in emerging white power structures. In the Far West these structures had to be formed and reformed under new sets of circumstances. Native American Indians, Hispanic Americans, African Americans, and Asian Americans all contributed richly to far western religious culture from their respective oppressed circumstances.[22]

Likewise European immigrants brought religious traditions outside the range of American white Anglo-Saxon Christian heritage. Fact and myth combined in the images of the Far West that had drawn them to beauty and opportunity, but also savagery and hardship, in their new homeland.[23] Yet they adjusted to life in the Far West without quite the harsh stigmas and class restrictions common in more established American Eastern cities and towns. Consequently the older stock American pioneers and their descendents also found religious adjustment to the far western environment necessary. If Yankee, southern, and midwestern-rooted pioneers, who altogether had the advantage of numbers and the power of native American citizenship in the Far West, intended to mold society into the image of their eastern cultural forms, they had to compete not only with natives but also with other strangers in the land. The Far West qualified all definitions of the religious mainstream and all pretensions to Christian hegemony.

Wilderness and Society

The wilderness, and errands into it, is an early and recurring theme in American religious historiography.[24] Spacious land provided the opportunity for holy experiments, whether understood as religious innovations, perfecting of traditions, or molding of public society. Yet the wilds of nature also threatened traditions, and material opportunity qualified lofty spiritual motives. Some rejoiced at the breath of fresh air, while others lamented the loss of high culture. Religious incentive varied; for some the frontier was the opportunity for social innovation, for others the cause for social reform.

In the Far West, wilderness untamed has offered spectacular beauty in contrasting forms and gigantic proportions. It also has contained plentiful natural resources available for human social benefit. To celebrate and preserve the natural environment for its own sake and for human enjoyment, or to develop and consume its resources for the sake of society and human needs--these tensions have engaged religious and political sensibilities.

Neither Emerson nor Thoreau, from their socially refined lodgings, could deeply appreciate the nature of far western wilderness. Rather it was John Muir (1838-1914), of Scottish birth, who truly experienced and described the far western sense of the beauty in untamed wilderness. Eclectic shades of transcendentalism, Christian orthodoxy, and pagan-like animism colored his wilderness preaching. He discerned scientifically the minute variations of nature while emotionally embracing the whole. He lobbied politically for conservation legislation even as he roamed in wilderness areas from Arizona to Alaska, over some of the "sacred mountains of the world." Those mountains and the cultured lands around them found twentieth-century appreciation and portrayal in the artful photography of Ansel Adams (1902-1984). For nearly thirty years he helped direct the Sierra Club, whose wilderness advocacy has permeated some circles of far western thinking with spiritual zeal and moral campaigning since it began under John Muir's presidency in 1892.[25]

Worship liturgies have proclaimed divine creativity in mountains and canyons, even as they taught in parables the planting of seeds and the harvesting of souls. Moral theologies and social ethics have pondered the meaning and implications of the biblical dictum that humankind should have dominion over the earth. Trapping, foresting, farming, mining, drilling, and damming the waterways have supplied people's felt needs, livelihoods, and commercial profits. Industrial plants and agribusiness have produced magnificently, but at great cost. Husbandry has not always prevailed. Resources have declined; the elements have become polluted; natural beauty has been blighted. In question is the relationship of the spiritual and the material--a profoundly religious question. One Far Western theologian has probed the historic issue by affirming that "we ourselves are not merely members of the human community, but also elements in the natural world."[26] Our regard for physical environment and our consequent behavior within it affect the quality of our society. An environment of space, freedom, and resources promising opportunity for the pursuit of happiness has been a theme affecting far western life styles, values, and views of human life. Perhaps no better expression of this theme can be found in secular form since the turn of the century than *Sunset*, "the magazine of Western living."[27] Religion vital to the people, whether appropriated and expressed in formal institutions or in less structured modes, has grappled with the conservation of resources and with the ecological aspects of human society.

The problems and possibilities of trying to create a society worthy of the natural beauty surrounding it found ample philosophic-religious expression in such contemporaries of John Muir as Josiah Royce, Jack London and Frank Norris. University of California professor of geology and natural history, Joseph Le Conte, taught theistic evolution and probed the interaction of the spiritual and physical relationships of people and their natural environment. In Santa Rosa Luther Burbank experimented with the human touch in nature by creating varieties of plant life in the interest of new beauty and food productivity. Then he transferred this humanly-affected evolutionary process to the concept of creating a new society out of varieties of people. Developing the land and its resources for the new society would be the final twentieth century step.[28] At the same time such pioneer educators in far western society-building as David Starr Jordan of Stanford University and Benjamin Ide Wheeler of the University of California in Berkeley, the Christian Brothers of Saint Mary's College, and John Swett--the "Horace Mann of the Pacific"-- sought to develop public and private institutional ways to train people's minds, talents, toward social creativity.[29]

Through political legislation, education, and social services far western religious leaders joined in the efforts to build the good society. Here far western religious history coalesces with the national story long recited and documented by eastern-oriented historians, but with an important exception. Far western cities were being forged out of the wilderness, built from scratch by an unusual variety of peoples. Whereas older eastern cities being transformed by industrialism and new immigration required reform and reconstruction as the twentieth century dawned, far western cities were being built from a mixture of raw materials in which industrialism, immigration, and social institutions all began simultaneously. Needing reform from the time of its origins, this rapid urbanization proceded on a scale of utopian-like intentionality that ranged from haphazard laissez-faire faith to complex social planning and more than a few communal experiments.[30] Organized religion permeated and was permeated by this process.

Historians have suggested that the carriers of eastern American church traditions were purveyors of culture in the Far West.[31] Perhaps so, but qualifications are in order. Church leaders brought eastern cultural forms that made limited headway in far western conditions. Churches had to alter their style and priorities to make this adjustment, often to the chagrin of their eastern architects. It is not that far western culture was lacking; rather it assumed its own character and became more diverse than its eastern tradition-bearers intended. This combination of factors provides clues to modern American religious history from a Pacific Coast perspective.

Early church plantings in the urban Far West did involve the Euro-American Christian impulse. Protestants and Catholics built schools, hospitals, missions, and other social institutions. Witness the early efforts of Dominican Catholic Archbishop Joseph Alemany of San Francisco, for example, along with Episcopal Bishop William Ingraham Kip, Congregationalist Joseph Augustine Benton, Baptist Osgood C. Wheeler, Methodist William Taylor, Presbyterian Samuel Hopkins Willey, and above all Unitarian Thomas Starr King.[32] Along with these men and their successors throughout the Far West were the Catholic women religious, the Protestant women's mission societies, and the Ladies Hebrew Benevolent Societies, whose ministries and social services contributed much to the extension of religion in the social fabric. The Women's Christian Temperance Union, the suffrage movement, and the crusades for peace and preparedness, moreover, brought religious-minded women into the realm of civil politics.

Twentieth-Century Patterns

By the twentieth century this social fabric woven with new cloth followed patterns ranging from the most conservative to the most liberal, spanning the spectrum of Christian social thought and action common to other parts of the nation. Organized religion engaged the social and political movements identified with Progressivism, the New Deal, the Great Society and the New Left, as well as the Old and New Right that countered these. Even the Ku Klux Klan made appearances. The Pacific Northwest's early radical heritage was personified in Seattle's Marxist Anna Louise Strong, who helped inspire that city's general strike of 1919. In contrast, though never representing more than a small minority of citizens, Seattle's fundamentalist Presbyterian minister of national fame, Mark Matthews, pressed for evangelical moral reform with some local political clout. In California, Berkeley's evangelical Methodist clergyman, J. Stitt Wilson, utopian Christian socialist, served a term as mayor during his years of social activism in the Bay Area. Across the Bay, within the tradition of Catholic social thought expressed in the papal encyclical *Rerum Novarum* (1891), Father Peter Yorke championed the cause of Irish laborers on the San Francisco docks. In San Diego, also during the early twentieth century, black Baptist preacher George Washington Woodbey spoke and wrote for radical socialist reconstruction.[33]

These years of Progressive reform at the turn of the twentieth century marked a new stage in far western religious history. Frederick Jackson Turner had declared the frontier closed, but the westward movement continued unabated. The gold rush in Alaska and the Yukon Territory stimulated new migrations and urban development in places like Seattle and Portland. As urban growth began to mushroom in Los Angeles and expand in most far western states federal conservation legislation promised to preserve the wilderness environment. At the same time, the Spanish-American War both represented the culmination of the New England-New Spain contest for North America and opened new involvements of the United States in the Pacific Islands and Asia. Pacific Coast International Exhibitions in Portland, Seattle, San Francisco and San Diego cast imperial visions of the dawning new era. These events affected the churches' world and home mission activities, especially as the immigration doors to Latin American and Asian peoples were opened and then closed in controversial measures of social legislation. The 1915 Panama-Pacific International Exposition at San Francisco displayed these new forces dramatically, as ecumenical religious congresses focused upon social themes, immigration patterns, peace concerns, and, most popular of all, women and missions. These congresses, while not as spectacular as the 1893 World Parliament of Religions in Chicago, did demonstrate the evolving integration of far western religious life into the larger national experience--not only as regional versions of Eastern-oriented patterns but also as regional originators of religious phenomena of national impact and international dimensions.[34]

Relations of church and state, for example, require regional examination both for understanding the local dynamics of religion in society and for assessing the region's impact on federal policy. In the Far West such issues have surfaced according to the relative power and influence of religious institutions in each area. Issues have focused especially on government-church interaction in work with Indian tribes, on taxation (which especially in California has questioned the very definitions of church, clergy, and religion), and on education. Schools, where religious and secular often meet in their common concern for social values, offer interesting case studies. Minority churches have stressed parochial schools where public schools reflect religious imprints of majority religious traditions. These varied in Utah (Mormon dominance), New Mexico (Roman Catholic control), Oregon (Protestant strength), and California (pluralistic orientation). Prayer and Bible reading never were widely practiced in public schools on the Pacific Coast, where secular orientations rigorously guarded church-state separation. The issue of evolutionism versus creationism has surfaced periodically, reflecting pockets of fundamentalism in far western localities, such as the Geoscience Research Institute at Loma Linda, California. More far-reaching than all of these, however, have been strides toward equal opportunity for racial and ethnic minorities with the white Anglo majority, especially as reflected in issues of school integration and bilingual-bicultural instruction.[35]

The modern history of religion and society in the Far West has carried further the processes of pluralism and migration. By the turn of the twentieth century the basic demographic pattern had formed. Most church-related citizens belonged to the large Roman Catholic and Protestant denominations. Pacific Coast "secularity" contrasted with Rocky Mountain church adherence. The Mormon empire, after polygamy was abandoned in 1898, began its Americanization. Mormon expansion would continue unabated, shifting into high gear after 1940 when during the next generation membership grew four hundred percent. New westward migrations, especially those from the South with the dust bowl migration of the 1920s and 1930s, the stampede to Pacific Coast wartime industries after 1940, and the more recent Sun Belt migration, have increased the proportional membership of conservative evangelical churches such as Southern Baptists, holiness and pentecostal churches, and the Seventh Day Adventists.[36] The 1940s migration also greatly increased the Black Church population on the West Coast. But the most dramatic change in Far Western religious demography involves the continual migration of Hispanic and Asian peoples.[37]

Mexican immigrants began arriving in large numbers by the late nineteenth century to provide cheap labor for the prospering mining and agricultural industries of the Southwest. Alternately recruited and deported, depending upon the economic needs of agribusiness, these Spanish speaking peoples experienced almost unchecked exploitation under the "Emergency Labor Program" until in the 1960s Cesar Chavez and the United Farm Workers Movement began successfully to organize for social justice. Many immigrants, of course, remained and became United States citizens. Since changes in immigration laws came about during the early 1960s, new arrivals from Latin American countries, both legal and "undocumented," including Salvadoran and Guatemalan refugees in recent years, have surged into the millions. They have moved throughout the Far West and beyond in search of livelihood and sanctuary. Largely of Catholic identity, but also including many Protestants, these people have become a major segment of far western American Christianity and a primary agenda for the churches' social justice ministries.[38]

Asian immigration began when Chinese people joined the mid-nineteenth century rush for gold and became another of the Far West's exploited labor forces. After the 1882 Chinese Exclusion Act, Japanese immigration increased. Most were Buddhists. Christian domestic missions, however, led to the founding of denominational Chinese and Japanese churches. Koreans and Filipinos, among them Christians descended from European and American foreign missions, began arriving in limited numbers after the turn of the century. They, too, formed churches. Emigrants from India came to California by way of the Pacific Northwest after 1910, bringing South Asian expressions of Hindu, Muslim, Sikh, Jain, Buddhist, Parsis, and Christian institutions. After World War II, and especially with the revoking of the 1924 discriminatory immigration law in the early 1960s, Asian immigration greatly increased. Like Indian, African, and Hispanic Americans, Asian Americans have struggled for their just civil rights and cultural identity. The major twentieth century event that brought to the surface the religious and ethnic tensions of the new society in the Far West and the Nation as a whole came during World War II, when Japanese American citizens were forcefully relocated in wilderness camps at much cost of their life, liberty, and pursuit of happiness. During the 1970s Asian caucuses were formed in some of the major Christian denominations, and institutional Buddhism became increasingly rejuvenated. Most recently Vietnamese and Laotian refugees have brought yet another new dimension to the Asian American community.[39]

As the major urban areas of the United States are becoming increasingly non-Anglo-European in the ethnic identity of their population, the global dimensions of the nation's immigration history becomes all the more significant. In this and other ways the Far West, where society has formed on the broad base of a national-ethnic-racial convergence of peoples, presents an insightful perspective on American social history. And religion, which both transcends culture and expresses itself at the heart of culture, provides an entree into the shaping of far western society.

Regional and National Religion

What, then, might we hypothesize about religion and society in the American Far West? To suggest uniqueness or to exaggerate distinctiveness vis-a-vis other regions of the nation would be a mistake. Much far western religion came from the eastern United States and from other countries whose emigrants also settled in the eastern United States. Moreover, aspects of far western religious culture have moved eastward in the Nation as well. Regionalism, in other words, can be misleading if examined in a vacuum. But neither can regionalism be ignored if the national picture is to be seen in its fullness. Religion may transcend times and places, but it actually lives only in times and places. Religion in the American Far West reflects and penetrates its regional cultural ethos, which helps locate both its distinctive qualities and its commonality with religion in other social contexts. Following are some ideas on these similarities and differences, generalizations that remain to be tested by comprehensive historical investigation.

Recalcitrant far western churches, not quite in tune with their eastern-based denominational structures, customs, and priorities, have asserted their independence. They have neglected (not ignored) the historic traditions of doctrine and practice, even the history itself, that eastern centers have cared more to preserve. Yet they have not produced their own traditions of theology in systematic literary form, although themes of ecology, liberation, and pluralism have drawn upon far western experience in modern theological expression. Neglect of traditionalism has not prevented--indeed it may help account for--instances of extreme sectarian-like expressions of religious traditions in the Far West. Likewise, new religious movements have been especially common on the Pacific Coast since the mid-nineteenth century. They have been present, too, in other parts of America; but in the Far West they have not contrasted so markedly with surrounding cultural and religious traditions that elsewhere had molded social institutions and community experience. In this sense the Far West manifests a certain secularity despite the history of a large variety of religious institutions and expressions in the region. The Spanish missions represent a religious past remembered almost romantically; but even Franciscan life in the Far West for the past century has reflected more the new German and Italian immigration than the old Spanish past. Modern Hispanic culture in the Far West makes contact with that earlier tradition, but its twentieth century migrant history has formed an ethos of its own tied in with modern social, economic, political, and religious forces. Similarly, early pioneer life in the Far West is remembered with a romantic-like quality that forms something of a tradition-mentality. But that mentality is itself largely hostile to the cultural traditions that defined the societies from which pioneers left. To some extent churches carried those cultural forms into wilderness settlements; but to at least an equal extent the churches provided a religious context and rationale for the pioneer declaration of independence from eastern traditions. Tradition, like history, whether preserving it or making it, has not preoccupied the far western mind. The great exception is the Mormon empire; but this indigenous American religion brought forth a new history and a new tradition that has flourished in the Far West as its primary home--from there exported around the world, with a self-conscious orientation toward its important role in the future.

With the exception of Mormonism and certain other new religious movements of the nineteenth and twentieth centuries, religious, ethnic, and racial identities and sensibilities have not asserted themselves with the same exclusiveness and preoccupation in the Far West that they have in the older eastern social structures and mores. Religious identity distinctions have existed in the Far West, sometimes rigidly, but they have interacted and remained separate on a more casual basis than often has characterized religious institutions in the eastern United States. Religious identities are neither challenged nor particularly enhanced in these more casual circumstances. Traditionalism has given in to other priorities in the Far West. The natural environment, the nature of a complex and developing society, the place of religion itself in far western life have forced issues in distinctive ways. In fact, except in Mormon territory, the majority of far westerners have cared little about traditional religious institutions and practices. They form the most secular society in the United States if gauged by church membership statistics, yet when questioned they claim to be religiously concerned and find religion to be important in their personal lives. They relate to varieties of religiously-oriented movements and informal gatherings and organizations that do not appear in statistics of religious institutions.[40]

In the San Francisco Bay Area, for example, where the entire history we are observing flourished from the the native Miwok and Costanoan cultures to modern pluralistic society, approximately one third of the citizens are members of churches and synagogues. Roman Catholics, Protestants, Mormons, and Jews account for the large majority of these. Others are spread among Orthodoxy, Islam, Buddhism, Vedanta, and many other small groups. Of the other two thirds of the population, many claim one of these religious identities without active membership. Others claim to be religious without any tradition or institutional orientation. Many others claim no religious orientation and welcome secular identity.[41]

During the 1960s the Bay Area became a center of Asian religious renaissance and of new religious movements in the counter-cultural context of social radicalism. Hare Krishna, Zen, the Unification Church, Scientology, Synanon, and other such groups became temporarily as visible as the traditional religions. The churches and synagogues, always involved in civic affairs, became unusually involved in campaigns against war, struggles for civil rights, and discussions of ecological issues. Around the University of California campus Unitas involved Protestants ecumenically in politics, while the Catholic Newman Center provided support for Cesar Chavez's United Farm Workers. The University Lutheran Chapel (Missouri Synod) became involved in providing sanctuary for Viet Nam draft resisters. The Radical Jewish Union carried leftist social criticism in its student publication, *The Jewish Radical.* Black churches, since pioneer days normally carrying on social ministries and justice advocacy, became more socially militant. Indian, African, Hispanic, and Asian identities challenged Anglo-European orientations. Across the Bay Episcopal Bishop James A. Pike preached the new Christian ecumenism from his Grace Cathedral pulpit, building on a long tradition of Northern California cooperative religious organization.[42] His social-theological-mystical orientation complemented the unique preaching style of mystic social theologian Howard Thurman preceding him in San Francisco's Church for the Fellowship of All Peoples. Different sounds, but some similar themes, could be heard in the Glide Memorial Methodist Church from preacher Cecil Williams, and different sounds yet from James Chuck in the First Chinese Baptist Church, or from the ultra modern architectural landmark--Saint Mary's Cathedral.

By the mid-1970s a more conventional, even conservative religious impulse had arisen within the context of the post-Viet Nam War ethos. The new evangelicalism became socially aggressive. Such new movements of the 1960s as Jesus People, Jews for Jesus, and The Christian World liberation Front had provided impetus for an evangelical commitment among young adults that helped evangelicals move beyond the old fundamentalist limitations and into social action. Apart from the reactionary, backlash extremism of the self-styled "Moral Majority" that surfaced nationwide during the 1970s, the more moderate conservative evangelical churches began to form a new identity with ecumenical vision. The founding of New College in Berkeley for training lay people with diverse secular vocations in theology and ministry in society exemplifies this new evangelical thrust. Among Catholics, too, the social upheaval of the 1960s had a profound impact. Despite a conservative backlash against the Vatican II revolution, Catholic social action assumed a new, seemingly permanent priority in the Church's life. The new Catholic spirituality embraced a social ingredient at its core. Religious social action, therefore, did not disappear in the 1970s.

Discussion of feminism, sexual orientation, and issues surrounding abortion became social priorities. By the end of the decade some churches also had resumed their protest of nuclear weapons proliferation and also begun providing sanctuary for illegal immigrant refugees from Latin America, which brought otherwise law-abiding citizens into situations of civil disobedience.

In these regional expressions of nationwide issues and movements, far western religious impulses both reflected and helped initiate the rhythms of the national social climate. A glance at some nationally prominent political personalities of far western identity suggests likewise. Religious auras have surrounded some western aspirants for the national Presidency during the past two decades. In 1964 the San Francisco Republican Convention nominated Arizona's Barry Goldwater, whose ethical certitudes and extreme individualist values presented one kind of western image. Meanwhile, another religious impulse resurfaced eastward as Michigan Governor George Romney projected a socially progressive Mormon image that enhanced his Utah-based church's public acceptance as part of the national mainstream. From Washington State, Democratic Senator Henry Martin Luther ("Scoop") Jackson, whose Norwegian immigrant parents instilled in him attitudes toward the virtue of work aptly described as "a living embodiment of the Puritan ethic," combined moderate economic policies with a liberal record on environmental conservation issues and a conservative hard line on national defense.[43] After Berkeley's 1964 Free Speech Movement, Ronald Reagan moved to Sacramento as California's Governor in 1966. Arch enemy of all 1960s social protests as well as liberal social philosophy generally, Reagan became a key expression of the nation's turn to the right in his movement eastward to the White House in 1980. His appeal to the ultra conservative "moral majority" represented a civil religious orientation that thrived more in midwestern and old southern sectors of the nation than in the Far West. Meanwhile California's Richard Nixon, whose nominal Quaker identity carried little public impact compared to his traditional American civil religious ideology, captured conservative popularity at the dawn of the 1970s before his Watergate debacle.

In conscious contrast to Nixon and Reagan alike, during the late 1970s the Jesuit-trained Jerry Brown governed the State of California with a counter-cultural flair. More congenial to the long-range social religiosity of the Far West overall, however, was Oregon's Governor and later U. S. Senator Mark Hatfield. Appealing since the late 1950s to a wide-ranging Protestant, Catholic, Jewish and secular constituency, Hatfield helped define a theologically conservative but socially progressive religious ethic with a commitment to environmental protection, human rights, and peace advocacy. Nevertheless, it was the Hollywood-trained Ronald Reagan who mastered the art of electronic mass-media communication and thereby brought one segment of far western religio-politics into the popular national realm.

Electronic religion had developed markedly during the post-World War II era. Radio religion long had sounded the Mormon Tabernacle Choir and homilies from Salt Lake City. "The World Tomorrow" had been broadcast from Pasadena for years. A variety of healers and revival preachers, as well as Protestant services and Catholic masses, had become commonplace over far western radios. Then television brought the nation's religious life into regional view and regional religious life into national view. The Hollywood-styled music, prayer, and oratory from the Crystal Cathedral (originally a drive-in church), for example, began to appear regularly on television screens. From Southern California it had become clear that TV religion was a form of mass evangelism, spiritual ministry, and theological indoctrination carefully orchestrated to reach millions of people and handle enormous amounts of money.

Los Angeles, perhaps on "the edge of history" since the new suburban metropolis began to explode a century ago, also suggests that religion in the American Far West has moved eastward and beyond. Ranging from Aimee Semple McPherson (1890-1944) and her International Church of the Foursquare Gospel to the powerful Cardinal Archbishop James Francis A. McIntyre (Archbishop 1948-1970), the Los Angeles Area religious scene has made an impact on the nation at large. Surrounded by several centers of graduate studies in religion, Los

Angeles became the hub of another form of religious activity that transcended its regional boundaries in September of 1972 as scholars from around the nation and the world gathered to attend an International Congress of Learned Societies in the Field of Religion.[44]

Meanwhile, also influential beyond the American Far West, in Berkeley plans quietly were being laid for an ecumenical, interreligious venture in theological education and advanced religious studies. In 1982 the Graduate Theological Union, a consortium of nine Protestant and Catholic seminaries plus a graduate program in religious studies in conjunction with the University of California, celebrated its twentieth anniversary. The GTU now also included a group of affiliated Centers of Judaic Studies, Urban Black Studies, Women and Religion, Ethics and Social Policy, New Religious Movements, Theology and Natural Science, an Orthodox Divinity Institute, a Pacific and Asian Center for Theology and Strategy, and a developing affiliation with an Institute of Buddhist Studies. The GTU library had become one of the largest collections of religious studies and theological literature in the nation.[45]

Finally, if we see the past five hundred years of American religious life from a Pacific Coast perspective with a view toward the future, tragedy counters celebration. We might think first of the religiously-motivated pan-Indian revitalization movements of the late nineteenth century and be reminded of the devastation of much of the tribal culture of the land's native peoples. Smohalla's Dreamer Religion of the Columbia River Plateau, the Shakers of Puget Sound, the Ghost Dance Religion, and the Peyote Cult represent a series of events that sought to integrate "teachings from the American earth" into the new society. The United States Government and churches alike have struggled to come to terms with the integrity of Indian American cultures that stretch the boundaries of pluralistic society and of religious freedom. During the past two decades Indian spirituality has surfaced anew, challenging as well as being challenged by the enormous problems of modern technocratic society.[46] That nature itself may be historical, with humanity a responsible natural agent of change, is a concept not central to Christendom or to American Indian heritage, but one that the two traditions in dialogue or dialectic might entertain.

Then we might think of the series of events by which human beings have organized natural elements scientifically, if not always ethically, threatening destruction of wilderness and society alike. From the Livermore and Los Alamos laboratories to Nevada test sites and the waters of Puget Sound, the nuclear age has dawned in the American Far West. The issue has become spiritually, morally, and theologically religious as well as politically, pragmatically, and ideologically scientific. "The very existence of humanity is at stake," wrote Seattle's Archbishop Raymond G. Hunthausen in his 1982 pastoral letter.[47] We can conclude that, just as regional religions have become national, all regions and religions coalesce as the whole earth itself appears a single vulnerable place in the cosmos.

Notes

I am grateful to Barbara Brown Zikmund of Pacific School of Religion and to Moses Rischin of San Francisco State University for their helpful comments from their reading of preliminary drafts of this essay.

1. Henry Warner Bowden, *American Indians and Christian Missions: Studies in Cultural Conflict* (Chicago: University of Chicago Press, 1981), provides an excellent historical analysis of Euro-American religious interaction with the Indians of North America, unfortunately not dealing with Pacific Coast Indians, but including a bibliography of the literature.

2. David Weber, *Spain's Far Northern Frontier, 1540-1821* (Albuquerque: University of New Mexico Press, 1979); John F. Bannon, *The Spanish Borderlands Frontier, 1530-1821* (Albuquerque: University of New Mexico Press, 1963).

3. Maynard Geiger, O.F.M., *The Life and Times of Fray Junipero Serra, O.F.M., or the Man Who Never Turned Back, 1713-1784* (2 vols.; Washington: Catholic University of America, 1959).

4. James R. Gibson, *Imperial Russia in Frontier America: The Changing Geography of Supply of Russian America 1784-1867* (New York: Oxford University Press, 1976); and Raymund F. Wood, "East and West Meet in California in 1806," *Pacific Historian*, 20 (Spring 1976): 22-33.

5. The classic account of Fort Ross was written by Ana Rosa Call, *The Russian Settlement in California, Known as Fort Ross*, first published in 1896 by R. A. Thompson, reprinted with Foreword by John C. McKenzie (Jenner, Ca.: Fort Ross Interpretive Association, Inc., 1982). See also Diane Spencer-Hancock and William E. Pritchard, "The Chapel at Fort Ross: Its History and Reconstruction," *California History*, 61 (1982): 2-17.

6. Neal Harlow, *California Conquered: War and Peace on the Pacific 1846-1850* (Berkeley: University of California Press, 1982); J. S. Holliday, *The World Rushed In: The California Gold Rush Experience* (New York: Simon and Schuster, 1981).

7. Robert Baird, *Religion in America, Or an Account of the Origin, Progress, Relation to the State, and Present Condition of the Evangelical Churches in the United States, with Notices of the Unevangelical Denominations* (New York: Harper & Row, 1844).

8. Ibid., Book I, Chapter XIV.

9. The modern critical abridgement of Baird's book by Henry Warner Bowden unfortunately omitted most of the far western references (New York: Harper & Row, 1970). On the Baird tradition see Eldon G. Ernst, "Beyond the Protestant Era in American Religious Historiography," in Joseph D. Ban and Paul R. Dekar, eds., *In The Great Tradition: Essays on Pluralism, Voluntarism, and Revivalism In Honor of Winthrop S. Hudson* (Valley Forge, Pa.: Judson Press, 1982). I wish to thank

Winthrop Hudson for his helpful comments on far western American religious history in personal correspondence over the past several years.

10. Cecil P. Drydon, *Give All to Oregon!: Missionary Pioneers of the Far West* (New York: Hastings House, 1968) is a popular account. See also Letitia M. Lyons, *Francis Norbert Blanchet and the Founding of the Oregon Missions, 1838-1848* (Washington, D.C.: Catholic University of America Press, 1940); Helene Margaret, *Father De Smet: Pioneer Priest of the Rockies* (New York: Farrar & Rinehart, 1940); and the works of Clifford Drury: *Marcus and Narcissa Whitman, and the Opening of Old Oregon* (Glendale, Calif.: A.H. Clark Co., 1973); and *First White Women over the Rockies*, 3 vols. (Glendale, Calif.: A.H. Clark Co., 1963-66).

11. Ted C. Hinckley, "Sheldon Jackson--Gilded Age Apostle," *Journal of the West,* 23 (1984): 16-25; Alice C. Cochran, *Miners, Merchants, and Missionaries: The Roles of Missionaries and Pioneer Churches in the Colorado Gold Rush and Its Aftermath, 1858-1870* (Metuchen, N.J.: Scarecrow Press, 1980); and Paul Horgan, *Lamy of Santa Fe* (New York: Farrar, Strauss & Co., 1975). An insightful analysis of the cultural-religious differences between the Spanish Catholic and Anglo Christian heritages in the Americas is Octavio Paz, "Reflections: Mexico and the United States," *The New Yorker,* September 17, 1979: 136-153.

12. For the historiography of the several Far Western regions see the articles appearing in *Pacific Historical Review,* 50 (November, 1981). On California see also Francis J. Weber, A *Select Guide to California Catholic History* (Los Angeles: Dawson's Book Shop, 1965); Douglas Firth Anderson, "California Protestantism, 1848-1935: Historiographical Explorations and Regional Method for a Nascent Field," unpublished manuscript, Graduate Theological Union Library, Berkeley, 1983; and Norton B. Stern, *California Jewish History: A Descriptive Bibliography* (Glendale: A.H. Clark, 1967).

13. Kevin Starr, *Americans and the California Dream 1850-1915* (New York: Oxford University Press, 1973); and Eldon G. Ernst, "Religion in California," *Pacific Theological Review*, 29 (Winter 1986): 43-51.

14. The best source for tracing the developing religious configuration of United States regions is Edwin Scott Gaustad, *Historical Atlas of Religion In America,* Revised Edition (New York: Harper & Row, 1976). See also Albert J. Menedez, "America's Religious Groups: Their Geography and Demography," in *Religion at the Polls* (Philadelphia: Westminster Press, 1977), chapter I.

15. Moses Rischin, "Beyond the Great Divide: Immigration and the Last Frontier," *Journal of American History*, 55 (June 1968): 42-53; and "Immigration, Migration, and Minorities in California: a Reassessment," *Pacific Historical Review*, 41 (1972).

16. For example, Robert J. Dwyer, *The Gentile Comes to Utah* (Washington, D.C.: Catholic University of America Press, 1941); and Francis J. Weber, "The Catholic Church among the Mormons in the 1880's," in William M. Kramer, ed., *The American West and the Religious Experience* (Los Angeles: Will Kramer Publisher, 1975).

17. Mark T. Banker, "Presbyterian Missionary Activity in the Southwest: The Careers of John and James Menaul," *Journal of the West*, 23 (1984): 55-61; R. Douglas Brackenridge and Francisco O. Garcia-Treto, *Iglesia Presbiteriano: A History of Presbyterians and Mexican-Americans in the Southwest* (San Antonio: Trinity University Press, 1974); Wilfred P. Schoenberg, S.J., *Paths to the Northwest: A Jesuit History of the Oregon Province* (Chicago: Loyola University Press, 1982); and William Toll, *The Making of An Ethnic Middle Class: Portland Jewry Over Four Generations* (Albany: State Univ. of N.Y Press, 1982).

18. For example, Erasmo Gamboa, "Mexican Migration into Washington State: A History 1940-1950," *Pacific Northwest Quarterly* 72 (1981): 121-131.

19. R. A. Burchell, *The San Francisco Irish, 1848-1880* (Berkeley: University of California Press, 1980); Deanna Paoli Gumina, *The Italians of San Francisco, 1850-1930* (New York: Center for Migration Studies, 1978); Dino Cinel, *From Italy to San Francisco: The Immigrant Experience* (Stanford: Stanford University Press, 1982). On the evangelical mindset, see Douglas Firth Anderson, "San Francisco Evangelicalism, Regional Religious Identity, and the Revivalism of D. L. Moody," *Fides et Historia*, 15 (1983): 44-66. See also Robert E. Levinson, *Jews in the California Gold Rush* (New York: KTAV, 1978); Fred Rosenbaum, *Architects of Reform: Congregational and Community Leadership at Temple Emanu-El of San Francisco, 1849-1980* (Berkeley: Judah L. Magnes Memorial Museum, 1980); and *Buddhist Churches of America*, Vol. I (History 1899-1974) (Chicago: Nobart, Inc., 1974).

20. Harland Hogue, "A History of Religion in Southern California, 1846-1880," Ph.D. dissertation, Columbia University, 1958); Gregory H. Singleton, *Religion in the City of Angels: American Protestant Culture and Urbanization, Los Angeles 1850-1930* (Ann Arbor: UMI Research Press, 1977); and Max Vorspan and Lloyd P. Gartner, *History of the Jews of Los Angeles* (San Marino, Ca.: Huntington Library, 1970).

21. Harold O. McCumber, *The Advent Message in the Golden West* (Mountain View, Ca.: Pacific Press Publishing Association, 1968); and Ferenc M. Szasz, "New Thought in the American West," *Journal of the West*, 23 (1984): 83-90.

22. James A. Fisher, "The Political Development of the Black Community in California, 1850-1950," *California Historical Quarterly*, 50 (1971): 256-266; Douglas Henry Daniels, *Pioneer Urbanites: A Social and Cultural History of Black San Francisco* (Philadelphia: Temple University Press, 1980); Newell G. Bringhurst, "The 'Descendants of Ham' in Zion: Discrimination against Blacks along the Shifting Mormon Frontier, 1830-1920," *Nevada Historical Society Quarterly*, 24 (1981): 298-318; Gail Madyum and Larry Malone, "Black Pioneers in San Diego: 1880-1920," *Journal of San Diego History*, 27 (1981): 91-114; Quintard

Taylor, "Slaves and Free Men: Blacks in the Oregon Country, 1840-1860," *Oregon Historical Quarterly*, 83 (1982): 153-170; and Elizabeth McLagan, *A Peculiar Paradise: A History of Blacks in Oregon, 1788-1940* (Portland: Georgian Press, 1982). On Native Indian, Hispanic and Asian peoples see notes 37-39 and 46 below.

23. Ray Allen Billington, *Land of Savagery, Land of Promise: The European Image of the American Frontier in the Nineteenth Century* (New York: W. W. Norton & Company, 1981). European writings generally were critical of the supposed nature of frontier religion in America (pp. 184-85). That myths have permeated the historiography of the American West is shown in C. L. Sonnichsen, *The Ambidextrous Historian: Historical Writers and Writing in the American West* (Norman: University of Oklahoma Press, 1981). The significance of the mythic, fictional, or "imaginary West" in the region's historical imagery is demonstrated by its inclusion in Howard R. Lamar, ed., The *Reader's Encyclopedia of the American West* (New York: Thomas Y. Crowell Company, 1977), which contains western-oriented articles on some religious traditions.

24. Classic essays are by Perry Miller, "Errand Into the Wilderness," and "Nature and the National Ego," in *Errand Into the Wilderness* (Cambridge, Mass.: Harvard University Press, 1956); and Roderick Nash, *Wilderness and the American Mind* (New Haven, Ct.: Yale University Press, 1973). An important recent study is Richard Slotkin, *The Fatal Environment: The Myth of the Frontier in the Age of Industrialization, 1800-1890* (New York: Atheneum, 1985).

25. Literature by and about Muir is vast. A useful anthology of his writings is Edwin Way Teale, ed., *The Wilderness World of John Muir* (Boston: Houghton Mifflin Co., 1954.). Excellent essays with a religious focus appeared in *Pacific Historian,* 25 (Summer, 1981). See also Ronald H. Limbaugh, "The Nature of John Muir's Religion," *Pacific Historian*, 29 (Summer/Fall 1985): 16-29; and Stephen Fox, *John Muir And His Legacy: The American Conservation Movement* (Boston: Little, Brown, &

Co., 1981). Ansel Adams's archives are deposited in The Center for Creative Photography at the University of Arizona; his personal library is housed at the University of the Pacific in Stockton, California.

26. Conrad Bonifazi, *A Theology of Things: A Study of Man In His Physical Environment* (Philadelphia: J. B. Lippincott Company, 1967), 13.

27. See "The Gospel According to Sunset," *Oakland Tribune,* May 29, 1984, B-7. Especially pertinent is "Wilderness in the West," *Sunset,* May, 1984.

28. On Leconte and Burbank, see Starr, *Americans and the California Dream,* 415-433.

29. Ibid., 307-344; Brother Ronald E. Isetti, *Called to the Pacific: A History of the Christian Brothers of the San Francisco District, 1868-1944* (Moraga, Calif.: St. Mary's College, 1979); and Nicholas C. Polos, "A Yankee Patriot: John Swett, the Horace Mann of the Pacific," *History of Education Quarterly,* 4 (1964): 17-32.

30. On rapid urbanization, see Gunther Barth, *Instant Cities: Urbanization and the Rise of San Francisco and Denver* (New York: Oxford University Press, 1975); Roger W. Lotchin, *San Francisco, 1846-1856: From Hamlet to City* (New York: Oxford University Press, 1974); and Roger Sale, *Seattle Past to Present* (Seattle: University of Washington Press, 1976). See also Robert V. Hine, *California Utopianism: Contemplations of Eden* (San Francisco: Boyd & Fraser, 1981); and Charles P. LeWarne, *Utopias on Puget Sound, 1885-1915* (Seattle: University of Washington Press, 1975).

31. Louis B. Wright, *Culture on the Moving Frontier* (New York: Harper & Row, 1955), 168.

32. John Bernard McGloin, S.J., *California's First Archbishop: The Life of Joseph Sadoc Alemany, O.P., 1818-1880*

(New York: Herder and Herder, 1966); Kenneth L. Janzen, "The Transformation of the New England Religious Tradition in California, 1849-1869," Ph.D. dissertation, Claremont Graduate School, 1964; and Kenneth Moore, "Areas of Impact of Protestantism upon the Cultural Development of Northern California, 1850-1870," M.A. Thesis, Pacific School of Religion, 1970.

33. Larry R. Gerlach, *Blazing Crosses in Zion: The Ku Klux Klan in Utah* (Logan: Utah State University Press, 1982); Carlos A. Schwantes, "The Churches of the Disinherited: The Culture of Radicalism on the North Pacific Industrial Frontier," *Pacific Historian*, 25 (1981): 54-65; Anna Louise Strong, *I Change Worlds* (New York: Henry Holt and Company, 1935); Walton Bean, "Ideas of Reform in California," *California Historical Quarterly*, 51 (1972): 213-226; J. Stitt Wilson, *How I Became a Socialist and Other Papers* (Berkeley: Published by the author, 1912); Philip S. Foner, ed., *Black Socialist Preacher: The Teachings of Reverend George Washington Woodbey and His Disciple Reverend George W. Slater, Jr.* (San Francisco: Synthesis Publications, 1983); and Joseph Brusher, *Consecrated Thunderbolt: A Life of Father Peter C. Yorke of San Francisco* (Hawthorne: Jos. F. Wagner, 1973).

34. Turner's famous 1893 address, "The Significance of the Frontier in American History," was published in *The Frontier in American History* (New York: Henry Holt and Company, 1920). On International Expositions see Robert Rydell, "Visions of Empire: International Expositions in Portland and Seattle, 1905-1909," *Pacific Historical Review*, 52 (1983): 37-66. The official published report of the 1915 Exposition is H. H. Bell, *A Modern Task or the Story of the Religous Activites of the Committee of One Hundred* (San Francisco: Federal Council of Churches of Christ in America, 1916). An estimated half million people attended the various meetings, the best attended being "the Woman's National Congress of Missions" series. Along with social themes, evangelism was a major thrust of these meetings. See also Burton Benedict, ed., *The Anthropology of World's Fairs: San Francisco's Panama Pacific International Exposition of 1915* (Berkeley: Lowie Museum of Anthropology, 1983).

35. On these issues see R. Pierce Beaver, *Church, State, and the American Indians: Two and a Half Centuries of Partnership in Missions Between Protestant Churches and Government* (St. Louis: Concordia Publishing House, 1966); Robert Michaelsen, *Piety in the Public School: Trends and Issues in the Relationship Between Religion and the Public School in the United States* (London: Macmillan, 1970); Mark J. Hurley, *Church-State Relationships in Education in California* (Washington, D.C.: Catholic University of America, 1948); Charles M. Wollenberg, *All Deliberate Speed: Segregation and Exclusion in California Schools, 1855-1975* (Berkeley: University of California Press, 1978); and Irving G. Hendrick, *The Education of Non-Whites in California, 1849-1970* (San Francisco: R. and E. Research Associates, 1977).

36. For the proportionate strength of denominations in each state in 1906 see Gaustad, *Atlas*, 48-51. On Mormon growth and expansion see Samuel W. Taylor, *Rocky Mountain Empire: The Latter-Day Saints Today* (New York: Macmillan, 1978); and Klaus J. Hansen, *Mormonism and the American Experience* (Chicago: University of Chicago Press, 1981). Mormons and Southern Baptists especially have increased their percentage of church-related population throughout the Far West, including Alaska and Hawaii. Contrast Utah, where 75% of the citizens are church members, with Washington, where only 31% are members, including over 8% Mormons. In Alaska, about 32% of church members are Mormons, Southern Baptists, and Holiness-Pentecostalists; whereas in Hawaii where 65% of church members are Catholic, half of the remaining church members (17%) are Mormon, Southern Baptist, and Holiness-Pentecostalists. Statistics are from Bernard Quinn, et al, *Churches and Church Membership in the United States 1980* (Atlanta: Glenmary Research Center, 1982).

37. The literature on the history of Hispanic and Asian peoples in the United States is increasing rapidly. Among the recent noteworthy historical studies of their rich and diverse religious life are the articles in *Pacific Theological Review*, 15 (Spring, 1982); and a session on Asian American Christianity at the annual

meeting of The American Society of Church History in San Francisco on December 29, 1983.

38. Among many studies, see Carey McWilliams, *North From Mexico* (Philadelphia: J.P. Lippincott, 1949); Rudolfo Acuna, *Occupied America: A History of Chicanos*, 2nd edition (New York: Harper & Row, 1981); and Antonio R. Soto, "The Chicano and the Church in Northern California, 1848-1978," Ph.D. dissertation, University of California, 1978.

39. See Isao Fujimoto, *Asians in America: A Selected Bibliography* (Davis, Ca.: University of California, Davis, 1971); Tricia Knoll, *Becoming American: Asian Sojourners, Immigrants, and Refugees in the Western United States* (Portland, Or.: Coast to Coast Books, 1982); Wesley Woo, "Protestant Work Among the Chinese in the San Francisco Bay Area, 1850-1920," Ph.D. dissertation, Graduate Theological Union, 1984; Kim Hyung-Chan, "History and Role of the Church in the Korean American Community," *Korea Journal*, August, 1974; Lester Suzuki, *Ministry in the Assembly and Relocation Centers of World War II* (Berkeley: Yardbird Publishing Co., 1979); and the articles by James Chuck, Roy I. Sano, and Warren W. Lee in *Pacific Theological Review* 15 (Spring 1982).

40. *Religion In America, 1982* (Princeton: The Gallup Organization, Inc., and the Princeton Religious Research Center, Inc., 1982).

41. For Bay Area statistics by counties see Quinn *et al., Churches*, p. 49. See also Don Lattin, "What We Believe," a report on religion in the Bay Area, *San Francisco Examiner,* March 27-April 3, 1983. A recent interpretation of Bay Area history is Charles Wollenberg, *Golden Gate Metropolis:: Perspectives on Bay Area History* (Berkeley: Institute of Governmental Studies, 1984).

42. Robert Bellah, "The New Consciousness and the Berkeley New Left," in Charles Y. Glock and Robert N. Bellah, eds., *The New Religious Consciousness* (Berkeley: University of California

Press, 1976); Jacob Needleman, *The New Religions* (Garden City, N.Y.: Doubleday, 1970); J. Stillson Judah, *Hare Krishna and the Counterculture* (New York: John Wiley and Sons, 1974); Michael L. Mickler, "A History of the Unification Church in the Bay Area: 1960-1974," M.A. Thesis, Graduate Theological Union, 1980; Helen E. Helton and Norman E. Leach, eds., *Heritage and Hope: A History of the Protestant, Anglican and Orthodox Movement in San Francisco on the Occasion of the 75th Anniversary Year (1978-1979) of the San Francisco Council of Churches* (San Francisco: San Francisco Council of Churches, 1979); and Ruth Hendricks Willard, et al., *Sacred Places of San Francisco* (Novato, Ca.: Presidio Press, 1985).

43. Neil R. Peirce, *The Pacific States of America: People, Politics, and Power in the Five Pacific Basin States* (New York: W.W. Norton, 1972), 235.

44. William Irwin Thompson, "Looking For History in L. A.," in *At The Edge of History* (New York: Harper & Row, 1971), Chapter 1; and James M. Robinson, ed., *Religion And The Humanizing of Man*, Second Revised Edition of the Plenary Addresses, International Congress of Learned Societies in the Field of Religion, 1-5 September, 1972, Century Plaza Hotel, Los Angeles, California (Waterloo, Ontario, Canada: Council on the Study of Religion, 1973).

45. Mark F. Fisher, *The First Twenty Years* (Berkeley: The Graduate Theological Union, 1982). Also founded in 1962 and located in Berkeley is the Judah L. Magnes Memorial Museum, a center for the study of Jews in the American West, including a major research library. For its historical context see Fred Rosenbaum, *Free to Choose: The Making of a Jewish Community in the American West* (Berkeley: The Magnes Museum, 1976), especially chapters 7-8. Among the other distinguished centers of religious studies in the Far West are Claremont Graduate School, The University of California at Santa Barbara, and the University of Southern California, all located in or around Los Angeles. In other regions are Arizona State University, The University of Oregon, Stanford University, and

the Graduate Theological Union. Data may be found in the 1981 edition of *The Council On the Study of Religion Directory of Departments And Programs of Religious Studies In North America,* edited by Harold Remus (Waterloo, Ontario, Canada: Council on the Study of Religion, 1981).

46. L. G. Moses and Margaret Connell Szasz, "Indian Revitalization Movements of the Late-Nineteenth Century," *Journal of the West,* 23 (1984): 5-15; Henry Warner Bowden, *American Indians and Christian Missions,* 198-221; Dennis Tedlock and Barbara Tedlock, eds., *Teachings From The American Earth* (New York: Liveright, 1975); and Vine Deloria, Jr., *God Is Red* (New York: Dell, 1975), especially Chapters 13-16.

47. Printed in Edwin S. Gaustad, ed., *A Documentary History of Religion in America,* volume II (Grand Rapids: Eerdmans, 1983), 598-99. For a recent collection of scholarly essays on religion and the environment, see Philip N. Joranson and Ken Butigan, eds., *Cry of the Environment: Rebuilding the Christian Creation Tradition* (Santa Fe: Bear and Company, 1984).

II

Missionaries

2.
Two Contrasting Views of the Indians: Methodist Involvement in the Indian Troubles in Oregon and Washington

Frederick A. Norwood

In the 1850s, when both Oregon and Washington were pioneer lands just emerging from wilderness conditions, sporadic Indian warfare made life dangerous and miserable for white settlers and threatened the very existence of the Indian subtribes which inhabited the mountains and valleys south and north of the great Columbia River basin. In the previous decade a provisional territorial government had been organized, even before the treaty of 1846 set the international boundary at the forty-ninth degree of latitude. Federal territorial government dates from 1849. In 1853 Washington territory was set off from Oregon.

During these crucial years two Methodist families arrived and sought to make a new life. One was that of the missionary appointed to the Puget Sound area, David E. Blaine. The other was that of John Beeson, who came west as a farmer. Both men, along with their families, were good Methodists. Blaine was a mininster, Beeson a layman. Both took their religion seriously and tried to express it in daily life. Both were caught up in the wild struggles which swirled around the mountains and valleys of pioneer Oregon and Washington territories.

The purpose of this essay is to place in contrast the attitudes of Blaine and Beeson toward the native inhabitants of these regions in a period when sporadic frontier Indian wars waxed and waned.[1] The essay thus serves as a case study in the relation of Christianity to culture--in this case of American Methodism to Indian culture in the westward movement. That such committed persons of almost identical religious backgrounds should have come to such diametrically opposed opinions is exceedingly strange. It is also disturbing, at least to this author.

Neither the Rogue River War of 1851-1856 in Oregon nor the Yakima War of 1855-1856 in Washington deserve to be called wars. They were both rather like exercises in reciprocal mayhem and murder. The Indians of the Pacific Northwest were not organized into grand tribes but rather existed in smaller communities under highly decentralized government. Under attack they might temporarily band together, thus providing one side for what is called a war. On the other side volunteer troops assembled haphazardly for the purpose of protecting homes, businesses and mines by the direct and simple means of killing the Indians. In these enterprises, laws and treaties could be as much an obstacle as military reprisal. Hence the so-called wars took on a three-cornered aspect: natives, volunteer troops and the regular army. The army was frequently caught between the other two. Most of the atrocities by whites were perpetrated by the volunteer troops.

1.

The Blaines arrived in Puget Sound via Panama late in 1853. They settled in the tiny village of Seattle in expectation of starting a Methodist mission, first to Indians, then to whites as they came. The situation was relatively calm, because so far the number of white people in the northern half of the territory was very small. Moreover, rumors of gold were not yet widespread. The isolated episodes connected with the Jason Lee Mission of 1833-1843 and the Whitman Mission of 1836-1847 were both largely affairs of the past, although memories lingered and institutions survived in the Willamette and Walla Walla valleys.[2] In a short while, however, the inexorable pressures of white expansion and settlement increased conflict with the native Americans, ending in "war."

The Blaines were caught in the so-called Battle of Seattle at the end of January 1856. They took refuge on the American sloop of war *Decatur* and presently moved to Portland. There David Blaine resumed his ministry, which by now was directed entirely toward the white inhabitants. Some of the influences which led the Blaines (as also Jason Lee before and others after) to abandon in effect the mission to the Indians, are abundantly clear in the letters which went homeward from the wild west. However, the truth of the matter is that the pioneer minister had his hands quite full making Christians out of palefaces.[3] Nevertheless, by November 1854 Kate Blaine was reporting, "Today they have raised our church." It was dedicated on 13 May 1855.[4]

Although ministers' salaries on the frontier were extremely low and rarely paid in full, the Blaines improved their worldly condition by acquiring choice real estate.[5] In addition, the first report to the Annual Conference recorded twenty-six church members. After the Blaines had moved to Oregon, one of the members of their Oregon City church was George Abernethy, Governor of the Provisional Territory. The Blaines had risen far from the squalor of the Seattle Indian mission.

Almost as soon as they arrived in Puget Sound the Blaines were disillusioned about the native inhabitants. Both man and wife were exceedingly frank in their appraisal of the condition and natural intelligence of those with whom they came into contact-- preferably not too close contact. As David wrote, "The intercourse between the white and Indians is such as to debase both. The Indians are at best but a poor degraded race, far inferior to even the lowest of those among us." The practice of flattening heads of infants accentuated the "absence of all appearance of intelligence in their countenances.... However, they are fast passing away and will soon disappear."[6] This last opinion was one commonly held by western settlers. Disappearance of the Indians was the simplest solution to the problem. Kate was incensed that the territorial legislature saw fit to give the vote to the half-breeds. She was sure all kinds of Indians would "pass" and vote. "You talk about the stupidity and awkwardness of the Irish. You ought to have to do with our Indians and then you would know what these words mean."[7]

The Blaines reported that the natives were too lazy even to hunt and fish, and besides they smelled. They had no sense of modesty. Kate admitted that she had become accustomed to seeing men parading around stark naked in warm weather, as well as the lively sight of children up to fourteen "running around without an article of clothing ... and they know as little of shame as the beasts of the field."[8] The tone of her letter suggests that in this case censoriousness was tempered by envy. But lack of modesty and shame about parts of the body would be listed among the evidences of degenerateness and savagery. The concept of natural freedom was entirely absent from the theological world view of either of the Blaines. Once, in pausing to admire the sight of a young Indian woman proudly carrying a flathead baby, Kate was moved to remark that mother and child expressed "no intellectual development whatever, and they have no intellect." In fact, Indians were utterly "pitiable," and "most undoubtedly beyond our reach."[9] This last conclusion undoubtedly relieved any sense of guilt over abandonment of a direct Indian mission.

One can almost feel the relief emanating from David's letter of 19 December 1854, in which he reported the plan of Governor Isaac I. Stevens to negotiate with the Indians for the sale of their lands and their removal. "It is supposed they will be removed from our midst. What a blessing it will be to both them and to the whites if this can be effected." As affairs now stand, he went on, each group degrades the other, and there is little hope of benefiting the Indians. A treaty was concluded, but the results were not immediately beneficial. "Since the treaty," David wrote, "we are blest with the presence, dwelling, noise, filth, vileness, and all manner of obscenity of more Indians than ever before."[10] The Blaines were discovering how wide and deep a cultural gap existed between their European-based American culture and native American Indian culture. They certainly erred in their judgment that all the excellent features lay with one and all the degenerate qualities with the other.

The Blaines' experiences illustrate the perennial problem of Christian mission anywhere: Christianity or the Christian's civilization--which comes first? Methodists had always been eager to proclaim the gospel of salvation in Jesus Christ directly to anyone who would listen. They assumed that civilizing efforts could follow at a more leisurely pace. But a few months with the Pacific Northwest Indians raised serious doubts about the convertibility of the Indians unless they were moved outside their native cultural setting. These considerations raise the even more fundamental question of just what is the gospel that is to be proclaimed and what connection it has, if any, with a given culture--in this case nineteenth-century white American culture. Christianity must exist in some cultural context--but which? Pioneers, the Blaines included, escaped this issue by the easy assumption that the whole problem would be resolved through the disappearance of the Indians.

In 1855 the Blaine correspondence introduced a new element: active trouble with the Indians. The tensions which gave rise to the Klamath War with its reverberations around Puget Sound were increasing. The Blaines give no evidence of understanding the issues which caused the conflicts. At first they expressed commonly held views that Indians were cowards and "afraid to contend with the whites."[11] Later on, after the native warriors had demonstrated their prowess all too well, affairs looked more serious.[12] The tribes were uniting in common opposition to white expansion. In fact, in less than a month nine whites were killed-- men, women and children. The Blaines were uneasy. Volunteer troops were being organized--if that is the word for assembly of an undisciplined rabble. At last David admitted the Indians were indeed a match for the white man.[13] The Methodist church was commandeered for use as a blockhouse. The Blaine family decided to move from their confortable residence to refuge on the *Decatur*, the welcome American sloop of war anchored in the harbor.[14] It was a wise decision; on 26 January 1856 the "Battle of Seattle" took place. Though a minor and indecisive engagement, the battle nevertheless completely upset the pioneer village which one day would become a great city.

The hostilities convinced the Blaines that their usefulness in that location was, for the foreseeable future, ended. They moved to Portland and continued to serve in Methodist ministry in the southern territory. In fact for a while only one Methodist missionary was left around Puget Sound.

Occasionally the Blaine correspondence shows awareness of a

moral issue of justice in the treatment of the Indians. David wrote about an incident in Seattle in which a white man shot three friendly Indians in cold blood. Kate reported at length a trial for murder in which the two white defendants were charged with murder of an Indian. One was acquitted forthwith. In the second case, the jury struggled for thirty hours, then finally acquitted him also on a technicality about the name of the murdered Indian. "The jury wanted to acquit him and knew the people wanted they should, and the evidence of his having assisted to hang the Indian was so plain they could not acquit him on any other ground."[15] Kate's moral scruples did not extend to an overt protest against this rank injustice. But her strait-laced Victorian standards were scandalized by the story of a man who bought an Indian girl from her father and proceeded to live with her. After unsuccessfully attempting to run away, the poor girl hanged herself. Although the whites were grudgingly willing that she be buried in the cemetery, the Reverend Mr. Blaine refused to perform a funeral ceremony. Kate thought his refusal was not too harsh, for the "squaw men" were as debased as the squaws. "Now what a situation he is in, with his little half-breed child, despised by the whites and hated by the Indians."[16]

All this correspondence reveals the degree to which one missionary family fell into the pattern common to the Western frontier: now and then qualms of conscience, pity for degraded savages, but not much else to demonstrate any distinctive impact of Christianity on the environment.

2.

Methodist John Beeson also experienced the troubles in the Pacific Northwest in the 1850s. He was a farmer, businessman and writer and a devout Christian of high principles. Born in England, he migrated to America in 1830 and settled in Illinois where he remained for nineteen years. He was interested in the temperance movement and took active part in the underground railroad. In March 1853, responding to the lure of the West, he moved with his family to a farm in the Rogue River valley of southern Oregon, where he spent the next three years. His book,

A Plea for the Indians, was based on his trip west and sojourn in Oregon. A high point later in his career was his appearance on 9 October 1859 in Faneuil Hall, Boston, together with Edward Everett and Wendell Phillips, to plead the Indian cause. He also talked with President Lincoln several times and wrote at least two letters to him.[17]

The Indian troubles in the Rogue valley began earlier than those in Washington territory but ended about the same time.[18] Violence began in 1851 with the murder of a white man by two Indians. This act brought the inevitable result of raising volunteers to exact "justice." Sporadic fighting continued over summer 1851. More action took place in summer of 1852. A harsh winter followed, exacerbating the troubles. In 1853 unemployed miners turned on the Indians and perpetrated atrocities to match those of the Indians. In August that year, the miners in Jacksonville summarily hanged two Shasta Indians. Later the same day they hanged a seven year old Indian boy who was brought to town. One observer commented that "in 1853 the Rogue River War was caused by bad whites and vindictive Indians."[19] The "war" was regularly punctuated by atrocities. For example, in winter 1854 unemployed miners attacked an Indian village inhabited by seven women, one boy and two little girls. All were driven into the forest to freeze, except for a pregnant woman and the two girls, who were shot. Such depredations were connected with fighting in the Klamath region of northern California, centering around Yreka. The struggle more or less ended in early 1856, when the surviving Indians agreed to move to a reservation near the Willamette valley.

John Beeson and his family arrived in the troubled Rogue valley in summer of 1853, proposing to engage in farming. However, Beeson's attention had already been drawn to the pitiable condition of Indians on the way west. Now he began to understand some of the forces which underlay the conflict. His book, *A Plea for the Indians*, attempted to offer another side of the story. He presented the Indians' side against the overwhelming pressure of white attitudes expressed in the pioneer press, inflammatory speeches, rabble-rousing assemblies and direct action by volunteer troops.

In his preface, Beeson expressed his hope that "a more thorough knowledge of the wrongs to which the Indian is subject may awaken attention."[20] In contrast to the general enthusiasm for a military solution through victory in war, Beeson insisted that such an approach would never satisfy justice. Nor would such activity bring any credit to the victors.

> Our military can never win honorable laurels in any contest with the Indians; for the world regards such warfare as they would a deadly strife between a giant and a dwarf. The strength is all on one side. But in the case mentioned our action could not be justified by even the pretense of war. It was a deliberate massacre of supplicating dependants--murder in its most revolting and aggravated form.

Moderation of expression was not one of Beeson's virtues. His attitude toward his fellow white citizens is characteristic: "The sum total of their religious and political faith consists in Squatter Sovereignty."[21]

He followed the news reports carefully and quoted specific items from the press in order to refute them. Some examples follow.

> "The Indians are ignorant, abject, and debased by nature.... Whose minds are as incapable of instruction as their bodies are of labor.... They are heroes only when women and children are to be murdered.... They have nothing in common with humanity but the form.... And God has sent us to destroy them, as he did the Israelites of old to similar tribes.... There is no evidence of sympathy or favor for Indians in the people or authorities of Oregon, in the present emergency."

In providing these quotations from the popular press Beeson gave some indication of what he was up against. He proceeded to refute each allegation and ended by pointing out that, in spite of the pressure, there were some exceptional individuals. The exceptions included Generals Palmer and Wool, "several clergymen," and many citizens. Even some of those who had volunteered for what they considered a patriotic duty were exceptions, "whose hearts yearned within them at the shameful impositions and unmerited sufferings they were compelled to witness."[22]

As a loyal Methodist John Beeson hoped to find a more enlightened understanding in the Methodist societies. He reported his disillusionment at length in a passage which deserves quotation in full. He had heard that punitive action was being planned by local volunteers. They were going to approach the Indians as if in peace, then fall on them and wipe them out.

As there was a Methodist Quarterly Meeting to assemble that day, within two hours ride of the scene of the intended massacre, I hoped there would be heard in that religious assembly some expression of brotherly kindness, and charity for the poor doomed outcasts in their immediate vicinity. Full of this hope I attended the meeting; but the services progressed with the rehearsal of *"Experiences"* common on such occasions, until speakers became scarce, and the Presiding Elder exhorted all who had anything to say for the Lord, to improve the time.

I arose and spoke with all the feeling, and all the power I had in behalf of the poor Indians. I entreated that Assembly who had gathered themselves together in the name of Christ--whose life and ministry was a living Gospel of Love--to put on the spirit and power of Christ. I begged them, by every principle of humanity and justice, to inflict no wrong upon the helpless. I drew in strong colors the scenes that would inevitably follow such an attack as was meditated. I thought if there was a soul, or a heart in them, I would find it, even if it could be reached through nothing but their own selfishness....
In conclusion, I strongly urged them, as citizens and Christians, to raise a voice of remonstrance, or to call on the Authorities for the administration of justice, and thus avert the impending calamity.

51

No voice responded to the appeal, and the meeting was closed; for no one had independence enough to speak his thoughts. But I afterward learned that there were members of that assembly who silently acknowledged its force; but the pressure of public opinion prevented open expression. I cannot resist the conviction that if the Presiding Elder, with his brethren of the Ministry, and leading members of the church, had taken a firm, manly, and Christian position, as advocates of the Gospel of Peace, the horrors of that week, and of the subsequent war, might have been prevented. I am confirmed in that opinion by one who became penitent for the part he had taken in those atrocities. He solemnly declared that he was led into it by the Preachers.[23]

After this experience with local Methodists Beeson was not too surprised to receive a cool reception from the editors of the church papers in the West. When he sought to have an article giving the Indians' side published in the *Pacific Christian Advocate*, he was refused on the ground that publication would lead to mob violence against the paper. Of course this argument did not satisfy Beeson. He received the same treatment from the *California Christian Advocate*.[24] His appeal for understanding and tolerance for opposing views was ignored.

Beeson's understanding of Indian religion was well in advance of his time--or of any time, for that matter. A long section of his *Plea* is devoted to an interpretation of native religious beliefs and an appeal for mutual respect. Indians tend to reject the Gospel, he averred, because they have never really been offered it. "A religion that came to them armed to the teeth, and ready to sanction any outrage that might be inflicted upon them, could not present a very winning aspect." Beeson thought Methodists were particularly at fault for despising Indians and bewailing the failures of mission work. He was sure Indians would respond more positively to a religion that did not "insult their common sense, by presenting itself with Whisky and Creeds in one hand, and Bibles and Bowie-knives in the other."[25]

He believed that diversity of understanding is written into the Bible itself: there is "a light that lighteth every man that cometh into the world." It is wrong, then, to assume that Indians are only savages who have no genuine faith, understanding of life or sense of moral right. In characteristically romantic style, but not therefore without truth, he wrote:

> It is true that their creed is not written in a book, neither have they temples built with hands, nor any idea of a Triune God, or of a Mediator through whom to approach and conciliate the Majesty on High. But they have, on their own mountains and valleys, the same Presence that dwelt with Moses, and Daniel, and the Prophets on the mountains and valleys of Palestine. The bright sun, and the fertilizing rain, are, to their simple minds, ministers of blessing. They look up to the blue canopy and meditate on the starry heavens; they bask on the sunny hill-side, or recline under the spreading trees; they retire into the deep aisles of the forest, and find there God's solemn temples, where the babbling brook, the sighing zepher [*sic*], and singing birds, all have ministries of love and worship; and with them they unite, in adoration of the Great Spirit, whose informing presence animates the whole, and in whom the Indian, as well as the Christian, lives, and moves, and has his being.[26]

In concluding his little book John Beeson listed several proposals for reformation of relations with the American Indians. The proposals may be neither better nor worse than innumerable others. (1) Provide enough suitable land for successful agriculture, for "a happier and easier transit from the savage to the civilized condition." (2) Clean up the federal Indian Service. (3) Place entire families rather than male individuals in the official agencies. (4) Encourage both fine and useful arts. (5) "They should be invested with the highest possible degree of freedom ... with full liberty to establish their own institutions." (6) Limit religious teaching to ethical principles and recognize that which is good in native religion. (7) Discourage use of tobacco, alcohol and drugs.[27] Whatever the limitations of this program, it is redeemed by emphasizing, over a hundred years before the principle was widely accepted, freedom for the Indians to determine their own destiny in the context of American life.

With these two contrasting case studies before us, the one reflecting commonly held views of frontier culture, the other protesting vigorously against the inexorable flood of white power westward at the expense of the native Americans, we may pause to ask the meaning of such a contrast for the understanding and proclamation of Christianity. Although it is not within the purview of this research article to attempt an answer, it is very important for our time to pose the question.

Notes

This article first appeared in *Church History* 49 (June 1980): 178-187, and is reprinted by permission of the American Society of Church History.

1. The two principal sources consulted in the preparation of this article are both located in the Huntington Library, San Marino, California. One is a manuscript collection of letters written by David Blaine and his wife Catherine Paine Blaine between 1853 and 1862, preserved in typescript copy and edited by Thomas W. Prosch. The other is a small and rare book by John Beeson, *A Plea for the Indians; with Facts and Features of the Late War in Oregon*, privately printed by the author in New York in 1857.

2. For general information on these earlier ventures see Cornelius J. Brosnan, *Jason Lee: Prophet of the New Oregon* (New York: Macmillan, 1932); Robert J. Loewenberg, *Equality on the Oregon Frontier, Jason Lee and the Methodist Mission 1834-43* (Seattle: Univ. of Washington Press, 1976); Clifford M. Drury, *Marcus Whitman, M.D., Pioneer and Martyr* (Caldwell, Idaho: Caxton, 1937); idem, *Marcus and Narcissa Whitman and the Opening of Oregon,* 2 vols. (Glendale, Calif.: A.H. Clark, 1973).

3. See for example David's letter, 21 June 1854, p.56, in which he reports that settlers, far from yearning for the gospel, were quite "indifferent" to it. Hereafter the designation David or Kate will indicate the letter writer.

4. Kate, 14 Nov. 1854, p. 101; David, 19 May 1855, p. 144.

5. Kate, 30 Oct. 1854, p. 96; David, 20 Nov. 1854, pp. 103-109; David, 24 Jan. 1855, p. 128; and many other references.

6. David, 20 Dec. 1853, pp. 19-20.

7. Kate, 3 May 1854, pp. 40, 42.

8. Kate, 4 August 1854, pp. 77-78.

9. Kate, 28 June 1854, pp. 59-60; David, 4 August 1854, p. 72.

10. David, 19 Dec. 1854, p. 123; David, 24 Jan. 1855, p. 127; and David, 5 Feb. 1855, p. 134.

11. Kate, 7 March 1854, p. 27; Kate, 28 March 1855, pp. 141-142.

12. Kate, 16 Sept. 1855, p. 163; the letter refers to the murder of four white miners by Indians who lived around the new diggings. The MS has two pages numbered 164.

13. David, 18 Dec. 1855, p. 169.

14. David, 29 Jan. 1856, p. 176.

15. David, 20 June 1856, pp. 191-192; Kate, 30 Oct. 1854, p. 98.

16. Kate, 23 Nov. 1854, pp. 111-112.

17. Beeson, *A Plea for the Indians*. Outside of this work the

main source for Beeson's life is an autobiography in *The Calumet* 1 (1860): 4-9. Beeson began this periodical with a view to promoting the cause of the Indian, but his effort was swamped in the controversy of the Civil War. Only one issue was published. Notice is taken of Beeson in Francis Paul Prucha, *American Indian Policy in Crisis: Christian Reformers and the Indian, 1865-1900* (Norman, OK: Univ. of Oklahoma Press, 1976), and Robert W. Mardock, *The Reformers and the American Indian* (Columbia, MO: Univ. of Missouri Press, 1971), esp. 10-14. In his later life Beeson continued to press the cause of the Indian through the Indian Aid Association of Philadelphia and other means. He also took up other causes, such as a dream for a universal system of thought, world government, universal language and a world university. He dabbled in spiritualism. See Beeson correspondence in Huntington Library: to his wife, 19 Feb. 1859; 5 Oct. 1862; to his son, 23 Dec. 1869; 26 May 1874. On the last mentioned date, he wrote: "I ask no favor of either God or Man for myself or for the Indians, but only that Justice, JUSTICE, JUSTICE may rule."

18. See Stephen Dow Beckham, *Requiem for a People, the Rogue Indians and the Frontiersman* (Norman, OK: Univ. of Oklahoma Press, 1971).

19. Beckham, *Requiem for a People*, 125.

20. Beeson, *A Plea for the Indians*, iii.

21. Ibid., 14, 15.

22. Ibid., 32-37; final quotation from p. 37.

23. Ibid., 47-48. Compare Beckham, *Requiem for a People*, 152. Beckham unintentionally garbles this episode through ignorance of Methodist polity and practice.

24. Beeson, *A Plea for the Indians*, 92, 104; compare p. 117.

25. Ibid., 100, 101.

26. Ibid., 112.

27. Ibid., 125-133.

3.
Missiology in New Mexico, 1850-1900: The Success and Failure of Catholic Education

Frances Campbell

To say that organized religion carried traditional American ideas and institutions into the Far West is to imply that, in acting as agents of the national ideology, the churches necessarily identified with America and extended loyalty to the nation. Such an identity and extension of fealty may be summed up in the phenomenon of nationalism as it is defined by Dorothy Dohen: an ideology which permits the nation to view itself and its common value system as the final interpreter of its own affairs.[1] In short, within a particular place and time the nation understands itself to be the primary agent of divine activity.

God's designs for the nation were apparent in the political and religious rhetoric of nineteenth century America. Territorial expansion, technological advances which provided increased control over the environment, and, early in the century, a religious awakening with its aftermath of benevolent, activist religion combined to instill within the national consciousness a spirit of power and confidence buttressed by a vision of national greatness.[2] The mixture of national events and public discourse produced in the 1840s a conviction that the nation was entrusted with a divine mission to extend its institutions globally either by example or by the acquisition of land and the assimilation of people. The United States considered itself a messianic light to all people and, as a guiding light, it had to be not only visible but also penetrating. Thus, as Americans advanced westward they implanted their traditional ideals and values along each successive frontier line. They did so primarily through the national institutions of representative government, common schools which taught national ideals and principles, and organized religion which endorsed not only worship but also morality, industry and patriotism.[3]

The religious societies and institutions which sent missionaries to the Far West overtly pursued organizational goals aimed at the extension and preservation of traditional American society. The missionaries of the Protestant Evangelical Home Missionary Society, for example, prized their religious and civil institutions and were anxious to conserve and spread them. The Society's recruits were instructed to view themselves not only as soldiers of Christ, but also as minutemen of democracy on the remote frontier, where they were to "educate the head and the heart of the people and make the West safe for Democracy."[4] Their task was to transform the untamed frontier into a moral and ordered society in order to realize fully the destiny of the nation.

Other pioneers besides the missionaries considered their settlements extensions of America's work in building God's kingdom. In Colorado, for example, frontier settlers were concerned with establishing representative government, productive labor, common education and acceptable religious observance, all components of society as it existed in the East. Through the cooperative effort of the gavel, the plow, the book and the Bible traditional American society was extended to the Rockies.[5]

The early appearance in pioneer California of traditional schools, churches and representative government suggests a nearly direct transfer of culture from the Atlantic to the Pacific coast.[6] Such continuity was facilitated by the services of two midwestern cities, Cincinnati, Ohio and Lexington, Kentucky. Both functioned as cultural and religious way-stations on the path between the East and the frontier. From their presses flowed a stream of textbooks, Bibles and tracts. These materials were carried into the Far West by graduates of seminaries which specialized in the methods of frontier religious and educational service.[7]

It was in the ordered and progresive atmosphere of Cincinnati and its environs that the young French priest, Jean Baptiste Lamy, encountered American society and ideals, acquired citizenship, and labored as a missionary among Catholic German immigrants. From Cincinnati Lamy was sent, in 1850, as apostolic vicar to the newly established territory of New Mexico where he was to work among another group of non-Americans.[8] The Hispanics of New Mexico, however, were to prove somewhat wary of Catholic missionaries and even less eager to assimilate to the ways of Americans.

This essay will outline the missionary philosophy and practice of the American Roman Catholic Church in New Mexico, as evidenced in its educational system. In order to clarify the Catholic Church's presence on the frontier its history will be compared with that of the Protestant churches in the same territory. The sectarian schools in New Mexico illustrate the way in which the missiologies of the Catholics and Protestants, while intent on the orthodox evangelization of the indigenous Hispanics, also pursued the goal of assimilating the people into the larger American culture. The experience of the mission schools indicates that the Hispanics were reluctant to assume such a cultural identity. However, because the Catholic missionaries led by Lamy appeared as defenders of the traditional faith against the Protestants and because they effectively used bilingual education to promote literacy, they were able to make larger inroads into the native population.

The encounter in New Mexico between the Hispanic and American cultures was complex. Despite the missiological efforts to evangelize and Americanize the people, particularly through education, neither American Protestantism nor American Catholicism were readily accepted by the Hispanics.[9] American religious efforts, strong and enthusiastic from earlier frontier successes, confronted in New Mexico a regional Spanish Catholicism which was revered as orthodox by a clergy and laity who explained their own frontier experience in messianic terms.

Like the rest of New Spain, New Mexico understood itself to be an agent of Spanish ideology, and New World colonists believed themselves to be God's chosen agents in the wilderness. As the authentic "auto de fe" (a generic term which summarized Spain's national identity and purpose as both were formed out of 700 years of resistance to Moorish occupation), Spain, New and

Old, saw itself as the divine champion of the true faith, a faith Catholic and Spanish. Wherever Spanish colonists were found, there also was a clearly defined holy mission to act as the true deposit of faith and as the conservators of that faith.[10] The Spaniards carried this religious identity into the northern frontier province of New Mexico. However, the isolation of the province left the settlements strongly Spanish yet fiercely independent, self-confident and self-sufficient.[11] Consequently, the province developed its own genre of colonial government, subsistence labor, primitive education and a religious system which served to assure the people of their righteousness and success in a lonely and hostile land. Thus, by the beginning of the Mexican period (1821), a regional way of life had evolved as had a clerico-popular Catholicism which was firmly established in the minds and hearts of the people.[12] Such was the religious and cultural system Jean Lamy and his Protestant rivals encountered.

Into the adobe villages of New Mexico Lamy carried all the zeal and optimism characteristic of American frontier expansion. An arduous journey marked by inclement weather, shipwreck, lost possessions, severe illness and the constant threat of Indian attack did not lessen Lamy's enthusiasm. Upon his arrival in Santa Fe, however, a quick survey of his impoverished vicarate and the Catholicism he discovered there dampened his spirits. Whatever his ecclesiastical plan had been for this rough place and its people, it was quickly eclipsed by a new agenda. This agenda was suggested by Lamy's vicar and close friend, Joseph Machebeuf, who, in 1852, penned a disheartened letter home to France:

> This is a country of ancient Catholicity. But, alas, how times have changed! Instead of that piety and practical religion which marked the days of the missions, we have but the forms of exterior religion.... In this semi-civilized land the people are ignorantly led by blind devotion mixed with fanaticism and superstition.[13]

From 1852 until his retirement in 1885 Lamy considered himself a civilizer representing knowledge and charity in a land where, in his opinion, ignorance and selfishness prevailed.[14] He worked to move the people from their accustomed paths by means of a multifaceted program of reform which included education of children (and thereby adults) through parochial academies, teaching orphanages and parish catechism classes. Lamy hoped to invade every area of Hispanic life and to plant therein a proper piety and acceptable citizenship. His goal paralleled, if it did not duplicate, that of Protestant evangelicals who wanted the indigenous population to be more American than Hispanic.

It is axiomatic that when two cultures meet they tend to reject each other. When they subscribe to different theologies and cosmologies, certain aspects of their initial rejection often create prejudices which, in turn, become additional barriers to mutual understanding and cooperation. Between 1848 and 1900, there was great dissimilarity in the cosmologies and theologies which guided the development of Anglo and Hispanic cultures. Anglos in New Mexico were highly critical of the Hispanics for their apparent lack of direction in life and lethargy in religion. Hispanics, in turn, were confused and even angered by what seemed to them a lack of respect among Anglos for the present moment and place and, consequently, outright manipulation of God's plan for the future. So different did the two peoples seem during this period that, at the time of his retirement, Lamy despaired over the cultural and religious gap he had tried for 33 years to close. In a report to the Vatican in 1881 Lamy revealed that he judged the Hispanics according to Anglo criteria, and they had failed:

> Very few of them will be able to follow modern progress. They cannot be compared to the Americans in the way of intellectual liveliness, ordinary skills, or industry. They will be scorned and considered an inferior race,... the morals, manners, and customs of our unfortunate people are quite different from those of the Americans.[15]

To be sure, Lamy's episcopal program often resulted in a volatile confrontation of values, religious ideas, traditional ways of life and new concepts of authority. He experienced, however, more than just conflict with the Hispanics. Within at least some sectors of New Mexico's religious society Lamy's reforms met with positive cooperation as well as popular resistance. The pattern of local religious history during this period is similar to a kaleidoscope turned slowly by each component of American Catholic and Protestant missiology, the shapes changing with every turn.

The focal piece in the kaleidoscopic pattern is the sectarian school system, which was made necessary by the failure, until 1891, of the territorial legislature to establish a public school system. To counter the Protestant day school system, begun by the Baptists in 1849, Lamy opened a boys school in his own living quarters in 1852.[16] The following year an academy for girls was established by the Sisters of Loretto who arrived from Kentucky. In succeeding years Loretto academies opened throughout the territory and in 1859 the Christian Brothers accepted their first students at St. Michael's College. These schools became the primary locus of positive interaction between Lamy and the Hispanics.

If the people seemed ready to cooperate with Lamy within the parameter of the schools, it was primarily because the academies offered a long-awaited and much-desired form of enlightenment. Since colonial days, New Mexicans had known sporadic efforts to conduct schools. Each attempt, however, was undermined and finally rendered futile by the lack of materials, teachers and funds. The reports of Mexican and, later, American officials reveal the weaknesses of the educational system Lamy and his Protestant counterparts inherited. As early as 1825 a commission established by the Mexican government reported that in New Mexico ignorance was rampant due to the absence of schools.[17] Eight years later the territorial legal advisor, Antonio Barreiro, reported:

> ... the benefit of primary letters is given only to the children of those who are able to contribute to the salary of the school teacher. Even in the capital it has been impossible to engage a teacher and to furnish education for everyone.[18]

Barreiro was able to locate private "schools" in the settlements of Santa Fe, Vado, Santa Cruz de la Canada, Taos and Albuquerque. However, concerning these he lamented:

The schools are in deplorable condition. No noticeable results are achieved by primary instruction, a condition which is due both to neglect, carelessness, and ignorance of many of the teachers, and to the lack of interest shown by the authorities.[19]

Barreiro also listed as obstacles to education the inadequate communications with the interior of Mexico and the general scarcity of books.[20] Children, if they ever mastered their letters, learned through a process that long ago had become a tradition in New Mexico. By recitation of homespun lessons in the form of *cuentos* (short moralistic stories) and *dichos* (proverbial folk sayings), children learned grammar, reading, the collective wisdom of the village and a religious faith vaguely remembered and half invented. The *cuentos* were copied by hand into rough pocket-sized manuals which were studied, memorized and then passed to the next generation or to the next settlement.[21]

In the missiological programs of Lamy and the Protestant evangelicals formal education was a high priority. The Protestants addressed the lack of competent teachers with their own force of graduates from the Home Missionary Society and other seminaries which trained students for frontier work.[22] For his part, Lamy begged his former bishop, John Purcell of Cincinnati, to send teaching sisters and priests to New Mexico. Along with the illiteracy and pre-modern habits of the natives, Lamy was alarmed by the potential Protestant threat to Catholicism. Repeatedly he wrote to Purcell of "the incredible efforts of Protestant proselytizers here who are daily opening schools, attracting our youth and rendering them religiously indifferent."[23]

Lamy may have been honestly concerned, but his fears were exaggerated. It is true that by the time of his own arrival in Santa Fe all the major Protestant Evangelical denominations had made their appearance in the territory. The Baptists had been first in

1849 in the persons of Reverend Hiram W. Read and his wife. At first their school prospered, but in the following years they and their fellow missionaries faced repeated frustrations among the Hispanics, who harbored a fundamental distrust of anything Protestant. Doctrinal matters posed but one problem. The difference in language made even basic communication difficult and rendered effective teaching virtually impossible. While language and doctrine posed problems for the Baptists and their Evangelical competitors, the Protestants also faced aggressive opposition from Lamy, who did more than write letters to the chancery in Cincinnati.

The Methodists have recorded in their New Mexico chronicles an incident which illustrates Lamy's obstructive tactics. In 1850, Methodist minister George Nicholson arrived in Santa Fe where he proselytized successfully among Hispanic adults. In 1853, Walter Hansen joined him and was instrumental in establishing a day school in the nearby village of Tecolote. In his journal Nicholson relates the short-lived history of the school which at first boasted an enrollment of 35 students with the promise of more. A Methodist shopkeeper in the village told Nicholson of an unannounced visit to the town by Bishop Lamy and his vicar, Machebeuf. The two rode into town on horseback and stayed but a few hours. Five days later the Methodist school was forced to close for lack of students.[24]

Between 1861 and 1871 there were no Methodist missionaries in New Mexico until Thomas Harwood was able to establish a Methodist presence among the increased number of Anglo settlers. His academies in Santa Fe and Albuquerque also won the support of several Hispanic families. The experience was mirrored by the Baptists, who had abandoned all missionary activities by 1860 and did not return to the territory until 1879 when they focused their energies not on the Hispanics but on the Anglo settlements along the recently completed rail lines.[25] The Presbyterians who arrived in Santa Fe in 1851 in the person of missionary W. J. Kephart repeated the pattern of the Baptists and Methodists. Unfortunately, that same year Kephart forsook his mission, leaving the Presbyterians with no official representative until 1866. Concerted missionary work by the Presbyterians did not resume until 1879 when they embarked on a program which over the following twelve years would result in twenty-three mission schools and two Anglo academies.[26]

The last two decades of the century were the "brick and mortar" years of the Protestants, who built several institutions reserved primarily for Anglo students and numerous mission day schools for the Hispanic population in the high desert villages. As the Anglo population increased and the campaign for statehood intensified, Protestant efforts to proselytize and Americanize the Hispanics also intensified especially in the mission schools. So strong and visible were the Protestants by this time that Lamy's fears voiced earlier to Bishop Purcell now found corroborative echoes in the correspondence of Catholic teachers in the territory. In 1883, for example, George Baldwin, a Christian Brother and former treasurer of St. Michael's College in Santa Fe, congratulated Blandina Segale of the Sisters of Charity on the "successful fight with those Protestant frauds who would rob the poor Mexicans of the only thing they have left--their faith."[27]

The Cincinnati Sisters of Charity had been in New Mexico since 1865 when they responded to Lamy's need for a hospital and an orphanage. The ophananges in Santa Fe and Albuquerque admitted both Anglo and Hispanic day students to their school curriculum and qualified, along with the Loretto academies, as territorial schools. This allowed them to receive public support from territorial funds.[28] The Sisters of Loretto had already opened their schools in Santa Fe, Taos, Mora, Albuquerque, Las Vegas, Las Cruces, and Bernalillo.[29]

School records and the journals and correspondence of the nuns illuminate the Catholic role in territorial education. Account books indicate that readers, spellers, and math texts were ordered from eastern publishers, as were catechisms and devotionals. It was the intention of the schools to bring both modern habits and the orthodox faith into the Far West through the media of classroom materials. Not even the most isolated, primitive settlements of New Mexico were exempt. Yet especially with the

Catholic nuns the harshness of this task was often tempered by a loving appreciation of their "primitive" charges.

One Sister of Loretto, Mother Magdalen Hayden, was prolific in her correspondence. In her letters she anguishes over her exile in a strange and foreign land, but she also speaks warmly of the indigenous people as a source of personal comfort and encouragement. Her impressions of the customs and faith of the Hispanics qualify the often bleak reports of Lamy and Machebeuf:

> In the people, and especially in the girls we have under our care, I have found a goodness of heart which I cannot help loving. The first missionaries to this country must have been very holy persons for they planted the Faith in a very singular manner, like that of St. Francis Xavier. Had they been otherwise, the people could not have retained so many pious and touching practices of Christianity as are seen here at present.[30]

In certain cases schools run by the nuns were a salve upon painful episcopal wounds caused by the conflict between native and American versions of Catholicism. For several years a controversy had raged in the town of Taos between Lamy and the local padre, Antonio Martinez, and the people had chosen sides. Lamy made several moves to mend the rift, one of which was to open a parish school in the town. According to Mother Magdalen Hayden,

> One of the reasons why the Sisters went to Taos rather than elsewhere was because of the schism which has existed there for several years. Thank God, it seems that the Sisters are doing at least a little to break it down. They already have forty girls and among this number three close relatives of the old schismatic priest.[31]

Bishop Lamy relied upon the nuns to generate the funds necessary to maintain their schools. In view of Lamy's despairing attitude it may come as a surprise that to support the schools many Hispanics readily volunteered labor, provided free materials for construction and maintenance, and generously donated money.[32] Yet many Hispanics cooperated with Lamy's schools for two reasons. First, these schools firmly educated their children in the Catholic faith--a much desired safeguard against the growing Protestant influence which was sharply felt by adults in the economic and political realms of territorial life. Second, despite some hostility to American ways most Hispanic parents believed that their children should learn English in order to function effectively in the territorial society.

The curricula in Lamy's schools were taught bilingually, with English offered as a separate subject.[33] From his first days in New Mexico Lamy insisted that his missionaries follow his working rule that Spanish was the primary language of the region and was to be used in all contacts with the native people. Although French was his mother tongue, he instructed each newly arrived group of religious workers that in New Mexico there were two languages: English, the language of government, and Spanish, the language of the people.[34] Because the bishop insisted on the bilingual ability of his personnel, he was able to use the schools to build avenues of communication and trust to the Hispanics. This proved an advantage not enjoyed by the Protestant teachers, who did not use the bilingual approach. When the Protestants finally secured Spanish bibles, they were unable to teach the children and their parents how to study them.

In the mountain villages and in the outlying desert towns Hispanic families welcomed into their homes the catechisms, the devotionals and prayers, the lithographs and religious medals and scapulars which the children brought home from the Catholic academies and schools.[35] Indeed, these schools served as central distribution centers for religious goods for the towns and villages. Lamy encouraged his pastors to teach the catechism, enroll children in religious societies and distribute religious articles. In 1862 Lamy informed the Society for the Propagation of the Faith that in support of the work being done in the academies he had sent ordained deacons to the villages to teach the catechism.[36]

Besides religious goods and doctrinal knowledge the children brought home a world of learning beyond that experienced by any of their family. With the nuns they studied writing, spelling, reading, English, mathematics, geography, and United States history. Students could also avail themselves of electives such as chemistry, botany, and music.[37] Until 1891, when the public school system was established in New Mexico, the Catholic academies and teaching orphanages were the primary Americanizing agent in the territory for Hispanic children and their families.[38] Even Governor W. W. H. Davis praised Lamy's schools for disseminating among the population knowledge of America and its institutions.[39]

Nevertheless, Davis and other territorial officials constantly pushed for a common public school system. Hispanic suspicion toward non-Catholics and their institutions clearly expressed itself in opposition to such a system. For Hispanics common education was a new idea imported from the United States which involved more than the academic education of their youth. At issue was unmonitored exposure to Protestant teachers, the disadvantage of a solely English curriculum, the prospect of increased taxes to support the public schools, and (for the wealthy) the disruption of social and economic systems firmly grounded upon an uneducated peon class.[40] In contrast to the proposed public schools, Lamy's schools addressed primarily the needs of Hispanics and only secondarily the needs of Anglo students.

The Hispanics were supported in their opposition to the public school system by Bishop Lamy and his priests, as well as by an organized legislative bloc of *ricos*, wealthy landowners who traditionally controlled the popular vote. The issue of public schools figured significantly in the larger issue of statehood. Quite simply, if New Mexico did not establish a system of public schools, Congress would not admit the territory to statehood. As the Hispanics grew accustomed to the territorial system they displayed little interest in seeking statehood. They were, therefore, willing to veto any bill which led to the creation of public schools. Anglo officials appealed to Washington for a solution or financial remedy to their problem. Congress made no move to meet the appeals so the territorial government resorted to foul play to secure the election of sympathetic legislators and to obstruct the *rico* bloc.[41] Anglo frustrations found a voice in Governor Davis, who described the New Mexicans as "so far sunk into ignorance that they are not really capable of judging the advantage of education."[42] Thirty-four years later Governor E. G. Ross echoed Davis' sentiments when, attacking those who had opposed school legislation, he protested, "They have denied us our most cherished right."[43]

Legislative lamentations were paralleled by the efforts of Protestants who, throughout the period, sought to enroll Hispanic children in their day schools. In 1920 Jay S. Stowell reported to the Home Mission Board in New York on the results of this effort. Based on a survey of all Protestant Evangelical schools for Hispanics in the southwest between 1880 and 1920, the report addressed unequivocally the goals of evangelization and Americanization. Stowell condemned the Catholic efforts as "failing to measure up to the demands of the situation," claiming that the Church's priests, who were themselves often non-American, failed to establish among Hispanics a satisfactory morality and pursued a ministry so permeated with "ignorance and superstition as to render it both unChristian and unAmerican." In Stowell's opinion it was the task of Protestant Evangelicals to take up the standard of Americanization so carelessly carried by the Catholics. The mission day school was the locus of salvation, the "one real Americanizing factor in the community." While praising the teacher's cottage as the one place where English was spoken, Stowell lamented the inability of the same teacher to speak Spanish and truly educate the people.[44] At the time of his survey there were sixteen Protestant day schools in the southwest, twelve in New Mexico. Although nearly all Evangelical energies among the Hispanics were engaged in New Mexico, Stowell concluded:

The Protestant Evangelical Churches have not had much influence here because the people insist upon clinging to their outdated customs and modes of livelihood.[45]

In the mind of the Anglo in New Mexico the indigenous people needed to be civilized and educated. Jean Lamy basically agreed, and he valued the academies and day schools as a positive and integral part of a total reformation. But the Catholic schools contributed to other aspects of Lamy's program besides Americanization. As adminstered by the nuns they were a point of contact and conciliation with native New Mexicans. Above all, they were a place to preserve the natives' Catholic faith against the Protestant challenge and to update it with instruction in orthodoxy rather than "superstition." Between the bishop and his people there was little understanding when it came to the popular practice of the faith and the everyday mode of living. But both shared an aversion to Protestants and a commitment to education--though sometimes for different reasons--and both found common ground in the schools. If beyond his chancery doors Lamy faced an unfriendly territorial government and a flock which resisted Americanization, the relative success of his Catholic schools was a source of comfort and encouragement.

Notes

1. Dorothy Dohen, *Nationalism and American Catholicism* (New York: Sheed and Ward, 1967), 6-7.

2. Norman Graebner, ed., *Manifest Destiny* (New York: Bobbs-Merrill Co., 1968); Frederick Merk, *Manifest Destiny and Mission in American History* (New York: Vintage Books, 1963); Ernest Lee Tuveson, *Redeemer Nation: The Idea of America's Millennial Role* (reprint, Chicago: University of Chicago Press, 1980); Albert K. Weinberg, *Manifest Destiny: A Study of Nationalist Expansion in American History* (reprint, Gloucester, Mass.: Peter Smith, 1958).

3. Louis Wright, *Culture on the Moving Frontier* (Bloomington: Indiana University Press, 1955); Leonard Pitt, *Decline of the Californios: A Social History of Spanish Speaking Californians, 1846-1890* (Berkeley: University of California

Press, 1966); Alice Cochran, *Miners, Merchants and Missioners: The Roles of Missionaries and Pioneer Churches in the Colorado Gold Rush and Its Aftermath, 1850-1870* (Metuchen, N.J.: Scarecrow Press and the American Theological Library Association, 1980); Alvin Sunseri, *Seeds of Discord: New Mexico in the Aftermath of American Conquest, 1846-1861* (Chicago: Nelson Hall, 1979); Colin Goodykoontz, *Home Missions on the American Frontier* (Idaho: Caxton Publishers, Ltd., 1939), 16, 35-39, 235-237.

4. Goodykoontz, *Home Missions*, 236.

5. Cochran, *Miners, Merchants and Missioners*, 168.

6. Wright, *Culture on the Moving Frontier*, passim.

7. Polly Welts Kaufman, *Women Teachers on the Frontier* (New Haven: Yale University Press, 1984), xvii-xxiii, 7-23, passim; Goodykoontz, *Home Missions*, 379-381; Wright, *Culture on the Moving Frontier*, 63-70, 92-110.

8. Paul Horgan, *Lamy of Santa Fe* (New York: Farrar, Strauss & Co., 1975).

9. See Horgan, *Lamy of Santa Fe*; Angelico Chavez, *But Time and Chance* (Santa Fe: Sunstone Press, 1981) and *My Penitente Land* (Albuquerque: University of New Mexico Press, 1974); Marta Weigle, *Brothers of Light, Brothers of Blood* (Albuquerque: University of New Mexico Press, 1976).

10. For *"auto de fe"* see Chavez, *My Penitente Land*, 119-154, and, by the same author, *La Conquistadora: The Autobiography of an Ancient Statue* (Santa Fe: Sunstone Press, 1975). The clearly defined sense of religious mission is discussed in Chavez, *My Penitente Land*, 1-52 and George Hammond, *Don Juan de Onate and the Founding of New Mexico* (Santa Fe: El Palacio Press, 1927), 74-79.

11. Antonio Barreiro, "Ojeado sobre Nuevo Mexico," in H. Bailey Carroll and J. Villasana Haggard, eds., *Three New Mexico Chronicles* (reprint, New York: Arno Press, 1967), 140-141.

12. See the reports of Fray Francisco Dominguez in Eleanor B. Adams and Angelico Chavez, eds. and trans., *The Missions of New Mexico, 1776: A Description by Fray Francisco Atanasio Dominguez, With Other Contemporary Documents* (Albuquerque: University of New Mexico Press, 1975), 86. For the observations of Bishop Antonio Zubiria during his visits to the region in 1832, 1845, and 1850 see José Espinoza, *Saints in the Valleys* (Albuquerque: University of New Mexico Press, 1967), 20-36. See also Chavez, *My Penitente Land*, 119-186; E. Boyd, *Saints and Saintmakers* (Santa Fe: Laboratory of Anthropology, 1946).

13. Quoted in W. J. Howlett, *Life of the Right Reverend Joseph P. Machebeuf, D.D.* (reprint, Denver: Register College of Journalism, 1954), 164, 181.

14. Paul Horgan, *Great River: The Rio Grande in North American History, Vol. 2: Mexico and the United States* (New York: Rinehart & Co., 1954) 866.

15. Quoted in Horgan, *Lamy of Santa Fe*, 407.

16. Lewis Meyers, *A History of New Mexico Baptists, 1849-1912*, Vol. 1 (n.p., Baptists Convention of New Mexico, n.d.), 41-53; Thomas Harwood, *History of New Mexico Spanish and English Missions of the Methodist Episcopal Church From 1850 to 1910 in Decades*, Vol. 1 (Albuquerque: El Abogado Press, 1908), 15-21; Stowell, *A Study of Mexican and Spanish Americans*, 9-14 and passim.

17. Sunseri, *Seeds of Discord*, 106.

18. Barreiro, "Ojeada sobre Nuevo Mexico," in Carroll and Haggard, eds., *Three New Mexico Chronicles*, 94.

19. Ibid., 95.

20. Ibid., 96; Horgan, *Lamy of Santa Fe*, 119; Howlett, *Life of Right Reverend Joseph P. Machebeuf, D.D.*, 167, 181-182; David Weber, *The Mexican Frontier, 1821-1846* (Albuquerque: University of New Mexico Press, 1982), 43-69; James Defouri, *Historical Sketch of the Catholic Church in New Mexico* (San Francisco: McCormick Bros., 1887), 49.

21. Borrego-Ortega Papers, Private Collections, New Mexico State Records Center and Archives, Santa Fe, New Mexico; Horgan, *Lamy of Santa Fe*, 124-126.

22. Kaufman, *Women Teachers on the Frontier*, 19-23, 102-115; Wright, *Culture on the Moving Frontier*, 222-223.

23. Jean Lamy to John Purcell, 2 September 1851 and 16 January 1859, Horgan Papers, Archives of the Archdiocese of Santa Fe, Albuquerque, New Mexico; Horgan, *Lamy of Santa Fe*, 119.

24. Harwood, *History of New Mexico Spanish and English Missions*, 26.

25. Meyers, *A History of New Mexico Baptists, 1849-1912*, 27-42, 54; anonymous, *Baptist Home Missions in North America, 1832-1882* (New York: Baptist Home Missions, 1883), 492, 553, 555, 559.

26. Mark Banker, "José Ynes Perea and Hispanic Presbyterians in New Mexico," *infra*; Carolyn Atkins, ed., *Los Tres Campos: A History of Presbyterians in Chimayo, Cordova, and Las Truchas* (Albuquerque: Menaul History Library of the Southwest, 1978); Gabino Rendon (with E. Agnew), *Hand on My Shoulder* (New York: Board of National Missions, Presbyterian Church in the U.S.A., 1953).

27. Brother George Baldwin to Sister Blandina Segale, 22 November 1883, Blandina Segale File, loose papers, Archives of

the Sisters of Charity, Mt. St. Joseph, Ohio.

28. Catherine Miriam Lawler, CS, "History of Sisters of Charity in New Mexico, 1865-1900" (M.A. thesis, Creighton University, 1938), 28-30.

29. Sister Mary Richard, SL, *Light in Yucca Land: Centennial Commemorative, 1852-1952* (Santa Fe: Schiani Brothers Publishing Co., 1952); Defouri, *Historical Sketch*, 36-43.

30. Magdalen Hayden, SL, to unnamed correspondent, 11 May 1854, Hayden Correspondence, RG Spec. 9, Box IV-3, Archives of the Sisters of Loretto, Nerinx, Kentucky.

31. Magdalen Hayden Correspondence, 20 December 1863, RG Spec. 9, Box IV-3, Archives of the Sisters of Loretto.

32. Brother George Baldwin to Sister Blandina Segale, 14 December 1883, Blandina Segale File, loose papers, Archives of the Sisters of Charity; See also the letters of Mother Hayden, 12 January 1863 and 12 May 1863, RG Spec. 9, Box IV-3, Archives of the Sisters of Loretto.

33. Catherine Miriam Lawlor, interview with author, Pueblo, Colorado, 25 August 1982; David Weber, *Foreigners in Their Native Land* (Albuquerque: University of New Mexico Press, 1973), 214-220; Howard Roberts Lamar, *The Far Southwest, 1846-1912: A Territorial History* (New York: W.W. Norton & Co., 1970), 89, 169, 187; Carolyn Zeleny, *Relations Between Spanish Americans and Anglo Americans in New Mexico* (New York: Arno Press, 1974), 274, 281-290.

34. Mother Hayden speaks of using Spanish also in daily prayers, individual confession, and retreats. See "Early Annals," 5, #8, RG-Sch XIII, Box XIVa-1 and Hayden correspondence of 28 September 1860 and 10 September 1861, RG Spec. 9, Box IV-3, Archives of the Sisters of Loretto; Horgan, *Lamy of Santa Fe*, 104, 160, 272.

35. "Price of School Books," Our Lady of Light Academy records, RG-Sch XIII, Box XIII-3, File: New Mexico, Santa Fe, Archives of the Sisters of Loretto.

36. Lamy to Purcell, 20 June 1859, Loose Documents, 1859, #13, and Lamy to Society for the Propagation of the Faith, 11 February 1862, Horgan Papers, Archives of the Archdiocese of Santa Fe.

37. Lawlor, "History of the Sisters of Charity," 53.

38. Ibid., 17, 35, 44; Jay Stowell, *A Study of Mexican and Spanish Americans and the United States* (New York City Library Archives: Home Mission Council and Council for Home Missions, 1920, microfilm), 12-14.

39. Quoted in Sunseri, *Seeds of Discord*, 109.

40. Zeleny, *Relations Between Spanish Speaking and Anglo Americans in New Mexico*, 265-271, 281-284; Stowell, *A Study of Mexican and Spanish Americans*, 62; Sunseri, *Seeds of Discord*, 109-112; Lamar, *The Far Southwest*,167, 187. For evidence that not all Hispanics opposed the public schools, see George Sanchez, *Forgotten People: A Study of New Mexicans* (Albuquerque: University of New Mexico Press, 1940), 17-25.

41. Sunseri, *Seeds of Discord*, 110.

42. Ibid.

43. Quoted in Lamar, *The Far Southwest*, 187.

44. Stowell, *A Study of Mexican and Spanish Americans*, 11-12.

45. Ibid., 71.

4.
Missionary to His Own People: José Ynes Perea and Hispanic Presbyterianism in New Mexico

Mark T. Banker

In October 1869 the Reverend John A. Annin arrived by stage in Las Vegas, New Mexico. His mission was to stake Presbyterian claim to the long-neglected region, which would soon be opened to the burgeoning Anglo-American society by the incoming Atchinson, Topeka, and Santa Fe Railroad. The railroad, however, did not reach Las Vegas for nearly a decade-- only the first of many setbacks and obstacles encountered by Annin. Without the anticipated influx of Anglo pioneers, Las Vegas remained small, isolated, and populated predominantly by Hispanic Catholics and a few Anglo cowboys and merchants. Finding the latter uninterested in his message, Annin decided to concentrate his work on the native Hispanics. Thus, without approval from his own Church, Annin took his Protestant message to a people who for several centuries had been steadfastly Catholic. Unfortunately, Annin in many ways undermined his own cause. His Spanish was poor and, more seriously, his ethnocentrism and personal piety made him repugnant even to those otherwise attracted to him. A more likely prospect for failure could hardly have been imagined.

That Presbyterianism did take root in Las Vegas and ultimately in the widely dispersed Hispanic communities of Northern New Mexico can mainly be attributed to a small number of native Hispanics who, for a variety of reasons, embraced and promoted the cause of the Anglo newcomers. Of these, none was more important than Don José Ynes Perea. Heir to one of New Mexico's wealthiest families, Perea had earlier converted to Protestantism while at school in the East. In 1869, alienated from family and friends, he was operating a sheep ranch eighty miles north of Las Vegas. Annin's arrival, he later wrote, was "an answer to prayer." Yet his own presence was more of a Godsend for John Annin than *vice versa*. As interpreter, financial benefactor and friend he was the pillar of Annin's struggling Presbyterian congregation. Most importantly, Perea was a bridge between Annin and a people the Anglo missionary little understood and who instinctively distrusted him. For thirty years after Annin's departure from New Mexico in 1880, Perea continued to spread the Protestant message to his fellow New Mexicans. His role as native purveyor of a foreign faith was neither easy nor enviable. Often rejected by his own people, Perea was not always accepted by the Anglo newcomers either.[1]

The story of the late 19th century Protestant intrusion is a little-known chapter in Southwestern history. Most general accounts devote only a few paragraphs to it. This neglect is justified if one considers numbers alone, for not once did the combined membership of all Protestant groups seriously challenge Catholic hegemony.[2] But church membership is not the only consideration of the religious historian. The most important themes in late 19th century Southwestern history are the complex social and cultural interchange between the native populations and the Anglo newcomers, and the beginning of the region's transition from traditional to modern society. Protestant missionaries and converts were key actors in this drama. Few were more significant than José Ynes Perea.

Perea was born in 1837 into a society perplexed by rapid change. Long an isolated and neglected outpost of Spain's far northern frontier, New Mexico was shakened in 1821 by Mexican independence and the subsequent opening of the Santa Fe trade. The region's rapid entrance into the modern world was further assured by the American conquest in 1846 and the transportation revolution, which by the last decade of the 19th century had tied it to the burgeoning Anglo society. Colonial New Mexico had been dominated by a few wealthy families and the Catholic church. Whereas the former were largely successful in adjusting to the new political and social conditions, the latter was in decline even before 1821. Always considered a mission field by the Spanish, New Mexico in 1760 had thirty Franciscan missionaries. Influenced by the increasing secularism of the 18th century, the number declined to only nine a few years after Mexican independence. Moreover, the erratic policies of the Mexican government eroded the strength of the ecclesiastical hierarchy and the church's economic base. In New Mexico, the church stagnated, believers were neglected, and the "morale and morality of the priesthood declined." The lay organization *Los Hermanos de Nuestro Padre Jesus Nazareno*, better known as the *penitentes*, emerged in early 19th century New Mexico to fill this spiritual void by organizing worship activities and providing social services. Their independence and penchant for physical penance disturbed the Mexican Bishop of Durango, who in 1833 denounced and banned the organization. But in a land where *obedezco pero no cumplo* had long been the rule, the Bishop's edict went unheeded and only antagonized the Native New Mexicans.[3]

Following the American conquest, both Catholics and Protestants took notice of New Mexico's spiritual malaise. "We now have but the forms and exterior of religion," one prominent Catholic wrote. In a population of 70,000, he added, the Catholic Church had only fifteen priests, six of whom were elderly while most of the others were "less than devoted" in their work. The well-known reforms of the French-born Archbishop Jean Baptiste Lamy were intended to correct these shortcomings.[4] That the Catholics were in such straits could not have been known from the early Protestant accounts of the region, which emphasized its "poverty, ignorance, and low state of morals" and most frequently described New Mexico as "priest-ridden." As José Ynes Perea wrote about his native land at the time of John Annin's arrival: "We were in the valley of the shadow of death."[5]

While occasional Protestant missionaries reached New Mexico shortly after the American takeover, few permanent inroads were made until the end of the Civil War. The Presbyterians were initially ambivalent about Hispanic missions. Henry Kendall, Secretary of the Board of Home Missions, was displeased with Annin's 1870 decision to work among Las Vegas's Hispanics. "Home" missions, he wrote, implied work with English-speaking people and thus New Mexico's Hispanics were "not a first priority."[6] But by the mid-1870s support from Dr. Sheldon

Jackson (Superintendent for Missions in the Rocky Mountain region), the promise of financial backing from the church's women, and the surprisingly positive response of some Hispanics to Protestantism convinced the Home Board to embrace Hispanic work. For the next several decades Presbyterians aggressively pursued this new challenge, with twin goals of Protestantization and Americanization. Pragmatically true to their Calvinist origins, the Presbyterians used education as the primary means of attaining their goals. In a land with almost no public schools and where private Catholic education only served the children of the elite, the Presbyterians opened 47 schools between 1867 and 1890, all but ten of which remained open at the latter date.[7]

José Ynes Perea was born too early to attend one of the Presbyterian schools. Moreover, his was one of the *rico* families that had long dominated New Mexico, and thus he was assured an education in the finest schools then available. Two powerful and countervailing forces shaped Perea's childhood and youth. The first of these, the deeply rooted Catholicism of his Hispanic heritage, was evident in the devotion of his mother, the large financial contributions his uncle made to the Church, and his sister's early decision to enter a convent. It is not surprising that José's first educational experiences were in Catholic schools. At the age of five he was sent to the school of a Father Becerra in the nearby village of Peralta, and two years later his father enrolled him in the acclaimed Chihuahua school of Dr. Guadalupe Miranda. There he received the rudiments of a classical education, was confirmed, and took his first confession. After the American acquisition of New Mexico, Don Juan Perea transferred his son to the "French School" of Mons. Peugnet in New York City.[8]

Despite this heavy Catholic influence, a few incidents from Perea's early youth portended his later repudiation of his parents' faith. The first occurred scarcely a few days after his birth, when an aunt and uncle, who were his Godparents, took him to be baptized. The nearest priest was at Isleta Pueblo, twenty-five miles south of the Perea ranch on the opposite bank of the Rio Grande. When their ox cart forded the river and was innundated, the party was delayed. Flustered by the unexpected bath and by the impatient priest, the aunt could not recall the middle name originally chosen by the infant's parents. The priest turned to his book of saints and came up with the name Ynes (Agnes), the saint on whose day the child was born. Despite the uncle's protests that it was a woman's name, the priest baptized the child accordingly. Though Perea never mentioned the matter in his own writings it is known that his parents were unhappy about it. It is at least plausible that his carrying the name Ynes (instead of Ignacio) contributed to Perea's early antipathies towards priests.[9] Perea gave clearer evidence of his future iconoclasm when, on a dare from a servant girl, he shot an arrow at his mother's beloved painting of the Holy Virgin. Though a boyish prank, the incident revealed an irreverence that sorely upset Perea's mother, who undoubtedly recalled it years later when José returned from the East renouncing "Catholic idolatry."[10]

The second shaping force of Perea's early development was his father's realization that the old order was rapidly changing and that his children had to adjust to the new conditions. Evidence of this was his decision to send José to Mons. Peugnet's school in 1849. There, however, the two forces shaping the youth collided. José joined a group of students who secretly read from the Bible in defiance of school rules--and official Vatican policy. Impressed by his scriptural discoveries, José soon refused to attend confession and became known by his teachers as "that Mexican heretic." When news about his precocious son reached the father, in the spring of 1851 Don Juan arranged for José's appointment to the United States Military Academy, where he enrolled the following fall. In less than a year José was as disgusted with the Generals as with his previous Catholic teachers. Shortly thereafter, Don Juan recalled his son to New Mexico, where he could watch him more closely.[11]

Many attempts were made to correct José, but he refused to recant. The matter was particularly scandalous because of the family's reputation. Finally, afraid José was beginning to influence other family members, Don Juan sent him to St. Louis to serve as a clerk in a dry goods store. Though he joined a Presbyterian Church there, he still felt the "continuing and growing opposition of his parents." True to the traditions of his adopted nation, on July 4, 1855, José declared his personal independence, took a steamboat to New Orleans, and signed on as a deckhand with a sailing vessel. For the next five years he traveled the world, making calls in such distant ports as Rio de Janeiro, Liverpool, Calcutta, and the Hawaiian Islands. In 1860 while in port in Boston, Perea received a letter from his father asking him to come home and indicating that his new faith would be tolerated. José accepted his father's plea and returned to New Mexico. However, lingering resentment towards his unorthodoxy and ill feeling over the growing sectional conflict convinced him to move to California. There he remained until 1864, when he received word that his father was seriously ill.[12]

Much had changed in the ten years since Perea's banishment from the family home. No longer a recalcitrant adolescent, he remained a strong but less flagrant Protestant. Similarly, while never renouncing Catholicism, Don Juan reconciled himself to his son's new faith and often read from the Spanish Bible José had given him. When Don Juan died in 1865, José alone of the eleven children was at his side and was appointed administrator of his estate. Perhaps the absence of other family members was evidence of the extent of the old man's acceptance of his son's "heretical views."[13]

Two years later Perea married Victoria Armijo, daughter of a *rico* of old Albuquerque. She apparently tolerated but never fully accepted José's Protestantism. The couple moved to *La Rinconda* (the Perea family ranch), but less than a year later Victoria died. A disheartened José withdrew from family and friends and soon thereafter took over one of the family sheep ranches at the isolated village of Salazar on the Rio Puerco. In 1869 he moved again, this time to even more distant La Cinta on the Pecos River, eighty miles north of Las Vegas, where he operated a ranch with 15,000 sheep. There he shared his Protestant convictions with his ranchhands and spread tracts and Spanish Bibles throughout the surrounding villages.[14]

Until 1869 José Ynes Perea maintained his Protestant beliefs but was uncertain about the course of his own life. John Annin's arrival erased Perea's doubts and convinced him he had a role in the "change and regeneration" of his own people. In a report to a Presbyterian magazine, Annin recounted meeting Perea when the rancher was on one of his regular trips to Las Vegas to purchase supplies. Always very direct, Annin pointedly asked Perea: "Do you think you are a Christian?" Perea responded: "I trust by the grace of God I am." This began a friendship that, despite occasional strains, proved propitious for both men and for the cause of Presbyterianism in the Southwest. Thereafter Perea's trips to Las Vegas were more regular, and he frequently visited the Annin home. In particular he enjoyed reading books from Annin's personal library. Finding himself increasingly devoted to the Presbyterian cause, Perea turned his ranch over to a foreman in 1871 and moved to Las Vegas, where he boarded with the Annins and became part owner of a general store.[15]

Had it not been for Perea, it is likely Annin would soon have given up the work at Las Vegas. His early letters describe New Mexicans as "heathenish, degraded, and thieving" and lament the Home Board's lack of interest in his work. Feeling pinched on both sides, he admitted to "a good deal of solicitude" about the success of his mission. Financial problems exacerbated his plight. His quarterly checks from the Home Board were never adequate and they rarely arrived on time. During the first year in Las Vegas, when Annin faced moving expenses and the costs of refurbishing a home, Perea advanced him more than $400. When Annin was finally able to make repayment, Perea only accepted $300, designating the rest a "contribution to the cause."[16]

Despite such setbacks, a group composed of Rev. and Mrs. Annin, Perea and four others gathered on March 21, 1870 to formally organize a church. Perea was unanimously chosen Ruling Elder and, since he alone among the Hispanics spoke English, also served as interpreter. Within six months membership grew to twenty-one. Only three of the new members were from Las Vegas; the rest were from distant villages in San Miguel and Mora counties. The latter areas had been neglected by the priests, and eventually would establish their own small

Presbyterian congregations. The presence of these people in the early Las Vegas church and the relative absence of members from Las Vegas itself (where there had long been Catholic priests) provides an important clue for understanding Presbyterian successes and failures in Hispanic New Mexico.[17]

Following formal organization of his church, Annin's next step was to construct a permanent building for worship and his school. In this effort, Perea was again a key figure. When a site was selected, Annin asked for pledges of support. Not surprisingly, the single biggest contribution came from Perea. It included $500 in cash, $100 worth of lumber, the use of ten yoke of oxen and two wagons, and sufficient sheep and cattle to provide meat for workmen on the project. With funds nearly depleted and the new structure still lacking a bell and belfry, Perea contributed additional money to complete the project. Perea was not only a financial benefactor; along with Annin, he secured needed materials and supplies, hired and supervised workers, and kept detailed financial records.[18]

The work of establishing and maintaining a congregation proved in some ways more difficult than building a structure in which it could meet. As the church's bilingual Ruling Elder, Perea examined those who wished to become members, most of whom spoke only Spanish. A more distasteful duty was maintaining church discipline, a task made difficult by Annin's rigorous expectations of his parishioners. On one occasion Annin and Perea rode fifteen miles to visit one of the original members, who had been charged with "violation of the 7th Commandment." When the man refused to give up his common law mate, Annin struck his name from the church role. The Session Minutes for these early years make many references to improprieties, such as "public drunkenness," "protracted absence from worship service," and "behavior unbecoming of a Christian." As Ruling Elder, Perea frequently followed up such cases, but when his efforts to rectify them failed, Annin was not loathe to dismiss the guilty party from the congregation. Though Perea left no public record on this, Gabino Rendon, who was raised in Las Vegas during this period and who later became a Presbyterian minister and friend of

Perea's, suggests that "Don Ynes and Annin did not see eye to eye on the matter of church discipline." Annin's letters and reports say nothing about this, but it seems plausible to conclude that the omission of any reference to Perea in Annin's correspondence between 1872 and 1875 indicates that he was not entirely happy with his Ruling Elder.[19]

It is difficult to know how the general population of Las Vegas viewed their fellow New Mexican who had so closely aligned with the Anglo minister. In recalling his youth in Las Vegas, Gabino Rendon commented that many people, including his own rabidly anti-Protestant father, looked up to Perea because he was wealthy and had seen so much of the world. Though no other observations about Perea from native Las Vegans remain, the importance of social deference in traditional New Mexican society and the absence of attacks on him (either physical or verbal) substantiates Rendon's assessment.

It would be a mistake to assume, however, that Perea's Protestant views were warmly accepted by his fellow Hispanics. Rendon recalled being warned to stay away from the *protestante* and, as a boy, imagined Perea "had horns and a tail."[20] Perea himself recalled that the Jesuits, who established a permanent mission and school in Las Vegas in the mid-1870s, were the major source of opposition to his and Annin's efforts. While their inflammatory sermons convinced some of the "better Catholics" to stay away, they never succeeded in completely subverting the Protestant cause, according to Perea. His dry comment, "I do not know of anyone being shot dead coming from church," is not only indicative of the casual attitude Las Vegans had towards violence but also suggests that the Presbyterian-Catholic dispute was relatively benign.[21] After 1875 a bitter journalistic war raged between the Jesuits' *La Revista Catolica* and Annin's *La Revista Evangelica*. For several years they debated issues such as public education and reading of the Bible by laypersons, both of which Annin defended as Christian and American. In response, the Jesuits editorialized that the world's highest crime rates were in those nations that provided free public education and pointed to the "Tower of Babel of American Protestantism" as evidence of the bitter fruits of open access to the scriptures.[22] While *La Revista Catolica* made several direct attacks on Annin during the period 1875-78, there is no mention at all of José Ynes Perea. Perhaps this was due to his frequent absences from Las Vegas; but it may be evidence that Perea, unlike his Anglo mentor, had learned that Catholicism could best be countered by avoiding antagonistic confrontations. His earlier experience with his father and his subsequent career suggest this might have been the case.

While the Presbyterians always considered education the primary vehicle for their mission, they soon realized the cause could be greatly enhanced by the development of a native ministry. At its November 1876 meeting, the Presbytery of Santa Fe decided to invite several responsible Hispanic church members to become full-time lay evangelists. As such, they would work in the field under direction from ministers, and it was expected that the more capable would prepare for the ministry. Shortly thereafter, the Rev. George G. Smith corresponded with Perea to inquire if he would join this endeavor. Perea initially was hesitant but eventually accepted the call.[23] Following an appearance before a committee of the Presbytery, he and Rafael Gallegos were appointed licentiates in the Las Vegas field, where they studied and worked under the direction of Rev. Annin. The Presbytery recommended Perea be paid $800, but the Home Board reduced this to $600, and he and the other licentiates were directed to give up all other professional pursuits and means of income. While for several of his co-workers this meant little, for Perea it was a major sacrifice. The first had truly become last, and the course was set for the remainder of his life.[24]

The two licentiates working with Rev. Annin followed a rigorous routine. After a week's preparation during which they worked with Annin "morning, noon, and night" studying scripture and preparing sermons, the two evangelists went out into the field. Often away from Las Vegas for more than a month, they visited isolated villages and ranches in San Miguel, Mora, and Taos counties, an area that proved unusually receptive to Presbyterianism. Each day they rose early and rode most of the morning to reach their destination. In the afternoons they visited homes and invited people to their evening services, following which they often visited with interested individuals until past midnight. Eager to take advantage of any gathering of people, they once preached at the wake for a person who had died of smallpox. Though exhausting, this routine provided excellent training. It was the kind of ministry Perea pursued the rest of his life.[25]

In the summer of 1878 Perea left Las Vegas. While details are unclear, some evidence suggests there may have been a rift with Rev. Annin. The latter tersely commented in his church's session book that "Mr. Perea left Las Vegas August last and has not returned and probably will not." Moreover, Perea's Hispanic co-worker had so many problems with Annin that he later left the Presbyterians for the Methodists. Yet it would be wrong to assume that these difficulties stemmed purely from ethnic factors. Annin had come to Las Vegas in 1870 following heated differences with his Minnesota congregation, and he departed ten years later in the wake of a protracted feud with the Anglo leaders of the church. The dispute was so heated that the Annins removed from the church a carpet which they had purchased with their own funds. While it seems unquestionable that Annin was difficult to work with, Home Missions officials greatly lamented the loss of his services and in private correspondence implied that he was not the cause of the problems in Las Vegas in 1879-80. Moreover, Perea's own later accounts of his Las Vegas years have nothing but praise for his mentor and friend.[26]

Upon leaving Las Vegas Perea served as guide and interpreter for Dr. Sheldon Jackson, who was touring the New Mexico missions. This was surely an honor, for Jackson was Superintendent of all Presbyterian work in the Rocky Mountain region and widely recognized as one of the church's most prominent leaders. At services organizing churches at Jemez and Laguna Pueblos, Perea translated Jackson's words into Spanish so they could be translated again into the native tongue. In early October the two parted company at Zuni Pueblo, where Perea had been appointed by the Board to serve as licentiate and interpreter under the Rev. Taylor F. Ealy. Ealy, his family, and his assistant,

Miss Susan Gates, arrived in Zuni a few days after Perea. They were already acquainted, because the Ealy party had stopped in Las Vegas the year before on their way to a newly created mission station in Lincoln, New Mexico. The violence and bloodshed there, known as the Lincoln County War, proved unconducive for mission work, and after several harrowing months the Ealys withdrew. For several weeks as the Ealys regained their strength in Las Vegas, Miss Gates attempted to establish a school at the village of Agua Negra, deep in the Sangre de Cristo mountains and on the evangelical circuit of José Ynes Perea.[27]

Perea's friendship and subsequent marriage to Susan Gates on Christmas Day 1878 were the only bright spots of his four months at Zuni Pueblo. Geographically isolated and culturally intransigent, the Zunis proved a more than formidable challenge for the Ealys and a host of other missionaries before and after them.[28] While at Zuni, Perea aided Ealy in digging a well and building a new mission house. Only once, when he read from Genesis 1 in Spanish so that it could be translated for a Zuni audience, did he perform anything resembling a ministerial role. When in February the newlyweds departed for a new assignment at Jemez Pueblo, Mrs. Perea had not been paid for her two months as teacher at Zuni, and Ealy owed Perea $85 he had borrowed to purchase supplies for the new home.[29]

The Home Board's appointment of Perea to the two Indian Pueblos during the winter 1878-79 is curious when one considers the great need for bilingual workers in the Spanish field. It seems even more inappropriate when one reads the anxious letters from Dr. J. M. Shields, missionary at Jemez, protesting that the Pereas would not help his cause. His reservations allegedly stemmed from the tense relationship between himself and the Catholic priest at the Pueblo, to whom most of the Indians were apparently loyal. Even before the Pereas left Zuni, Shields wrote Pueblo Agent B. M. Thomas, indicating that the arrival of more missionaries, particularly a man, would only worsen the situation.[30] When the Pereas arrived at Jemez, Shields again voiced these concerns and suggested they move several miles beyond the village and work at the Spanish community of Canon de Jemez until further word arrived from the Board. In a letter informing Sheldon Jackson of the unexpected change, Perea suggested a better location for work in the Spanish field would be one of the less isolated towns along the Rio Grande. Since Bernalillo and Albuquerque were "full of Jesuits," he suggested he be sent to the village of Corrales, and concluded: "I wish to settle in one place and make it my life's work." Not coincidentally, Corrales was only a few miles from the Perea family ranch. In April, the Board approved a recommendation from Jackson that Perea be transferred to Corrales, making him truly a missionary to his own people.[31]

The Pereas' first year at their new station was hectic. The field extended on both sides of the Rio Grande and encompassed more than twenty-five Spanish villages. As in Las Vegas, Perea utilized a circuit rider approach; a roundtrip, whirlwind visit to his dispersed flock took over two weeks. Though the Board originally advised that a school should not be established until autumn, Perea protested that by then his evangelistic work would probably alienate some who might initially be willing to bring their children to school. In short, he saw a school, in addition to its normal educational role, as bait to draw people to his work. His argument was apparently convincing, for on May 26 a school opened with "seven very nice little girls of the well-to-do people of the town" and Mrs. Perea as their teacher. By the following January, over thirty were enrolled, though not all attended regularly. After the birth of the Pereas' first child, José became increasingly involved in school work, and both his preaching duties and preparations for the ministerial examinations were neglected. The illness and death of the infant, and the severe financial strain brought on by a reduction in Board support left Perea disheartened. On April 3, 1880, he wrote Sheldon Jackson: "We have been trying to do *too* much." But, when the Board later considered transferring him to Albuquerque, Perea wrote Jackson again stating he had not expected "easy success" at Corrales and that the results there already surpassed his expectations.[32]

Perea's evangelical work under Dr. Shields was in most ways similar to that under Rev. Annin. As in the previous field, his task was largely preparatory. Working among people who had known him since his childhood, Perea was cautious and sensitive to pressure from the priests on those who might stray from their direction. Rather than hold formal worship services, he visited families in their homes and distributed Spanish tracts and Bibles. Shortly after his arrival in Corrales, he reported that a few men were reading from the scriptures; but, he added, they were unwilling to discuss them. As the enrollment of his school grew, so did the opposition from the priests. Perea reported that at mass they denounced him as a "corrupt and wicked heretic" and commanded their parishioners not to associate with him. Some of the people were friendly and even defiant of the priests. The father of a child who attended the mission school condemned the priests for "living off the fat of the land" and suggested to Perea they opposed his school because they wanted "to keep the people ignorant." But most of the villagers, including practically all of his family and friends, kept their distance. When Perea's wife and child were ill and he faced severe financial problems, his pleas for temporary employment and financial help went unheeded.[33] In Hispanic New Mexico, where family ties are very strong, this was an unmistakable indication of the negative reaction to his decision to preach the Protestant message.

While Perea's relations with his Anglo co-workers at Zuni, Jemez, and Corrales were probably more cordial than they had been with Annin, one senses occasional strain. Often the attitude towards Perea seemed paternalistic and patronizing. One wonders why Dr. Ealy did not use Perea more fully in the areas for which he was assigned and whether Perea was not resentful that he spent almost the entire four months at Zuni working as a manual laborer. Moreover, Dr. Shields' almost frantic opposition to Perea's working at Jemez Pueblo may have had other sources than the one he officially gave. Though always outwardly supportive of Perea, he once complained to Sheldon Jackson about Perea's "miserable Mexican way of doing business." From Perea's point of view probably nothing was more disquieting than the Board's decision in 1880 to reduce the assignments for the Hispanic evangelists to six months. This meant salaries would be cut in half and that the evangelists would have to find secular employment for the remainder of the year. This, Perea protested to Jackson, would be disastrous for both his work and his family. Fortunately, the matter was resolved without having to cut the assignments, but it nevertheless disturbed Perea and left his faith in his Presbyterian friends shaken.[34] Rejected by many of his own people, Perea could not count on being considered an equal by the Anglos, whose cause he had made his own.

The September 1880 meeting of the Presbytery of Santa Fe was an historic occasion for American Presbyterianism. An original expectation of the Spanish evangelist program was that some of the licentiates would pursue studies and ultimately be ordained Presbyterian ministers. At this meeting José Ynes Perea became the first candidate to go before Presbytery for this purpose. After successful completion of exams in church government, the sacraments, theology, and church history, Perea preached a trial sermon which was unanimously approved by the Presbytery. The next day he became the first Hispanic in the United States to be ordained a Presbyterian minister.[35] Perea's elevation to ministerial status at least outwardly changed his role in the Church. Though reappointed to his old field, his annual salary was increased to $1,000, commensurate with the salaries of the Anglo ministers in the Presbytery. In subsequent years he played a more prominent role in the Presbytery and Synod, and in 1882 his colleagues chose him to represent the Presbytery of Santa Fe at the Church's General Assembly in Chicago. In short, José Ynes Perea became the elder statesman of Hispanic Presbyterianism and living proof of the Anglos' commitment to it. Yet except for a change in location Perea's day-to-day work changed little after his ordination. Until his retirement in 1905 Perea labored much as he had since his early days as an evangelist under John Annin-- dispensing tracts and Bibles, visiting in homes, sharing his views with any who would listen, and preaching to the few who risked condemnation by priests and neighbors and attended his services. Ironically, far fewer records remain of Perea's work after his ordination than for the earlier periods.[36] What is clear, however, is that the last thirty years of Perea's life were devoted to one of the most difficult Presbyterian assignments in the New Mexico Territory.

Following his ordination, Perea returned to Corrales, where signs of progress seemed apparent. Under the direction of Miss Elizabeth Smith, school enrollment in February 1881 exceeded forty students. Around the same time Perea began holding regular worship services. Though attendance occasionally exceeded twenty-five persons, he remained cautious about formally organizing a church. He commented to Jackson that Catholic opposition had receded and that "the Bible is being read and commented on in every home." Less than a year later, however, Perea reported renewed Catholic opposition and added that "those who do not come to services are reached by going to them."[37]

Within a few years Perea's attention was drawn away from Corrales. Greater potential for Presbyterianism seemed to exist in a cluster of small villages along the Rio Grande, south of Albuquerque, and Perea spent an increasingly large amount of time there. By the mid-1880s, Minutes of the Presbytery listed Perea as working in this latter area, and in 1890 he moved his family to the village of Pajarito, seven miles south of Albuquerque. No official explanation was given by Perea or the Church for his abandonment of Corrales. Despite ardent efforts, he left without formally establishing a church, and within a short time the Presbyterian school was closed. Apparently Perea and his fellow Presbyterians finally conceded that his home soil was too barren for the seeds he had so hopefully planted.

It is unlikely Perea moved to his new field because he believed the work would be easier. Like every area he worked, the one south of Albuquerque was huge and contained a large number of small and isolated Hispanic villages that had long been dominated by Catholicism. In particular, Perea's work concentrated on the villages of Pajarito and Los Lentes. He had initially visited the former in the early 1880s, established a church there with fourteen members in 1883, and four years later opened a school. After moving to Pajarito in 1890, he began preaching in Los Lentes, a small village several miles further down the Rio Grande, and he established a church there in 1896 with fifteen members. A few years thereafter he opened a school.[38] Perea's work in both areas was plagued by strong Catholic opposition, but, as in Las Vegas and Corrales, Perea found this was mostly the work of the priests and that most of the lay people, while unwilling to accept his religion, accepted him personally. Occasionally there were reasons for optimism, such as a revival in Pajarito in 1904 that led several long-time Catholics to convert to Presbyterianism, and a service in Los Lentes in 1898, where Perea and Synodical Missionary Robert Craig preached to a crowd of over 200, forty of whom were outside of the church building. But, in general, the work was slow, and as late as 1902 the combined membership of the churches was less than thirty.[39] Shortly after a flood destroyed the Los Lentes school and church in 1904, Presbyterian activity in the village was discontinued. The work in Pajarito continued sometime longer, but after Perea's 1905 retirement it went into decline. Within a few years of his death in 1910, the Presbyterians withdrew altogether.[40]

Despite apparent failures, the waning years of Perea's life and of Presbyterian work in his field were not completely devoid of accomplishment. Though old age slowed Perea down considerably, it provided him an opportunity to work with a number of young men who, like himself a few years before, were training for the ministry. As early as 1899, Synodical Missionary Craig advised the Synod of New Mexico that Perea needed help in ministering to his widespread field; the result was the assignment to Perea of students from the "Albuquerque Training School." Created by the Home Missions Board in 1902 and located on the Menaul School campus, the "Training School" was designed to provide practical and academic training for native New Mexicans who hoped to enter the ministry. During the week, students pursued course work at the school, and on Sundays they applied what they learned by assisting in churches in Albuquerque and surrounding areas. In the summers, advanced students were appointed to longer assignments as lay evangelists under the direction of ordained ministers. From 1902 until his retirement Perea rarely found himself without the assistance of one or more of the students. Not only did they relieve him of some of his duties, but they were welcome evidence that the work to which he had devoted his life would continue. At the 1904 meeting of the Presbytery Perea spoke glowingly of the program and modestly conceded he had learned a great deal from the young men working with him. Needless to say, the latter benefited greatly from Perea's experience and example.[41]

Perea's bilingual skills were yet another important contribution to the broader cause of Hispanic Presbyterianism. Most of the Anglo missionaries arrived in New Mexico speaking Spanish poorly, if at all, and most Hispanic converts felt more comfortable using their native tongue. Thus, Perea's ability to communicate articulately in both languages made him indispensable. In recognition of the growing number of Hispanics in their midst, the Presbytery of Santa Fe in 1880 designated Perea official interpreter of their proceedings. When the Synod of New Mexico in 1900 considered establishing a bi-monthly Spanish newspaper, Perea was one of its strongest supporters and proposed the name *La Aurora* (the dawn or beginning). Over the final ten years of his life he regularly contributed original and translated articles to the paper. Among his translations were theological treatises, hints for ministers, temperance tracts, and accounts (often apocryphal) from American history. Perea's choice of articles reflected his own experiences and predilections. For example, at the end of a 1905 translation describing George Washington in the midst of enemy fire at Yorktown, Perea likened the British bullets to attacks on Christians by their enemies. They were, he concluded, *balas gastadas* ("wasted bullets") and thus "nothing to fear." After Perea's death in 1910 the absence of the line *"traducido por JYP"* left a noticeable void in *La Aurora*.[42]

Perea also contributed many original articles to *La Aurora*, including accounts of his early experiences in the mission field and periodic updates on his work at Pajarito and Los Lentes. Undoubtedly Perea's most ambitious effort was a long series of articles written after his retirement, entitled *Extractos de la Historia de la Iglesia Cristiana*. Published semi-regularly by La Aurora from September 1907 to November 1910, *Extractos* recounted in flowing Spanish prose Christian history up to the era of the Reformation. Its blatantly anti-Catholic orientation was influenced greatly by the writings of the Rev. James Wharley and the 18th Century German Lutheran, Johann Lorenz Mosheim. As the latter's works have never been translated into Spanish or English, Perea apparently read French or Latin translations; his classical education had not gone to waste. The last segment of the *Extractos* was published posthumously in *La Aurora*'s memorial issue to Perea in 1910. Gabino Rendon's eulogy to Perea in this issue suggested that Perea's interest in church history provided "constant reinforcement of his own Protestant principles." This is evident in Perea's emphasis on the corruption of the papacy, priestly neglect of spiritual duties, and the Council of Trent's proscription of the reading of scriptures by laypersons. For Perea, these characteristics of the Medieval and Renaissance Catholic Church had parallels in 19th century New Mexican Catholicism. Similarly, he saw himself and his fellow Protestants following the examples of Martin Luther and John Calvin, the heroes of his account of Christian history. The series of articles served as a valedictory for Perea's long career and justified for himself and others the difficult and sometimes painful course of his own life.[43]

The life and career of José Ynes Perea provides insight into the little-known phenomenon of Protestantism in Hispanic New Mexico. Most obviously, the failure of this missionary to convert more than a handful of his countrymen reflects the general failure of Protestantism to challenge Catholic hegemony in the region. While Catholicism's deep roots and the fierce traditionalism of the New Mexican society were undoubtedly the major causes of this, Perea's experience suggests that other factors also hindered the Protestant cause. The reluctance of Anglo newcomers like Reverend Annin and Doctors Shields and Ealy to fully accept and utilize Perea's talents limited his effectiveness among his own people. Even after ordination into the ministry, Perea labored in small, isolated, and generally unfruitful fields. However, the full blame for this cannot be laid solely on the Anglos. In 1880 Perea balked at an opportunity to move from Corrales to a more promising field in Albuquerque, and when he ultimately left Corrales, he apparently chose to work in the equally unpromising field south of Albuquerque. While Perea's commitment can hardly be questioned, one wonders about how he chose to apply it. Was he simply unambitious? Or did the Anglo reluctance to accept him fully, plus opposition from his own people, make him cautious about his missionary endeavors? Yet another possibility was that because his primary concern was with individuals (and their souls) he rejected emphasizing quantity over quality in his work. The evidence does not fully answer these questions, but we do know that the Presbyterians held so little hope for Perea's fields that they relinquished all of them before or within a short time after his death. While Presbyterians continued their emphasis on preparing and utilizing native evangelists, the single most important factor in their accomplishments in New Mexico came from their widespread educational missions. Perea promoted schools in all of his fields, but he was never a major participant in the Presbyterian educational enterprise, one that later proved so attractive to his people.

Perea's experience reveals much about the broad social and cultural changes that occurred in the late-nineteenth-century American Southwest. His conversion to Protestantism stemmed directly (though not intentionally) from his father's recognition that New Mexico's Hispanics had to come to terms with the Anglo newcomers. Enmity from his own people and the deaths of his father and first wife seem to have driven him to further acculturation and into the arms of John Annin and the Presbyterians. Just how far he moved into the world of the Anglos is revealed by his subsequent marriage to Susan Gates and their choice of English names for their children. But it would be unfair to conclude that Perea was a "traitor" to his own people and culture. Even while embracing Presbyterianism he helped Hispanicize it. His entire missionary career was spent among his own people in remote and unpromising fields. He steadfastly advocated retention of the Spanish language, and by his own example promoted the development of a native ministry. His effort to share his Presbyterian faith with his fellow New Mexicans was motivated by belief that they would find meaning and benefit in it. The substance of this conviction may be questioned, but Perea's sincerity cannot.

The cultural interchange between Anglos and Hispanics in the late nineteenth century Southwest sometimes occurred reluctantly, but it was never a one-way process. As precursor and pioneer of the Presbyterian cause among his own people, José Ynes Perea acted as a cultural broker. His status as a *rico* and his deep love of his own people earned him their respect, and his knowledge of English, acculturation into the Anglo world, and commitment to Protestantism made him invaluable to the incoming Presbyterians. Perea's role was never easy, but his experience clearly reveals the human dimension of the cultural interchange that is perhaps the most important theme in the history of the late-nineteenth-century American Southwest.

Notes

1. Information about Presbyterian beginnings in Las Vegas may be found in J. A. Schufle, *Preparing the Way* (Las Vegas: First Presbyterian Church, 1970), Chapters 1-3; and Douglas Brackenridge and Francisco Garcia-Treto, *Iglesia Presbyteriana: A History of Presbyterians and Mexican Americans in the Southwest* (San Antonio: Trinity University Press, 1974), 38-44.

2. Frank D. Reeve, "The Church in Territorial New Mexico" (paper read at Minister's Continuing Education Conference, Albuquerque, 1964) cites census figures from Coan, *History of New Mexico*, indicating that of 105,748 New Mexico church members in 1890, 100,576 (95%) were Catholic. Of the Protestant denominations, the Methodists had 2,360 members and Presbyterians 1,285. Methodism, however, was strongest in the heavily Anglo southern part of the territory. The Presbyterians were undoubtedly the strongest Protestant group among the Hispanics of Northern New Mexico. The number of Hispanics to become Presbyterians has not yet been exactly determined; the most reliable estimates suggest that between 5 and 10% of the Hispanics in Northern New Mexico became Presbyterian by 1900.

3. David J. Weber, The Mexican Frontier, *1821-46: The American Southwest Under Mexico* (Albuquerque: University of

New Mexico Press, 1982), 69-81; Howard R. Lamar, *The Far Southwest, 1846-1912: A Territorial History* (New York: Norton, 1970), 18-19. The best source available on the *Penitentes* is Marta Weigle, *Brothers of Light, Brothers of Blood: The Penitente of the Southwest* (Albuquerque: University of New Mexico Press, 1974).

4. Schufle, 25. Two excellent biographical sketches of prominent New Mexico Catholics of the era are Paul Horgan, *Lamy of Santa Fe: His Life and Time* (New York: Farrar, Strauss and Co., 1975); and W. J. Howlett, *Life of the Right Reverend Joseph P. Machebeuf* (Pueblo, Colorado: Franklin Press Co., 1908).

5. José Ynes Perea, "Trabajos Tempranos," *La Aurora*, 16 July, 1903. *La Aurora* was a bi-monthly newspaper of the Synod of the Southwest. It was usually published in Spanish, though a few issues were in English and some were bilingual. Some of the originals and microfilm of all remaining issues are in the Menaul Historical Library (hereafter cited as MHL), Albuquerque, New Mexico.

6. Henry Kendall to Sheldon Jackson, 18 July 1870, Sheldon Jackson Correspondence Collection (hereafter cited as SJCC). The original SJCC is at the Presbyterian Historical Society, Philadelphia. Microfilm of the parts of it pertinent to the southwest are at the MHL.

7. Good general accounts of Presbyterian work in New Mexico are Ruth K. Barber and Edith Agnew, *Sowers Went Forth* (Albuquerque: Menaul Historical Library, 1981); and Brackenridge/Garcia-Treto, Ch. 2.

8. José Ynes Perea to Norman Skinner, 19 January 1897, J. Y. Perea file, MHL; "Memorial Sketch of Rev. José Y. Perea," *La Aurora*, 15 November 1910.

9. Robert Craig, *Our Mexicans* (New York: Board of Home Missions, Presbyterian Church in the U.S., 1904), 89-90.

10. There are several different accounts of this incident. In her unpublished manuscript "Missions in the Southwest," Alice Blake recounts a very different version that has Perea as a teenager shooting the picture with a gun. But written in the margin of Miss Blake's original copy is a comment from Rev. Gabino Rendon that Perea's own account of the incident was very different. The account Rendon then gave is the one given here. It is corroborated by a letter from Perea's son, Clifford, in the J. Y. Perea file, MHL.

11. José Ynes Perea to Rev. Norman Skinner, 19 January 1897; "Memorial Sketch . . . ", 15 November 1910.

12. Ibid.; Craig, 91; Schufle, 7.

13. José Ynes Perea to Norman Skinner, 19 January 1897; Schufle, 7.

14. Ibid.

15. Annin's account of meeting Perea was written on August 17, 1880, and was printed in the magazine, *The Presbyterian.* A clipping of the article is preserved in the Sheldon Jackson Scrapbook Collection (hereafter cited SJSC) on microfilm in the MHL. Perea's account of meeting Annin is found in "Original Missions in N.M.," *La Aurora,* 21 March 1912; and Perea's letter to Rev. Skinner, 19 January 1897.

16. John A. Annin to Sheldon Jackson, 5 January 1871, SJCC.

17. Session Minutes: 1st Presbyterian Church, Las Vegas, N. M., citation for 21 March 1870. (Note: The original minutes for the Las Vegas church are lost; the source used here is a typed/ handwritten transcription from the original. Las Vegas Presbyterian Church file, MHL); José Ynes Perea to Rev. Norman Skinner, 4 January 1897, J. Y. Perea file, MHL; John A. Annin to Sheldon Jackson, 24 October 1870, SJCC.

18. John A. Annin to Sheldon Jackson, 24 October 1870; Schufle, 19-24.

19. Session Minutes: 1st Presbyterian Church, Las Vegas, 1870-72; Gabino Rendon, *Hand on My Shoulder* (New York: Board of National Missions, Presbyterian Church in the U.S.A., 1953), 23-24.

20. Rendon, 17-18, 51.

21. José Ynes Perea to Norman Skinner, 4 January 1897.

22. Elizabeth Annin to Sheldon Jackson, 23 January 1878, SJCC; *Revisita Catolica*, 6 May 1875, 22 May 1875 (In History Library, Museum of New Mexico, Santa Fe); Schufle, 26-27.

23. Minutes of Presbytery of Santa Fe, November 1876; George G. Smith, "Reminisences of Early Days," *La Aurora*, 1 November 1905.

24. Minutes of Presbytery of Santa Fe, November 1877.

25. José Ynes Perea, "Original Missions in New Mexico," *La Aurora*, 21 March 1902; Perea, "Early Gospel Labors in N. M.," *La Aurora*, 13 August 1903.

26. Appendix (entitled "Records of John A. Annin") to Session Minutes: 1st Presbyterian Church, Las Vegas; J. M. Shields to Sheldon Jackson, 20 October 1879, SJCC. For more detail about Annin's problems at Las Vegas see the following letters from the SJCC: B. B. Borden to Sheldon Jackson, 15 December 1879 and 21 February 1880; Henry Kendall to Sheldon Jackson, 17 December 1879. Perea's letter to Norman Skinner, 4 January 1897 and his historical articles in La Aurora express very positive memories of Rev. Annin.

27. Ruth R. Ealy, *Water for a Thirsty Land* (published privately by Ealy family; original copy in MHL), 94-95; T. F. Ealy to Sheldon Jackson, 14 September 1878, SJCC; José Ynes

Perea to Susan Gates, 18 August 1878, J.Y. Perea file, MHL.

28. For an account of Presbyterian work at Zuni see M. T. Banker, "Presbyterians and Pueblos: A Protestant Response to the Indian Question," *Journal of Presbyterian History*, 60 (Spring 1982): 23-40.

29. T. F. Ealy to Sheldon Jackson, 9 November 1878, December 1878, 1 February 1879, 27 February 1879; Mrs. Ealy to Sheldon Jackson, 18 November 1879 -- all in SJCC; also see Ealy's diary entry for 26 January 1879 in *Water for a Thirsty Land*.

30. B. M. Thomas to Sheldon Jackson, 21 January 1879; Henry Kendall to Sheldon Jackson, 26 February 1879; J. M. Shields to Sheldon Jackson, 25 January 1879, 14 March 1879 -- all in SJCC.

31. José Ynes Perea to Sheldon Jackson, 20 February 1879; Henry Kendall to Sheldon Jackson, 7 May 1879.

32. José Ynes Perea, "Original Missions in N. M.," *La Aurora*, 21 March 1902; José Ynes Perea to Sheldon Jackson, 30 April 1879, 8 May 1879, 8 December 1879, 9 January 1880, 27 January 1880, 3 April 1880, 11 May 1880; J. M. Shields to Sheldon Jackson, 24 January 1880; Henry Kendall to Sheldon Jackson, 4 April 1880; all in SJCC.

33. José Ynes Perea to Sheldon Jackson, 30 April 1879, 8 December 1879, 20 January 1880, SJCC.

34. Henry Kendall to Sheldon Jackson, 4 April 1879; José Ynes Perea to Sheldon Jackson, 27 January 1880; J. M. Shields to Sheldon Jackson, 19 April 1880, SJCC.

35. Minutes of Presbytery of Santa Fe, September 1880; "Memorial Sketch . . .," *La Aurora*, 15 November 1910.

36. There are several reasons for the dearth of records for the latter part of Perea's career. First, one of the major sources for his earlier career is the SJCC. After 1880 Jackson's efforts turned increasingly to Alaska, and thus few letters from New Mexico are in that collection after that time. Second, Perea never established a church at Corrales, and the two churches he did establish (at Pajarito and Los Lentes) closed early in the 20th century and their official records no longer exist.

37. José Y. Perea to Sheldon Jackson, 19 October 1880, 29 February 1881, 10 February 1882; Elizabeth Smith to Sheldon Jackson, 5 November 1880, SJCC.

38. José Y. Perea, "Original Missions . . .," *La Aurora*, 21 March 1902; *Home Mission Monthly*, September 1887, 274; Minutes of Synod of N. M., 1901, 1902.

39. "Synodical Missionary Report," Minutes of Synod of New Mexico, 1898, *La Aurora*, 15 February 1904; *Home Mission Monthly*, November 1899, 20.

40. Minutes of Synod of New Mexico, 1904; Blake, "Missions in the Southwest," 47.

41. Craig, 86; *Home Mission Monthly*, November 1904, 9.

42. Minutes of Presbytery of Santa Fe, September 1880; "Memorial Sktech . . .," *La Aurora*, 15 November 1910.

43. "Extractos de la Historia de la Iglesia Cristiana," printed semi-regularly in *La Aurora*, 1 September 1905 - 15 November 1910. Information about Mosheim's histories (written in German) was provided by Dr. Donald Sullivan, Department of History, University of New Mexico.

5.
Baptist Railroad Churches in the American West, 1890-1946

Salvatore Mondello

Itinerant Baptist missionaries driving horse-drawn mission wagons filled with Bibles and religious tracts appeared in the American West as early as the eighteenth century. While some ministers went west with their migrating congregations from the east, other preachers and missionaries spent a season or two along the western frontier, establishing small churches before returning to the South and Northeast. Since some Baptist groups traveled long distances from their original settlements in the South and Northeast, they were required to worship in "traveling churches" during their westward journeys. Other Baptists moved west as family groups, however, and itinerant preachers such as Thomas Tinsley, John Taylor, and Joseph Redding made their way to Kentucky and Tennessee, to organize the faithful into new congregations and to provide them with religious literature.[1] The westward migration of Eastern Baptists contributed significantly to the establishment of the itinerant preacher as an important figure in church history and western folklore.

Baptist evangelicals journeyed westward not only to preserve the faith among the brethren, but to convert Indians, blacks, and non-Baptist whites--or at least to shield them from the teachings and influence of Roman Catholics and Protestants of other denominations. In the late eighteenth and early nineteenth centuries, Baptist officials began to consider the West a fertile field for their evangelical efforts, though the foreign field was their major missionary enterprise. As early as 1802, the Baptists of Massachusetts organized mission societies to assist financially the work of converting non-believers. In the second decade of the nineteenth century, Baptist leaders recognized the need to coordinate their missionary efforts in the West. A convention met in 1814 in Philadelphia to create a national missionary organization. Seventeen of the thirty-three delegates in attendance at that meeting were members of the Philadelphia Association, the oldest Baptist association in America. They established a permanent organization known as the Triennial Convention because its meetings were held once every three years.[2]

By supporting the missionary effort of Baptist evangelicals and revivalists already present in the West, the Triennial Convention contributed significantly to making itinerant missionary work on the frontier a permanent part of Baptist evangelism. The Convention's most important itinerant preacher in the American West, John M. Peck, worked tirelessly in St. Louis and its surrounding region. As early as 1818 Peck and his assistant, James E. Welch, established in St. Louis a Baptist church of eleven members, which had "no house in which to worship God, except a school-room, and that we rent."[3] In that year, Peck and Welch also organized a Sabbath school for blacks. When the war between the Cherokees and their allies and the Osages ended in late 1818, Peck approached Indians who showed an interest in Baptist teachings. In seeking financial assistance for this work, Peck noted that he intended not only to teach the Indians Christian principles but "to show them the value of property, of labour, and of industrious habits." When he commented on his activities among white settlers, he stressed the long distances he was required to travel for his house-to-house visitations and the need for Sunday schools and competent teachers.[4]

Peck pleased many Baptists because his evangelistic efforts were directed toward all minorities in his mission field, and because such efforts connected conversion to Christianity with such commendable institutions as Eastern-inspired Sunday schools and female missionary societies, as well as with the capitalist work ethic. Supported by the Triennial Convention, Peck became the vital link connecting mission bodies spread across a large region. In 1818 he organized the various mission groups he had helped to create in Missouri and Illinois into one missionary society. The new organization appointed the Reverend Peck its agent and superintendent and authorized him "to obtain subscribers, collect monies, originate auxiliary societies, [and] establish schools."[5] Peck's dynamic evangelism elevated the status of itinerant western missionaries and connected them on a permanent basis with regional Baptist associations.

Strong regional organization led to more effective national organization when in 1832 the American Baptist Home Missionary Society was established, with Peck one of its leading missionaries. The creation of the new Society within the Triennial Convention marked the triumph of those like Peck who championed centralization of the denomination's activities in the expanding nation.[6]

Prior to the Civil War, itinerant missionaries and colporters were sent throughout the western states and territories, and they worked with all of the major minority groups in the region in order to teach them the Scriptures and the importance of assimilating Anglo-American Protestant values. Evangelism among the Indians and Mexicans in New Mexico was viewed as a mighty crusade against "the dark and cruel rites of gross paganism" and the "cruel impositions of a degrading Romanism." Benjamin M. Hill, corresponding secretary of the Home Mission Society, reflected in 1854 that "the powerful young giant of the West" could be won over to Baptist principles "only by arming the pulpit of the West with sanctified intellect and holy feeling." The Baptists in the West, he argued, had to successfully challenge "the numerous forms of corrupt religion" and the "subtle infidelity prevalent in the land."[7]

The Baptists' great missionary zeal, their promotion of home missions, and their "vision of winning the West for Protestantism" continued into the late nineteenth and twentieth centuries.[8] In pursuing traditional aims, however, Baptists increasingly called upon modern technology for assistance. With their belief in progress and their commitment to reach the unchurched, post-Civil War Baptists were in the front rank of those American Christians who wished to dedicate "the machinery of civilization" to the work of God. Among the most fascinating results of this modernization process was the Baptists' widespread use of "the mightiest transportation facilities of the earth"--the American railroad system--to spread the gospel in the West.[9]

Though the Baptists devoted increasing attention and resources after the Civil War to evangelism among European immigrants in the East and ex-slaves in the South, they also renewed and expanded their crusade in the West. Worried about western outlawry and intemperance, fearing the influence of the Mormons and the swelling settlements of foreign-born Catholics in the West, American Baptists hoped to intervene decisively to cleanse and convert the region for God and country. To be successful in the undertaking, itinerant missionaries believed they had to make extensive use of the expanding railway network, which grew from 35,085 miles in 1865 to 254,037 in 1916.

No one understood this better than Wayland Hoyt, pastor of the First Baptist Church of Minneapolis, Minnesota. Reverend Hoyt believed that Baptist capitalists should take the initiative in financing the construction of the first Pullman churches to service the West and the South. He proposed his plan for establishing churches on trains to his brother Colgate, a railroad tycoon. Riding through Wisconsin and Minnesota in his brother's private Pullman, Wayland frowned on towns and hamlets with saloons but no churches. Stopping at a station in a lumber region, the minister spotted thirty or forty log houses, several stores, and a saloon. "It was not difficult," he later wrote, "to imagine the serpent slime of blight and wretchedness it [the railroad] would draw through that humble settlement." After the train pulled out of the station, he admonished his brother, "You railroad men ought to be doing more for this new country than you are now doing."[10]

Apparently agreeing, Colgate Hoyt invited John D. Rockefeller, Charles L. Colby, James B. Colgate, John B. Trevor, and Eugene J. Barney, all wealthy Baptist businessmen, to join him in forming the Chapel Car Syndicate. They met in New York City and decided to finance the construction of *Evangel*, the first Baptist Church Pullman. Rockefeller, convinced of the importance of Christian education, may have exerted his great influence in having *Evangel* placed under the jurisdiction of the American Baptist Publication Society rather than the American Baptist Home Mission Society. Unlike the Home Mission Society, which established missions and churches, the Publication Society, more to Rockefeller's liking, emphasized the dissemination of religious literature and the establishment of Sunday schools in its evangelistic programs.[11]

In May 1891 the members of the American Baptist Publication Society, convening in Cincinnati, proceeded to the Grand Central Depot to accept *Evangel* as a gift from the tycoons and to dedicate it to the Lord's service. "Roll On, Thou Bright Evangel," a hymn written for the occasion by Reverend W. H. Geistweit of Minnesota, was sung. Wayland Hoyt "made a felicitous address of presentation in behalf of the donors," and Boston W. Smith of Minneapolis, recently appointed general manager of chapel-car evangelism and one of its first proponents, accepted the Pullman for the Publication Society. The conferees gave "a vote of thanks with cheers" to the philanthropists and another vote of appreciation "with cheers" to the Northern Pacific and other railroads for offering to move *Evangel* free of charge.[12]

The donors had spared no expense in building the rolling church. Constructed by the E. J. Barney Company, *Evangel*, sixty feet long and ten feet wide, seated one hundred worshippers. Colonel J. J. Estey of Vermont donated the organ and Lucy A. Littlefield of the Mount Morris Baptist Church of New York City contributed a brass lectern. New York Central's experimental *Exposition Flyer* of 1893, a magnificent passenger train carrying thousands of New Yorkers to the Columbian Exposition, may have been inspired by the beautiful *Evangel* introduced two years earlier.[13]

In 1893, the Chapel Car Syndicate, perhaps hoping to squelch mounting public criticisms of railroad practices and management, contributed a second rolling church, *Emmanuel*, to the Baptist denomination. S. F. Smith, the author of "America," wrote "Chapel Car Hymn" for *Emmanuel*, dedicated at Denver. Reverend Kerr B. Tupper, delivering the dedicatory address, asked rhetorically, "And why should not the wheel, and all that is connected with it in the way of achievement and progress be consecrated to Jehovah?"[14]

Exterior of <u>Grace</u> with a local congregation.
Courtesy American Baptist Historical Society

From 1894 to 1900 the Baptists built four more rolling churches. In 1894, while *Evangel* traveled through Minnesota and *Emmanuel* toured California, *Glad Tidings*, a gift from William Hills of the Mount Morris Baptist Church, was dedicated in Saratoga, New York. At the ceremony Colonel C. H. Banes, corresponding secretary of the Publication Society, noted that Christians were "beginning to use the swiftness of steam." While the cathedrals symbolized the "everlastingness of religion," the chapel cars represented "its holy restlessness." Chapels stood for "continuity" and "preservation," said Banes, while chapel cars called for "conquest" and "pioneering."[15] Such an enthusiastic response to the chapel car ministry reflected the hope that the railroads would prove vital to the success of reaching non-believers. Technology, many Baptists believed, had come to the assistance of religion.

But the faithful had to contribute to the work. William Hills stipulated that his donation of *Glad Tidings* had to be matched by a similar grant from the denomination as a whole for a fourth car. Baptists from the Northeast responded by contributing the funds required for building *Good Will*. At its dedication ceremony at Saratoga in 1895, Wayland Hoyt commended the railroads for not charging any fees to carry chapel cars. "As the Roman roads were pathways for the feet of the apostles, so the railroads have made themselves free avenues for the swift-goings of the chapel cars." At the ceremony he complimented his fellow Baptists for making such marvelous use of the new technologies: "You have hitched your gospel to the nineteenth century."[16] After the women of the denomination contributed the *Messenger of Peace* in 1898, the men responded by paying for the *Herald of Hope* two years later. The Baptists built their seventh and last chapel car in 1915. B. F. Conaway of Los Angeles donated *Grace*, a steel-framed car with a wood interior. Presented in Los Angeles, *Grace* served California and Arizona during its first year of operation.[17]

Modeled after the Pullman sleepers, the chapel cars attracted attention wherever they went. They served to advertise the work of the denomination. "The very beauty and cleanliness of the cars command the respect and admiration of all who see them," said

Interior of <u>Grace</u> during a church service.
Courtesy American Baptist Historical Society

Reverend J. P. Jacobs, a railroad missionary. "Not only are the cars themselves respected but the missionaries are respected because of them and many a time find their way into homes and hearts that could not be reached otherwise."[18] When a storm in Galveston damaged *Good Will*, the Texas Baptists, proud of its work, made large contributions for the repairs.[19] In 1904, Baptist officials, glowing with admiration for their chapel cars, exhibited *Messenger of Peace* at the St. Louis World's Fair. "On one day over ten thousand people passed through the car," the Publication Society boasted in 1905. "The commissioners have awarded a silver medal to the car for its excellence."[20] Chapel cars had become showcases for Baptist evangelism.

In 1909, the Baptists announced that their pioneering chapel-car work had convinced the Roman Catholics to build a car of their own. Six years later, the Baptists noted that the American Catholics had three chapel cars while the Greek Catholic Church maintained an equal number on the Trans-Siberian Railways.[21] The Baptists had been first in chapel-car evangelism not simply because Wayland Hoyt had quickly won the endorsement of Baptist railroad barons, but because as early as the eighteenth century they had placed a greater stress on a mobile ministry than any other denomination.

The Publication Society flooded its annual reports with statistical evidence showing the success of its chapel-car program. In 1894, *Evangel* in Minnesota and *Emmanuel* in California together traveled a total of 17,834 miles, distributing 681 Bibles and 74,945 pages of tracts. With the chapel cars usually sidetracked for two to three days in most of the towns visited, the missionaries delivered 1,313 sermons and addresses, held 207 prayer meetings, visited 589 families, celebrated eighteen baptisms, constituted seven churches, and organized eleven Sunday schools.[22]

Statistics might impress the faithful, but biographies and memoirs give a more vivid picture of the missionaries and their daily work. In 1893, Boston W. Smith, general manager of the Chapel-Car Department of the Publication Society, selected Edwin

G. Wheeler as the first railroad missionary. Wheeler, a successful telegrapher and businessman in Minnesota and South Dakota, experienced a profound spiritual conversion in 1877. Becoming a devout Baptist, Wheeler established morning and evening prayer services for his employees in Winona, Minnesota, but found his greatest pleasure in setting up Sunday schools in the surrounding region. Indeed, he devoted so much time to organizing Sunday schools that he became known in Minnesota as "Sunday-school" Wheeler. He eventually accepted the appointment as district missionary of the Publication Society for the Pacific Coast. After working in this capacity for ten years, Wheeler assumed his duties as chapel-car missionary. Soon called "Chapel-car" Wheeler, he won the respect of the railroad workers and other mobile men who attended services in *Evangel.* "I doubt if ever a service was held in the car that did not result in conversions," said a pastor from San Francisco in praising Wheeler. Later, Wheeler and his wife took charge of *Emmanuel* when it was put into service in California. Their work in El Paso, Texas, led to the establishment of a Chinese Baptist mission. On August 7, 1895, Wheeler died in a railroad accident in New Mexico.[23]

Unlike Wheeler, whose wife recorded his experiences, Charles H. Rust, a prolific writer and public speaker, left many personal accounts of his activities as a chapel-car missionary. Charles and his wife Bertha, well-educated young missionaries in Boston, hoped to go to Africa until Boston W. Smith assigned them to *Glad Tidings.* "And I confess all was very dark to us," wrote Rust, "because we had never been west of New York, and while I knew Chicago and Minneapolis were excellent cities, yet what we might find west of them frightened us." However, they grew to enjoy their work as chapel-car missionaries traveling through North and South Dakota, Minnesota, Wisconsin, Iowa, and Nebraska. Though the parsonage on the car gave the couple and their two daughters practically no privacy, they were pleased that farmers, miners, and lumberjacks packed the audience room wherever the car went. With a seating capacity of more than one hundred, the audience room accommodated an organ donated by the Estey Company, a brass lectern, a blackboard, and two libraries, one for Rust and the other filled with books to lend to small towns. The audience room, fifty-two feet long, offered a striking contrast to the cramped parsonage, eighteen feet long and ten feet wide, consisting of a bedroom with two berths, a dining room, a study, a kitchen, a toilet room, and a heater to warm the entire car!

Chapel-car missionaries needed nerves of steel as well as rugged constitutions to survive living on the road. "If the car is not on a special spur of its own it must be switched nearly every day and night," wrote Rust in 1905. "During one night last summer we were switched five times, and handled quite roughly." Few missionaries kept orderly kitchens. "I would like to have some neat housewife who prides herself on daintiness, see our refrigerator after a switching crew had banged our car up and down the track for a half-hour," remarked Rust. "Such a sight. Milk, potatoes, jelly, pickles, all together."

Children gathered around the car upon its arrival in every town, wondering if it was the circus. Some adults and children hoped to relieve their drab existence by attending services in the chapel car. Rust had "a wonderful voice," his daughter Majorie noted in a recent interview, and liked to illustrate his sermons by writing on the blackboard. Bertha sang and played the organ. She also visited the women in their homes, hoping to ease their loneliness. Although many westerners were "rough," the personable minister nonetheless attracted them to the church services. Eventually Rust rode the rails alone, leaving his family in Minneapolis. Since chapel-car missionaries received passes from the railroads to ride free of charge on any line, he could visit his family often. He worked ten years as a chapel-car missionary, leaving that field in 1905.

Rust points out that the chapel car was a beautiful urban-style church made available to people living in drab hamlets and small towns. While western farmers and miners might imagine what the private Pullman cars of the rich and famous were like, the chapel cars gave them a direct experience with gracious urban living. Since the chapel cars traveled hundreds of thousands of miles through the hinterlands of the South and West, they must have stimulated interest in the urban areas of America. That Christian brothers and sisters like Charles and Bertha Rust might also greet newcomers to the cities must have been a comforting thought to many farmers and miners preparing to leave their natal homes.

At first, no one considered using the cars for religious services for railroad workers. "The possibilities along that line developed after the work was started," wrote Rust. As Boston W. Smith talked with railroad officials about the importance of the work, chapel-car missionaries were soon encouraged by the railroad managers to provide more religious services for the mobile railway crews. Railroad managers hoped such services would elevate the moral standards of their employees, thus improving the public's impressions of the railroads while reducing workers' discontent with labor conditions. Writing in 1905, Rust noted that "there has never been a time previous to the present when railroad companies were so free to recognize the demand and need for moral character among their employees . . . . They are enforcing rules regarding drinking and frequenting saloons that would not have been tolerated a few years ago." Rust believed that "the chapel car is a railroad institution and the missionary is a railroad man."

According to Rust, the chapel-car work changed considerably during its first decade. Initially, chapel-car missionaries remained only a few days in most towns. Their task was to organize Sunday schools. "We hardly dared to stay very long for fear we might have enough conversions for a church, and thereby open up the possibility of criticism as a demand for a church organization came to the front."[24] Soon, however, the Baptist state conventions recognized that the enthusiasm people felt for the chapel-car services might represent a first step toward building permanent church facilities in many towns. State officials started to cooperate with the Publication Society in using the chapel-car missionaries to save weak churches and to establish new ones. In this way urban church standards as reflected in the chapel cars influenced the establishment of more modest churches at the turn of the century.

Baptist missionaries benefited from special privileges granted by the railroad companies. In 1902 Rust expressed gratitude to the officials of "the many lines of railroad" who provided the missionaries free transportation and trackage. According to Rust, railroad companies had built a special spur track for his car, *Glad Tidings*, in six towns in the past year and a half. The companies, he added, gave special rebates on freight in some instances, reducing the cost of building Baptist churches.[25]

Beginning in 1906, however, the expenses of running and maintaining the chapel cars became increasingly burdensome for the Publication Society. This situation was the consequence of more stringent government regulation of the railroads. Before the Progressive movement, government attempts to curtail railroad abuses had been ineffective. Established in 1887 as the first federal regulatory agency, the Interstate Commerce Commission had the power to regulate railroad rates, but of the sixteen cases it had brought before the Supreme Court between 1887 and 1906, all but one had been decided in favor of the railroads. The Sherman Antitrust Act of 1890 had proved equally ineffective in regulating big business, including the railroad interests. This trend was reversed during the Progressive era. The Elkins Act of 1903 strengthened the Interstate Commerce Act of 1887 by defining more clearly the penalties for railroad rebates. Three years later, the Hepburn Act increased the powers of the Interstate Commerce Commission to establish maximum railway rates, to determine through routings, to decide fair division of rates among cooperating carriers, and to set up uniform accounting procedures. The Mann-Elkins Act of 1910 clarified the short-haul versus long-haul provisions of the Interstate Commerce Act, enabling the Interstate Commerce Commission to regulate more effectively the rates charged by the railways. Three years later, the Physical Valuation Act gave the Commission the power to assess railroad property so that fair rates could be fixed.

In December 1905, the presidents of the Pennsylvania, the New York Central, and the Reading railroads announced that beginning January 1, 1906, free passes would be issued only to their own employees. In 1907, the Publication Society reported that new government regulations compelled some railroads to charge fees for transporting the rolling churches. Seven years later, the Publication Society announced that restrictive regulation against all free rail services made it necessary for the Baptists to pay "for transportation quite generally, and as a result the operative expense has been considerably increased." In 1917, the Baptists cancelled an arrangement for bringing *Grace* to the East for an evangelical campaign when the Pennsylvania System rescinded "all promises of trackage rights." By the second decade of the twentieth century, some churches adopted chapel cars in order to reduce the expenses of the Publication Society. The Board of Managers of the Publication Society reported in 1915 that the First Baptist Church of Dayton, Ohio adopted *Herald of Hope*.[26] This represented an extension of an old Baptist practice of individual churches adopting missionaries, thereby cutting down the expenses of the denomination's mission societies.

Baptists also hoped to reduce costs by securing endowments for the cars, but such plans failed to materialize. Noting in 1910 that "we have more applications for the cars than we can possibly meet," the Publication Society decided to reduce expenses by restricting one of the cars, the *Messenger of Peace*, for work among railroad men only. Beginning this work on the Frisco System in Missouri, the Publication Society in 1911 extended its cooperative program with the Railroad Y. M. C. A. by allowing the missionary on the *Messenger of Peace* to work among railroad men in other states as it traveled eastward to take its place in the exposition of "The World of Boston."[27] Whatever their intentions, Progressive reformers had seriously curtailed the effectiveness of the railroad ministry.

To cover its mounting costs, the Publication Society entered into an agreement with the Home Mission Society in 1920. The Home Mission Society agreed to pay the salaries and direct the missionary activities of the chapel-car workers while the Publication Society continued to direct their Bible and religious activities and to pay all expenses involving equipment and transportation.[28]

This joint agreement applied to the gospel-boat as well as

chapel-car missionaries. As early as 1906, the *Mamie Beal* under Reverend D. W. Townsend had been put in operation in Puget Sound with the endorsement of the Baptists of Washington: "The wheels of the steamer are in motion in the interests of Christ's kingdom."[29] By 1914, two other colportage boats had been added to the Baptist flotilla on the Pacific Coast: the *Life Line* working in western Oregon and the *Osceola* (also called the *Crozer Cruiser*) operating in northern California. Thanks to the boats, one missionary reported, "a Sunday-school of thirty-five" had been started "in a large dance-hall controlled by a saloonkeeper."[30] Since their introduction in 1906, gospel boats complemented the work of the chapel cars.

Unlike the gospel boats, however, automobile and truck chapels equipped with trailers posed a direct challenge to the existence of the railroad chapel cars. In 1922, the Publication Society purchased its first auto chapel "with a special trans-continental home touring body" for missionary work among the Mexicans of the Los Angeles area. Placing Reverend Pablo Villanueva, a Mexican, in charge, the Society noted that the auto chapel reached hamlets and small towns far removed from other transportation facilities. One year later, the Baptists added the *Ernest Leigh Tustin Memorial Auto Chapel Car No.2* for missionary work in northern California. In 1925, Reverend Villanueva, still in charge of the *Crawford Memorial Chapel Car No.1*, received high marks from the Society for his services among the Mexicans of Belvedere Park. Four years later, with a fleet of five auto chapels serving California, Arizona, Cuba, and Puerto Rico, the Publication Society noted that their maintenance was less costly than that of the railroad chapel cars.[31] Each auto chapel, like every railroad chapel car, carried a large tent for religious services.

During the 1920s and 1930s the railroad chapel cars continued to build churches and stimulate religious revivals in the South and West, though they now shared these functions with the auto chapels. In 1924, the railroad rolling churches performed missionary activities in Wyoming, Colorado, Nevada, Arizona, Washington, California, and West Virginia. During the Twenties, A. C. Blinzinger and his wife, missionaries on *Grace*, led a revival in Las Vegas, the "most wicked town west of the Mississippi." Blinzinger met stiff opposition but refused to leave until he organized a group of Baptists who would "help clean up" the place.[32]

By the end of the Thirties four railroad chapel cars were retired because of obsolete equipment and costly maintenance. *Evangel*, cut in half and widened sufficiently to make four Sunday-school rooms and a large social hall, was incorporated in the Baptist church of Rawlins, Wyoming. *Herald of Hope*, placed on a solid foundation, became a Baptist church and parsonage at Mar-France, West Virginia. *Good Will* was reconstructed as the headquarters for missionaries in northern California. *Glad Tidings* ended its days as the church building and parsonage of the First Baptist Church of Flagstaff, Arizona.[33]

Howard Parry and his wife Mary Ellen labored as chapel-car missionaries in the final years of the railroad ministry. During the 1930s, Parry traveled on *Emmanuel* in Colorado, establishing and strengthening congregations in such towns as Peyton, Briggsdale, Crowley, Ordway, and Deertrail. In South Fork and Del Norte, the Parrys "had a battle with cold as well as with sin," noted *The Coleman News*. "The altitude is some 8,200 feet, and temperatures register below zero more than 180 days out of every 365."[34] They worked among people suffering from the harsh economic hardships caused by the Great Depression. In February 1940, Reverend Parry wrote: "No work at all in South Fork and very little in Del Norte, with people in both areas required to rely either on government relief or dip into reserves of the income producing period in summer and fall."[35] When Parry left in 1941, the Baptists in South Fork had built a community chapel and the Del Norte congregation had been revived. The two churches, aided by the Colorado Baptist Convention, appointed Theodore Mayberry, a recent graduate of Eastern Baptist Theological Seminary, as their permanent pastor.[36] In South Fork, Parry worked so successfully with Mexican Americans that Catholic officials in Colorado were worried. Parry reported: "The Roman Catholics have apparently been stirred to provide some services for their Mexicans since our coming, for the priest came down and has been talking about building a church here."[37]

Because public and denominational interest in the chapel cars declined by the 1930s and 1940s, Parry always seemed concerned about meeting the expenses connected with his work. At South Fork the Parrys suffered from the bitter cold because funds could not be found for more than a year to purchase an adequate heater. In 1938, he feared that the Colorado Baptist Convention might stop paying for half of the expenses of transporting and spurring out *Emmanuel*. "Your representatives feel that some churches served are able to assume a portion of this expense," he complained to the chairman of the Colorado Convention.[38] Parry and his superiors at the Publication Society must have been greatly relieved when the Colorado Convention agreed to continue to pay for half of these fees.

Emmanuel and the other two remaining railroad chapel cars were serving Baptist communities in Colorado, Washington, and Wyoming in 1942. But the Publication Society reported that "in no state is there a large field for the use of these cars."[39] Baptists preferred their automobiles and trailers instead. When the new *Nuveen Trailer*, a Howard 21 DeLuxe donated by John Nuveen of Chicago was displayed at Wichita, Kansas, 3,030 visitors signed the "Trailer Guest Log."[40] In the same year, *Emmanuel* was retired to the Swan Lake Assembly Grounds in South Dakota to "stand as a memorial to the chapel-car ministry in the west."[41]

Defense plants during World War II opened up new opportunities for the last chapel-car missionaries. C. W. Cutler and the *Messenger of Peace* went to Vancouver. Cutler presented a frustrating account of his work in 1944: "The closing days of our current year find us back to the city with its teeming multitudes living in defense housing projects, with its terrible juvenile crime wave, with its frightful unconcern, and with the combined efforts of all religious organizations not reaching one-tenth of the itinerant people."[42] After the war the *Messenger of Peace* was stationed in Everett, Washington, its last known location. Howard Parry and *Grace* spent the war among defense workers in Orem, Utah where the chapel car became known as the Grace Baptist Community

Church. But Orem was a Mormon stronghold, and following the war the Baptists there were too few to support a permanent church. In 1946, *Grace* was retired to Green Lake, Wisconsin. Officials of the Denver and Rio Grande Western Railroad Company told Parry they could not transport *Grace* to Wisconsin at a reduced rate because of Interstate Commerce Commission rulings.[43] Stringent government regulation of the railways, increasing preference for the automobile for missionary work, and the rising costs of maintaining the chapel cars had finally ended the era of the railroad ministry in the West.

In his recent study of the American railroads, John R. Stilgoe enhances our appreciation of their contributions to American culture and society in the half century following 1880. "Understanding their half century of importance," he writes, "may indeed facilitate understanding rural, suburban, and urban environments, for trains and right-of-way created a fourth distinctive environment-- the metropolitan corridor." Stilgoe also observes: "In the remotest corners of rural America, in suburbs of broad lawns, in small towns, the luxury express advertised the crackling energy of urban industrial zones."[44] The work of the Baptist rolling churches suggests that the "metropolitan corridor" contained some "chapel rooms." The Baptist Pullmans, themselves elegant cars, proclaimed the vigor and vitality of urban churches to the rural West.

But that was not their principal aim. Their primary purpose was to revitalize and expand the Baptist mission in the American West, a mission which had suffered from neglect during the era of the Civil War and Reconstruction. The railroad ministry proved to be a resounding success, yielding significant results. Facilitating the efforts of the Baptists to spread Christian teachings, the railroad ministry established the policy of denominational support for itinerant missionaries in the modern era, a policy continued by the automobile ministry. The enthusiasm crowds at city and state fairs showed for chapel-car exhibitions taught Baptist leaders that advertising and showmanship were sometimes vital in successful fundraising campaigns for missions. Another important consequence of the railroad ministry was its totally accidental creation of a new community of the faithful, the mobile railroad men of the West. The chapel cars were the permanent places of worship for the railroad men as well as the temporary churches of others.

By establishing and strengthening churches in the West, by extending literacy to remote settlements, and by organizing Sunday schools, the Baptist chapel cars played a prominent part in taming the West. In building modern rolling churches, American Baptists announced that the new technologies could serve eternal spiritual needs. Using the chapel cars to reach the poorer classes of rural America, the Baptists were reaffirming their historical commitment to Christianize a democratic society.

Notes

1. Robert G. Torbet, *A History of the Baptists* (Valley Forge: Judson Press, 1963), 356. Research for this paper was conducted at the American Baptist Historical Society in Rochester, New York [ABHS].

2. Torbet, *History*, 249-250.

3. John M. Peck and James E. Welch, "Mission to the Westward of the Mississippi River," *The Latter Day Luminary* 1 (May 1818): 89.

4. John M. Peck, "Station at St. Louis," Ibid. (February 1819): 303-04.

5. Ibid., 307.

6. Torbet, *History*, 252.

7. *Twenty-Second Report of the American Baptist Home Mission Society* [ABHMS] (New York: ABHMS, 1854), 26-39.

8. Torbet, *History*, 253.

9. *Eighty-First Anniversary of the American Baptist Publication Society* [ABPS] (Philadelphia: ABPS, 1905), 13. On the modernization of the American churches, see Benjamin Primer, *Protestants and American Business Methods* (Ann Arbor: UMI Research Press, 1978).

10. *Sixty-Sixth Anniversary of the American Baptist Publication Society* (Philadelphia: ABPS, 1890), 69-73.

11. *Church on Wheels* (n.p., n.d.), 1-2; Torbet, *History*, 327, 410.

12. *Sixty-Seventh Anniversary of the American Baptist Publication Society* (Philadelphia: ABPS, 1891), 36-37.

13. John J. Stilgoe, *Metropolitan Corridor: Railroads and the American Scene* (New Haven: Yale University Press, 1983), 59.

14. *Sixty-Ninth Anniversary of the American Baptist Publication Society* (Philadelphia: ABPS, 1893), 36-37; Churches on Wheels, 8.

15. *Seventieth Anniversary of the American Baptist Publication Society* (Philadelphia: ABPS, 1894), 23-24.

16. *Seventy-First Anniversary of the American Baptist Publication Society* (Philadelphia: ABPS, 1895), 15.

17. *Ninety-First Anniversary of the American Baptist Publication Society* (Philadelphia: ABPS, 1915), 1044.

18. *Eighty-Second Anniversary of the American Baptist Publication Society* (Philadelphia: ABPS, 1906), 13.

19. *Seventy-Ninth Anniversary of the American Baptist Publication Society* (Philadelphia: ABPS, 1903), 58.

20. *Eighty-First Anniversary of the ABPS*, 97.

21. *Ninety-First Anniversary of the ABPS*, 1045.

22. *Seventieth Anniversary of the ABPS*, 58-59.

23. Rose Farrington Wheeler, *Chapel-Car Wheeler* (Philadelphia: ABPS, 1897), passim.

24. Charles H. Rust, *A Church on Wheels or Ten Years on a Chapel Car* (Philadelphia: ABPS, 1905), passim; memorandum of interview with Majorie Rust Morrison, December 10, 1980, in the author's possession. Rust later became pastor of churches in Minneapolis, Minnesota, and Rochester, New York. He served as an army chaplain in World War I. During his seventies, Rust, given a free pass by the railroads, traveled through the states he had served as a young missionary. He was warmly greeted by his former pupils in every town he visited.

25. *Seventy-Eighth Anniversary of the American Baptist Publication Society* (Philadelphia: ABPS, 1902), 41-80.

26. *Ninety-First Anniversary of the ABPS*, 1044-1045.

27. *Eighty-Sixth Anniversary of the American Baptist Publication Society* (Philadelphia: ABPS, 1910), 36; *Eighty-Seventh Anniversary of the American Baptist Publication Society* (Philadelphia: ABPS, 1911), 28.

28. *Ninety-Sixth Anniversary of the American Baptist Publication Society* (Philadelphia: ABPS, 1920), 38.

29. *Eighty-Second Anniversary of the American Baptist Publication Society* (Philadelphia: ABPS, 1906), 77.

30. *Ninety-First Anniversary of the ABPS*, 1044.

31. See the Anniversary Reports of the Publication Society for 1923-25 and 1929. The Crawford Memorial Auto Chapel Car

was dedicated on November 5, 1922, at the Near Baptist Christian Church in Los Angeles.

32. *One-Hundreth Annual Report of the Board of Managers: The American Baptist Publication Society* (Philadelphia: ABPS, 1924), 30-31; A. C. Blinzinger to Mark Rich, March 15, 1942, ABHS.

33. *So Were the Churches Established in Faith,* brochure (n.p., n.d.); *One-Hundred-Eighth Anniversary of the American Baptist Publication Society* (Philadelphia: ABPS, 1932), 44: *One-Hundred-Fifteenth Anniversary of the American Baptist Publication Society* (Philadelphia: ABPS, 1939), 48; R. Dean Goodwin, "On the Rails with the Gospel," *The Chronicle* 10 (January 1947): 29.

34. *The Coleman News,* May, 1941.

35. Howard Parry to John C. Killian, February 15, 1940, ABHS.

36. "Parrys Move from South Fork to Lakewood," *The Colorado Baptist,* 42 (April 1941), p. 1.

37. Parry to Linda Dearmond, September 5, 1939, ABHS.

38. Parry to C. D. Poling, January 11, 1938, ABHS.

39. *One-Hundred-Eighteenth Anniversary of the American Baptist Publication Society* (Philadelphia: ABPS, 1942), 42.

40. Ibid., 41.

41. *One-Hundred-Nineteenth Anniversary of the American Baptist Publication Society* (Philadelphia: ABPS, 1943), 35.

42. *One-Hundred-Twentieth Anniversary of the American Baptist Publication Society* (Philadelphia: ABPS, 1944), 24-26.

43. "Orem Project, American Baptist Home Mission Society, Utah Baptist State Convention, Situation as of May 14, 1945," ABHS; Parry to Mark Rich, January 28, 1946, ABHS; Goodwin, *Chronicle*, 29.

44. Stilgoe, *Metropolitan Corridor*, 71.

III

Mormons

6.

"Reluctant Polygamists": The Strains and Challenges of the Transition to Polygamy in a Prominent Mormon Family[1]

Lawrence Foster

The practice of Mormon polygamy in nineteenth-century America has aroused curiosity and intensely ambivalent emotions for more than a century and a half. At its peak plural marriage was officially accepted by over one hundred thousand Latter-day Saints in the Intermountain West as the highest ideal of marriage and was an integral part of Mormon religious and social life. The nineteenth century saw strident attacks on polygamy by non-Mormons and equally polemical defenses by Latter-day Saints. After 1890 when the Mormon Church gradually moved to eliminate the practice, tensions with the outer society over plural marriage gradually subsided. During the past twenty-five years in particular, Mormon and non-Mormon scholars increasingly have been able to step back from earlier polemical approaches and begin to analyze plural marriage more dispassionately as an important social institution--the largest and most sustained alternative to monogamous marriage ever developed in the United States. Despite this growing attention to polygamy as a social system, however, far less has yet been written about the difficult process, both in Illinois and in the West, by which a practice which differed so sharply from Anglo-American monogamous norms was successfully introduced and institutionalized among the Mormons.[2]

This article will address that latter issue by looking at the difficult transition to polygamy in one prominent early Mormon family, that of Heber C. Kimball. Kimball was one of the closest associates of both Joseph Smith and Brigham Young, and he also was officially the most married of all Mormon polygamists, with over forty wives. Extensive primary records from the Kimball family have survived, both published and unpublished. In addition, an award-winning biography, *Heber C. Kimball: Mormon Patriarch and Pioneer,* by Stanley B. Kimball, one of Kimball's many descendants, provides a nearly-exhaustive overview of the external details of Kimball family relationships, both in Illinois and in Utah. Yet even this fine study still remains more descriptive than analytical. It tells a story, yet does not fully probe some of the larger issues which the experiences of this remarkable family raise both for its time and for our own. This article will try to complement Stanley Kimball's work, using analytical approaches which might suggest a fresh perspective on the difficult experiences of this courageous, intensely dedicated, and often intensely troubled family. While the Heber C. Kimball family certainly was not "typical" of Mormon polygamous families, the very extremes present in the family highlight the difficulties and challenges of introducing a radically new system of belief and practice in nineteenth-century America. If one way to study the process of social change is to use aggregate data and statistics, another is to focus on one complex case which can reveal the dynamics of the larger situation in microcosm.[3]

Perhaps the core problem which Heber C. Kimball's family life raises is the dichotomy between his close and loving relations with his first wife Vilate and eldest daughter Helen and the emotionally detached and at times almost cavalier quality of his relations with many of his plural wives and their children. If these two sets of relationships are juxtaposed, Heber C. Kimball at times seems to be almost a different man. Throughout his life, he wrote and spoke with great tenderness to Vilate. During the difficult 1840s, he observed: "My heart aches for you and some times I can hardly speak without weaping [sic] to think that I for one moment have been the means of causing you any sorrow. . . ."[4] And again, "I assure you that you have not been out of my mind many minutes at a time since I left you."[5] Reportedly Heber was so distraught that he felt on the verge of apostasy in 1842 when he was was commanded by Joseph Smith to take another wife secretly.[6] And throughout the Utah period, Heber continually reaffirmed Vilate's priority in his affections and his unshakeable devotion to her, no matter what might happen. His letters, journals and speeches contain frequent warm references to Vilate and her children.

Heber's daughter Helen recalled: "He was often heard to say that he did not care how soon he followed her [to the grave], and he lived but nine months to mourn her loss [before his own death in 1868]."[7]

By contrast, Kimball's relations with his many plural wives appear considerably less than congenial or satisfactory. He could be blunt and unflattering regarding his wives (and women in general) and he did not hesitate to discuss his domestic discord in his sermons. He announced that he would deed his property to the church so that his family would not quarrel over it.[8] He admonished wives not to rebel, and said that he had one or two wives he could not control.[9] At one point, Kimball declared that if any of his wives wanted to leave him they could, and he would give them assistance to get away.[10] At another point, he declared that if any of his wives were to object to his sustaining Brigham Young over them and threaten to leave, "I should reply, 'leave and be damned!'"[11] According to family lore, Heber once blessed the son of a troublesome wife with all the strengths of his father and none of the weaknesses of his mother.[12] These scattered vignettes suggesting disharmony are borne out by quantitative indicators, such as the ten wives who left him and the six others who remain unaccounted for in Utah.[13] Although Kimball evidently did take seriously his economic and social responsibilities, at least toward his core group of twelve wives, he appears to best be characterized as something of a "benevolent autocrat," a "dutiful" husband who expressed little affection for most of his plural wives.

What accounts for the apparently sharp dichotomy between Heber C. Kimball's relations with his first wife Vilate and his relations with his other plural wives? A complex family system such as that of Heber C. Kimball magnified the potential for interpersonal tensions many times over, of course. Simply to keep track of an actual and adopted family that eventually totalled at least 108 persons would have tried the patience of the most even-tempered and judicious of men. In such an extreme situation, perhaps a brusque and autocratic style was almost to be expected. Yet surely more was also involved in Heber C.

Kimball's case. Stanley B. Kimball perceptively speculates: "It is as if he never loved anyone but Vilate."[14]   While this may be an overstatement, it does highlight an important point. Even though Kimball had children by seventeen of his wives, his primary emotional loyalties appear to have remained with Vilate and her family. What significance could Kimball's dichotomized reaction have for understanding the dynamics of the development of Mormon polygamy? Is there, perhaps, a personal tragedy here which, if properly understood, could shed light on the problems of extreme commitment to any cause?

One inadequate explanation for Kimball's family difficulties deserves brief mention. Numerous apostate and anti-Mormon sources criticize Kimball's motives and integrity, seeing him as a lustful authoritarian with serious personality flaws. He was, one writer declared, "a large man, with oily sensual face, and a bald head."[15] Others stressed his "vulgar or course speech," accusing him of making indelicate references to female anatomy which suggested his own indecency.[16]   Sir Richard Burton noted in 1861: "Mr. Kimball is accused by Gentiles of calling his young wives from the pulpit, 'little hiefers,' of entering into physiological details belonging to the Dorcas Society, or the clinical lecture room, rather than the house of worship, and of transgressing the bounds of decorum when reproving the sex for its *penchants* and *ridicules*."[17]

No doubt Kimball, like many other frontier leaders, was prone to the use of blunt, salty language which offended Victorian sensibilities. No doubt, too, he could make demands for total commitment which seemed excessive to those not struggling to survive and establish themselves in the arid, inhospitable Great Basin region. But Kimball's sincerity is not really at issue--if anything, he tried too hard. In a lengthy expose of Mormonism, the apostate T. B. H. Stenhouse--certainly no apologist for polygamy or for Mormonism--nevertheless spoke only in superlatives of the "valiant men" and "excellent women" to whom Joseph Smith initially presented the polygamy revelation. According to Stenhouse, it was Joseph Smith's good sense in taking only his finest and most devoted followers into his confidence on this issue that made possible the eventual establishment of a full-scale polygamous system after his death.[18] Certainly Heber, Vilate, and Helen Kimball were among that select group about whom Stenhouse wrote; they sacrificed even their most deeply held personal beliefs in support of what they believed to be a divine revelation.

Instead of trying to attribute the strains in the Kimball family life to personality defects, a more promising approach might be to try to understand the larger social forces that were at work, particularly the problems of individuals caught in the transition between two partially contradictory standards of behavior. How does a man or a woman who had been taught to believe strongly in monogamy and sexual exclusiveness react to what he or she believes to be a command from God that they radically change their behavior by accepting polygamy? This was a problem that faced many early Mormon men and women.

Like others who were commanded to take plural wives, Heber C. Kimball reportedly was so disturbed in 1842 by Joseph Smith's command to take another wife secretly that, unquestioningly loyal though he always had been, he had to be commanded to do so three times in the name of the Lord before he obeyed. Even then he feared that he would apostatize. It would be more than two years after Kimball took his first plural wife Sarah Noon in 1842, before he would marry again. And with only a handful of exceptions, almost all of his additional plural wives were sealed to him either immediately prior to the forced exodus from Nauvoo, Illinois, or during the tense Mormon Reformation of 1856-57, times when herculean levels of commitment were called for by the Saints.[19] Being in a subordinate position to Heber C. Kimball, his first wife Vilate and daughter Helen would have faced a much more difficult situation had they chosen to oppose the new system. It is clear, as we shall see, that they experienced at least as high a level of ambivalence as did Kimball himself.

Here is a classic case of individuals caught in an inescapable moral dilemma, between two partially contradictory standards--an old standard and relationship to which they are committed and a new standard which they are trying to bring themselves to accept. This dilemma was never fully resolved by Kimball and his family. Even in Utah, Kimball appears to have remained only a reluctant polygamist, concerned at the hurt polygamy caused Vilate and often all too brusque in dealing with his other plural wives. Like many other early polygamists, Kimball bravely attempted to restructure his behavior, but he could not by will alone change his deepest emotional responses.

One useful framework for understanding the ambiguities and contradictions with which the Kimballs and other early polygamous families tried to grapple in such situations is that suggested by the anthropologist Victor Turner in his book *The Ritual Process: Structure and Anti-Structure*. Turner discusses both the external structural characteristics and the internal emotional significance of major social transitions. He begins with Arnold Van Gennep's analysis of ritual "rites of passage" or transition, which are marked by three phases: first, a separation, disaggregation, or breakdown of an old status or order; second, an intermediary "liminal" or threshold period when neither the old nor the new standards are in effect; and third, a reaggregation or establishment of a new order.[20]

Turner's most provocative insights are found in his analysis of the "liminal" or transitional period between two opposed or partially contradictory states of being, whether as parts of individual "rites of passage" or of larger social transitions. During such a transitional period, a person's status is ambiguous; he is caught "betwixt and between the positions assigned and arrayed by law, custom, convention, and ceremonial." This temporary symbolic breakdown of normal secular distinctions of rank, status, and obligation in the liminal period releases intense feelings of egalitarianism and a sense of emotional unity. With the breakdown of the arbitrary social regulations which normally separate individuals comes an overriding sense of direct personal communion, a blend "of lowliness and sacredness, of homogeneity and comradeship."

Accompanying this sense of egalitarianism is a personal malleability which, paradoxically, is conducive to an opposite extreme--an intense stress on the subordination of the individuals undergoing the experience to a higher authority. Frequently initiates are represented as possessing nothing, are expected to obey their instructors completely and accept arbitrary punishment or seemingly irrational demands without complaint. "It is as though they are being reduced or ground down to a uniform condition to be fashioned anew and endowed with additional powers to enable them to cope with their new station in life." During the liminal period, therefore, the ambiguous potential and the extreme polarities of social life are most vividly highlighted. [21]

Heber C. Kimball's understanding of his experiences and of the experiences of other early Mormons is remarkably compatible with Victor Turner's discussion of liminality. Perhaps the best example of what Davis Bitton has called Kimball's "authoritarian imagery" is his metaphor of mankind as clay in the hands of a divine potter. Kimball described how clay was immersed in water and then molded, ground, and ground again until it became passive and could be shaped into whatever shape the potter wanted to make it, into a "vessel of honor." Frequently this process would be a long and difficult one in which the potter might turn the clay into as many as fifty to one hundred different shapes before it became a jug. And if the clay proved refractory and unable to be worked, it would eventually be thrown back into the mill until it was ground down and became passive and could be worked at last into the desired form. Even so, Latter-day Saints were to be passive and allow themselves to be formed by their leaders into a new people and adopt a new way of life.[22]

This image of Heber C. Kimball's grew out of his own experience working as a potter, as well as from biblical metaphor. It also almost perfectly represented his own experiences in offering total and undeviating loyalty to the commands of Church authorities, and the similar implicit obedience that he expected from those who were under him in the hierarchy. There was a sense of exhilaration associated with this intense dedication to attempting to bring the kingdom of God on earth. Kimball himself had been through the fire not once but many times and had faced seemingly almost impossible assignments. He had served as one of Joseph Smith's most trusted associates during the difficult Zion's Camp trek from Ohio to Missouri; he had helped Brigham Young oversee the Mormon flight from Missouri when the assaults on Mormon settlements in the state forced the group's departure; and he eventually served on eight demanding missionary assignments in the United States and in England. Between 1839 and 1846 alone, Kimball was away from home on missionary trips 55 per cent of the time.[23] Having unflinchingly carried out so many difficult assignments, Kimball correspondingly expected that others would also give total and unquestioning loyalty to the dictates of the church.

As applied to family relations, however, such absolute standards of virtue and loyalty posed severe problems. Mormon leaders sometimes developed unrealistically high expectations about what they should be able to accomplish in family life. It may not be accidental, for instance, that many of the most fanatical early proponents of polygamy were individuals who initially had been so opposed to the practice that they had almost apostatized. Orson Pratt, for example, had verged between apostasy and madness in 1842 over polygamy, yet a decade later in 1852, he had a large plural family and eloquently delivered the first public defense of the system. Jedediah M. Grant resisted taking a plural wife for more than three years after being appointed to high church office in early Utah, yet he became one of the most extreme advocates of the practice during the Mormon Reformation of 1856-57. Kimball himself, though evidently always a reluctant polygamist emotionally, took officially the largest number of wives of anyone in Utah, perhaps in part to prove his loyalty to the Church. And Kimball's daughter Helen, who like some other strong female supporters of polygamy found plural marriage to be one of the greatest trials of her life, nevertheless in 1884 wrote what may well be one of the most eloquent personal testimonies to the divine nature of the principle. One suspects that these cases may reflect overcompensation.[24]

Even under ideal circumstances, the practice of polygamy

significantly complicated personal relationships. The most sensitive monogamist would have been hard pressed to handle the range of church responsibilities and problems that Heber C. Kimball faced and still have time to maintain a close and intimate family life. But when a figure as busy as Kimball attempted to deal responsibly with a core group of twelve wives and as many as seventy immediate dependents in all, concerning himself with their economic, social, and religious well-being, severe strains were placed on emotional relations. Kimball attempted to be even-handed in dealing with his wives and their families, but even going out for an evening social gathering raised major logistical problems. In order to be fair, Kimball rotated taking his wives to social events. Given such constraints, maintaining special emotional closeness with most of his wives simply was not possible. One might argue that by taking on so many church responsibilities and by adopting the practice of polygamy Kimball had sacrificed his family in the service of his church.[25]

To keep this picture in perspective, it should be noted that Heber C. Kimball's family life was far from typical of the family life of all Mormons in the Intermountain West during the nineteenth century. Even during the height of polygamy practice in Utah, probably more than three quarters of all married men were monogamists, and of the polygamists, the vast majority had no more than one additional wife. Although other Mormon families did engage in great sacrifices to help build a Zion in the West, the extremes of total commitment and its associated problems were less likely to be found in monogamous families or in polygamous families with only two or three wives. While polygamy did have inherent tendencies to limit the emotional closeness of husbands and wives, by the 1860s and 1870s the initial transitional problems suggested by the Kimball family's experiences had been at least partially overcome in many polygamous families. Lowell Bennion's recent demographic studies of the incidence of Mormon polygamy in 1880, based on United States census data, suggests that by that time the practice had become firmly established throughout Mormon country and would, in all probability, have continued to persist strongly had not the intense federal pressure of the 1880s led to the Mormon

Church's formal decision not to sanction any further plural marriages in the United States after 1890.[26]

Even in the Kimball family, there were occasional touches of romance and suggestions of a lighter side to polygamy after the initial transitional period was past. For example, Heber's last marriage, in 1857, was to the nineteen year-old Mary Smithies, who eventually bore him five children. In one of his most-quoted statements, perhaps partially inspired by this relationship which had just been sealed and consummated three months earlier, Heber Kimball noted:

> I would not be afraid to promise a man who is sixty years of age, if he will take the counsel of brother Brigham and his brethren, that he will renew his age. I noticed that a man who has but one wife, and is inclined to that doctrine, soon begins to wither and dry up, while a man who goes into plurality looks fresh, young, and spritely. Why is this? Because God loves that man, and because he honors his work and word. Some of you may not believe this; but I not only believe it--I also know it. For a man of God to be confined to one woman is small business; for it is as much as we can do now to keep up under the burdens we have to carry; and I do not know what we should do if we had only one wife apiece.[27]

While this statement could be taken to suggest that Kimball's polygamy was motivated simply by excess sexual energy, the observation actually is entirely compatible with his religious and social philosophy. Nineteenth-century Mormons did not dichotomize religious and sexual life so sharply as did many of their Victorian contemporaries, who looked with suspicion even at sex within marriage. Instead nineteenth-century Mormons, like their Puritan forbears, viewed sexual relations that were properly conducted within a sanctioned marriage relationship as good--an integral part of God's purpose for the world. Polygamy for nineteenth-century Mormon men could accentuate both the responsibilities and the pleasures of marriage. It is thus not surprising that despite the manifold and often extreme difficulties that polygamy caused Heber C. Kimball, the practice brought him benefits as well.[28]

Far more has been written about the effects of polygamy on women than on men in nineteenth-century Utah. These brief comments have tried to redress that balance by shifting the focus to men in order to suggest the strains that the practice also could place on them. Nevertheless, women undoubtedly faced the most difficult adjustments to polygamy. If they often shared with their husbands the exhilaration of total dedication to their church, they also were more frequently confronted with the difficult and more mundane demands of day-to-day living and family responsibilities. In particular, they faced the difficult emotional adjustment of sharing their husbands with other wives. Vilate appears to have remained quietly unhappy with polygamy throughout her life, pouring much of her emotions into self-sacrificing concern for her children and into assistance to other plural wives. She once advised an unhappy plural wife that "her comfort must be wholly in her children; that she must lay aside wholly all interest or thought in what her husband was doing while he was away from her" and simply be as "pleased to see him when he came in as she was pleased to see any friend."[29] Heber also commented on Vilate's unhappiness with polygamy, saying:

> I know there is no Woman can ever feel worse than my Wife has done, and she is just as good a Woman as ever lived, and I never blamed her for feeling bad but loved her the more.[30]

One result of such dissatisfaction was the high divorce rate in nineteenth-century Utah. During the thirty years of Brigham Young's leadership in Utah (1847-1877), the Mormon Church authorized at least 1,645 divorces, the bulk of which appear to have involved dissatisfied plural wives. The 72 highest Mormon Church leaders who practiced polygamy had a total of at least 391 wives, with 54 divorces, 26 separations, and 1 annulment. Utah territorial law in 1852 allowed divorce for a wide range of causes, including incompatibility. Mormon Church policy made divorce relatively easy when requested by women but difficult when requested by men. Mormon men were expected to honor their family responsibilities, but had the option of taking additional wives. Mormon women whose affections were alienated from their husbands found little difficulty or stigma in getting divorced and remarrying, a safety valve that resulted in *de facto* serial polygamy for some women. Despite the difficulties such evidence suggests, there were many happy plural marriages in Utah as well. In particular, second or third wives who chose to enter into plural marriages frequently fared somewhat better than first wives, since later wives had a better idea of what to expect. Nevertheless, polygamy did prove a severe trial for many women, especially during the early period. Only the conviction that plural marriage was necessary for the highest exaltation in the afterlife caused many women reluctantly to accept the practice.[31]

Among the most articulate of the women who candidly discussed their responses to the introduction of polygamy was Heber C. Kimball's daughter Helen. Her extreme ambivalence about the practice parallels that of her father and mother. At the age of fifteen in Nauvoo, Helen became a plural wife of Joseph Smith, and later she became the first wife of Horace K. Whitney, who would serve as one of the Twelve Apostles in Utah. Helen's experiences in Nauvoo were especially traumatic. Not only was she in the midst of the usual difficulties of the transition to womanhood, but she also was caught in the middle of a larger social transition, as polygamy was simultaneously being introduced among a select group of leading Mormons.[32]

In a handwritten statement dated March 30, 1881, Helen wrote about her reactions and those of her mother Vilate. Although recorded in retrospect and reflecting a somewhat exceptional case, her statement nevertheless highlights the great emotional strain which the introduction of polygamy could cause for women. Helen wrote:

> Just previous to my father's starting upon his last mission but one, to the Eastern States, he taught me the principle of Celestial marriage, & having a great desire to be connected with the Prophet, Joseph, he offered me to

him; this I afterwards learned from the Prophet's own mouth. My father had but one Eue Lamb but willingly laid her upon the alter: how cruel this seamed to the mother whose heart strings were already stretched untill they were ready to snap asunder, for he had taken Sarah Moon to wife & she thought she had made sufficient sacrifise but the Lord required more. I will pass over the temptations which I had during the twenty four hours after my father introduced me to this principle & asked me if I would be sealed to Joseph who came next morning & with my parents I heard him teach and explain the principle of Celestial marriage--after which he said to me, "If you will take this step, it will insure your eternal salvation & exaltation and that of your father's household & all of your kindred." This promise was so great that I willingly gave myself to purchase so glorious a reward. None but God & his angels could see my mother's bleeding heart--when Joseph asked her if she was willing, she replied "If Helen is willing I have nothing more to say." She had witnessed the sufferings of others, who were older & who better understood the step they were taking, & to see her child, who had scarcely seen her fifteenth summer, following in the same thorny path, in her mind she saw the misery which was sure to come as the sun was to rise and set; but it was all hidden from me.

Helen continued with a poem suggesting her guilelessness upon entering into her first polygamous relationship. It began:

I thought through *this life* my time will be my own
The step I now am taking's for eternity alone,
No one need be the wiser, through time I shall be free,
And as the past hath been the future still will be.

To my guileless heart all free from worldly care
And full of blissful hopes--and youthful visions rare,
The world seamed bright--the thret'ning clouds were kept
From sight and all looked fair but pitying angels wept.[33]

143

Despite the intensely ambivalent feelings that she had toward polygamy--feelings that are also suggested by her reticence in even mentioning that she had once been a plural wife of Joseph Smith-- Helen Mar Kimball Whitney in 1884 wrote *Why We Practice Plural Marriage*, one of the most thoughtful and moving defenses of the divine inspiration of Mormon polygamy. She began the pamphlet by sharing an extraordinary exchange of letters between her and a sensitive non-Mormon man who was living in a bigamous relationship. The man, whose first wife's debility had led him to maintain a clandestine second relationship, inquired about the Mormon rationale for polygamy. Helen courteously but severely reproved him. Although a non-Mormon might view the relationship as similar to some Mormon plural marriages, Helen told the man in no uncertain terms that he was living in heinous sin. The only justification for plural marriage was its practice under the authority of God in the Mormon Church. As she put it: "To live with more than one woman, except you are sealed by one holding the Priesthood and authority from the Great Master, is nothing less than adultery. . . ."[34] The pamphlet then provided an eloquent defense of plural marriage, though Helen also candidly observed: "I did not try to conceal the fact of its having been a trial, but confessed that it had been one of the severest in my life; but that it had also proven one of the greatest blessings. I could truly say that it had done the most toward making me a saint and a free woman, in every sense of the word. . . ."[35]

What is one to make of such devotion to a practice which, at the most personal level, one apparently finds deeply distasteful? Stanley Kimball's observations about a very different situation in which a sick Heber C. Kimball was called on a mission to England, necessarily leaving behind an even sicker wife and children, might well also apply to early polygamy: "Only totally dedicated men can do such things, and only even more dedicated women can endure such things."[36]

In the final analysis, therefore, the most important questions which the experiences of the Heber C. Kimball family raise have to do not so much with polygamy as with commitment. How is one to achieve the best possible balance between the needs of the individual and the requirements of society, two factors which often seem to be in tension, especially during periods of major social transition? Mormon history characteristically has stressed the importance of the group, celebrating the extraordinary dedication of early figures as they gave total loyalty to the Church in missionary ventures, the difficult trek westward, or the demanding settlement of the Intermountain West. This approach is entirely understandable and legitimate; the intense dedication shown by early Mormons was, in fact, a social necessity if the group were to be able to accomplish what it did. As Leonard J. Arrington has noted: "Only a high degree of religious devotion and discipline, and superb organization and planning, made survival possible" in the arid and initially inhospitable Great Basin region.[37] The process of social and industrial development that much of the rest of the world achieved in a haphazard and piecemeal fashion, was achieved by Mormons largely through rational planning and deliberate sacrifice of short-term individual concerns for long-term group goals.

Yet it is also well to remember the other side of such commitment, the enormous human cost of self-consciously attempting to bring the kingdom of heaven on earth. There certainly is a dark side to great commitment that must not be forgotten. Not without reason has much of Mormon theology turned on the concept of being tried in the fire, being tested, being in a probationary state, and the necessity of opposition in all things.[38] Although the Heber C. Kimball family did not always achieve a satisfying balance between the needs of the individual and the demands of the group, their struggle to come to terms with plural marriage highlights broader issues of commitment which the religious effort to transform society necessarily entails.

Notes

1. An earlier version of this paper was presented as a response to a paper by Stanley B. Kimball at the Mormon History Association adjunct session of the annual meeting of the Organization of American Historians in St. Louis, Missouri, on April 8, 1976.

Stanley B. Kimball's full analysis subsequently appeared in his biography, *Heber C. Kimball: Mormon Patriarch and Pioneer* (Urbana: University of Illinois Press, 1981). Chapter 20 of that study was entitled, "Reluctant Polygamist." This article is based upon information from the study by Kimball, upon my own book, *Religion and Sexuality: Three American Communal Experiments of the Nineteenth Century* (New York: Oxford University Press, 1981), and upon other records in the Archives of the Historical Department of the Church of Jesus Christ of Latter-day Saints in Salt Lake City, Utah, hereafter cited as Church Archives.

2. For examples of influential apostate attacks on Mormon polygamy, see John C. Bennett, *The History of the Saints, or, An Exposé of Joe Smith and Mormonism* (Boston: Leland & Whiting, 1842), and John Hyde, Jr., *Mormonism: Its Leaders and Designs* (New York: W. P. Fetridge, 1857). The most thorough nineteenth-century Mormon defense of polygamy is found in *The Seer*, a periodical edited and published by Orson Pratt in Washington, D.C. between 1853 and 1854. For scholarly analyses of the role polygamy played in stimulating hostility toward the Mormons, see Leonard J. Arrington and Jon Haupt, "Intolerable Zion: The Image of Mormonism in Nineteenth Century American Literature," *Western Humanities Review* 22 (Summer 1968): 243-260, and Jan Shipps, "From Satyr to Saint: American Attitudes Toward the Mormons, 1860-1960" (paper presented at the 1973 annual meeting of the Organization of American Historians, Chicago, Illinois). Scholarly studies of Mormon polygamy are analyzed by Davis Bitton in "Mormon Polygamy: A Review Article," *Journal of Mormon History* 4 (1977): 101-118. Polygamy practice in Utah is treated in Stanley S. Ivins, "Notes on Mormon Polygamy," *Western Humanities Review* 10 (Summer 1956): 229-239; James E. Smith and Philip R. Kunz, "Polygyny and Fertility in Nineteenth-Century America," *Population Studies* 30 (1976): 465-480; Kimball Young, *Isn't One Wife Enough?: The Story of Mormon Polygamy* (New York: Henry Holt, 1954); and D. Michael Quinn, "Organizational Development and Social Origins of the Mormon Hierarchy, 1832-1932: A Prosopographical Study" (M.A. thesis, University of Utah, 1973). On Joseph Smith's role in introducing

polygamy, a Mormon analysis is Danel W. Bachman, "A Study of the Mormon Practice of Plural Marriage before the Death of Joseph Smith" (M.A. thesis, Purdue University, 1975). The first non-Mormon analysis of the origins of Mormon polygamy based on full access to the relevant records in the LDS Library and Archives is in Lawrence Foster, *Religion and Sexuality*, cited previously. A compelling recent study, which for the first time convincingly analyzes the complex personal dynamics between Joseph Smith and his first wife Emma is Linda King Newell and Valeen Tippetts Avery, *Mormon Enigma: Emma Hale Smith-- Prophet's Wife, "Elect Lady," Polygamy's Foe* (Garden City, N.Y.: Doubleday, 1984). Many of the most important recent scholarly analyses of Mormon polygamy will appear in the forthcoming anthology being edited by David J. Whittaker and Lori Winder Stromberg, tentatively entitled *A Twin Relic Reconsidered: Essays on Mormon Polygamy.*

3. In addition to Stanley Kimball's biography, major sources on Heber C. Kimball and his family include Orson F. Whitney, *Life of Heber C. Kimball* (Salt Lake City: Published by the Kimball Family, 1888); a series of reminiscences by Helen Mar Kimball Whitney in the *Woman's Exponent* in 1881 and 1882, especially "Scenes and Incidents in Nauvoo," *Woman's Exponent* 11 (1882): 26, 39-40, and 57-58; sermons reported in early volumes of the *Journal of Discourses,* 26 vols. (Liverpool, Eng.: F. D. Richards and others, 1854-1886); and Kate B. Carter, ed., *Heber C. Kimball: His Wives and Children* (Salt Lake City: Daughters of Utah Pioneers, 1967).

4. Letter dated October 23, 1842, as quoted in Helen Mar Whitney, "Scenes and Incidents in Nauvoo," *Woman's Exponent* 11 (1882): 26.

5. Letter dated October 25, 1842, ibid. These two letters were written during the period when Heber and Vilate were struggling to come to terms with the introduction of polygamy. Continuing concern over this issue is suggested in the letter from Heber to Vilate Kimball on February 12, 1849, quoted in Stanley Kimball, *Heber C. Kimball*, 101.

6. Orson Whitney, *Life of Heber C. Kimball*, 335-338, quoting a statement by Helen Mar Whitney. Another wrenching test reportedly preceded the demand that Heber Kimball secretly enter into polygamy. Joseph Smith is alleged to have asked Heber to give him Vilate to be his wife, and when Heber finally with the greatest of reluctance agreed to do so, Smith wept, embraced Heber, and told him that he had not really wanted Vilate but had only been testing whether Heber's loyalty to him were absolute. Ibid., 333-335. The context of this extraordinary episode is discussed in Foster, *Religion and Sexuality*, 159-166.

7. Helen Mar Whitney, "Scenes and Incidents in Nauvoo," 26.

8. *Journal of Discourses* 2: 153. Sermon of April 2, 1854. This statement presumably was made for rhetorical effect. Kimball actually died intestate. On the distribution of his estate, see Stanley Kimball, *Heber C. Kimball*, 317-320.

9. *Journal of Discourses* 5: 277. Sermon of September 27, 1857.

10. Ibid., 5: 274. Sermon of September 27, 1857.

11. Ibid., 5: 28. Sermon of July 12, 1857.

12. Stanley Kimball, *Heber C. Kimball*, 232.

13. Ibid., 307-316.

14. Stanley B. Kimball, "Heber C. Kimball and Family: The Nauvoo Years," *Brigham Young University Studies* 15 (Summer 1975): 466.

15. Albert D. Richardson, editor of the *New York Tribune*, as quoted by Stanley P. Hirschon, *The Lion of the Lord: A Biography of Brigham Young* (New York: Alfred A. Knopf, 1969), 267.

16. Samuel Bowles, *Across the Continent* (Springfield, Mass.: Samuel Bowles, 1866), 87; Andrew F. Rolle, ed., *The Road to Virginia City: The Diary of James Knox Polk Miller* (Norman: University of Oklahoma Press, 1960), 53.

17. Sir Richard Burton, *The City of the Saints, and Across the Rocky Mountains to California* (New York: Harper & Brothers), 263.

18. T. B. H. Stenhouse, *The Rocky Mountain Saints: A Full and Complete History of the Mormons* (New York: D. Appleton, 1873), 200.

19. Stanley Kimball, *Heber C. Kimball*, 227-231. It should be noted that a number of Kimball's wives were non-connubial and were taken on essentially as his wards. For a related practice, see Gordon Irving, "The Law of Adoption: One Phase of the Mormon Concept of Salvation, 1830-1900," *Brigham Young University Studies* 14 (Spring 1974): 291-314.

20. Victor W. Turner, *The Ritual Process: Structure and Anti-Structure* (Chicago: Aldine, 1969), 94-203. The quotations in this and the following two paragraphs are from pp. 94-97. Arnold Van Gennep's classic account is *The Rites of Passage*, trans. Monika B. Vizedom and Gabrielle L. Caffe (Chicago: University of Chicago Press, 1960). Related topics are also discussed in Victor W. Turner, *Dramas, Fields, and Metaphors: Symbolic Action in Human Society* (Ithaca, N. Y.: Cornell University Press, 1974).

21. Some of the most important analyses suggesting the ambiguous potential of movements for radical transformation include Anthony F. C. Wallace, "Revitalization Movements," *American Anthropologist* 38 (April 1956): 264-281; Kenelm Burridge, *New Heaven, New Earth: A Study of Millenarian Activities* (New York: Schocken, 1969); I. M. Lewis, *Ecstatic Religion: An Anthropological Study of Spirit Possession and Shamanism* (Baltimore: Penguin, 1971); and William Sargant, *Battle for the Mind: A Physiology of Conversion and*

Brainwashing (Garden City, N.Y.: Doubleday, 1957)

22. Davis Bitton, "Heber C. Kimball's Authoritarian Imagery," in *Conference on the Language of the Mormons* (Provo: Language Research Center, Brigham Young University, 1974). Examples of the imagery are found in the *Journal of Discourses* 1: 161, 5: 131.

23. Stanley Kimball, "Heber C. Kimball and Family," 447.

24. For Pratt's difficulties, see Thomas Edgar Lyon, "Orson Pratt--Early Mormon Leader" (M.A. thesis, University of Chicago, 1932), 34-44. On Jedediah Grant, see Quinn, "The Mormon Hierarchy," 153, and Gene Allred Sessions, *Mormon Thunder: A Documentary History of Jedediah Morgan Grant* (Urbana: University of Illinois Press, 1982).

25. The complexities of Heber Kimball's family relationships and daily life are discussed in Stanley Kimball, *Heber C. Kimball,* 227-259. Heber Kimball had a total of at least 108 wives and children, but because of deaths, marriages, and separations it appears that he never had more than seventy in his immediate family at any one time. Ibid., 228.

26. For an introduction to the practice of polygamy in nineteenth-century Utah, see Lawrence Foster, "Polygamy and the Frontier: Mormon Women in Early Utah," *Utah Historical Quarterly* 50 (Summer 1982): 268-289. A pathbreaking recent analysis which challenges many earlier assumptions is Lowell Bennion, "Patterns of Polygamy Across Mormon Country in 1880" (paper presented at the annual meeting of the Mormon History Association in Provo, Utah, May 1984). Bennion's preliminary findings, based on a sample of some sixty towns from the entire area that had become Mormon country by 1880, show that between 20 to 30 per cent of all Mormons at that time were living in polygamous families, with a range of participation between 6 and 66 per cent. There appeared to be no obvious correlation between the incidence of polygamy and the size, location, or ethnic composition of the towns in the sample.

Bennion's analysis would appear to show that, contrary to earlier interpretations such as that of Ivins, "Notes on Mormon Polygamy," the practice was not dying out at that time but retained great vitality.

27. *Journal of Discourses* 5: 26. Sermon of April 6, 1857. Regarding Mary Smithies, Stanley Kimball remarks: "Only once, after his first marriage, does something more than obligation and duty seem to have surfaced. The fifth Utah bride and last of all his wives was an English teenager." *Heber C. Kimball*, 227. Details on Mary Smithies and her children are provided, ibid., 313.

28. For a brief discussion of the ideological defense of plural marriage in Utah, see Foster, *Religion and Sexuality*, 199-204. Puritan attitudes are discussed in Edmund S. Morgan's classic article, "The Puritans and Sex," *New England Quarterly* 14 (December 1942): 591-607. The transformation to Victorian attitudes in the nineteenth century is analyzed in John S. Haller, Jr. and Robin M. Haller, *The Physician and Sexuality in Victorian America* (New York: W. W. Norton, 1977), 92-102.

29. Mrs. S.A.Cooks, "Theatrical and Social Affairs in Utah," (Salt Lake City, 1884), 5-6. The original copy of this manuscript is in the Hubert Howe Bancroft Collection of Mormon Manuscripts at the Bancroft Library of the University of California at Berkeley.

30. Mary Haskins Parker Diary, typescript, 31-32, University of Utah, Salt Lake City, as quoted in Stanley Kimball, *Heber C. Kimball*, 237.

31. Overviews of divorce and polygamy in Utah are found in Eugene E. Campbell and Bruce E. Campbell, "Divorce Among Mormon Polygamists: Extent and Explanations," *Utah Historical Quarterly* 46 (Winter 1978): 4-23; and in Foster, *Religion and Sexuality*, 216-220. Data on the extent of divorce and separation among the Mormon hierarchy is provided in Quinn, "The Mormon Hierarchy," 248-291.

32. On the problems that the introduction of polygamy caused Mormon women in Illinois, see Foster, *Religion and Sexuality*, 151-159.

33. Handwritten statement in the form of a letter, without salutation but presumably to her children, dated March 30, 1881, and signed by Helen Mar Kimball Smith Whitney, LDS Archives, Helen Mar Kimball Whitney papers. Reproduced here with the original capitalization and spelling. Based on an extrapolation from this poem, Stanley Kimball concludes that Joseph Smith's marriage to Helen Mar Kimball was unconsummated. *Heber C. Kimball,* 98. This conclusion goes beyond the evidence. The poem merely indicates that Helen anticipated that the relationship would be for eternity alone. Such an anticipation was also held by Eliza R. Snow, who subsequently did appear to have sustained a sexual relationship with Joseph Smith. Foster, *Religion and Sexuality*, 157.

34. Helen Mar Whitney, *Why We Practice Plural Marriage* (Salt Lake City: Juvenile Instructor Office, 1884), 21.

35. Ibid., 23.

36. Stanley Kimball, "Heber C. Kimball and Family," 450.

37. Leonard J. Arrington, *Great Basin Kingdom: An Economic History of the Latter-day Saints, 1830-1900* (Cambridge, Mass.: Harvard University Press, 1958), 38.

38. See Stanley Kimball, *Heber C. Kimball,* xii, quoting 2 Nephi 2:11 in the Book of Mormon.

7.

Priestess Among the Patriarchs: Eliza R. Snow and the Mormon Female Relief Society, 1842-1887

Maureen Ursenbach Beecher

Inside a church dominated by a male clergy, a female network with Eliza Roxcy Snow at its center achieved for Mormon women a power base and a degree of public influence unequalled by "gentile" women on the frontier. Through their central organization, the Female Relief Society, the women expanded their outreach into every Mormon settlement in the intermountain West, sustaining each community not only through the prayer meetings and charitable activities typical of such societies, but also through home industries, trading ventures, educational programs, and public health facilities. Eliza Snow, at the hub of the women's work, held the key to their autonomy, clearing their programs at the highest administrative levels and overseeing their introduction at the local level. At her death in 1887, and with the end of the frontier phase of Mormon colonization, the Relief Society declined in power and influence. Mormon women lost the advantages gained over two decades of initiative, achievement, and organizational autonomy.

The commercial productivity and personal accomplishment of Mormon women is well established. Leonard Arrington's 1955 seminal work on the economic contribution of Mormon women has been followed by several published discussions of cooperative projects and individual achievements which show Mormon women as the unquestioned opposite of the "poor, downtrodden harem slaves" portrayed by the eastern press at the time.[1] A brief accounting will suffice here. The parent organization among the women, their Relief Society, originally founded in 1842 and reestablished in 1867, rose to three hundred branches by 1884. Beginning in 1872, the women supported a semi-monthly newspaper which enjoyed a a forty-two year run. Under the auspices of one or another of the organizations which followed the Relief Society, the women conducted a widespread education program in public health and midwifery. Prompted by a burgeoning population and increasing specialization of medical treatment, the Salt Lake City Mormon women sponsored and staffed their own hospital in 1882, and later built maternity hospitals in outlying regions. Active political involvement of Mormon women followed the granting of universal suffrage in Utah in 1870, fifty years before the nineteenth amendment allowed the franchise to women in the nation as a whole. Commercially, Mormon women followed an Eastern United States tradition of cottage industries by sponsoring silk culture, hat manufacture, and other home projects. Transcending their Eastern models, however, they established several cooperative and commission stores as outlets for their production. In these and other projects growing out of economic and social necessity, the women pioneers deomonstrated organizational skill and community responsibility commensurate with Mormon society's needs as they perceived them.[2]

Such productive activity resulted from a far-reaching and efficient female network and the leadershop of a powerful central figure aided by a group of like-minded under-officers. Elsewhere I have attempted to demonstrate the coming together of the women who formed that core, with Eliza Snow at their center. She and the other "leading sisters" who sustained her are a significant study in female administration in the nineteenth century.[3] For the purposes of this essay I will look more specifically at Eliza Snow, the origins and workings of the Mormon Female Relief Society, and the forces in Mormon society that allowed Snow and her followers to function so effectively.

For the women of intermountain Mormondom, public involvement began before the hegira to the west, in Nauvoo, Illinois, an eight-year Mormon settlement on the banks of the Mississippi. The founding of the Female Relief Society of Nauvoo in 1842 is neither unique nor surprising in a community whose roots were transplanted from Protestant eastern United States. In tracing women's religious auxiliaries from 1798 onward, historian Keith Melder delineates such purposes as mission support, prayer and spiritual uplift, relief for the poor, temperance, abolition of slavery, moral reform, and "mutual improvement."[4] It is not surprising, then, that a group of Mormon women would gather in Sarah M. Kimball's parlor on a spring day in 1842 to organize a sewing circle with charitable aims.[5]

The ease with which the women moved from informal intention to *fait accompli*, in fact, bespeaks their acquaintance with the ways of organizations. Within one week, Eliza Snow, then a spinster noted for little more than her literary gifts, had produced for the group a constitution which won the praise of the Mormon founder and prophet Joseph Smith. He saw in the organization, however, potential for more than the ladies' aid societies which may have been their models.

A decade earlier, Smith had dictated a revelation directed to his wife Emma Hale Smith in which she had been charged with responsibilities of leadership and instruction, and termed, in a phrase from the New Testament, "elect lady." The new organization seemed the appropriate vehicle for the fulfilling of that prophetic calling. Citing the revelation as justification, Smith reorganized the group with her as its president. His changes were not limited, however, to replacing the young Sarah Kimball with his more mature and experienced wife as leader. After the pattern which had evolved in his organizing of the male governing bodies of the young church, he established this group "in," "under," and "after the order" of the priesthood, until then the exclusively male prerogative. Though he did instruct the women in the secular methods of parliamentary procedure, Smith's pattern for the women was not that of women's benevolent societies, but that which he had used successfuly in the past in organizing "quorums" of priesthood.[6]

That the male pattern was intended is apparent throughout the minutes of the first Relief Society: the women were to have a president to "preside just as the Presidency preside over the church"; they were to keep minutes which "will be precedents for you to act upon--your Constitution and law." They were to regard those records as sacred, he continued, comparing them to the minutes which should have been kept of meetings of the powerful Quorum of the Twelve Apostles, which "had we now, would decide almost any point of doctrine which might be agitated." But the essential ecclesiastical aspect of the organization, which was missing from "auxiliary" organizations inside and outside the church, was the authority granted the institution. As he had done with prominent priests, Joseph Smith "ordained" the women to their leadership positions. Just as he had reminded the Quorum of the Twelve of the "keys" with which they had been endowed, so he made several mentions to the women of *their* appropriate keys.[7]

The concept of authority, as symbolized in the term "key," was for Mormons an essential distinction between their religion and those of their contemporaries. It was their belief that Peter, the apostle of Christ, had restored to Joseph Smith the priesthood, and with the "keys of the kingdom of heaven" in a context similar to that recorded in Matthew 16:19. Though women in the new church had exercised ecclesiastical voting rights along with male members, to this point there had been no talk of their holding priesthood keys along with their brothers.

Keys are mentioned in several contexts in the Relief Society minutes, but most significantly in a sermon Joseph Smith delivered on April 28, 1842. Throughout the sermon he admonished the women to be responsible for their own salvation, and encouraged them to be autonomous in their organization. "He spoke of delivering the keys to this Society, and to the Church," wrote the minute-taker. "The keys of the kingdom are about to be given them [the women], that they may be able to detect every thing false, as well as to the Elders." And finally, he concluded, "I now turn the key to you in the name of God. . . ." It was to be the beginning of better days for the Society.[8]

That the women accepted the responsibility of the keys is demonstrated through the remainder of their history in Nauvoo. They conducted their own meetings, directed their own projects, and kept their own counsel. Their work of benevolent service continued with or without the encouragement of male leaders until the spring of 1844.

156

To set the Relief Society in a broader context, it may be helpful to look briefly at the religious experiences of women generally. A useful paradigm divides the religious functions into three sometimes overlapping, but usually disparate sets of activities: the charismatic, the liturgical, and the ecclesiastical.[9] As the ecclesiastical realm we might well consider the organizational matters recounted above. The women of the church organized their own society, operated within their chosen sphere, and took responsibility for a share of the work of the church.

A second set of religious functions comes under the heading of the liturgical. The priestly functions of religious observance in the mainstream churches of western cultures have until recently been exclusively the province of males. There have been from the early Christian beginnings women ascetics, cloistered women, and women charismatics, but the official "priesthood" authority by which they might exercise their spiritual gifts for the good of others has been denied them. Mormonism has for the most part been no exception. "Priesthood" in the sense of a ceremonially bestowed and acknowledged right to "act in the name of the Lord" was and is in doctrine and in practice considered not available to Mormon women of the Utah-based church. The right to "expound scriptures," and to "exhort the church," is an exception--the "elect lady" revelation (now known as Doctrine and Covenants 25) specifically granted that right to Emma Smith, and Eliza Snow years later considered the right to preach an office apart from the presidency to which she had been called and one she was later granted. However, in the beginning of the Nauvoo Relief Society and the accompanying events another, more specifically liturgical function was given to the women.

Evidence suggests a connection between the founding of the Relief Society in 1842 and the introduction one year later of the Mormon "endowment" ceremonies in which the women would be given authority--*ordained*--to perform priestly functions for other women candidates for the blessings.[10] Bishop Reynolds Cahoon said to the women of the second year's Relief Society that "You knew not [*sic*] doubt but this Society is raised by the Lord to prepare us for the great blessings which are for us in the House of the Lord in the Temple."[11] Women to this day administer holy ordinances in the procedures of the highest worship available to Latter-day Saints, the rituals of the temple.

Nineteenth-century Mormon women retained a sense of the connection between that authority, those functions, and their Nauvoo-based Relief Society. Thus, Emma Smith served as a functional "matron" over the endowments for women in the Holy Order while she remained president of the Relief Society, and Eliza Snow, Zina D.H. Young, and Bathsheba Smith served *ex officio* as presidentess of the women's work of the Endowment House and Salt Lake Temple while they presided over the Utah Relief Society. However quietly observed, there remains among the Mormons a set of priestly functions performed by women in the temples, though their specific link to the Relief Society is no longer evident.

Of the charismatic expressions among Mormon women, more has been written. Linda King Newell's chronological survey of women's exercise of the pentacostal gifts--the prophesying, speaking in tongues, and healing characteristic of the Biblical church--reveals that the practice pre-dated the Nauvoo Relief Society.[12] With Joseph Smith's blessing, however, the gifts of healing, tongues, interpretation of tongues, and prophecy became an integral part of the women's organization. Rather than criticize the practice, Smith would "rejoice that the sick could be healed" by the women's ministrations. Even so, he said, prophecy and tongues were to be subservient to the order which he established in the society: doctrine would never be enunciated in tongues, and even prophecy would be limited: "This Society is to get instruction thro' the order which God has established--thro' the medium of those appointed to teach," he promised.[13]

With the blending of these aspects of religious experience into the organizational framework of the Relief Society many Mormon women there found their spiritual, ritualistic and functional needs fulfilled. The Nauvoo society attracted about 1200 women in the two summers of its existence, and spread to create sister groups among Mormons on the east coast and in Britain.

From the outset the Nauvoo Relief Society was charged to look after the morals of the community. As it entered its third season, the Society embarked upon what was a traditionally accepted mission of American women's societies: "moral reform," in most cases the abolition of prostitution. But this time the mission, as the president interpreted it, pitted the women directly against church leadership. To Emma Smith, moral reform meant abolishing the newly-founded practice of plural marriage, espoused secretly by many of the church leaders, her own husband included. In March of 1844 she spoke out against "polygamy" and "bigamy" in a tirade which marks the last entry in the Nauvoo Relief Society minutes. The absence of further minutes suggests that either the meetings were interdicted by priesthood authority or discontinued by the women themselves.[14]

At this crucial juncture the fates of the two most influential Mormon women were intertwined: Emma Smith, presidentess, "elect lady," designated by revelation to "judge...those over whom you are plac'd in authority," and Eliza Snow, secretary, amanuensis to Emma Smith, and plural wife since 1842 to Joseph Smith, Emma's own husband. Though she claimed ecclesiastical authority over the women, Emma Smith by opposing polygamy was undercutting the source of that authority: the priesthood as administered through her prophet-husband. The society, which was to "move according to the ancient Priesthood," "in concert" with it, was being led to oppose one of the injunctions of its male leader. Meanwhile, Eliza Snow, in secretly marrying Joseph Smith as a plural wife, had vowed obedience to the officially espoused doctrine. That demonstration of fealty had put her in a position of preference in the eyes of church leaders. When in 1844 Joseph Smith was murdered, Emma was left out of favor with the larger group of his successors, that headed by Brigham Young. When the Saints began their exodus from Nauvoo Eliza, not Emma, carried the Relief Society minute book across the plains to the new settlement in the mountains. Emma Smith remained behind.

For a time, the society, and with it any remaining sense of

female autonomy, was forced underground. Brigham Young, successor to Smith in the leadership of the Church, saw in the Relief Society a threat of such magnitude that he said to priesthood leaders: "When I want Sisters or the Wives of the members of the church to get up a Relief Society I will summon them to my aid but until that time let them stay at home & if you see Females huddling together veto the concern and if they say Joseph Smith started it tell them it is a damned lie for I know he never encouraged it. . . ."[15] When Young was finally ready to permit the women's organization, it was ten years later and a thousand miles away.

Why Brigham Young was eventually to reorganize the Relief Society, in small branches at first, and later throughout the church, has much to do with Eliza R. Snow. After Joseph Smith's death, Young had married her, most likely to provide for her temporal support. The daughter of a wealthy Ohio farmer and politician, she had never had to fend for herself, except for a few widely separated periods of schoolteaching and the occasional making of a gentleman's suit of clothes. Widowed by Joseph Smith's death, bereft of parental support, she was left to cross the plains with what little support Young could provide. More than food, however, she found in Young's family--his other wives and their families--a kind of nurturing which sustained her while she learned the lessons of self-sufficiency. She proved her loyalty to Young and the establishment he represented by publishing a poem supporting his presidency: he had been "call'd of the Lord o'er the Twelve to preside,/And with them o'er the Church and the world beside."[16] Her support of plural marriage was unquestioned; her doctrine, articulated publicly through her verses, was orthodox; and her spiritual strength, even through a decade of physical weakness after the crossing of the plains, led Young to set her before his own family as exemplar. She had achieved what he sermonized as "true independence of spirit," that assurance of transcendent rightness in the eyes of God.[17] In 1867 Young gave Snow an official calling to re-establish the Relief Society in Utah and the surrounding settlements, primarily to promote home manufacturing among Mormon women.

How Snow was able to expand that Society's mandate and work its presidency into the powerful position it eventually became depended less upon Brigham Young than upon her own qualities, and how they were perceived by Morman women and their local priesthood leaders. And that perception brings us back to the paradigm of ecclesiastical, liturgical, and charismatic religious expressions with which we began. For Eliza Snow represented to the women of the Mormon church the pinnacle of achievement in all three areas.

In Nauvoo only her writing had distinguished Eliza Snow as outstanding. "Zion's poetess" carried little religious credibility in a male-dominated church. Her work in the Relief Society of the 1840s was slight--she is absent from the minutes for almost the entire second year. And, though she served as recorder in the temple during much of its hurried activity just prior to the exodus, she was not one of the administrators there. But there was in Nauvoo a beginning of her later rise to power: her practice of the spiritual gifts. Sarah Kimball later recalled when Eliza Snow gave her first blessing: "Sister Snow," she reported saying to her friend, "you come and lay your hands on my head and bless me. She arose and l[o]oking at my mother said it seems more propper [sic] to bless the elder first. I said do so. There were only three of us present but the occasion was memorable."[18] Later in the Relief Society Eliza Snow publicly prophesied over one of the women.[19]

As the women gathered along the trail west, especially during the long winter of 1846-47 at the Nebraska layover called Winter Quarters, Snow's aptitude for the charismatic increased. The "blessing meetings" in which she participated centrally sustained the women, and her reputation as "prophetess" spread beyond the elite group of the families of general authorities, growing to near-legendary proportions by the time the main body of the church was settled in Salt Lake City.

At the very early stages of the work of the Endowment House in Salt Lake City, the proto-temple where the high rituals were performed, Eliza Snow was named officiator, and women who presented themselves for endowment and marriage came to regard her as "priestess." Her practice of pronouncing blessings, prophecies and other pentacostal expressions carried over into the new office. By 1867, when the title "presidentess" was added, there was no woman so highly regarded in all Mormondom. Her power was second only to that of her prophet-husband among the women--and her accesibility to them greater.

Eliza Snow possessed exactly the qualities for the task. Raised in frontier Ohio, she was nevertheless confident of her position in the social order. The daughter of a line of first settlers, she considered her rightful place in society the same as her place in school had been: at the head of the class. Married successively to two presidents of the Latter-day Saints, by 1867 she sat at mealtime to the left of her second husband and presided over the spiritual affairs of his large plural family, always meticulously under his direction. The trek across the plains had taught her independence and self-sufficiency, but her experiences in Nauvoo had taught her obedience and discretion. The ability to function in the tension between the two extremes was her chief virtue. "We will always do as we are directed by the priesthood," she would write to a local Relief Society leader in later years, at the same time challenging the woman to find ways of converting her male leader to the women's program. Empowered by her husband in 1867 to reestablish the society in the local units of the church, Snow was given no counselors, no budget other than her own resources, no staff, not even a secretary to keep minutes. Uniquely free of the domestic duties of most women--she lived, childless, in Young's cooperative Lion House with some fifteeen wives and their children--she managed on her own to give sufficient leadership to the new societies to boost the movement very quickly into an established program.

For two years she worked virtually alone in the Salt Lake City wards. At that point, her need for an organization to carry the work beyond the immediate vicinity coincided with another development in Brigham Young's temporal state: the need to curtail the cash flow out of Utah. Seeing women as chief culprits in the purchase of "states" goods, he called for "retrenchment" in the lavish styles of dress and tablesetting. En route to the southern colonies of Mormon country in the fall of 1869, he presented the problem to Mary Isabella Horne, then visiting her son in Gunnison. Horne interpreted Young's challenge to her to "lead out" in the movement as a charge to rally the women. Going first to Eliza Snow, she took direction from her to establish a group of their intimate sisters into the Senior and Junior Retrenchment Association, meeting twice a month in Salt Lake's Fourteenth Ward.

Far removed from the usual pattern of Mormon organization, this body crossed ward boundaries, was responsible to no priesthood leader except Young himself, and consisted of a president and not the usual two, but seven counselors. Horne was titular head of the body, but it is evident from the minutes that Eliza Snow directed its activities. Here was the organized support she needed for her direction of the activities of the Relief Societies throughout the Mormon colonies. Long after the immediate need for "retrenchment" had passed, the group continued to meet, adopting various purposes and projects the women believed would promote the cause of Zion.

That such a female group could maintain autommy of program and practice in a society in which male priesthood leaders were assembling themselves in increasingly hierarchical pyramids challenges traditional ideas of the role of women in Mormon society. Jill Mulvay Derr and C. Brooklyn Derr see as a partial explanation the propensity of women to function sucessfully in informal networks, a concept familiar to observers of the contemporary world of men and women.[20] Given a skeletal organization and a nebulous purpose, "to build the kingdom," the women would perceive a need, talk about it at their semi-monthly meeting, defer to Sister Snow for confirmation (except in those cases in which she introduced the idea in the first place), and volunteer or assign each other to carry the program to the outlying organizations.

Perhaps a more profound explanation of the successful operation of this Mormon women's group lies in the paradigm of religious experience delineated above, the blend of charismatic, liturgical and ecclesiastical expressions involving Mormon women. Eliza Snow's various titles reflect the roles women were able to appropriate in the Mormon church: "prophetess" for her exercise of the pentacostal gifts; "priestess" for her participation in the rituals of the endowment house, which the women regarded as the holy of holies; and "presidentess" for her organizational role in directing spiritual and economic projects undertaken by the group, and her continued intermediary function as their voice with the male hierarchy.

Some of the methods Snow used to weave her calling as Relief Society president into a pattern of female activism in a patriarchal church can be glimpsed in accounts of her visits to local congregations of the Saints. Diaries extant seldom fail to mention her visits, and minute books recording most meetings in a few lines award pages to verbatim accounts of her speeches. One example of her communication with the Saints in outlying areas of Mormon country provides in its details some clue to her approach and its response.

In 1880, together with Zina D.H. Young, her sister wife in sealings both to Joseph Smith and Brigham Young, Snow undertook a four-month long visit to St. George, center of the Southern Utah colonies. Her purposes were personal as well as ecclesiastical: she wanted to spend some time in the recently dedicated temple there, the temple in Salt Lake not yet being completed; but also she would visit Relief Societies and organize in the settlements there the newly-approved Primary Association for the children.

By her own account, she and Zina Young traveled "on the cars," that is, by train, almost three hunded miles to the station nearest St. George, and from there, in the course of their visit, more than a thousand miles by wagon, buggy, or whatever mode the community provided.[21] At the temple, noted diarist Charles L. Walker, the two women "felt much pleased and gratified in having the glorious privilege of entering in and participating in the ordinances."[22] Walker and the other temple workers would have felt themselves under inspection by Snow, she having so long presided over the work in the Salt Lake Endowment House. That she was pleased augured well for the rest of the visit.

The women's visits to the various Relief Societies went equally well. A Parowan diarist notes: "In the eavening [sic] Sister Eliza R. Snow and Zina D. Young . . . gave some excellent instruction to the sisters, at which meeting the Brethren attended also."[23] Mormon men as well as women regarded their "leading sisters" as visitors to be heard.

The most significant mission of the two women on this trip was the organization of the Primary Associations, children's groups recently inaugurated in the central wards and now spreading to more distant settlements. There is no record of any opposition to the program, despite its coming without male priesthood representation. It had originally been founded on the suggestion of a woman, encouraged by her bishop, and presented for highest level approval by Snow herself (Brigham Young by then deceased, she had to win the support of the new president, John Taylor). In St. George, the minutes record the response of Bishop Judd, typical of the reactions of his fellow parish leaders: "Bishop Judd said he felt deeply interested in these Primary Associations and felt to bless all endeavors to promote the talents of the children of this ward, felt to bless the efforts of Sister Eliza R. S and Zina Y. . . ."[24]

Personally and organizationally, the women of the Relief Society accomplished a great deal. But the basis of their lasting impact on the various congregations lay even more in the spiritual dimension of their work. Not an isolated case is the report of one child who later remembered hearing of a boy brought "very sick and weak" to the Primary organization meeting in the tiny town of Pinto:

> He wanted to be prayed for, so at the close of the meeting
> Sister Snow told the children to arise to their feet, close
> their eyes, and repeat after her the prayer, one sentence at
> a time. She prayed for the sick boy. When they got

through praying he got up, walked home, and got into a
wagon without help. He was well from that time.[25]

Whether the incident occurred as the child wrote it thirteen years
later, or whether the hearsay story gained in the retelling is
immaterial; what is salient here is that such healing powers were
attributed to Eliza Snow, and such demonstrations in the course of
church meetings were accepted and even expected.

Given their marital connection to the founder of the Mormon
church, it is not surprising that part of the celebration of the visit
of Eliza Snow and Zina Young to St. George was their presence
as honored guests at a party commemorating the birthday of
Joseph Smith. Two hundred guests heard the memorial speeches,
after which the two widows "withdrew, and while they were
withdrawing the whole audience, rose upon their feet and stood,
in honor of the wives of . . . the Prophet whose birth they had met
to commemorate."[26] But the fact that a month later a similar party
honored Eliza Snow on her own birthday suggests that she had
achieved a reputation quite independent of her husband's. And
while the St. George Saints were enjoying her company at their
celebration, members of the church in Salt Lake City, Ogden, and
perhaps other places as well, were also gathering in her honor.[27]

Such, in brief, was the character of Mormonism's strongest
woman leader and its most powerful women's organization. The
Relief Society resulted from a fortuitous coming together of
community needs and solutions; of isolation from the larger
society; of a utopian ideology sanctioning a unique form of
polygamy; and of a woman in whom personal attributes and social
position blended to fill the female void in an otherwise male
leadership. In the patterns of institutionalization typical of human
organizations (even churches), however, the sources of Eliza
Snow's strength gradually became mired in administrative
policies. Before her death in 1887, Snow was mourning the
diminution of spiritual expressions in the Relief Society, and
official publications of the church were diminishing the importance
of the keys and authority the women felt they had been given.
Brigham Young, whose confidence granted to Eliza Snow

substantial power, had died ten years earlier. Under his successor John Taylor's direction in 1880 the one umbrella organization became four separate ones, the sisterhood gradually splintered, and ecclesiastical authority dissipated. With Eliza Snow's death and the dissolution of those familial and associational ties came the beginning of the end of female autonomy in the Mormon organizational structure.

Notes

1. Gail Farr Casterline, "'In the Toils' or 'Onward for Zion': Images of Mormon Woman, 1852-1890," (Master's thesis, Utah State University, 1974), delineates the views of Mormon women created for and held by non-Mormon Americans.

2. Leonard J. Arrington, "The Economic Role of Pioneer Mormon Women," *Western Humanities Review* 9 (Spring 1955): 145-64 was the pioneer. Since then the following specialized studies, having to do with the programs mentioned here, have appeared: Sherilyn Cox Bennion, "The *Woman's Exponent:* Forty-two Years of Speaking for Women," *Utah Historical Quarterly* 44 (1976): 222-39; and "Enterprising Ladies: Utah's Women Editors," ibid. 49 (1981): 291-304; Chris Rigby Arrington, "The Finest of Fabrics: Mormon Women and the Silk Industry in Early Utah," *Utah Historical Quarterly* 46 (1978): 376-96; Jessie L. Embry, "Relief Society Grain Storage Program, 1876-1940" (Master's thesis, Brigham Young University, 1974); Christine Croft Waters, "Pioneering Physicians in Utah, 1847-1900" (Master's thesis, University of Utah, 1976); Thomas G. Alexander, "An Experiment in Progressive Legislation: The Granting of Woman Suffrage in Utah in 1870," *Utah Historical Quarterly* 38 (Winter 1970): 20-30; Beverly Beeton, "Woman Suffrage in the American West, 1869-1896" (Ph.D. dissertation, University of Utah, 1976). More are listed in Carol Cornwall Madsen and David J. Whittaker, "History's Sequel: A Source Essay on Women in Mormon History," *Journal of Mormon History* 6 (1979): 123-145.

3. Maureen Ursenbach Beecher, "The 'Leading Sisters': A Female Hierarchy in Nineteeth Century Mormon Society," *Journal of Mormon History* 9 (1982): 25-39, traces the individual women who formed this central group from their first contact with each other, through their trials along the trail west, to their positions of rank and power in Utah.

4. Keith E. Melder, *Beginnings of Sisterhood: The American Woman's Rights Movement, 1800-1850* (New York: Schocken Books, 1977), 30-47.

5. Official Relief Society histories include *A Centenary of Relief Society, 1842-1942* (Salt Lake City: Relief Society General Board, 1942), and *History of the Relief Society, 1842-1966* (Salt Lake City: Relief Society General Board, 1966). Both tell the bare story of the Nauvoo beginnnings, essentially without interpretation or background.

6. An essentially lay ministry governs Mormon congregations. Male priesthood leaders, organized into local "quorums" of deacons, teachers, priests, elders, seventies, and high priests, and central quorums of apostles and a first presidency, have responsibility for various facets of church administration. The present organization evolved a quorum at a time, each one repeating basically the same pattern of initial organization and ongoing administration.

7. In 1880, when he presided over a reorganization of the women's groups, John Taylor reinterpreted the term "ordain" to mean "set apart," a term which, he said, more accurately implied Joseph Smith's intent. *Woman's Exponent* 9 (1 September 1880): 53-[55]. "The ordination then given," he explained, "did not mean the conferring of the Priesthood upon those sisters." This subsequent redefinition may as easily reflect the changing attitude of the time as it does Taylor's recollection of Smith's intent.

8. Minutes of the Nauvoo Female Relief Society, 1842-1844, manuscript, 28 April 1842, LDS Church Archives, Salt Lake City.

9. I owe the suggestion of this paradigm to my friend and colleague Laurel Thatcher Ulrich, who first applied it to Mormon women in a discussion in Nauvoo, May 24, 1982.

10. The "endowment" is the highest religious rite in Mormon practice. Promised to the Saints as early as 1830, it was finally formalized by Joseph Smith into a lengthy ritual designed to be performed in the temple then under construction. In lecture and dramatic presentation, the ceremony provided for the faithful a continuity of human experience, exacted from them covenants of obedience to divine law, ordained them with priestly power, and promised them heavenly rewards for their faithfulness. It was considered by 19th century Mormons as essential to their afterlife.

11. Nauvoo Relief Society Minutes, 13 August 1843. Andrew Ehat and Lyndon Cook connect the founding of the Relief Society and the beginnning of the endowment in their notes to *The Words of Joseph Smith* (Provo: Religious Studies Center, Brigham Young University, 1980), 141-42.

12. Linda King Newell, "A Gift Given, A Gift Taken: Washing, Annointing, and Blessing the Sick Among Mormon Women," *Sunstone* 6 (September/October 1981): 16-25.

13. Joseph Smith, as recorded in Nauvoo Relief Society Minutes, 28 April 1842.

14. The blame was laid at Emma Smith's door by John Taylor in 1880, but Eliza Snow in 1867 suggested that Emma may have had laudable reasons for discontinuing the society: rather than see the splintering of the church, she would give up the women's organization entirely. See my "Women at Winter Quarters," *Sunstone* 8 (July-August 1983): 11-19.

15. Seventies Record, manuscript, 9 March 1845, LDS Church Archives.

16. "To President Brigham Young," *Times and Seasons* (Nauvoo), 15 February 1845.

17. Brigham Young, in *Journal of Discourses* 1: 312, discourse of 20 February 1853. Snow's progression from child to responsible adult is delineated briefy in my "Eliza Roxey [*sic*] Snow's Way to Sainthood," *Exponent II* 10 (Winter 1984): 10-12.

18. Sarah M. Kimball, "Record of the Relief Society from First Organization to Conference April 5th, 1892, Bk. II," manuscript, LDS Church Archives.

19. Nauvoo Relief Society Minutes, 19 April 1842.

20. Jill Mulvay Derr and C. Brookly Derr, "Outside the Mormon Hierarchy: Alternative Aspects of Institutional Power," *Dialogue: A Journal of Mormon Thought* 15 (Winter 1982): 21-43.

21. *Woman's Exponent* 10 (1 November 1881): 82.

22. Charles L. Walker, Journal, 27 March 1880 to 27 June 1882, entry for 24 November 1880, photocopy of typescript, LDS Church Archives.

23. Samuel H. Rogers, Diary, 14 December 1880, LDS Church Archives.

24. St. George First Ward, St. George Stake, Primary Minute Book, 1880-86, 29 November 1880.

25. Mabel Knell, "Our Primary," in *Juvenile Instructor* 28 (1 May 1893): 301.

26. "History of the Life of Oliver B. Huntington, Written by Himself," typescript, LDS Church Archives.

27. Franklin D. Richards, Diary, 21 January 1881, LDS Church Archives.

8.
"We Are Rather Weaker In Righteousness Than In Numbers": The Mormon Colony at San Bernardino, California, 1851-1857

M. Guy Bishop

During the summer of 1851 the *Los Angeles Star* briefly noted the arrival of a sizable contingent of new settlers. "A body of people, numbering about 500 souls are now encamped in the neighborhood of Cajon Pass," the story related. The prospective residents were said to be engaged in negotiations with the family of Don Antonio Maria Lugo, the current landowners, for the purchase of several thousand acres located in the San Bernardino Valley.[1] This announcement heralded a quasi-official colonizing project being undertaken by the Church of Jesus Christ of Latter-day Saints (Mormons) in southern California. A few months before, Brigham Young, successor to Joseph Smith, had appointed two ecclesiastical leaders, Apostles Charles Coulsen Rich and Amasa Mason Lyman, to initiate a settlement on the West Coast.[2]

The motivation for the founding of the San Bernardino colony has been subjected to varying historical hypotheses. The followers of Young had initially arrived on the shores of the Great Salt Lake in July 1847 and a steady flow of Latter-day Saints continued for years afterward. The World War II era writings of Milton R. Hunter have helped to popularize the notion of an imperialistic Mormon church hierarchy determined to control the entire Great Basin by encircling Salt Lake City with an outer cordon of satellite colonies which Hunter labeled "control settlements".[3] Such an interpretation may have predated the mid-twentieth century. A study by A. Harvey Collins printed in the *Annual Publication of the Historical Society of Southern California* in 1919 attributed the Mormon colonization of San Bernardino to "the fulfillment of this dream of empire" which the church authorities nurtured.[4] While the origin of the imperialism school of thought remains obscure, its thesis continued to be accepted, explicitly or implicitly, by many writers of Utah and Mormon history. By 1958, when Leonard J. Arrington published his exhaustive economic history of nineteenth century Mormonism, the outer cordon had been modified somewhat to the "Mormon Corridor".[5] This interpretation, which described a string of outposts ranging from the Great Salt Lake to the Pacific Ocean, had a more sound historical basis than did the encirclement position. Finally, an essay by Eugene E. Campbell in the *Utah Historical Quarterly* (1973) convincingly took to task all previous interpretations. Campbell questioned not just the theory of Mormon expansion beyond the Great Basin, but also the actuality.[6] This study will address the lingering question of why San Bernardino was settled, and also examine the causes of the colony's eventual demise, and assess what, if anything, was accomplished by the undertaking.

If the church-controlled imperialism idea is to be rejected, specifically for Mormon activities in southern California, other motives must be uncovered. In an unpublished doctoral dissertation, Joseph S. Wood pointed out two reasons for the church to have desired the establishment of a strong settlement in the area: first, to solve the logistical problems encountered in moving people and products to the isolated Salt Lake Valley, and second, to originate a Mormon foothold in the rich Pacific region.[7] Although the latter motive appears closely related to the discredited expansionism stance, a distinction must be made between spreading the gospel of Mormonism to new areas and aspiring to inaugurate a theocratic empire. Furthermore, the creation of a West Coast terminus for the church is supported by the available evidence.

The dual goals of spreading the gospel and gathering the faithful to Zion were vital concerns to the Latter-day Saints from the religion's infancy. While the place of assembly had been relocated, under much duress, from Ohio to Missouri to Illinois and, finally, to the Great Basin, the twin objectives had remained constant. And both motives were apparently at work in the San Bernardino venture.

In the minds of Rich, Lyman, and, of course, Brigham Young, the settlement of southern California meant building up the Kingdom of God. The two apostles referred to their assignment as a "mission" undertaken on instructions given by Young as early as November 1850. In fact, the duo had previously been dispatched to California in 1849 to determine the expediency of establishing a base for the church somewhere in the area. After careful consideration, Lyman recommended the vicinity of Los Angeles for Mormon occupation, the primary reason being the easier accessibility of land in the southern portion of California.[8]

One goal of the mission of 1851 was clearly to establish a godly enclave in the locale on Mormon terms. It is obvious from extant sources that the two apostles perceived this aspect of the undertaking. Charles C. Rich saw the object in simple, direct terms--to locate a standard of righteousness on the West Coast. His apostolic associate, Amasa Lyman, admonished the Saints shortly after their arrival at San Bernardino, "We came here to plant and cultivate the principles of virtue and morality."[9]

However, the founding of a western terminus for Mormonism was also of primary importance. Access to West Coast port facilities was viewed as an essential component for expediting the gathering of the faithful Saints to the new denominational headquarters at Great Salt Lake City. As Mormon missionaries began to teach on Pacific isles and in Australia, a settlement near the southern California harbor of San Pedro was deemed necessary. Mary Ann Rich, who accompanied her husband on the colonization attempt, recollected in her autobiography that the church leaders had authorized the settlement "for the gathering of the Saints."[10] Brigham Young's thoughts on the goals of the colony were best outlined in the General Epistle of 1852 to the Saints throughout the world. This directive announced that "[t]hose who are accustomed to a warm climate, and have the opportunity, may journey to California, and take counsel of the Presidency at San Bernardino [Rich and Lyman]."[11]

From the very beginning, however, the aims of devout leaders

173

were compromised by some unwieldy followers. Word of the impending foray into California circulated quickly through the Mormon community in Utah. The fertile soil and temperate climate of the West Coast, in some instances accompanied by dreams of gold and quick wealth, were a strong temptation for some Saints. According to James Henry Rollins, who had been called to participate in the settlement, "there were many of the brethren [who] came to them [Lyman and Rich] and wanted to go."[12] Among these eager colonists were not only devout Mormon missionaries but adventurers and gold seekers who longed for the chance to emigrate, some dissidents who grated under the confines of Salt Lake City and Brigham Young's firm control, and former members of the Mormon Batallion who fondly remembered the area. The church hierarchy had anticipated that the initial party would consist of about twenty-five people, but in the spring of 1851 nearly five hundred prospective settlers assembled at the departure point. Brigham Young, who had planned to deliver a farewell address, was so dismayed by the group's inflated size that he would not render his blessings. Young reportedly said that he was "sick at the sight of so many of the [S]aints running off to California, chiefly after the gods of this world."[13] While Brigham Young would continue to recognize the potential usefulness of San Bernardino as a way station for converts, he never again exhibited enthusiasm for the settlement.

The original intention of Lyman and Rich was to purchase the property of Isaac Williams in what is now the Chino area. Henry Bigler, a Mormon who was in the area during 1849-50 when the two apostles surveyed southern California for a potential settlement, recorded the following in his journal:

> This morning Col. Williams offered to sell his Ranch and all the Stock on it; his figure is two hundred thousand dollars, this offer was made to Br. Rich .... His reason for wishing to sell, he was not satisfied and wished to go to the states to live.[14]

By the time of the party's arrival in the Los Angeles area in the spring of 1851, however, Williams had changed his mind. In an attempt to mask this disappointing development, Amasa Lyman wrote Brigham Young that the Rancho Del Chino "was not the right place for our settlement."[15] It was said to lack sufficient water and timber resources. Consequently, a search for an alternate site was immediately launched.

During the summer of 1851 Rich and Lyman negotiated for the purchase of a rancho owned by the Lugo family, who upon learning of the Mormons' need for land had offered several thousand acres in the San Bernardino and Yucaipa valleys. Recent Indian hostility had made the Lugos willing to accomodate the newcomers. Lyman and Rich hoped to make the purchase for between fifty and sixty thousand dollars, but they eventually agreed to a price of $77,500, with a down payment of $7,000. The property was believed to encompass between eighty and one hundred thousand acres and included existing structures.[16] The Mormon colonists quickly moved onto the land, began to construct homes within a solid stockade enclosure, and made preparations for the winter.

During the interim between their arrival in the area and the purchase of the Lugo ranch a conference of the Saints had been convened in the San Bernardino Valley. At that time an ecclesiastical hierarchy was established in accordance with the accepted Latter-day Saint pattern. David Seely was nominated by the apostles to serve as president of the new San Bernardino Stake (a central entity in local church governance) and a High Council consisting of twelve brethren was chosen. In his concluding remarks, Amasa Lyman cautioned the people concerning their conduct in California. They were admonished to settle their difficulties within the church and avoid the legal system of the United States--undoubtedly a thinly-veiled Mormon criticism of American judicial equality.[17]

By February 1852 Amasa Lyman was able to inform Brigham Young that crops had been planted and the settlement was blossoming. In a letter to a fellow apostle, Franklin D. Richards, written in June of that year, Lyman related the colony's progress in detail. Some two thousand acres of the tract had been surveyed, a school had been established, a grist mill and saw mill were under construction, a vineyard had been planted, and plans were being drawn for a future city. Since his correspondent was at the time serving a mission in England, the San Bernardino churchman added with a touch of glee that "the climate . . . is as pleasant as we could wish.... At no time during the winter was the weather so cold that an overcoat was necessary."[18]

Not only was material progress being made during this early period, but the winning of souls was also moving forward. Other California emigrants, as well as some natives, embraced Mormonism with some regularity. Richard R. Hopkins, who served the San Bernardino colonists as clerk and recorder, kept a detailed account of the developments. His history mentions numerous conversions, including the baptism of several individuals identified as "Mexicans or Spaniards" and said to be the first of that ethnic background to join the church.[19] In recounting the local denominational conference of April 1852, Hopkins joyfully noted the stalwartness of the community: "The heart of every Saint appeared to join in praises and thanksgiving to the dispensor of all good for the happiness which surrounds us."[20] Indeed, the first year or two in southern California was a time of harmony and mutual cooperation for the San Bernardino Mormons. Unfortunately, such tranquility would begin to be shattered by the mid-1850s.

The cause, or causes, of the eventual disaffection of many of the settlers and the resulting abandonment of the colony represent a tangled and recurring story in early Mormon history. Seeds of discontent among some members of the community can be found in the issues of land distribution and political independence. These factors were aggravated by the growth of a non-Mormon minority which opposed the theocratic control of the church. In order more clearly to understand these problems, the workings of the Latter-day Saint governmental system must be briefly considered. Mid-nineteenth century Mormon ecclesiastical leaders like Charles C. Rich and Amasa Lyman had no intention of fostering democratic rule. God had chosen his servants and the faithful were obliged to follow their counsel in all matters spiritual and temporal. Brigham

Young and his associates in the Utah Territory held firm control, and the apostles at San Bernardino hoped to exercise a similar benevolent stewardship. Actions by the church hierarchy were instituted with the best of intentions, since they believed that the young colony needed to be carefully guided to maturity, but in this case the worst possible results were the eventual product.

Land distribution at the Mormon settlement was dictated by Lyman and Rich, who held legal title to the rancho and also bore the responsibility for the sizable debt which had been incurred. By early 1852 the settlers were able to pay a second installment on the property, thus bringing the total amount tendered to $25,500. This allowed them to secure a warranty deed. A note for the additional $52,000 was signed by the apostles at this time.[21] The money was obtained through financial connections in the San Francisco area, solicited from the Saints scattered throughout California, and from the occasional contributions of the San Bernardino church members. But still the debt hung heavy over the community and particularly weighed upon Lyman and Rich. In July 1854, the two men organized a joint-stock company to help disperse the obligation, and later that year sent some agents to the northern California gold fields to try to raise additional monies.[22] The experiences of Henry G. Boyle highlighted the problem which the rancho debt imposed. In March 1854 he was sent with several other Mormon men to prospect for gold along the Kern River in the southern Sierra Nevada Mountains. When this project proved unsuccessful, Boyle accompanied a party sent to the north later that summer to solicit support.[23]

Indebtedness was not the only land-related problem which troubled the Mormon settlement. At the local conference held in April 1852, less than one year after the Saints' arrival at San Bernardino, Amasa Lyman alluded to the question of private ownership when he told those gathered to be satisfied with the "use of the land" until such a time as it became practical to allow each his own inheritance.[24] The two apostles held the property for later sale to the residents, feeling that such a safeguard insured their ability to make good on the real estate loan by which they were bound. When a dispute with the federal government over the dimensions of the Lugo land grant arose in 1853, the tensions mounted. The Mormon claim was reduced to almost half of its original size by decision of the United States Land Commission. This determination caused the apostles to question their ability to sell the property for the needed amount, and they acted indecisively in dividing the remaining holdings. Their actions led some of the disgruntled settlers to accuse the men of holding out the best sections for themselves.[25]

Mormon dissidents as well as local "gentiles" (non-Mormons) seized upon the land issue in an attempt to thwart church strength in southern California. Two such cases occurred during 1856. The first involved Jerome Benson, an apostate Mormon, who refused to vacate property claimed by Rich and Lyman. Upon notification of his impending eviction, Benson rallied the support of other disconcerted individuals, fortified the house which he occupied, and vowed to resist any attempts to remove him from the land. Charles C. Rich warned the Saints to stay calm and avoid aggression, thus depriving the opposition of any confrontation. Benson remained illegally on the tract until the majority of the Latter-day Saints had vacated San Bernardino nearly two years later, at which time he chose to purchase more desirable property which was then unencumbered.[26]

Perhaps a more telling incident in the growth of anti-Mormon sentiment which focused on the land situation was a lawsuit brought against Lyman and Rich by Louis Roubidoux, an early pioneer of the San Bernardino Valley. Roubidoux had initially been quite friendly to the Latter-day Saints; on one occasion the two apostles had secured a loan from him to apply toward the rancho debt. However, in April 1856, following his arrest in the Mormon community on charges of public intoxication, he demanded immediate payment of the note. Richard Hopkins, in his record, identified this judicial proceeding as "one of the first acts of persecution against us."[27] Fortunately the defendants were able to secure the needed funds and make payment to Roubidoux. The question of land distribution and issues related to the indebtedness were a source of escalating concern for the colonists and a vehicle by which the disaffected could enlist support. However, it was in the arena of politics that the opposition provided the most antagonism.

In 1853 Jefferson Hunt, a Mormon representative to the California State Assembly, presented a petition to the legislature seeking a division of Los Angeles County and the creation of a new San Bernardino County. The act was passed in April of that year. Originally the division was a boon to Mormon interests since they held the balance of power in the new county. In fact, the election of June 1853 saw a sweep of all offices by the Latter-day Saint candidates.[28] This easy victory, nonetheless, proved to be a harbinger of future problems. In the 1855 election three Mormons--Benjamin Grouard, F. M. Van Leuven, and Valentine Herring--chose to run against the official church ticket.[29] All three were soundly defeated, but the note of disunity had been introduced. Grouard, a New England convert who had served with distinction as a missionary to the South Pacific, reacted to his defeat with unexpected rancor. He publicly blamed the local ecclesiastical leaders for his loss.[30] All three men were called before a church court to explain their actions.

In accordance with a plan laid down by the Mormon prophet Joseph Smith in 1844 and perpetuated by Brigham Young and his colleagues in Utah, the political kingdom of God on earth was administered by a council of fifty men.[31] Amasa Lyman and Charles Rich were members of this select body and, as such, had the prerogative to dictate candidates for public office. Faithful Latter-day Saints were expected to second their decision without question. A diary entry by Henry G. Boyle described what transpired at the inquest for Grouard, Van Leuven, and Herring:

> Brother Lyman proceeded to explain the nature of the wrongs committed by them, and the evil consequences that would grow out of such a course of conduct ....They [the dissidents] raised the hue and cry that we were Slaves and not men [a charge to which Boyle took exception].... The men above mentioned would not confess or retract. Therefore they were cut off from the Church.[32]

Since the dissidents' main reasons for seeking election apparently hinged upon the point of political freedom rather than any doctrinal differences, the response of the San Bernardino leadership may have been ill-advised. Rather than stemming any further opposition, political factionalism and apostasy increased steadily in its aftermath.

As had been predicted by Lyman and Rich at the time of the Saints' arrival in southern California, the greatest hostility toward the church came from within its own ranks. Among those who either left the settlement at San Bernardino or joined the political factionalists (who called themselves "Independents") were Robert M. Smith, a member of the High Council, Henry G. Sherwood, who had long been an active churchman, and Quartus S. Sparks, a prominent local politician who had served as city attorney. The Anti-Mormon Party, founded in 1855, counted F. M. Van Leuven as well as Sparks among its foremost advocates. The stability of the struggling colony was badly shaken by these developments. It is small wonder that Richard R. Hopkins surmised in August 1855, "There is not the same spirit of unity existing here as formerly."[33]

Conditions worsened as time passed for the colony. To Hopkins this represented a shocking course of events.

> The spirit of Apostasy is daily becoming more evident, men who for years apparently have labored zealously in the Church are turning against the brethren, abusing the authorities . . . and swearing vengeance on all saints.

The defection of Henry G. Sherwood brought to the surface a very real fear, as he threatened to bring a mob against the Mormons at San Bernardino.[34] For those of the Saints who had been through a mobbing in Missouri or Illinois such fulminations certainly struck a note of terror.

A brief respite from the upheaval took place early in 1856 as a portion of the inhabitants renewed their covenants to support the church leaders and, according to Hopkins, the spirit of piety began once again to manifest itself. This sense of recommitment was undoubtedly bolstered when Charles C. Rich admonished the people to conduct themselves properly or face excommunication.[35] Still, the entire situation continued to weigh heavily upon Rich and Lyman as they contemplated the settlement's future. Letters penned by Rich to members of his family in Utah openly reflected his despondent state. In reference to financial matters at San Bernardino he wrote, "Times is Verry [sic] bad in this country." This same theme continued into the following year as he noted that "there is nothing that would be more congenial to my feelings than to be placed in the midst of Salt Lake Valley."[36] The writings of Charles C. Rich during the later San Bernardino period reflected a discouraged and homesick man. Amasa Lyman's correspondance with Brigham Young also exhibited similar disillusionment:

> In relation to our strength here we are rather weaker in righteousness than in numbers. [T]he constant influance [sic] of discordant feelings is but calculated to increase an evil already in existence to a great extent.[37]

While the disaffection of some at San Bernardino can be traced to politics or land use, the prior disposition of others must also be considered. Many of the settlers, perhaps even a majority, were devout Latter-day Saints looking to build the Kingdom of God. But, as mentioned previously, some had entered the undertaking with less worthy purposes. Many had come to California primarily for self-aggrandizement. Others had histories of discontent and were on their way to apostasy even before they arrived. For example, Amasa Lyman mentioned Charles Crismon, an eventual apostate, as having been a problem in both Salt Lake City and San Bernardino. Henry G. Sherwood, for reasons which remain unclear, left Utah already strongly opposed to Brigham Young and the church hierarchy. And Quartus Sparks had experienced earlier difficulties in the San Francisco area. He had arrived on the West Coast late in 1846 with a contingent of Saints who had sailed from New York City under the direction of Samuel Brannan. Due to weak leadership and internal conflicts the party had deteriorated into varying degrees of inactivity, and several, including Sparks, had to be rebaptized in 1851.[38] While he demonstrated renewed fidelity following his appearance at San Bernardino, Sparks soon became associated politically with the Anti-Mormon Party, took a mistress, and was eventually cut off from the church for immorality.[39]

Added to the turmoil engendered by the apostates was the ever-increasing non-Mormon population of the community. According to a late nineteenth century history of the county, their arrival multiplied the current hard feelings. This Mormon-Gentile animosity continued even after the majority of the Saints had departed from southern California.[40] Throughout the summer of 1856 Richard Hopkins made regular notations regarding the influx of non-Mormons into the city. He was appalled by the increase in gambling and drunkenness which reportedly accompanied them. The challenge which these newcomers presented to the Mormon leadership was great. "It is almost impossible to insure a concert of action upon any object of public interest," wrote Hopkins.[41] Of particular concern was an increased orientation within the community toward private interests. Such disunity along with the emergence of worldliness and materialism was devastating to the church's aspirations for the settlement.

With these internal developments as well as other external factors, the tenure of the Saints in southern California was drawing to a close. In March 1856 Charles C. Rich began to allude to the possibility of the apostles' recall--under the pretext of a missionary assignment in Europe.[42] By this juncture such a new calling must have offered an attractive possibility for the embattled churchmen. Clearly, Brigham Young had already written off San Bernardino as an experiment that failed. The church hierarchy at Great Salt Lake City seemed to regard the California community as a magnet which attracted the undesirable elements of Utah Mormon society, and they were happy to part company with such individuals.[43]

During the late summer of 1856 the anti-Mormon forces raised funds to publish a pamphlet which viciously attacked the church. The work, alledgedly written by Quartus Sparks in collaboration with others, played upon the supposed threat of the Latter-day Saints' political power and was directed toward the citizenry of San Bernardino County. It called for a "new order" of government which would be free of Mormon domination. The document abounded with the charge of theocracy and reminded its readers that in the Utah Territory "there are no political conventions, mass meetings, or Caucuses." It further asserted that locally the Mormon leaders tried to arrange every ticket as well. And, in reference to the aborted candidacies of Grouard, Herring, and Van Leuven, the diatribe warned that, under such a system, to "disobey council would be [to] forfeit . . . standing in the community."[44]

At the close of the year Lyman and Rich instituted one final attempt to salvage the Mormon colony at San Bernardino. Following the lead of church officials in Utah, the two men tried to introduce the "Reformation Movement" in southern California. As in Salt Lake City, the purpose of the reform was to stem the tide of apostasy and build faith among the Saints. Church members were encouraged to affirm their commitment by openly confessing their sins, being rebaptized, and striving more fully to obey God's laws. Throughout Mormondom the devout followers were urged to "live your religion" and "hold to your covenants."[45]

According to local church records, the reformation at San Bernardino commenced in December 1856 and lasted into the following spring. Scores of rebaptisms were enumerated.[46] In a letter to a friend dated January 8, 1857, Ellen Pratt McGary wrote, "There is quite a reformation going on here [San Bernardino] at present. All the true-hearted Mormons are being baptized over again, those who are not [rebaptized], are not considered members of the church. I think it is doing great good." Yet within this enthusiastic assessment was an indication that the movement might ultimately have done additional harm. If all the Saints developed attitudes similar to Ellen McGary--that is, a clear distinction between the "true-hearted" and everyone else--then antagonism would most certainly have increased.[47]

Whatever consequences the reformation may have brought, it

was only a temporary reprieve. To magnify the problems for the San Bernardino Saints, Amasa Lyman and Charles C. Rich were recalled by Brigham Young in the spring of 1857. Mary Ann Rich recollected in her autobiography that Young had reassigned the two men since "everything was flourishing [and] their special aid was no longer needed there."[48] This belated statement, perhaps dulled by the years or embellished by the woman's close affiliation with the colony, was, at best, a drastic understatement of the true facts.

At their final church conference before departing, the two apostles touched upon the pressing concerns still confronting the Saints. Charles C. Rich formally announced a forthcoming "mission to Europe" and then rendered some remarks concerning the necessity of unity--certainly a problem in San Bernardino. In his farewell address, Amasa Lyman reminded the congregation:

> We told you then [in 1851]...that if opposition and persecution came upon us, that it would originate right in our midst; you know whether it has been so or not.... To those that had the ability without the disposition to aid the cause, we have naught but pity. You [were] not here to build up a city with a certain number of inhabitants... You [were] here to serve God.[49]

With this rehearsal of the causes for failure, at least as he understood them, Lyman washed his hands of the colony.

The Lyman-Rich party left southern California for Utah in April 1857. It must have been a time of mixed emotions for the two apostles. In one sense they were undoubtedly relieved to put so much turmoil behind them, but the colony represented an enormous but futile effort. For Charles Rich the tragedy was heightened by the death of his small daughter during the return trip.[50]

If the loss of the apostles had not been damaging enough to the Mormons remaining at San Bernardino, further events hastened the abandonment of southern California. During the fall of 1857 the federal government seemed bent on a military confrontation with the Rocky Mountain Saints. National public opinion, provoked by stories of polygamy and sedition in Mormondom, had forced President James Buchanan to dispatch troops of the United States Army to the Great Basin to reassert proper control. The major goals of the Buchanan administration's expedition were to investigate reported infringements upon the rights of non-Mormons in Utah Territory, to suppress Mormon home rule, and to eradicate the practice of plural marriage.[51]

Based on their previous encounters with persecution in the Midwest, church members in Utah expected the worst from the rapidly escalating military threat. This attitude ultimately caused more problems for the San Bernardino Mormons than did any governmental actions. In August 1857, amidst growing tensions and anger, a combined force of Latter-day Saint militiamen and their Indian allies annihilated a civilian wagon train at Mountain Meadows in southern Utah. The perpetrators of the attack mistakenly believed the party to be an advance body of the U. S. Army.[52]

The repercussions in southern California were significant. When news of the Mountain Meadows massacre reached San Bernardino the apostates and anti-Mormons quickly seized hold of the potentially volatile issue. Throughout October 1857 the Saints reported fears of imminent violence. It was rumored that the opposition was at work exciting the populace of Los Angeles against the church members. As one resident of San Bernardino lamented, "[the] day of trouble for the Saints in this land appears to be nearby."[53] The *Los Angeles Star*, a newspaper which had been favorably disposed toward the Latter-day Saints, intimated that the Mormons had instigated the attack upon the emigrant wagon train because the church leadership was "corrupt and bloodthirsty."[54]

Increasing tensions in southern California, along with a strong desire on Brigham Young's part to reunite the Saints from outlying areas with the main body in Utah, resulted in the recall of the San Bernardino settlers in November 1857. Instructions received from Salt Lake City on November 2 bid them to return with all possible haste. The internal dissension of the apostates plus the threat from federal troops provoked this decision by the Mormon hierarchy. As the faithful prepared to bid farewell to yet another home many were forced to sell their property for a "mere trifle." At the end of the month Richard Hopkins, still serving as scribe, reported:

> A large number of Saints have sold out, intending to leave for Utah.... The outsiders [non-Mormons] are purchasing our property at very reduced rates. They expect our people to take whatever is offered.[55]

The Mormon settlement at San Bernardino had been undertaken for a variety of reasons. Possibly it was the result of an expansionist tendency on the part of the church leadership. However, missionary zeal and the logistics of gathering the righteous to Zion represent a more plausible explanation. While Amasa Lyman, Charles C. Rich, and some colonists may have viewed the project as a calling from God, many others sought worldly wealth or an escape from Brigham Young's domain. And while the underpinnings of its demise were evident from the beginning, the continual influx of non-Mormons further eroded the church's control.

Many of the faithful Saints were probably ready to leave by 1857. Henry G. Boyle, who returned in that year from yet another mission to northern California, was greatly disturbed by the situation at San Bernardino. On November 17, 1857 he noted in his diary, "The Apostates and Mobbocrats [sic] are prowling around trying to stir up the people to blood shed and every wicked thing. O it is hell to live in the midst of such spirits." Just over three weeks later, in one of his last entries from San Bernardino, Boyle wrote that the locale had gotten to be "a den of Apostates, thieves, drunkards, Methodists, and every kind of foul character."[56]

In the final analysis, the Mormon colony at San Bernardino must be judged a failure. A recent study of transoceanic Latter-day Saint emigration between 1840 and 1890 has identified only three such voyages which terminated at the southern California port of San Pedro.[57] The desired pipeline for the gathering from San Bernardino to Salt Lake City thus never materialized. While missionary forays were launched from San Bernardino to sites all along the West Coast, their main purpose was to raise funds to pay the land debt. Although the missionaries won converts, it could well be that more souls were lost through apostasy. The entire project, from start to finish, received only token support from a church hierarchy in Salt Lake City which feared the wide dispersal of its members. Apostles Rich and Lyman, in their zeal to build up the kingdom, failed to recognize the necessity of gently leading their charges to the desired end. Local leadership, which had its talents stretched too far by a multitude of tasks and problems; a populace not unanimously committed to furthering the church; and virtual neglect by the ecclesiastical authorities in Utah all combined to bring about the demise of this Mormon experiment in building a frontier outpost.

Notes

1. *Los Angeles Star*, 5 July 1851. See also *Harper's New Monthly Magazine* 4 (December 1851-May 1852): 192.

2. Leonard J. Arrington, *Charles C. Rich: Mormon General and Frontiersman* (Provo: Brigham Young University Press, 1974), 157-61; and Joseph S. Wood, "The Mormon Settlement in San Bernardino, 1851-1857" (PhD diss., University of Utah, 1967), 48.

3. Milton R. Hunter, "The Mormon Corridor," *Pacific Historical Review* 8 (1939): 190-92; and *Brigham Young, The Colonizer*, 3rd ed. (Independence: Zion's Printing & Publishing Company, 1945), 66-67. Hunter never used the terms "inner" or "outer" cordon, preferring instead the designation "control settlements".

4. A. Harvey Collins, "At the End of the Trail: The Mormon Outpost of San Bernardino Valley," *Annual Publication of the Historical Society of Southern California* 2 (1919): 66.

5. *Great Basin Kingdom: An Economic History of the Latter-day Saints, 1830-1900* (Cambridge: Harvard University Press, 1958), 86.

6. Eugene E. Campbell, "Brigham Young's Outer Cordon--A Reappraisal," *Utah Historical Quarterly* 41 (1973): 220-25.

7. Wood, "San Bernardino," 48.

8. See Eugene Edward Campbell, "A History of the Church of Jesus Christ of Latter-day Saints in California, 1846-1946" (PhD diss., University of Southern California, 1952). Regarding the investigation of possible sites for settlement see Brigham Young Papers, Incoming Correspondence-Amasa Lyman, 23 July 1850, Historical Dept. of the Church of Jesus Christ of Latter-day Saints, Archives, Salt Lake City (hereafter LDS Archives).

9. Arrington, 158; Journal History of the Church of Jesus Christ of Latter-day Saints, 6 April 1852, LDS Archives.

10. Mary Ann Phelps Rich, "Autobiography" (n. d.), 27, LDS Archives; [Andrew Jensen] Manuscript History of San Bernardino, 6 July 1851, LDS Archives.

11. *Deseret News* (Great Salt Lake City), 13 October 1852; see also Robert V. Hine, *California's Utopian Colonies* (New Haven: Yale University Press, 1966), 133.

12. James Henry Rollins, Reminiscences (c. 1888), Spring 1851, LDS Arcives.

13. For Young's comment, see Hubert Howe Bancroft, *Works*, Volume XXVI, *History of Utah 1540-1886* (San Francisco: The History Company, 1889), 320.

14. Henry W. Bigler, Journal, 18 December 1849, Henry E. Huntington Library, San Marino.

15. See Richard D. Thompson, *Pioneers of San Bernardino Valley* (Rialto, California: n. p., 1976), 6-7; and Wood, "San Bernardino," 56. For Lyman's statement regarding the Chino Ranch, refer to Brigham Young Papers, Incoming Correspondence-Amasa Lyman, 30 July 1851.

16. Roy Elmer Whitehead, *Lugo: A Chronicle of Early California* (Redlands, California: San Bernardino County Museum Association, 1978), 372, 378.

17. Manuscript History, 6 July 1851.

18. Brigham Young Papers, Incoming Correspondence-Amasa Lyman, 14 February 1852; quotation in Manuscript History, 25 June 1852.

19. Richard R. Hopkins, Journal of the San Bernardino Branch of the Church of Jesus Christ of Latter-day Saints, 20 July 1852, LDS Archives. Much of the Manuscript History was based on Hopkins's journal.

20. Ibid., 6 April 1852.

21. Manuscript History, undated, c. March 1852; also Whitehead, *Lugo*, 378.

22. Manuscript History, 10 July 1854 and 22 October 1854. The most complete coverage of the entire financial situation can be found in Wood, "San Bernardino."

23. Henry Green Boyle, Diary, undated, c. March 1854 and 4 July 1854, LDS Archives. Boyle was one of the few participants in the San Bernardino colonization who was actually "called" to the task. For this reason the apostles relied upon him for much assistance.

24. Journal History, 6 April 1852.

25. See Wood, "San Bernardino," 10-12; Brigham Young Papers, Incoming Correspondence-Amasa Lyman, 1 September 1853; David Lavender, *California: A Bicentennial History* (New York: W. W. Norton and Co., 1976), 133; and Loretta Lea Hefner, "The Apostasy of Amasa Lyman" (Master's thesis, University of Utah, 1977), 30.

26. Manuscript History, 4 March-29 March 1856.

27. Hopkins, Journal, 6 April 1856; Rich, Diary, 22 April 1856; and Campbell, "A History of the Church," 207-8.

28. Manuscript History, 2 July 1853.

29. On the election of 1855, see Manuscript History, 21 April 1855; and Eugene E. Campbell, "The Decline and Fall of the Mormons in San Bernardino: A Second Look," unpublished manuscript, LDS Historical Department. While Grouard and Van Leuven were clearly participants, the identity of the third man is less certain. The Manuscript History named him as "Valentyn Johnson", as does Eugene Campbell in his dissertation (206). Joseph S. Wood states that he was "V. J. Herring", while Henry G. Boyle's diary used "Heron" and George William Beattie and Helen Pruitt Beattie (*Heritage of the Valley: San Bernardino's First Century* [Pasadena: San Pasqual Press, 1939]) said that the third candidate was "V. J. 'Rube' Herring." The Special California Census of 1852 for Los Angeles County listed only a "Valentine Herring", a native of Kentucky and former resident of Utah. Based upon the census data the author has concluded that the third man was Valentine Herring.

30. Concerning Grouard's missionary background, see Conway B. Sonne, *Saints on the Seas: A Maritime History of Mormon Migration 1830-1890* (Salt Lake City: University of Utah Press, 1983), 5.

31. See Klaus J. Hansen, *Quest for Empire: The Political*

Kingdom of God and the Council of Fifty in Mormon History (Lincoln: University of Nebraska Press, 1974), Chapters III and IV.

32. Boyle, Diary, 4 December 1857.

33. Manuscript History, 6 April 1855, Aug.14&17, 1855.

34. Quotation from Manuscript History, 28 November 1855; see also 5 December 1855.

35. Manuscript History, 16 March 1856. Four months previously Rich had declared to the leaders of the San Bernardino Stake that it was his intention to "purify" the community (Manuscript History, 11 November 1855).

36. Charles Coulsen Rich, Letters, 1 August 1855 and 1 June 1856, LDS Archives.

37. Brigham Young Papers, Incoming Correspondence-Amasa Lyman, 8 January 1855.

38. It has been suggested that San Bernardino may have become a place where disaffected Utah Mormons were either sent or voluntarily relocated to. See Edward Leo Lyman, "The Demise of the San Bernardino Mormon Community, 1851-1857," *Southern California Quarterly* 65 (Winter 1983): 326-28. On Charles Crismon, see Brigham Young Papers, Incoming Correspondence-Amasa Lyman, 21 March 1854. Paul D. Bailey, *Sam Brannan and the California Mormons* (Los Angeles: Westernlore Press, 1943) provides adequate background on that group of Saints. On the falling away at San Francisco, see Rena Holdaway Stanley and Charles L. Camp, eds., "A Mormon Mission to California: From the Diary of Parley Parker Pratt," *California Historical Society Quarterly* 14 (1935): 182.

39. Manuscript History, 24 April 1856 and 15 June 1856. It is interesting to note that Sparks's mistress was jailed for her immorality, but he was not.

40. *History of San Bernardino, California, with Illustrations* (San Francisco: W. W. Elliott, 1883), 85.

41. Manuscript History, 14 May 1856.

42. See Manuscript History, 16 March 1856. In the mail later that month, Young advised Rich to stay at San Bernardino through the fall (25 March 1856).

43. Lyman, "The Demise of San Bernardino," 327-28.

44. "Mormon Politics and Policy: Political and Judicial Acts of the Mormon Authorities in San Bernardino, California" (Los Angeles: n. p., 1856), Bancroft Library, University of California-Berkeley. Also see Manuscript History, 8 August 1856, for references to the pamphlet and its authorship. The attacks in the treatise were directed primarily against the Mormon-dominated San Bernardino City Council.

45. Paul H. Peterson, "The Mormon Reformation" (PhD diss., Brigham Young University, 1981), 65; and Gene A. Sessions, *Mormon Thunder: A Documentary History of Jedediah Morgan Grant* (Urbana: University of Illinois Press, 1982), 259-60.

46. Manuscript History, 20 December 1856; 7 February 1857. It was reported that nearly five hundred persons were rebaptized in less than three months.

47. Quoted in S. George Ellsworth, *Dear Ellen: Two Mormon Women and Their Letters* (Salt Lake City: University of Utah Press, 1974), 36-37. Eugene E. Campbell ("Decline and Fall of the Mormons") and Paul H. Peterson ("The Mormon Reformation") have concluded that the movement caused further polarization within the community.

48. Mary Ann Rich, "Autobiography", 30.

49. *Western Standard* (San Francisco), 1 May 1857.

50. Amasa M. Lyman, Journal, 21 May 1857, Huntington Library.

51. See Leonard J. Arrington and Davis Bitton, *The Mormon Experience: A History of the Latter-day Saints* (New York: Alfred A. Knopf, 1979), 164-68; and Norman F. Furniss, *The Mormon Conflict, 1850-59* (New Haven: Yale University Press, 1960), 67.

52. On the entire incident, see Juanita Brooks, *The Mountain Meadows Massacre* (Norman: University of Oklahoma Press, 1970).

53. Manuscript History, 27 November 1857.

54. *Los Angeles Star*, 17 October 1857.

55. Manuscript History, 27 November 1857.

56. Boyle, Diary, 17 November 1857; 4 December 1857.

57. Sonne, *Saints on the Seas*, 168.

IV

Denominations and
Ethnic Groups

9.

Judaism as a Civic Religion in the American West

William Toll

The history of American Jewry has often been interpreted by its leaders as both a declension from European standards of piety and an emulation of Protestant liturgical and social models. In a recent monograph, however, Stephen Cohen has freed Jewish history from such self-serving moralism by emphasizing two points. First, many traditional Jewish social patterns were themselves typical of a more generalized European peasant culture. Second, Jews compared to persons of Anglo-American parentage have had to adjust in a highly compressed way to a modernizing host society.[1] In Europe, Judaism sanctified a form of peasant behavior; its corporate communities integrated body and spirit through sacred practice and denied the importance of a private soul.[2] In America, however, Jews encountered a society which relegated religion to a private and voluntary realm, and which required individual initiative in the public realm. Individual ambitions were expected to supercede the will of a collective community, and the drive for personal autonomy was inculcated in the home. The pursuit of personal autonomy, efficiency and social improvement, which Cohen and others see as the hallmark of the modern psyyche,[3] suggests how the Jewish communal consciousness faced a comprehensive challenge. But the breadth of a concept like modernization can obscure the specific circumstances which in different locales determined the content of a new civic consciousness. Modernization as a theme establishes a context, but it does not explain how the tension between tradition and opportunity shaped the entry of Jews into the new civic arena of the American West.

To appreciate how Judaism sustained new social enclaves one must first examine the evangelical culture of 19th century America. Its emphasis on moral reform especially affected the relationship between Jews and the majority of predominantly Protestant Americans among whom they settled. Two groups in particular who came West for religious reasons--Protestant missionaries and Mormons--helped place Jews in the social landscape. It is also crucial to understand how the second generation of American-born Jews inherited communities from their parents. Although the second generation innovated to an extraordinary degree over the parental models, the precedent of extensive and self-confident participation by first-generation Jews in the larger community while building their own agencies of self-support encouraged their children to do likewise. Indeed, as Judaism developed a rationale for community in the urban West, it cooperated uniquely with Protestant institutions to integrate a leadership strata in a rapidly changing civic order.

I

How did Jews, who were socially ostracized in Europe, and whose religion was villified as archaic, find secure niches in the 19th century American West? The answer lies partly with the individual Jews who came West, and partly with the character of the societies they entered. Jews who ventured West between the Gold Rush and the Civil War were predominantly young men who had quite self-consciously cut themselves loose from the routines of their fathers. Their social habits were flexible and they did not practice an intensive ritual orthodoxy, but like their gentile counterparts they utilized networks of brothers and cousins to marshall security for their venture. Bernard Goldsmith, born in Weddenburg, Bavaria in 1832, came first to New York at age fifteen, where his cousin taught him the watchmaking trade. By 1850 the lure of California drew him. "I never had any definite idea of what I was going to do," he recalled. "I simply wanted to strike out where there was more elbow room." Abandoning the traditional jeweler's trade for merchandising and land speculation, he settled in Portland and brought seven younger brothers at different times to join him.[4]

Just as important as Goldsmith's ambition and his social network, however, was the fact that the unstable society which he entered not only tolerated religious diversity, but saw in religious affiliation support for civic stability. From the 1820s forward wealthy merchants in New York, Boston and Philadelphia, observing the social dislocations of rapid population growth and equally rapid geographic dispersal, had sponsored a series of institutions to identify the Protestant religion with self-control and social discipline. Through temperance societies which spanned the denominations they sought to channel modern drives for mobility by sanctifying orderly labor. A network of itinerant salesmen distributed tracts which spread the evangelical message of thrift and family stability to the unorganized frontier. An Educational Society subsidized the instruction of Congregational and Presbyterian theological students, and the overarching Home Missionary Society supported hundreds of graduate clergymen at subsistence wages in remote areas.[5] In 1860, the Jewish traveller I.J. Benjamin found Presbyterian and Methodist churches in county seats throughout California, Oregon, and Nevada. Churches, temperance societies and fraternal lodges had become pillars of local authority within two to five years of the founding of towns like Grass Valley, Marysville, Placerville and Stockton in California, and in Portland, Oregon.[6]

The evangelical focus of cultural institutions might have portended an uncomfortable welcome for Jews, who were often depicted in the popular fiction of the day as reprobates against the millennial kingdom of Christ.[7] Although Protestant missionaries in eastern cities did attempt to convert Jews,[8] in the West circumstances downplayed the image of the Jew as pariah and encouraged his inclusion among those groups supporting social order.

First, Protestant missionaries in the West in the 1830s were initially preoccupied with the native population, particularly with bringing them into the Christian fold. Occasionally they might ennoble their efforts with the cosmic myth that the Indians were descendants of the Ten Lost Tribes of Israel whose redemption would speed the millennium. But the descent of the Indians into heathenism and savagery, missionaries believed, raised a more practical dilemma: could conversion of the Indians precede their "civilization," that is, their acceptance of white patterns of settlement, family life, and even language?[9] Although Protestant

199

missionaries desired that confessions of faith be accompanied by adoption of the social habits of Middle Western family farms, Western Indians rarely acceded to these admonitions.[10] By the 1840s in the Oregon country, for example, Methodist missionaries had abandoned preaching in remote outposts, and established boarding schools for Indian children among the white agricultural settlements in the Willamette Valley.[11]

Second, since the Protestant missionaries were married, they had to create a stable society for their own families. As professionals they had to expand their focus to accommodate rejection by the Indians and the accumulation of their own social needs.[12] By the time Jews arrived in the area between the Rocky Mountains and the Pacific Coast missionary work had been transformed from conversion of heathen souls to the sustenance of white civilization. The most politicized evangelical causes became temperance and the Sunday closing laws. While most Jews were indifferent to both, a few, especially in California towns, were conspicuous for their support.[13]

Third, in the wake of the Gold Rush, civilization became identified with the commercial activities which would make mining and then agriculture profitable. Meeting the consumer demands of the socially mobile was precisely the function which most Jews performed. From the 1850s through the 1890s, Jewish stores in the towns of Oregon's Willamette Valley, in the Sierra of northern California, in southern California, and along the eastern slope of the Rockies in Colorado were often the most stable commercial institutions. Many miners were able to entrust their nuggets to storekeepers like I.W. Hellman of Los Angeles, who soon began small banks and more regular wholesale supply networks. Relatively high rates of Jewish persistence belied the myth of the "wandering Jew," and Jewish participation with gentiles in fraternal lodges, especially the Masons and Odd Fellows, contradicted the view that Jews were socially secretive and culturally archaic. Indeed, in most western towns there were no more obvious symbols of the Protestant virtues of thrift, sobriety and stability than the brick buildings of the Jewish merchants. The British liberal Norman Angell, spending his young manhood as a ranchhand in southern California in the late 1880s, referred to the Weil brothers--the leading merchants of Bakersfield--as "the type of Jew who represented at that time in the new country the most cultured and civilized element in the community."[14]

Jews, however, also created social networks around their own religious and benevolent institutions. Though integrated as individuals into the mercantile elite, as a group they stood apart for ideological reasons. To better understand how Jewish separateness supported rather than challenged social order, one should compare it to a similarly distinct religious separatism which played an even more dramatic role in the West, that of the Mormons. Mormons arrived in large numbers only slightly before the Jews, beginning in 1846, when Brigham Young led a band of scouts beyond the territorial limits of the United States to stake a claim to the valleys around the Great Salt Lake. Unlike Protestant missionaries, the Mormons did not come to save the souls of natives, though Indians did occupy an honored place in their theology. Instead, Mormons were a sect of theological and social rebels. Their prophet, Joseph Smith, and his followers had outraged established Protestant denominations by claiming that divine revelation continued and could be experienced by any believer.[15] Indeed, he argued that it must provide the justification for any social policy. Ecclesiastically, Mormons not only rejected the hierarchical notion that ministers must be trained in seminaries, but they elevated all males to different ranks of priesthood, depending largely on age and experience. Furthermore, by the 1840s they had become notorious by rejecting conventional views on marriage, the institution which Protestant clergymen saw as the last bastion of social control. By 1856, the Republican Party linked Mormon polygamy with slavery as the dual evils besetting an otherwise perfectable American social order.[16]

Mormons also rejected the market economy upon which American growth was predicated. They espoused instead a communitarian ethos based on storehouses and barter.[17] Despite the reduction of their theocracy to a territory of the federal government just before the Civil War, the Mormons developed new technologies of irrigation and by the 1860s had created rural settlements in eastern Arizona, the San Bernardino area of southern California, and the river valleys of southern Idaho. Their control of trade routes to the Pacific coast challenged not only the expansion of the capitalist market but the moral authority of Protestant clergymen and the sexual economy of the middle class family.[18] The presence of such Mormon subversion throughout the West made the Jews, despite their separatism, seem agents in support of Protestant moral authority.

II

While Mormons separated to maintain pre-capitalist values, Jews maintained separation as a bridge between their corporate sense of social responsibility and their individual commitment to entrepreneurship. Most Jews who came West had travelled from the margins rather than the center of German Jewry. In the wake of the Napoleonic era, most German cities had accepted the new emphasis on free trading, and had admitted new categories of people, including Jews.[19] By the mid-19th century, Jews had become the most urbanized of all German groups, and their birth rate, often used as an indicator of shifts to more modern social attitudes, was lower than that of Protestants and Catholics.[20] Most Jews in the American West, however, had come from the small towns of Bavaria, Hesse and Alsace, or from the Posen area of Poland.[21] Despite their drive for achievement, they tried to reestablish traditional practices in the most intimate areas of their lives. In their villages of origin they had been identified as an ethnic minority and had been legally responsible for their own welfare, which had become encrusted with religious sanction. The German authorities, by contrast, were identified with a Christian social order, which Jews did well to avoid.[22]

In the American West Jews understood that the separation of church and state meant that all persons could apply for the meager public aid available. But they invariably assumed responsibility for their own welfare. They usually waited to marry until they were established as sedentary merchants, and often they returned to Germany for a bride.[23] Quite at variance with their counterparts in urban Germany, however, they often selected women much younger than themselves and proceeded to rear large families.[24] Furthermore, the distinction between the realms of male and female, which marked traditional European towns, was retained, as each sex cared for the needs of the respective gender groups, as well as for the members of their individual families.[25] In Jewish settlements in San Francisco, Denver, Los Angeles, and Portland men and women organized separate benevolent societies.

Because San Francisco was the port of entry and supply for the Pacific coast, and its Jewish population through 1900 was by far the largest,[26] social innovations observed there in the 1850s were often repeated elsewhere ten or twenty years later. This is not to suggest that communities had a "natural history," but that if local economic conditions allowed, settled residents would be able to meet the accruing demands of their life cycle by utilizing fragments of their cultural memories. Because of its large size, San Francisco also supported a range of institutions and provided intellectual and economic leadership not matched elsewhere.

Within the context of this metropole-hinterland relationship, the general pattern of Jewish self-sufficiency proceeded. Because the young immigrants were neither scholars nor yet heads of families, their sense of religious obligation extended primarily to ritual burial and observance of the holiest days of the Jewish year. The traveller I.J. Benjamin noted in 1860 and 1861 that invariably the first religious institution founded was the cemetery society, and that the only holidays observed were the Jewish New Year and the Day of Atonement, which followed eight days later.[27] The second institution usually founded in conjunction with the cemetery association was a Hebrew Benevolent Society, which would provide health and death benefits for members, and companionship during illnesses. Sacramento and San Francisco had such Associations by 1850, and their membership grew in proportion to the local population. By 1857 similar societies existed in small towns like Marysville, Placerville and Nevada City. Portland and Denver did not develop such societies until the 1870s, perhaps because the latter, despite its closer proximity to the east, was settled later, while Portland was a more remote outpost, many of whose Jewish young men were migrating back and forth to San Francisco.[28]

While the benevolent societies fulfilled traditional male welfare needs, they also reflected many departures. Leadership, for example, was exercised within a voluntary association, not by an incorporated body of elders. Jewish newcomers were not automatically enrolled, but were subjected to an election procedure which reflected the influence of secular fraternal orders where Jewish men were mingling with gentile peers. The Folsom, California, Hebrew Benevolent Society, for example, which I.J. Benjamin helped to organize in 1860, required that new applicants be sponsored by two members and that they undergo a two-step black ball evaluation. Officers were subject to annual election, and the admittance fee, dues, and sick and death benefits were uniform, rather than being determined idiosyncratically by a patriarchal elite.[29]

Finally, by 1872 in Portland, and probably earlier in San Francisco, the benevolent society raised small amounts of venture capital for its members by extending interest-free loans for short periods to men starting new businesses or expanding older ones. Throughout the country local banks contemplating loans often depended on the Dun & Company credit rating service, which hired young lawyers in each city to provide confidential information about the trustworthiness of local merchants. Frequently entries on Jews would cast aspersions on the integrity of individuals simply by citing their religious affiliation. As Peter Decker reports for San Francisco, "One among many examples which might be cited is a Dun & Co. report on two Germans who owned rather substantial assets. 'They are Hebrew. May be good [for credit] if *well watched*; they are tricky.'"[30] While Jews were nevertheless able to borrow from local banks, the Hebrew Benevolent societies came to fulfill many emergency credit needs.

Usually the third institution created in western Jewish enclaves was the synagogue, and here at the ideological core of the community the tension between tradition and modernization was most acute. The resolution that occurred suggests how Jews wished to be integrated, but on a communal basis, into the civic order. It is difficult to know to what extent the synagogues replicated tradition, because we know so little about the institutions of southern Germany and Posen. But as a social institution, synagogues in the West reflected the meager religious education of the men. Sabbath services were generally not well attended, and except for the elegant Temple Emanu-el in San Francisco, most buildings were modest. Congregations were often happy to save the expense of a rabbinical salary by having one of their own lead the Sabbath ritual. Despite the limited number of ordained rabbis, they were hired and fired with great rapidity.[31] The only exception seems to have been Elkan Cohn, who brought Reform to Emanu-El from 1860 through his death in 1889.[32] Despite their limited training, synagogue members usually wished to follow the patterns of their province of origin.[33] Conflicts over liturgy often led those from southern Germany and Alsace to separate from the "Poseners," and most cities soon found themselves with two or more synagogues, burial grounds, and even benevolent societies. But Jews from southern Germany especially might be influenced by new rabbis or enthusiastic laymen to shift their liturgy to less traditional formats. The adoption of a shorter or more anglicized ritual, however, did not necessarily mean that the synagogue was affiliated with a national reform organization, and practices within nominally Reform congregations varied considerably.[34]

As an American institution, the synagogue's greatest departure was in educating the young.[35] In Europe Jewish boys had been educated at separate institutions, while the synagogues had housed study centers for Talmud and Torah for men. In America rabbis and lay teachers alike abandoned those traditions in part because of the limited public educational opportunities in western towns, and in part because the teachers themselves were not traditional religious instructors. Schools in Portland, San Francisco, Denver and Los Angeles reflected the influence of public education by abandoning the rote learning of the *heder* and emphasizing instruction in modern languages like French and German, as well as biblical Hebrew. Most rabbis coming West were steeped in secular learning and saw education in Jewish matters as a means of invoking ethnic consciousness in young people who would be participating as equals in a pluralistic society.[36] Perhaps most important, boys and girls were educated together, thus providing Jewish women for the first time with a formal education and preparing them for social equality with Jewish men and intellectual parity with gentile women.

The fourth institution to integrate Jewish men into the social order was a new fraternal lodge, the B'nai B'rith. Initially, it seemed to share some of the functions of the benevolent society, and in Portland and Denver it even preceded the latter. It, too, provided mutual benefit insurance to care for sick members and it occasionally used its national network--which the benevolent societies lacked--to find employment for members in other cities.[37] But its unique function must be understood in conjunction with the growth of fraternal orders, especially the Masons, in western Europe and America. The Masons seem to have been organized originally in early 18th century Britain by men on the margins of urban corporate society who needed personal security and who cultivated subversively liberal ideals. Most were journeymen or entrepreneurs who despised the guilds and trade monopolies and who professed a deist philosophy in opposition to denominational orthodoxy. Individual Jews, who were also seeking freedom from communal control, were admitted to Masonic lodges in Britain and Holland by the 1740s. Somewhat later in the century, however, when Jews sought admission in larger numbers, they were often refused. By 1800 there were at least six separate Jewish Masonic lodges in London. Likewise, in German cities, where anti-Semitism was stronger, Jews formed their own Masonic lodges, and like American blacks they sought charters from Grand Lodges in London or Paris.[38]

Why young Jewish clerks in New York city in the early 1840s should have wanted their own fraternal order is not clear, since American Masonic lodges did admit Jews. Probably as in London, the large number of young Jews seeking admission precluded their entry into any single lodge, and Masonry by the "Age of Jackson" had already become a preserve for local elites.[39] The founding of an ethnically exclusive lodge also reflected the desire for mutual support among the young men flooding into

New York from German towns. Whatever the specific reason, the B'nai B'rith lodges spread very quickly to the edge of Jewish settlement, so that San Francisco had two and Sacramento one by 1860, Portland had one by 1866, and Denver and Los Angeles one each by 1871.[40]

As in New York, the lodges were founded primarily by men in their late 20s and early 30s, many of whom were just marrying and who needed insurance for themselves and their families. But most of all the lodges provided a social gathering for men just settling down after years as peddlers in rural outposts. Where the benevolent societies rarely met and provided only limited social outlets, the weekly or monthly lodge meetings allowed men to discuss public issues or just to unwind. In addition, where the Masons might contribute to the respectability of individual Jews, the B'nai B'rith provided a collective civic voice. Since Jews in the West upheld the civic order by joining volunteer fire companies and the militia and were consistently elected to city councils and state legislatures, anti-Semitism lacked respectability. But where it did appear in newspapers or the vaudeville stage, the lodge protested and projected a communal image that demanded the enforcement of constitutional guarantees.[41] By the late 1870s when lodge members had become more affluent, the national organization, at the instigation of several locals, assumed greater fiscal responsibility for communal welfare. By 1880, a series of regional orphanages had been established, including one in San Francisco, and by 1900 the Denver lodge had convinced the Order to support a hospital for the tubercular patients flocking to that city.[42]

Despite its innovative welfare functions, the B'nai B'rith prior to the 1890s reinforced the sexual division of services within Jewry and contributed to the domination of the civic realm by men. When Jewish women arrived in the West they were almost always young wives of small merchants or of tailors or expressmen with entrepreneurial aspirations. Almost invariably they became immersed in child-rearing. Cut off from their mothers and sisters, they had to look beyond the family for support. By the late 1850s in San Francisco and by the early

1870s in other cities, Ladies Hebrew Benevolent Societies appeared.[43] What these organizations contributed to modernization is not clear because we know so little about traditional social welfare patterns in central Europe. Jacob Marcus, for example, found that separate women's organizations arose rather late and had quite limited functions.[44] Some which supported religious ritual, like the bath house which Orthodox women were supposed to use after their monthly menstruation, seem never to have been instituted in the West by German women.[45] By contrast, the Ladies Benevolent societies assumed comprehensive responsibility for the welfare needs of women and children. Since infant mortality was the most frequent form of death until the 1890s when the immigrant generation reached old age, women assumed responsibility for the majority of funerals. They also comforted the bereaved, cared for the children of sick women, and nursed one another through innumerable pregnancies and illnesses. Because very few women of German Jewish origins worked outside the home, widows seem rarely to have opened businesses. Instead, the Ladies Benevolent societies occasionally supported widows for brief periods or helped them rejoin relatives.[46]

Like the men's benevolent societies, when the women accumulated savings they began to contribute to Jewish charities beyond the local communities. But like the men of their generation, the women never widened their philanthropy to include non-Jews or to accept the professionalization of social service. And the fact that the Ladies Benevolent Societies were virtually the only organizations which immigrant women created suggests how isolated their sphere remained.

III

With the maturity of the children of the immigrants in the 1890s, women's sphere changed dramatically until it became the source of civic innovation within the Jewish community. Indeed, to understand the new social concerns of the community one must begin with the roles of women, which were given focus by a new institution initiated nationally in the 1890s, the Council of Jewish Women. Regretably we know very little about the national organization and the debates which shaped it. It was founded in Chicago in 1893 by a group of women who allegedly resented their limited role in preparing the Jewish exhibit at the Chicago World's Fair.[47] Because no history of the organization has appeared and it has been given short shrift in communal histories, I can at best suggest its pivotal role from my own research in Portland and on inferences drawn from brief accounts of Council work elsewhere.[48]

Who were the women of the Council, and how did they alter the relationship between the Jewish community and the general public? In Portland in the late 1890s the initial Council officers were older women, some of whom had held office in the Ladies Benevolent Society. But the majority of the members were in their late 20s or early 30s, and within five years of the founding the younger women had assumed control and shifted its focus. Although they had generally been raised in large households, most Council members did not reproduce such a home. Those who married usually did so at a higher age than had their mothers, and most important they had far fewer children. Many Council members were unmarried, and a few had begun careers as teachers, librarians and social workers.[49] In short they were the American-born and educated sisters and wives of successful merchants who had the time, education and interest to examine new issues. Although some may have belonged to predominantly gentile women's clubs, they retained an ethnic sense of loyalty.

Local Councils were ostensibly founded to spread knowledge of Jewish liturgy to a generation whose religious education had been meager. In Portland, however, bible study, usually under the direction of men, was discontinued within a few months and the rabbi was rarely asked to attend a Council meeting. Members were instead attracted to the conditions of the Jewish poor, who were congregating in a new immigrant district. The intensive over-crowding and sweatshops which characterized New York's Lower East Side were not duplicated in the West. But because East European Jews usually arrived in family groups, the problems of childhood disease and unsteady incomes, and the adjustment of children to the schools and streets arose immediately.[50]

Having taken an interest in the immigrants, the women of the Council wished to apply to their philanthropy new professional standards. In Portland the Council began with cooking and sewing classes in rented quarters, but under the leadership of young Rabbi Stephen Wise and his wife Louise, who had done social work in New York, they soon constructed the city's only settlement house.[51] The neighborhood setting, the timing of the settlement's founding and its activities parallel the founding of a Jewish settlement house in the Colfax Avenue area of Denver.[52] Though the Neighborhood House lacked resident social workers as at Hull House or the Chicago Commons, it became even more so the instrument of the ethnic community. By the 1920s it sponsored not only recreation, well-baby and dental clinics, but a modern Hebrew school which almost 200 local youngsters attended after public school sessions four afternoons each week. Council officers also followed the needs of the immigrant children into the courts, public school, and the city council.[53] Indeed, the Council as the leading organization of second-generation Jewish women differed from institutions created by their male cohorts because, in conjunction with gentile women's organizations, it expanded both the ethnic group's and the city's social agenda.

As second generation Jewish men emerged as merchant leaders of the community, they settled into the comfortable niches pioneered by their fathers. In the city at large lawyers like Abe Ruef in San Francisco and Joseph Simon in Portland controlled political machines, but they were supported within the ethnic community by cliques centered in the lodges.[54] Within the Jewish enclave the most characteristic new institutions were greatly expanded synagogues, city clubs and B'nai B'rith lodges, all of which served new cultural tastes. The second generation, like the first, saw religion as one of several attributes of ethnic identity. But where the fathers had seen it as a ritual sanctifying transitions in the life cycle, the sons saw it as a social grace. Since members of the second generation were products of large families, they swelled synagogue membership starting in the 1880s, and the pressures for larger facilities led to the erection of more elaborate buildings along major thoroughfares close to their homes in the new streetcar suburbs.[55]   Their limited religious training may have predisposed them to embrace Reform practices, while their broad contacts since childhood with gentile business families led them to seek spiritual leaders who could represent them with dignity in contact with gentile ministers. The new graduates of Hebrew Union College like William S. Friedman (Denver), Sigmund Hecht (Los Angeles), and Jacob Voorsanger (San Francisco), or with American university education like Stephen S. Wise (Portland) were attractive preachers and were retained for long periods.[56] They took great pride in sharing pulpits with elite Protestant ministers and in instituting joint worship services on quasi-religious holidays like Thanksgiving. The status of their ethnic group was reinforced when Friedman and Wise were apponted shortly after their arrival by the respective governors to state Assocociated Charities boards.

The consolidation of the Temple as an elite cultural institution signified the end of the frontier era in the urban West, however remote from civilization the Pacific slope cities might seem to the Jews of Philadelphia and New York. By eliminating esoteric ritual and by identifying Judaism with a mission to preach ethical monotheism, rabbis like Voorsanger virtually required that Jews join with Protestants to reinforce social order.   Indeed, they reiterated the dicta on civil religion enunciated initially by Rousseau in *The Social Contract*, "that it unites the divine cult with love of the laws, and making country the object of the citizens' adoration, teaches them that service done to the State is service done to its tutelary gods."[57] Liberal Judaism, like its Protestant counterpart, was declared to rest on faith in the progressively revealed word of a rational God rather than on immutable ritual. The liturgy was shaped to the cosmopolitan atmosphere of America by ending the prohibition against musical instruments and by allowing non-Jews to serve as members of a choir. Worship services could be held on Sundays and non-Jews were encouraged to attend. Because Reform was most concerned with retaining the allegiance of a secularized youth, it developed a new ceremony called "confirmation" for both boys and girls of ages 15 or 16. Unlike the *bar mitzvah* of boys at age 13, the conformant was prepared through instruction in ethical precepts and history rather than through rote learning of liturgy and bible, and was inducted into the community through a co-educational graduation ceremony.[58]

To further celebrate their elite status, Jewish merchants primarily of the second generation erected elegant city clubs in central business districts between the mid-1880s and 1900. Why they did not join the new city clubs begun by gentile merchants as they continued to join the Masons and Odd Fellows, is not clear. Some scholars have noted that the new Concordia and Standard Clubs begun by Jews often had some gentile members and usually showed a special interest in German culture. In a city like Milwaukee where German cultural influences predominated, or in Atlanta where German Jews were the largest immigrant contingent, the celebration of cultural remnants may have been a major innovation.[59] But on the Pacific Coast members of Concordia showed little more than the usual interest in German symphonic music which marked Victorian culture everywhere, and as in no other part of the country their elite status was recognized. But just as the Jews condemned intermarriage and could expel synagogue members who married a non-Jew, so the gentile elite drew the line in their most intimate social intercourse. In San Francisco, although Jews were included in the first *Elite Directory* (1879) far out of proportion to their numbers in the local population, they were confined to a separate list. In Portland they were integrated into the general list in the first *Blue Book* (1891), but they were not admitted to elite gentile clubs.[60]

The outlook of the young Jewish mercantile elite was also expressed in the evolution of the B'nai B'rith lodges, which gradually eliminated mutual benefit services and turned their attention to modern forms of social intercourse. Lodge meetings far more often than previously included entertainment, which was often provided by the wives and fiancees of members, who sang or played musical instruments.[61] This voluntary introduction of women into what had been a male domain suggests how Jewish men and women were coming to share a common cultural sensitivity and to rely on one another for companionship far more than their parents had done. Indeed, as a consequence of shared social experience, the lodges were gradually drawn into the social work of the women. In addition to their growing support for orphanages and hospitals the local lodges might purchase equipment for a vocational school in the immigrant district or contribute funds for a new settlement house.

A handful of Jewish men in Portland, San Francisco or Denver would support progressive legislation to regulate utilities, limit child labor or bring professional expertise to city government. But the majority preferred membership on the board of trade or the expanded chamber of commerce to maintain mercantile direction of civic affairs.[62] They had achieved autonomy in a bourgeois niche to which they gave elegant veneer by their conspicuous public philanthropy and occasional cooperation with both religious and lay spokesmen for elite Protestant churches. As a civic religion Judaism had freed its practitioners from vestigial ritual to exercise the same rational choices in the private realm as they were required to do in public. It had helped internalize a patrician civic consensus which had in turn revolutionized Jewish status as in no other corner of the world.

Notes

1. Stephen M. Cohen, *American Modernity and Jewish Identity* (New York: Tavistock Publications, 1983), 7-8.

2. Marshall Sklare, *America's Jews* (New York: Random House, 1971), 111.

3. Cohen, *American Modernity*, 16, where individual choice is also related directly to the expansion of the capitalist market economy. See also, Martin Cohen, "Structuring Amerian Jewish History," *American Jewish Historical Quarterly*, 57 (December 1967): 139-140; and Richard D. Brown, *Modernization: the Transformation of American Life, 1600-1860* (New York: Hill and Wang, 1976), 15, 56, 150.

4. Bernard Goldsmith (interview), November 29. 1889, H.H. Bancroft Collection, Bancroft Library, University of California, Berkeley; Don Doyle, *The Social Order of a Frontier Community: Jacksonville, Illinois, 1825-1870* (Urbana: University of Illinois Press, 1978), 116-17; William Bowen, *The Willamette Valley: Migration and Settlement on the Oregon Frontier* (Seattle: University of Washington Press, 1978), 26, 27, 43; William Toll, *The Making of an Ethnic Middle Class: Portland Jewry over Four Generations* (Albany: State University of New York Press, 1982), 10-11; Albert Vorspan and Lloyd Gartner, *History of the Jews of Los Angeles* (S.Marino:Huntington Library, 1970),5, 37.

5. Brown, *Modernization*, 95, 101, 103; Clifford P. Griffin, *Their Brother's Keeper: Moral Stewardship in the United States, 1800-1860* (New Brunswick, N.J.: Rutgers University Press, 1960), 23-43, 202-04. As Robert Bellah has noted, "The God of [America's] civil religion is not only rather 'unitarian,' he is also on the austere side, much more related to order, law, and right than to salvation and love." See Bellah, "Civil Religion in America," in Joseph E. Faulkner, ed., *Religion's Influence in Contemporary Society* (Columbus, Ohio: Charles E. Merill Publishing Co., 1972), 356.

6. I.J. Benjamin, *Three Years in America, 1859-1862* (Philadelphia: Jewish Publication Society, 1956), vol. I, 236-37, vol. II, 12, 42, 64.

7. Michael N. Dobkowski, *The Tarnished Dream: The Basis of American Anti-Semitism* (Westport, Conn.: Greenwood Press, 1979), 22-26.

8. Griffin, *Their Brother's Keeper*, 211; Robert T. Handy, *A Christian America: Protestant Hopes and Historical Realities* (New York: Oxford University Press, 1971), 59.

9. Robert J. Loewenberg, *Equality on the Oregon Frontier: Jason Lee and the Methodist Mission, 1834-43* (Seattle: University of Washington Press, 1976), 82-83.

10. Combining model farms with Christian preaching seems to have begun among the Iroquois in upstate New York in the 1790s, when Quakers established a small demonstration project. See Anthony F.C. Wallace, *The Death and Rebirth of the Seneca* (New York: Alfred Knopf, 1970), 272-77.

11. Loewenberg, *Equality on the Oregon Frontier*, 99-100.

12. Ibid., 112-114; Handy, *Protestant Hopes*, 110.

13. Robert E. Levinson, *The Jews in the California Gold Rush* (Berkeley: KTAV Publishing House, Inc., 1978), 72-73.

14. Ibid., 29, 37, 47, 50, 57; Allen D. Breck, *The Centennial History of the Jews of Colorado, 1859-1959* (Denver: Hirschfeld Press, 1960), 16, 50, 127; Vorspan and Gartner, *Jews of Los Angeles*, 37-38; [Norman Angell], *After All, the Autobiography of Norman Angell* (London: Hamish Hamilton, 1951),,51.

15. Leonard J. Arrington and Davis Bitton, *The Mormon Experience: A History of the Latter-Day Saints* (New York: Alfred Knopf, 1979), 47, 53, 96-97.

16. Ibid., 164, 184, 199, 205; Griffin, *Their Brother's Keeper*, 206-07.

17. Arrington, *Mormon Experience*, 39, 53; Mark P. Leone, *Roots of Modern Mormonism* (Cambridge, Mass.: Harvard University Press, 1979), 1, 13-14.

18. Leone, *Roots of Modern Mormonism, 52, 86, 108, 155-59. See also Benjamin, *Three Years*, II, 224-26.

19. Jacob Katz, *Out of the Ghetto: the Social Background of Jewish Emancipation, 1770-1870* (Cambridge, Mass.: Harvard University Press, 1973), 75-76.

20. John E. Knodel, *The Decline of Fertility in Germany, 1871-1939* (Princeton: Princeton Univ. Press, 1974), 136-38.

21. Rudolph Glanz, "The 'Bayer' and the 'Polack' in America," *Jewish Social Studies,* 10 (January 1955): 29-33; Leon Jick, *The Americanization of the Synagogue, 1820-1870* (Hanover: University Presses of New England, 1976), 29-31; Vorspan and Gartner, *Jews of Los Angeles,* 6; Breck, *Jews of Colorado,* 8; Mitchell B. Gelfand, "Jewish Economic and Residential Mobility in Early Los Angeles," *Western States Jewish Historical Quarterly,* 11 (July 1979): 336-37; Toll, *Ethnic Middle Class,* 9, 11.

22. Katz, *Out of the Ghetto,* 203.

23. Toll, *Making of Ethnic Middle Class,* 16.

24. Ibid., 47 (Table 10), 54 (Table 14). Edward Shorter, *The Making of the Modern Family* (New York: Basic Books, 1975), 24-25, 38, notes that in old towns in 18th century England and early 19th century Bavaria, merchant families and households were larger than those of laborers.

25. Shorter, *Modern Family,* 5.

26. Benjamin, *Three Years,* I, 232, estimated that about 5,000 Jews lived in San Francisco in 1860, when Sacramento had about 500, Portland and Los Angeles about 150. Denver, which had just been settled, had far fewer.

27. Ibid., II, 25, 28, 36, 47; Levinson, *Jews in Gold Rush,* 100; Toll, *Ethnic Middle Class,* 20. Accounts of Passover observances are sporadic, and because it was a holiday celebrated within the family, many young men may not have participated.

28. Benjamin, *Three Years,* I, 210, 227; II, 10, 25, 38, 47, 49; Breck, *Jews of Colorado,* 27; Toll, *Ethnic Middle Class,* 18-19; Vorspan and Gartner, *Jews of Los Angeles,* 19.

29. Benjamin, *Three Years,* II, 49-53.

30. Peter Decker, "Jewish Merchants in San Francisco: Social

Mobility on the Urban Frontier," in *The Jews of the West: The Metropolitan Years*, ed. by Moses Rischin (Berkeley: American Jewish Historical Soc., 1979), 15; Toll, *Ethnic Middle Class*, 17.

31. Breck, *Jews of Colorado*, 61; Toll, *Ethnic Middle Class*, 24.

32. Fred Rosenbaum, *Architects of Reform: Congregational and Communal Leadership, Emanu-el of San Francisco, 1849-1980* (Berkeley: Judah Magnes Memorial Museum, 1980), 23.

33. Jick, *Americanization of Synagogue,* 101-02; Benjamin, *Three Years*, I, 199, 210, 227; Toll, *Ethnic Middle Class*, 25.

34. Toll, *Ethnic Middle Class*, 24; Rosenbaum, *Architects of Reform*, 9, 13; Breck, *Jews in Colorado*, 32.

35. Jick, *Americanization of Synagogue*, 62.

36. Rosenbaum, *Architects of Reform*, 26; Benjamin, *Three Years*, I, 229-31; Toll, *Ethnic Middle Class*, 20.

37. Toll, *Ethnic Middle Class*, 25-26.

38. Jacob Katz, *Jews and Freemasons in Europe, 1723-1939* (Cambridge, Mass.: Harvard University Press, 1970), 11-18, 69, 82, 90. On discrimination against Jews in English Masonry, see Todd Endelman, *The Jews of Georgian England, 1714-1830* (Philadelphia: Jewish Publication Society, 1979), 270-71.

39. Lee Benson, *The Concept of Jacksonian Democracy: New York as a Test Case* (Princeton: Princeton University Press, 1961), 24-28; Doyle, *Frontier Community*, 178-84, 186-87.

40. Toll, *Ethnic Middle Class*, 25-27; Benjamin, *Three Years*, I, 227-28; Breck, *Jews of Colorado*, 29.

41. Breck, *Jews of Colorado*, 25, 35. For Jewish participation in fire companies see Levinson, *Jews in California*

Gold Rush, 66, "Bernard Goldsmith," (interview). Peter Decker, *Fortunes and Failures: White Collar Mobility in Nineteenth Century San Francisco* (Cambridge, Mass.: Harvard University Press, 1978), 144, notes that in San Francisco, a more dense social atmosphere, Jews did not gain admittance to fire and militia companies.

42. Breck, *Jews of Colorado*, 98-101; Rosenbaum, *Architects of Reform*, 38; Steven Hertzberg, *Strangers Within the Gate City: The Jews of Atlanta 1845-1915* (Philadelphia: Jewish Publication Society, 1978), 120.

43. Benjamin, *Three Years*, I, 229.

44. Jacob Rader Marcus, *Communal Sick Care in the German Ghetto* (Cincinnati: Hebrew Union College Press, 1978 ed.), 139-45.

45. East European Jewish women did organize *mikvot*. See Breck, *Jews of Colorado*, 81; Toll, *Ethnic Middle Class*, 71.

46. Toll, *Ethnic Middle Class*, 49-52.

47. Charlotte Baum, Paula Hyman, Sonya Michel, *The Jewish Woman in America* (New York: New American Library, Inc., 1975), 48.

48. Rabbi Jacob Voorsanger of San Francisco discouraged the Council as a rival to his temple sisterhood, and there it lagged behind local chapters in Portland. See Rosenbaum, *Architects of Reform*, 51.

49. Toll, *Ethnic Middle Class*, 55-58; Baum, *Jewish Woman*, 48-51.

50. Toll, *Ethnic Middle Class*, 56.

51. Ibid., 58-62; Melvin Urofsky, *A Voice that Spoke for Justice: the Life and Times of Stephen S. Wise* (Albany: State

University of New York Press, 1982), 27, 36.

52. Breck, *Jews of Colorado*, 108-09.

53. Toll, *Ethnic Middle Class*, 62.

54. Rosenbaum, *Architects of Reform*, 61-62.

55. Decker, *Fortunes and Failures*, 205; Toll, *Ethnic Middle Class*, 27, 29. A similar trend in Protestant churches is explained in Sydney Ahlstrom, *A Religious History of the American People* (New Haven: Yale University Press, 1972), 737.

56. Breck, *Jews of Colorado*, 84-86; Toll, *Ethnic Middle Class*, 97-98; Rosenbaum, *Architects of Reform*, 45-50; Vorspan and Gartner, *Jews of Los Angeles*, 102, 156-58.

57. Rosenbaum, *Architects of Reform*, 45-48, emphasizes Voorsanger's disgust with ritual. See Jean Jacques Rousseau, *The Social Contract and Discourses*, translated by G.D.H. Cole (Everyman's Library, Dutton: New York, 1979 reprint), 272.

58. Breck, *Jews of Colorado,* 85; Jick, *Americanization of Synagogue*, 191-93. On the influence of liberalism on Protestant social consciousness see Ahlstrom, *Religious History of American People*, 779-80, 845. On the missionary role of liberal Protestantism in the late 19th century see Henry May, *Protestant Churches and Industrial America* (New York: Harper & Brothers, 1948), 42.

59. Hertzberg, *Strangers Within Gate City,* 50; Louis J. Swichkow and Lloyd Gartner, *The History of the Jews of Milwaukee* (Philadelphia: Jewish Publication Society, 1963), 117.

60. Decker, "Jewish Merchants," 21-22; Toll, *Ethnic Middle Class*, 33-34.

61. Toll, *Ethnic Middle Class*, 35.

62. Vorspan and Gartner, *Jews of Los Angeles*, 80; Toll, *Making of Ethnic Middle Class,* 94-96; David G. Dalin, "Jewish and Non-Partisan Republicanism in San Francisco, 1911-1963," in Rischin, ed., *Jews of the West,* 108-114.

10.
The "Non-Evangelical Alliance": Freemasonry In Gilded-Age San Francisco

Tony Fels

Evangelical Protestantism occupies an established place of prominence in the history of the American West. Successive outbursts of revivalism, which enlivened rural areas and cities alike during the nineteenth century, and the great interdenominational associations to promote Bible-reading, Sabbath-keeping and temperance which followed in their wake did much to bring social order and civilization to the vast regions of new settlement. Symbolically capping this united spiritual effort during the post-Civil War decades stood the Evangelical Alliance, a national body of Protestant leaders in roughly forty cities formed to coordinate the multi-faceted evangelical crusade.[1]

Emotional, "experiential" religion, however, always had its Protestant opponents. Nor were these confined to the small though influential enclaves of haughty Boston Unitarians and bookish Princeton Presbyterians. Indeed, it is likely that non-evangelical religion enjoyed a national appeal which nearly equalled that of revivalism among Protestants generally and surpassed it among Protestant men in particular. One of the chief reasons why popular non-evangelicalism has escaped the notice it deserves is the fact that one must look outside the established denominations in order to find some of its most significant expressions. In terms of sheer numbers, the enormously popular fraternal organizations of the nineteenth century, foremost among which were the Freemasons and the Odd Fellows, probably supplied more strength to the non-evangelical position than did the male followings of all the non-revivalistic Protestant denominations combined.[2] An examination of the Masonic fraternity in Gilded-Age San Francisco (1870-1900) provides a case study in the type of ritualistic, theistic rationalism which the fraternal experience had to offer.[3]

I

The brotherhood of Freemasons fulfilled a diverse set of needs for its adherents--the exercise of mutual aid, the provision of fellowship and sociability, entrance into the social and economic life of a community on a respectable basis--but none of these functions existed apart from religious aims and practices. Recent studies of Masonry have helped to bring the religious character of the organization into sharper focus.[4] Still, there is a tendency to regard the institution as only "quasi-religious," employing the trappings of faith to enhance predominantly secular purposes. Although it may never be possible to learn what proportion of men derived primarily religious as opposed to social or economic satisfactions from their experience in the order, the same limitation besets the historian's knowledge of the compelling motivations behind church membership generally. Especially during the late nineteenth century, when the religious character of Masonry was so much in evidence, the fraternity deserves to be treated on an equal footing with the established denominations as an additional and important variant within the tradition of Judeo-Christianity.[5]

To begin with, the fraternity required a belief in God and in the immortality of the soul as a precondition for membership.[6] In no sense was this mere formality. Grand Masters and Grand Orators made frequent reference to the Divine inspiration which was assumed to underlie both the genesis and continued existence of the fraternity. Thomas Guard, addressing the Grand Lodge in 1878, was only more expressive than most grand officers when he asked rhetorically, "Who knows when it [Freemasonry] lay in the hollow of God's hand, even as a dew-drop within a rose-bud, until He carved for it a dwelling-place in earth's deep bosom, and there set it to be the everlasting mirror of His own infinitude?"[7] Throughout the period, the California fraternity leveled criticism at the French Freemasons, who in 1876 had removed all references to a Supreme Being from their Constitution and made the display of the Bible optional in the lodgeroom.[8] When the only two cases of freethought to be reported within its own ranks arose, the California Grand Lodge acted quickly and forcefully against the offenders. In one case, in which the candidate had attested only to a belief in a vague supreme power, the Grand Master bluntly directed that the degree fees be returned, adding:

> Masonry has no use for men who will 'hesitate' and quibble about *God*, or belief in His *Omnipotence, Omniscience,* and *Omnipresence....* The first, the essential and the indispensable qualification of a candidate for initiation is that he must have *faith in God*. Not a nameless something, but the true GOD of ABRAHAM, ISAAC, and JACOB; the same by whose Divine command MOSES wrought the deliverance of the children of Israel; and the same Who gladdened the heart of DAVID by the promise of a house that should be dedicated to His Holy Name, and finally verified that promise in the person of SOLOMON.... [9]

No less central to Masonry was the doctrine of immortality. Fervent hope for life after death animated the most important of the fraternity's initiatory themes--the legend of Hiram Abif, King Solomon's Master Architect. The heroic Israelite project of constructing the Temple at Jerusalem, related in the Biblical books of Kings and Chronicles, provided the setting for this symbolic story. According to Masonic legend, three apprentice workmen surprised the Master Builder one day in the Temple, slaying him while attempting to extort knowledge and privileges which were not rightfully theirs. King Solomon ordered a group of craftsmen to capture the traitors and recover the body of the Architect, but though the workmen were successful in the first task, they discovered the corpse to be too decomposed to make any movement of it possible. Moreover, the full weight of the tragedy now dawned as they learned that certain crucial secrets had perished irrevocably along with the murdered leader. But then an extraordinary event touched with mystery occurred. By means of a special grip, the King was able to raise Hiram from his make-shift grave, marked by his killers with an (evergreen) acacia plant, in order to prepare him for a proper burial. Simultaneously, the assembled workmen acquired knowledge (the Master Mason's Word) which would henceforth substitute, though imperfectly, for that which had been squandered.[10]

Fraternal members attached several layers of meaning to this story, which was considerably more elaborate than my short summary imples. Of course, it is not easy to know what lessons any given individual drew from a particular set of symbols, but on one aspect of the Hiram story Masonic interpretation spoke quite clearly: the disinterment of the Master Architect was intended to signify the persistence of life after death--immortality of the soul for most Masons, bodily resurrection as well for some.[11] Here, too, it would be a mistake to gloss over the strength of the religious impulse expressed. "Above all," proclaimed Thomas H. B. Anderson, Grand Orator in 1882, "[Masons] believe in the personal immortality of the soul after death--not the unsubstantial 'immortalities' of race, or thought, or fame.... The evergreen that marked the last resting place of one illustrious in Masonry [Hiram Abif] tells its own story. You and I shall live--live long after these hills shall have passed away; long after these star-fires shall have expired on heaven's high archway."[12]

Not surprisingly, the Hiram story served as the basis for the funeral service which the brotherhood held for its deceased members. These rites entailed an opening section held at the lodgeroom, a procession to accompany the carriage bearing the coffin to the gravesite, a burial service, and a procession returning to the lodgeroom, where the ceremony ended. At many key points, the funeral service harkened back to the story of the Master Builder. Its references to this portentous legend, with which every fraternal member had originally become acquainted under the dramatic circumstances of his initiation, were oblique enough to protect the story's secrecy (since non-Masons would be attending the funeral) yet evocative enough of that formative event in the careers of the assembled lodge members to give added emotional weight to the wish for immortality. Thus, for example, when the lodge members circled the tomb, each pausing at its head to deposit a sprig of acacia upon the casket, everyone present could appreciate the universal symbol of rebirth embodied in the evergreen, but members of the order also knew that the plant signified the finality of a treacherous deed yet at the same time the confounding of its evil intent. Knowing "more," the lodge members could feel more. The richness of the fraternity's sacred symbols, like those of any religious denomination, offered them channels for both encouraging and organizing their thoughts and feelings about death.[13]

Freemasonry not only taught faith in God and the immortality of the soul, it also offered its adherents a highly developed set of ritualistic practices through which to express convictions concerning man's nature, his relationship to the Divine and to his fellow men. Masonic rituals included ceremonies held at the laying of cornerstones for public buildings, the aforementioned funeral services, and observances to honor annually installed lodge officers and newly dedicated temples. At the center of this symbolic complex stood the fraternity's initiatory rites. Actually, the term "initiation" fails to convey the full religous dimensions of this central Masonic practice, to which the great majority of lodge meetings were devoted. What was meant was really a progression of ceremonies, called "degrees," each dramatizing different aspects of the fraternity's sacred tales of origin. I use the term "sacred" because these stories--and there were seven major classes of them, ranging from fully developed myths, such as the one about Hiram Abif, to mere fragments of historical or philosophical narrative-- were designed to direct the mind of the membership toward a consideration of spiritual values and heartfelt sentiments, not to promote a literal investigation of the organization's actual origins. The legends of Masonry, while grounded in historical plausibility, were meant to be taken figuratively, and the initiatory ceremonies breathed life into their symbols through the use of sensory representation and dramatic impersonation.[14]

The fraternity's uninhibited use of costumes, emblems, relics, special lighting, movements and postures in its ceremonies set it strikingly apart from the austere environments in which the mainstream evangelical tradition worked its own very different emotional effects. For Masonry the intent was always to reach the heart via the senses, to produce a linkage of ideals and emotions through an appeal to beauty. Amasa Bishop, editor of San Francisco's officially endorsed *Masonic Mirror*, offered one of the most forceful statements contrasting the religious sensibility of the brotherhood with the predominant style in American Protestantism when he wrote:

> [Ceremonialism] serves to please, to instruct, to make agreeable, and is the best medium for raising man in the scale of being, and inculcating in him the attributes of perfection, bringing him into closer resemblance to his Divine Maker.... It were just as easy for the great Architect of the Universe to have spoken this world into existence, as to have used forms and ceremonies to accomplish the great design. But then, in that case, the great plan would have lost its beauty of simplicity. It might have been more wonderfully and mysteriously grand, but too hard for human minds to grasp.[15]

Here was the Masonic critique of introspective piety at its most direct. Damning with faint praise the characteristic reliance by evangelical preachers on the power of the Biblical text alone to inspire their followers (as if God had "spoken this world into existence"), Bishop heartily defended the use of ritual as a spiritual approach that was at once more beautiful and more effective.

Considering Freemasonry's profoundly religious character, it is at first glance surprising to learn that men unaffiliated with any church comprised an overwhelming majority of the fraternity's membership in late nineteenth-century San Francisco. Just 12% of the brotherhood's members in 1890, the only Gilded-Age year for which church affiliation may be meaningfully ascertained, belonged to one of the city's Protestant houses of worship. It is true that San Francisco ranked low among the nation's major cities in Protestant church membership. Founded amid the materialistic orgy of the 1849 Gold Rush, elevated rapidly to the status of the country's ninth largest city in 1890 by the aggressive pursuit of commerce, finance and light manufacture in support of its mining and agricultural hinterland, San Francisco carried its libertine, Jacksonian spirit well into the post-Civil War era. Protestant churchmen--from Methodist street preachers to the settled Episcopal bishop--were present even during the first frontier decade, but they and their lay followers always seemed to be waging an uphill struggle against the city's many unobservant Protestants on the one hand, and its large, well–churched Irish Catholic minority on the other. From a minister's perspective, the situation of the male population appeared even more critical, for men everywhere in the United States were about one-half as likely to join a Protestant church as were women.

As a result of these factors, a meager 9% of the city's adult, white, non-Catholic, male inhabitants (the subpopulation from which Masonry recruited its members) belonged to a church. Thus, the brotherhood actually attracted to its ranks a slightly higher proportion of church members than existed in the city at large. More significant, however, is the fact that the Masonic order drew as weakly as it did from the churched Protestants of San Francisco, far more weakly than one would have expected for such a demonstrably religious institution. In other words, the brotherhood functioned for a great many of its members as a denomination in its own right, providing all of the religion that most men in the order seemed to require.[16]

II

Let me now take a closer look at the key suppositions underlying the Masonic faith and attempt to place the fraternity within the religious history of nineteenth-century America. First, Masonry envisioned an unbridgeable gap between God and man. Whether invoking the stern Judeo-Calvinistic "God of Abraham, Isaac and Jacob," the comforting Unitarian "Fatherhood of God and the Brothernood of Man," or the neutral deistic "Great Architect of the Universe," in each case these common Masonic usages stressed the transcendent otherness of the Divine.[17] Conversely, the fraternity's rituals and rhetoric presented a deeply chastened view of man, notwithstanding his great capacity to reason. The term "original sin" would have been foreign to the brotherhood's Enlightenment vocabulary, but many of the order's chief allegorical symbols, like the craftsman's compass which lay atop the Bible on the lodgeroom's altar, taught the constant need to "circumscribe one's passions."[18] As the acts of the rebellious workmen in the Hiram legend exemplified, greed and ambition lurked in every human situation, and this drama of treachery and martyrdom was echoed in other sacred tales of the fraternity, most notably the story of the medieval Knights Templar, whose leader, Jacques de Molay, lost his life at the hands of a Papal-royal conspiracy.[19]   Most Masons would have agreed with Grand Orator John Nelles Young when he declared in 1887 that "the practical tendency of the unaided human race is to moral degeneracy. This fact will be conceded by every student of history."[20]

Yet these sobering spiritual assumptions did not preclude Masonry from generating hope concerning man's future. Again, the Hiram story illustrates the crucial points in the Masonic theology: Man, the legend taught, is forever searching after true knowledge about the meaning of life and his place in the cosmos. But once man accepts that ultimate knowledge, being Divine, will always elude him and that he must remain satisfied with an imperfect human approximation, he will realize that faith alone can supply the substance he is lacking. Through faith, not only truth but also immortality becomes attainable. As the popular nineteenth-century Masonic scholar Albert G. Mackey put it,

> It is one of the most beautiful, but at the same time most abstruse, doctrines of the science of Masonic symbolism, that the Mason is ever to be in search of truth, but is never to find it. And this is intended to teach the humiliating but necessary lesson, that the knowledge of the nature of God and of man's relation to him, which knowledge constitutes divine truth, can never be acquired in this life. It is only when the portals of the grave open to us, and give us an entrance into a more perfect life, that this knowledge is to be attained.[21]

The important Royal Arch degree within the fraternity's initiatory progression drew the same lesson, relying in part upon more familiar Old Testament material. This ritual, dramatizing the sacred story of how Zerubbabel led the Israelites in the rebuilding of the Temple following its destruction by the Babylonians, reached its climax in the discovery of the holiest symbol for

Masonry, the name of the Lord himself, signified by the Hebrew initials *JHVH*. Represented paradoxically in a name that remained theoretically unspeakable, a symbol that in itself embodied mysteriously the properties of both symbol and referent, of both approximation and truth, this Judaic-Masonic formulation expressed perfectly both the limits of human knowledge and the great possibilities opened through faith. Each Masonic degree ceremony, moreover, in conveying to the candidate the special Word appropriate to his level of achievement within the ritualistic progression, referred ultimately to this holiest of symbols in which approximation and truth would finally be united.[22]

Compare the axioms of this spiritual position with those of the liberal theology just emerging out of the evangelical tradition during the Gilded Age, and the contrast is unmistakable. For liberal Protestants, God's presence in nature and in human culture became the dominant theme, replacing the older transcendent conception of the Deity. Liberals assumed man to be infused with Divine spirit, as represented in the person of Jesus. They "affirmed God's sovereignty," writes historian William R. Hutchison, "but refused to consider this the cornerstone of the Christian system." Rather, Christ's Incarnation was the key spiritual event, and for liberals salvation became even less problematic than it had been under the Arminian assumptions of the early evangelical movement. The Christian Saviour took on the character of a great universalistic principle, a symbol of the unity that already existed between the human and the Divine. Although liberal ministers turned away from the cathartic conversion techniques of their revivalistic forebears in favor of the slower methods of Christian education and ethical counsel, their "new theology," which would become dominant by the turn of the century, did little to weaken the underlying belief in man's perfectability that had long fueled the evangelical impulse. In each of these assumptions concerning the relationship between God and man, Masonry and liberal Protestantism stood at odds.[23]

A second distinguishing characteristic of the Masonic faith lay in the fraternity's commitment to religious rationalism. Freemasons believed that man's God-given capacity to reason formed the underpinnings of his faith. Although this viewpoint appears to contradict the fraternity's cautions concerning the limits of human knowledge, the issue here was not a question of faith versus reason but rather one of the proper *route* to faith. The Masonic position can be best understood in reference to the brotherhood's two major spiritual antagonists, the Catholic Church and evangelical Protestantism.

Throughout the Gilded Age, the fraternity frequently denounced the "superstitious" practices of Catholicism. One finds, for example, in 1874 Grand Orator Samuel C. Denson pointing with pride to the medieval knights' "splendid triumphs" against "assaults of superstition and fiendish folly in religion's guise," and in 1899 C. Moody Plummer, editor of the semi-official San Francisco Masonic *Trestleboard*, printing a copy of the "requirements for Lent" in order to make fun of the "nonsense" of fasting.[24] Members of the brotherhood sparred ideologically with the city's Irish Catholics over lingering controversies concerning the public school system.[25] Many Masons ventured outside their organization to contribute leaders, followers and, most significantly, the fraternity's organizational model (including a lodge structure, ritual degrees, secrecy and hierarchical formality) to San Francisco branches of the era's chief anti-Catholic political formations--the American Protestant Association in the 1870s, the American Party in the 1880s, and the American Protective Association in the 1890s.[26]

The brotherhood's hostility to the Catholic Church grew out of a variety of causes, many of them political, not the least of which included Rome's unrelenting attacks on Freemasonry as part of its fierce struggle with the fraternity for control in several European countries. On religious grounds, however, the Masonic order condemned Catholicism as a faith based on magic and blind obedience to priestly authority. "No organization, be it religious or otherwise, is above criticism," wrote the editors of the *Masonic Mirror* in 1872 in the midst of a dispute with San Francisco's Catholic magazine, the *Monitor*, over Masonic participation in the cornerstone ceremony for the new City Hall. "[P]rinciples or tenets which will not bear the light of discussion are rotten, and the sooner they are interred the better."[27]

By contrast, the fraternity took pride in its historical connection to Enlightenment learning, to developments in the natural sciences, and to the general diffusion of secular knowledge. It endorsed wholeheartedly the tenets of Common Sense epistemology, by which the mind could be trusted to apprehend the facts of nature as the self-evident building blocks of truth. Carrying forward into the Gilded Age the Christianized version of this Enlightenment epistemology which so dominated American Protestant thought during the ante-bellum years, the fraternity regarded the "facts" and testimonies recorded in the Bible, no less than the great lawfulness observed in nature, as the only sound basis for faith in God. Masons viewed their rituals as fully consonant with this rationalist approach, centered as they were on motifs derived from the Bible or from other verifiable texts. "Men like mystery," asserted Grand Orator Aaron A. Sargent in 1877, referring to the fraternity's general appeal, "...but if the reason is left unsatisfied, all soon becomes stale, flat, and unprofitable."[28]

When facing its evangelical opponents, the brotherhood defended religious rationalism against a somewhat different threat. Where Masonry regarded Catholicism as superstitious and authoritarian, it attacked its Protestant antagonists for their "fanaticism" and "sectarian zealotry." Memories of the 1820s and 1830s, during which the young evangelical movement had spearheaded a crusade against the fraternity for its supposed idolatrous practices (leveling many of the same charges against the brotherhood which Masonry later hurled at Catholicism), all but extinguishing lodge activity in many states of the North, provoked some of these derogatory comments about "enthusiastic" religion. Moreover, groups like the National Christian Association, led by the Presbyterian minister Jonathan Blanchard and the renowned ante-bellum revivalist Charles Grandison Finney, as well as several Protestant subdenominations kept religious anti-Masonry alive after the Civil War by denouncing secret societies and expelling any followers who joined a lodge. Though these groups did not exert a strong influence in San Francisco, Grand Orator Thomas Henry Laine had such organizations in mind when he characterized these enemies of Masonry as "self-righteous religious fanatics, . . . a zealous, fuming, frothing lot...."[29]

However, animosities between Masonry and the largest evangelical bodies--the Methodists, Baptists, New School Presbyterians, and Congregationalists--cooled off considerably during the late nineteenth century, and individual lodges sometimes carried on quite amicable relations with particular churches. The penetration of theological liberalism within the major denominations, with its rejection of Biblical literalism and greater tolerance for varied interpretations of the Protestant message, helped to foster this rapprochement. Yet even amid the new cordiality, one can still discern a difference in mood between the fraternity and the evangelical-liberal mainstream stemming from divergent positions on the issue of reason's relationship to faith. All Protestants, of course, vested final authority in the Scriptures and in the individual's ability, with God's help, to make sense of the revealed word recorded within them. To this extent all Protestants were rationalists. But the historic development of revivalism had elevated "experience" to a position of preeminence over Biblical understanding. In nineteenth-century evangelicalism, a new religion of the heart and of personal feeling triumphed over an older Calvinist tradition thought to be too reliant on a learned ministry and the techniques of rational persuasion.[30]

These radically romantic tendencies within evangelicalism did not disappear with the rise of liberalism in the late nineteenth century. Following the lead of Congregationalist theologian Horace Bushnell, whom William Hutchison has called the evangelical counterpart of Emerson, Gilded-Age liberals replaced the revivalist's use of emotion with the minister's emphasis on intuition as the appropriate means for apprehending God's indwelling in nature and in culture. The European philosophers and theologians to whom the liberal movement looked for inspiration--Maurice, Coleridge, Schleiermacher, Hegel--expounded an idealist epistemology that called into question the self-evident truth of empirical facts, respecting the powers of the mind to shape reality as much as to mirror it. Poetic imagery became an important rhetorical style for preaching this subjectivist faith. All of this stood in marked contrast to the religious and philosophical temperament of Masonry. True, the fraternity had its poets, and its orators on occasion broke into rhapsodies on the sublimities of nature. But a didactic style that appealed to the reasoned weighing of human actions and consequences, as if moral dilemmas were problems in mathematics or physics, composed the essence of Masonic rhetoric. Commonly, in fact, fraternal spokesman referred to their institution as the "science of Masonry." Through the end of the nineteenth century, the fraternity's European heroes remained the Enlightenment figures, Locke, Newton and Priestly, and their scientific predecessors, Copernicus and Galileo.[31]

An emphasis on moralism of an exemplary rather than a crusading type constituted a third distinguishing feature of the Masonic religious outlook. Few aspects of Masonry were as well known to the public as the fraternity's reputation for looking after its own members in sickness or distress and, in the case of a member's death, his widow and children. Charity relief of this sort--which did not operate on the principle of a guaranteed benefit, as did most of the fraternal benevolent societies springing up during this period--in fact lay embedded within a larger structure of ideas and practices which aimed at instilling a stringent code of ethical conduct in every member of the order. Common Sense epistemology served the fraternity admirably here, for it affirmed the existence of absolute moral principles and laws as "scientifically" sound as the facts and laws of nature were presumed to be.[32]

Characteristically, the brotherhood expressed its moral code symbolically--through the allegory of King Solomon's Temple. In this instance the focus of attention was not the Master Architect, Hiram Abif, but rather the building project itself. The perfect harmony with which such a vast endeavor had been executed, the self-discipline of the craftsmen, the wise guidance of King Solomon, the application of honest skills to purposes of both beauty and spirit, and the magnificently proportioned Temple itself were all themes which lent themselves to emblematic elaboration of almost endless variety. Through the specific symbols of this Masonic allegory--such as the craftsman's tools, each conveying its own moral lesson--the fraternity taught the general principle that one builds a life of virtue with the same deliberation that characterized the construction of the ancient Biblical Temple.[33]

In addition to this symbolic expression, the fraternity's spokesmen reiterated moral themes in their speeches and writings. Grand officers and Masonic editors frequently exhorted the membership to be temperate in the use of both alcohol and tobacco, to avoid profanity in speech, to shun the gambling table and the house of prostitution, and to exercise self-restraint over the passions of greed, ambition and violence.[34] Beginning in 1870 under the four-term Grand Mastership of Leonidas E. Pratt, moreover, the Grand Lodge embarked on a largely successful effort to tighten the moral (as well as ritualistic and record-keeping) standards of the lodges in the state, believing that the Gold Rush era had bequeathed a looseness of manner that was now out of place in a civilized California society noted for its commercial and agricultural development.

Yet what is striking about Masonic moralism is that its intensity was directed inward, rather than, as with the evangelical denominations, toward the outside world. Furthermore, the fraternity's moralism demonstrated a leniency uncharacteristic of its evangelical counterpart. Grand Master Pratt himself, in the midst of rising temperance agitation precipitated by evangelical women and agrarian reformers, defended the ability of a saloon keeper to be both a moral man and a good Mason, ridiculing "the ultra reformers, who set up a standard of perfection for others than themselves to conform to." While lodges (though not all of the bodies of higner-degree Masonry) gradually abolished drinking from their official celebrations during the Gilded Age, the California Grand Lodge twice defeated attempts in the 1890s to bar liquor dealers from holding Masonic office or from joining the fraternity. Although Masons were generally not active in moral reform causes outside the fraternity, some did participate in the California temperance movement. Yet, significantly, the state temperance movement itself seems to have been split into fraternal and evangelical wings. In northern California the former branch, including the Sons of Temperance, Good Templars, and

Rechabites--groups which took in women but organized on a "fraternal" model--persevered doggedly but could achieve successes only when joined by strong bursts of energy from evangelical activists in the Women's Christian Temperance Union and later the Anti-Saloon League.[35]

In a common expression of the fraternity's restricted moral aims, Grand Master Hiram Newton Rucker declared, "...Masonry does not seek the reformation of men. It seeks to bind good men and true in closer bonds of fellowship and love, and to perfect the good work already begun." Foremost among the Masonic virtues was the internal one of charity (called by many Masons "true, practical religion"): visiting a lodge brother who was sick or providing for those undergoing hard times. If a lodge's members followed respectable standards of behavior and practiced such charity, its moral mission--to serve as an "example of brotherly love" to the community around it--would be fulfilled.[36]

Fourth, the brotherhood stood for religious universalism. "Thoroughly cosmopolitan and universal as it is in its character, it [Masonry] tends to unite those who would otherwise remain at a perpetual distance," asserted George C. Perkins, Grand Master in 1875.

> Men of every nationality and creed,--with no religious qualification, except the one requisite belief in God, the Supreme Intelligence which pervades all nature--Jew and Gentile, Mohammedan and Christian, meet within our Lodges upon one common level, working harmoniously together for their moral improvement and social regeneration.[37]

The fraternity buttressed its claim to universal appeal by barring the discussion of religion (or politics) from the lodgeroom, and by seeking precursors of its faith in the rites of pagan societies.

Actually, this principle was not quite as ecumenical as it seemed, even if we leave aside the question of its practice. Masonic toleration had arisen in early eighteenth-century England in reaction to the intense religious controversies that had brought that country to civil war in the previous hundred years. In light of these origins, the fraternity's nonsectarianism had always contained a good measure of *anti*-sectarianism as well. In nineteenth-century America, the order's persecution at the hands of the ante-bellum evangelical movement kept alive this tendency in its thought. Thus one finds many Gilded-Age spokesmen for the fraternity lauding Masonic universalism and castigating Protestant evangelicalism in the same breath. C. Moody Plummer of the *Trestleboard* was only more extreme than most when he declared Protestantism itself to be a religion of warring sects "as intolerant often of each other as human action can be," while Masonry was "the only religion which can become universal and is [therefore] true religion."[38]

Ironically, the evangelical thrust within Protestantism, with its call to constitute a religion of the heart, had itself emerged as a universalistic reaction to the narrow dogmatism of early Calvinism. Evangelical universalism did indeed make possible the great interdenominational crusades for Christianizing and moralizing the nation during the nineteeth century. Yet following a brief marriage during the American struggle for independence, the two universalisms of Masonry and evangelicalism had parted company to assume the posture of antagonists.[39] Only in the face of a renewed "European" threat--that of the equally universalistic Roman Church--could these two Protestant traditions unite in anti-Catholic vituperation, and even then only by adopting quite different styles and organizational forms. In San Francisco, as I have noted, anti-Catholic Masons both created and gravitated to specific associations that affirmed their own religious values of ritualism, hierarchy and sexual distinction. On the other hand, anti-Catholic activists from the city's evangelical and liberal denominations, just as strident in tone as their fraternal counterparts, adopted their own equally characteristic mode of expression: charismatic preachers--Reverend John Hemphill of Calvary Presbyterian Church in the 1870s and Baptist minister John Q. A. Brown in the 1890s provide the two best examples--who appealed to a loosely organized, egalitarian and sexually mixed following. Just as the case of temperance organizations illustrated, even such issues of ostensible Protestant unity as anti-Catholic agitation brought forth differences in outlook and action between the evangelical and non-evangelical camps.[40]

In sum, Gilded-Age Freemasonry carried forward the philosophical outlook of Enlightenment rationalism as it had been modified by the forces of Christianity in the early decades of the nineteenth century. I have contrasted the suppositions of this fraternal faith with the radically romantic tendencies of subjectivism, optimism and crusading moralism that animated the evangelical Protestant mainstream, including its new liberal formulation which emerged toward the end of the century. Yet Masonry was not satisfied with a rationalistic religion alone. Its ritualistic sensibility, its fascination with hierarchy and medievalism, its love of symbols and forms all demonstrate that it too owed much to romantic currents of thought. Masonry borrowed, however, from the conservative side of the romantic spectrum, invoking the values of tradition where evangelicalism extolled change. Conservative romanticism had been in a clear minority during the first half of the nineteenth century, residing most typically in the cultures of the slaveholding South (where Freemasonry was quite popular) and in the upper-class mercantile centers of the North. But the Gilded Age witnessed a subtle shift in the nation's cultural and religious center of gravity toward formality, traditionalism and estheticism, from which the Masonic fraternity and fraternalism in general benefited greatly.[41] Fashioned out of this mixture of Enlightenment, Christian and romantic motifs, Freemasonry captured a dominant place among the non-evangelical forces of its era.

III

In the previous section I have attempted to define the central tendency (to borrow a statistical metaphor) of the Masonic religious outlook. Yet the actual distribution of spiritual positions among individual members showed considerable dispersion around this mean. That religion was not the sole reason why men chose to join the fraternity, of course, accounts for some of this variation. But the Masonic non-evangelical temperament itself may also take credit for the wide latitude of religious beliefs tolerated within the organization's ranks. The fraternity's stated principle of universalism, its denial of human perfectionism, its suspicion of moral reform, and perhaps most of all its respect for ceremony over creed, enabled any man sharing in these conservative spiritual assumptions--provided he was white, non-Catholic, and able to afford the fees and dues of membership--to possess a strong chance of being accepted into the order.

A look at the Protestant church members within the San Francisco fraternity, admittedly a small minority of the brotherhood's total membership, tends to confirm both Masonry's non-evangelical orientation and its ability to draw together men of varying religious backgrounds. By comparing the denominational affiliations of this Masonic subgroup in 1890 with the proportional distribution of denominational members in the city's male population for the same year, one finds that Episcopalians, Unitarians and Swedenborgians were overrepresented in the fraternity, Methodists were evenly represented, while Presbyterians, Congregationalists, Baptists, Disciples of Christ and Lutherans were underrepresented. A much more detailed discussion than can be presented here would be needed to interpret these findings fully, but in summary form three conclusions may be drawn. First, the disproportions indicate that Masonry attracted men whose denominational affiliation showed a bias in favor of non-evangelical observance. (Indeed, one would not be far wrong to think of Freemasonry as a cross between Episcopalianism and Unitarianism.) Second, men belonging to churches of every major Protestant denomination could nevertheless find a place within the order. Third, there is reason to assume that those Masons belonging to churches within evangelical denominations subscribed to less evangelical interpretations of their respective faiths.[42]

Even the cases of the two denominations--Methodism and Lutheranism--whose extent of representation within the San Francisco fraternity appears somewhat at odds with these generalizations on closer examination bear them out. Although American Methodism was the virtual prototype of an evangelical faith, the denomination had grown so large during the nineteenth century that by the time of the Gilded Age it encompassed members of divergent spiritual inclinations. By mid-century, in fact, Methodists were divided over the question of secret fraternal societies. This issue had precipitated in 1859 a split in the Genesee Conference of western New York, and the alignment of forces there indicated that those standing unalterably opposed to fraternal membership also upheld the more steadfast evangelical positions not only in matters of worship but also as against worldliness in dress and behavior, compromise on slavery, and "love of money." Similar passions disturbed the California Conference. That body's nineteenth-century historian noted that when one preacher in a mountain district attacked Masonry and all secret societies, even the Sons of Temperance, "[t]his produced some friction in certain quarters of the district." Differences in religious temperament had also flared over the slavery question at the conference's third meeting in 1855. There, Methodists belonging to the Know-Nothing movement, a secretive, anti-Catholic political party organized along fraternal lines and enjoying considerable Masonic support, fought unsuccessfully to moderate anti-slavery sentiments--"hating 'fanaticism' more than they hated sin," in the words of the conference's historian. These bits of evidence suggest that those Methodists who did join the Masonic fraternity occupied the less evangelical wing of their faith, and that the denomination produced no shortage of such men.[43]

In the case of Lutheranism, a generally non-evangelical faith, a detailed picture of the denomination in San Francisco helps to explain the disproportionately low number of Lutheran men who chose to join the Masonic fraternity. In fact, members of two major German-speaking Lutheran churches in the city and the one important English-speaking church were well represented inside the brotherhood. Rationalistic currents of thought had penetrated all three congregations, making them hospitable to many of the ideas of Freemasonry. But San Francisco also housed a large congregation of Lutherans belonging to the Missouri Synod, a branch of the faith that adamantly opposed membership in secret societies. Founded by Saxons who had emigrated to the United States in the 1840s to escape modernistic tendencies within their provincial Lutheran Church, the Missouri Synod moved steadily toward a position of strict confessionalism and Biblical literalism, bearing an increasing resemblance to pre-evangelical Calvinism in its renunciation of all worldly signs of piety. It happened that the pastor called to the early, united Lutheran community in San Francisco, Jacob Buehler, became partial to the Missouri Synod's theology. When he refused to bury a Mason in the late 1860s, latent differences in outlook surfaced among the laity, and the congregation split. But the continued existence of a large number of strict, anti-rationalistic Lutherans in the city reduced the proportion of Lutheran Masons to a smaller figure than the non-evangelical character of the denomination would have implied.[44]

Perhaps the most surprising representatives in the Masonic non-evangelical alliance were the large number of Jews. In Gilded-Age San Francisco, Jews comprised 12% of the brotherhood's membership, about the same proportion which they formed in the city's adult, white, male, non-Catholic population as a whole.[45] Considering the strictly Protestant origins of Freemasonry, this high proportion of Jewish members is extraordinary. Jews cited the fraternity's adoption of Old Testament themes, including an abundance of Judaic symbols (some of which originated in the Jewish mystical Kaballah, which passed into Freemasonry via the post-Reformation Christian interest in the occult), as well as the Masonic commitment to strict monotheism as two important sources of compatibility between Masonry and their own faith. Indeed, it was these affinities which prompted an anonymous Jewish Mason, writing in the San Francisco *Hebrew* in 1865, to proclaim, "if there be any religious system more closely connected with the institution [of Masonry] than others, *it is Judaism.*"[46] Above all, however, Jews gravitated to the brotherhood's universalistic appeal. Acceptance by non-Jews on a basis of equality held tremendous secular importance to these German and Polish immigrants and their sons. And the brotherhood's spiritual combination of universalism and rationalism, which could be interpreted as pointing toward a nonsectarian world religion, was especially attractive to the members of San Francisco's large Reform-minded synagogues, who flocked to Masonry in disproportionately large numbers.[47]

There were also some Masons who insisted upon an explicitly Christian interpretation of their institution. Toward the beginning of the period some lodges used prayers that linked Hiram Abif to Jesus, drawing a clear parallel between the Master Architect's "resurrection" and that of the Christian Saviour, although when Jewish members registered complaints these prayers were discontinued.[48] Occasionally, references to "the Redeemer" or statements asserting Masonry's affinity with Christianity appeared in the addresses of Grand Orators.[49] In general, however, the great bulk of the membership seemed content to accept the Judeo-Protestant character of Masonry without specifically connecting the brotherhood with either of these two established faiths.

Greater conflict on this issue was no doubt averted because the fraternity maintained a Christian "safety-valve" in one of its small higher-degree organizations, the Order of Knights Templar. This body had always restricted its membership to Christians, and during the Gilded Age the Knights Templar underwent a shift toward further Christianization. Most grand commanderies (as the supreme organizations of the Knights Templar were called), including California's, came to require "a firm belief in the Christian religion," while some jurisdictions went so far as to insist additionally on a profession of faith in the Trinity. The growth and Christianization of the Knights Templar during these years indicated both the increased spiritual pull of "high church" formality and, paradoxically enough, the rise of an Enlightenment-based Protestant fundamentalism within the brotherhood. The success of the commanderies probably also signified that tendencies toward status-driven exlusivity and "social anti-Semitism," which historian John Higham has found in the nation at large during the Gilded Age, were operating within the Masonic fraternity as well.[50]

Jewish and Christian interpretations of Masonry were not the only oppositions to be found within the religious range of the fraternity. The brotherhood included theistic humanists like William C. Belcher, a prominent lawyer in Marysville and later San Francisco and for twenty-eight years the guiding spirit of the Grand Lodge's prestigious Jurisprudence Committee. It was said of Belcher that he "believed in humanity" and would never join a church because it would narrow his field for doing good.[51] Another humanist, the *Trestleboard*'s editor, C. Moody Plummer, rankled the sensibilities of more conventional members when he suggested holding Sunday "Masonic services" consisting of lectures and moral instruction. (Lodge meetings were generally held on week nights.) Plummer's idea was never enacted. It was considered to be unnecessarily challenging to the city's churches, though the fraternity customarily held its funeral services on Sunday.[52]

On the other hand, the fraternity produced rationalistic defenders of Biblical literalism, whose mode of argument would again not have been out of place in the fundamentalist movement just beginning to take shape during the Gilded Age. Early in the period, the editor of the *Masonic Mirror* cited works by astronomers and geologists to confirm that Christ's crucifixion had indeed occurred on April 6, 31 A.D. Nearly twenty years later, Grand Orator Young asserted that Masonry's

> great light is the volume of the Sacred Law, accepted as the unerring standard of truth and justice, which, while it harmonizes with and irradiates natural religion, supplements it with new and additional truths, and teaches by direct declaration what could be acquired from natural law only by inference from close observation combined with inductive reasoning.[53]

The controversial question of Darwinian evolution similarly evoked divergent opinions within the order. An anecdote related by Edwin A. Sherman, a California Mason and the fraternity's nineteenth-century historian, humorously revealed both favorable and unfavorable attitudes. Commenting on the fraternity's fourth degree ritual (York Rite), in which each candidate was called upon to identify himself by entering a personal emblem in the degree's sacred book, Sherman recalled, "In one Chapter book of marks in San Francisco some years ago the device which a member chose was that of a ring-tailed monkey climbing a pole, proving his belief in the Darwinian theory...." But in so doing, Sherman added sarcastically, the member proved "that his [own] simian ancestry was not very remote...."[54]

Thus, under its peculiar banner of ritualistic, theistic rationalism, Masonry was able to unite men of wide-ranging religious backgrounds and creeds. Despite the brotherhood's great size, its contribution to the moral and religious life of the nation, as compared with that of the evangelical denominations, has been overlooked. Undoubtedly this is because evangelical Protestantism exerted such a demonstrable influence on the country's cultural and political life--distributing Bibles to every village, enforcing observance of the Sabbath, moderating drinking habits, setting up schools and colleges, and sparking the campaigns to abolish slavery and to enfranchise women. In contrast, the accomplishments of fraternal groups like Freemasonry were much quieter. Grand Master Perkins boasted in 1875 that for many years Masonry had constituted the prevailing moral influence in the mining districts, kept men within the bounds of moderation, and taught them the Golden Rule. It had ministered to the sick, relieved the destitute, and paid last tributes to the dead.[55] Members of the San Francisco fraternity did play conspicuous parts in running and staffing the school system, in holding municipal and state office, and in contributing to the city's philanthropic services. But the non-evangelical temperament of Masonry remained most suited to furthering the everyday work of the institutions of the market--the merchant house, the insurance agency, the transport company, the skilled shop, and the law office. Religious underpinnings of such secular endeavors are often thought to be nonexistent, but in the conservative practices of the lodge a great many men filling these Gilded-Age roles found their faith.

Notes

I wish to thank the volunteers at the Library of the Grand Lodge of California, Free and Accepted Masons, for their assistance in making the historical materials of the California Masonic fraternity available to me. I am grateful also to Michael Kazin, Carl

Guarneri, Barton J. Bernstein, Ronald Schatz, Douglas F. Anderson, and S. Brent Morris for their comments and suggestions.

1. Sydney E. Ahlstrom, *A Religious History of the American People* (Garden City, N. Y.: Image Books, 1975) I, 469-470, 568-570; Robert T. Handy, *A Christian America: Protestant Hopes and Historical Realities*, second edition, revised and enlarged (New York: Oxford University Press, 1984), 24-56; Timothy L. Smith, *Revivalism and Social Reform: American Protestantism on the Eve of the Civil War* (New York: Harper and Row, 1965), 7-8, 15, 34-44. On the Evangelical Alliance, see Paul Boyer, *Urban Masses and Moral Order in America, 1820-1920* (Cambridge: Harvard University Press, 1978), 133, 329.

2. In 1890, for example, there were 3062 men in the Masonic fraternity in San Francisco, whereas for the same year one may estimate the total number of men belonging to non-evangelical churches (Episcopalian, Unitarian, Lutheran and Swedenborgian) at 2100. The male membership of the evangelical denominations (Methodist, Baptist, Presbyterian, Congregationalist and Disciples of Christ) totaled 3800 in 1890. This is a rough comparison, since there were some evangelicals among Episcopalians and some non-evangelicals among Presbyterians. As the text will bring out, there was little overlap between Masons and members of Protestant denominations. *Report on the Statistics of Churches in the United States* (Washington: Government Printing Office, 1894), 98-99; *Religious Bodies: 1906. Special Reports of the Bureau of the Census* (Washington: Government Printing Office, 1910), I, 162-165. Since the 1890 Report on Statistics did not give denominational totals broken down by sex, I applied the denominational sex ratios reported in 1906 to the 1890 totals. The estimated total for the Church of New Jerusalem (Swedenborgian) comes from my examination of local church records. Nationally, the Masonic brotherhood claimed 609,000 members in 1890. Lynn Dumenil, "Brotherhood and Respectability: Freemasonry and American Culture, 1880-1930," PhD Dissertation (University of California, Berkeley, 1981), 389.

3. I have restricted my study to the white Freemasons of San Francisco and to the proceedings of the grand bodies of California whose jurisdictions included all white Masonic organizations in the state. During these same years, a smaller and separate organization of black (Prince Hall) Freemasons also existed in the city and state. I have omitted as well from consideration the Order of the Eastern Star, the women's auxiliary to the Masons, which had its beginnings during the Gilded Age.

4. Dorothy Ann Lipson, *Freemasonry in Federalist Connecticut* (Princeton: Princeton University Press, 1977); Lynn Dumenil, "Brothernood and Respectability;" Pamela M. Jolicoeur and Louis I. Knowles, "Fraternal Associations and Civil Religion: Scottish Rite Freemasonry," *Review of Religious Research* 20 (Fall, 1978): 3-22; John Wilson, "Voluntary Associations and Civil Religion: the Case of Freemasonry," *Review of Religious Research* 22 (December, 1980): 125-136.

5. In treating the fraternal lodge as a religious organization, I am pursuing the suggestion of Sydney Ahlstrom, who has written: "Despite its obvious importance, the 'lodge' as an American social and religious institution has been inadequately studied.... For many [lodge members] they [the lodges] seemed to satisfy social needs and a yearning for rites and ceremonies that Protestantism lacked. For many others they seemed to have provided a religious alternative to the churches." *Religious History*, II, 212; I, 669. Following Peter Berger, I take religion to mean the system of beliefs and practices that establishes for a person and his social group a meaningful order in the cosmos and does so through an appeal to the sacred, "a quality of mysterious and awesome power, other than man and yet related to him...." Peter L. Berger, *The Sacred Canopy: Elements of a Sociological Theory of Religion* (Garden City, New York: Doubleday and Company, 1966), Ch. 1, esp. p. 25.

6. "The person who desires to be made a Mason must be...a believer in God and a future existence...." General Regulation 11, *Proceedings of the M. W. Grand Lodge of Free and Accepted Masons of the State of California* [hereafter referred to as

Proceedings] (1874), 646.

7. *Proceedings* (1878), 592. Other examples may be found in *Proceedings* (1871), 165; *Proceedings* (1887), 167, 170; *Proceedings* (1897), 199.

8. *Proceedings* (1877), 186; *Proceedings* (1878), 564; *Proceedings* (1879), 16; *Proceedings* (1882), 639-640; *Proceedings* (1894), 786.

9. *Proceedings* (1888), 463-464. For the second case, see *Proceedings* (1900), 644, 902.

10. Malcolm C. Duncan, *Duncan's Masonic Ritual and Monitor* (republished, New York: David McKay Company, no date), 102-125. Internal evidence makes clear that the original version of this ritual guidebook (in its third edition) came out in the late 1860s or early 1870s. Not only is it a faithful representation of American Masonic practice generally, but it followed the same system which was in most general use in California at the beginning of the period. My dissertation, "The Square and Compass: San Francisco's Freemasons and American Religion, 1870-1900," (in progress, Stanford University) goes into greater detail concerning the authenticity of this source.

11. The clearest exegesis of the immortality theme may be found in Albert G. Mackey, *Manual of the Lodge* (New York: Macoy and Sickels, 1865), 96. Mackey was the most prominent American Masonic scholar of the mid-nineteenth century, and his writings were cited by California Masons more often than those of any other nationally known Masonic figure.

12. *Proceedings* (1882), 635.

13. *A Masonic Burial Service*, as arranged by Alex. G. Abell (San Francisco: F. Eastman, 1856); *Funeral Service of* _____ *Lodge, No.* _____ , *F. & A. M.,* _____ ,California (San Francisco: Office of the Masonic Monthly, 1978). The latter was a guidebook intended to be used by any lodge in the jurisdiction.

14. The Masonic degree system, linked to organizational subdivisions within the fraternity, was exceedingly complex. For purposes of this examination of the brotherhood's religious practice, I have treated the entire degree progression as if it were a single entity. Substantial similarities of meaning among the various groups of degrees make this procedure justifiable.

15. *Masonic Mirror* (October, 1869), 43-44.

16. The statistical comparison is based on a random sample of 371 members belonging to the fraternity in 1890, whose names were checked against surviving church records. The Masonic totals found for each denomination were then adjusted by a ratio based on a comparison of the surviving church records and the denominational totals given in the 1890 *Report on the Statistics of Churches*. For further details on this statistical procedure, for my rules of record linkage, for the sources of church records, and for the computation of the adult, white, male, non-Catholic subpopulation in San Francisco, see my dissertation. On the general weakness of evangelical forces in San Francisco, see Douglas Firth Anderson, "San Francisco Evangelicalism, Regional Religious Identity, and the Revivalism of D. L. Moody," *Fides et Historia* 15 (Spring-Summer 1983): 44-66, which also gives comparisons of church membership rates between San Francisco and other American cities (pp. 63-64). My understanding of San Francisco's history has been strongly influenced by Alexander Saxton, *The Indispensable Enemy: Labor and the Anti-Chinese Movement in California* (Berkeley: University of California Press, 1975), and Kevin Starr, *Americans and the California Dream, 1850-1915* (New York: Oxford University Press, 1973).

17. Examples of the Judaic formulation may be found in the quotation cited earlier in the text and in *Proceedings* (1882), 631-632; for the "Unitarian" phrase, see *Proceedings* (1892), 483-484, and the *Trestleboard* (June 21, 1888): 161-162; for the deistic usage, see usage in *Proceedings* (1885), 15, and *Proceedings* (1875), 122.

18. On the compass, see John W. Shaeffer, "The Monitorial Work of the Three Degrees of Masonry," in James Wright Anderson, ed., *A Masonic Manual, Comprising Decisions of the M. W. Grand Lodge, F. & A. M. of the State of California from Its Formation to the Present Time* (San Francisco, 1906), 284.

19. The story of the Knights Templar is presented in Frank William Sumner, *Tactics and Monitor for Knights of the Order of the Temple* (San Francisco: Grand Commandery of Knights Templar of California, 1897), 735-745; *Pacific Coast Guide and Programme of the Knights Templar Triennial Conclave at San Francisco, August, 1883, as Prepared by the Triennial Committee* (San Francisco: Ira G. Hoitt, 1883), 167-171; and in Edwin A. Sherman, compiler and editor, *Fifty Years of Freemasonry in California* (San Francisco: George Spaulding and Company, 1898), II, 628, 630, 639.

20. *Proceedings* (1887), 166.

21. Mackey, *Manual of the Lodge*, 93-94.

22. On the Royal Arch degree, see *Duncan's Manual*, 217-265.

23. William R. Hutchison, *The Modernist Impulse in American Protestantism* (Cambridge: Harvard University Press, 1976), 2, 4, 79, 84, 95-105 (the quotation is on p. 98), 121; Sydney E.Ahlstrom, "Theology in America: A Historical Survey," in James W. Smith and A. Leland Jamison, eds., *The Shaping of American Religion* (Princeton: Princeton University Press, 1961), 287; Ahlstrom, *Religious History*, II, 243-246.

24. *Proceedings* (1874), 576; *Trestleboard* (March 1899), 131.

25. *Masonic Mirror* (February 18, 1871): 9; A. L. Mann [a Mason and Superintendent of San Francisco Schools], "Our 'Godless' Common Schools," *The Pacific School and Home Journal* 3 (January, 1879): 42-43; *The Common School Question:*

A Discussion between Rev. William Gleeson (of East Oakland) and Frank M. Pixley, Editor of the [San Francisco] *Argonaut* (San Francisco: P. J. Thomas, 1883); *Trestleboard* (January, 1893): 36-38. Other Masons, however, could be quite pragmatic in their dealings with Catholics. Many members of the fraternity served on the San Francisco Board of Education during the Gilded Age, where most pursued the course established by John Swett, a Mason and early State Superintendent of Public Instruction, of approving a settlement on religious issues in the public schools that was more amicable toward Catholics than was common throughout the United States during these years.

26. Evidence supporting Masonic influence within these anti-Catholic organizations can be found in my dissertation. As one example: a membership list of 183 names from one American Protective Association lodge in San Francisco, when compared against a master list of the city's Masons, yields 25 fraternal members, three times the number which would be expected if there were no statistical association between Masonry and APA membership.

27. *Masonic Mirror* (March 9, 1872): 8. The fraternity continued to fight Catholic objections to its public cornerstone rituals throughout the Gilded Age. *Trestleboard* (April, 1889): 114-116, and (January, 1897): 42. The Roman Church, for its part, threatened any Catholic with excommunication for joining a Masonic lodge.

28. For examples of the fraternity's pride in secular knowledge, see *Proceedings* (1871), 167; and Sherman, *Fifty Years*, II, 548. On Common Sense rationalism and its Christian interpretation in the United States, see Theodore D. Bozeman, *Protestants in an Age of Science: the Baconian Ideal and Antebellum American Religious Thought* (Chapel Hill: University of North Carolina Press, 1977), esp. Chs. 3 and 7; and Henry May, *The Enlightenment in America* (New York: Oxford University Press, 1979), 61-65. The quotation from Grand Orator Sargent's address is in *Proceedings* (1877), 176.

29. For examples of attacks on sectarian Protestantism, see *Masonic Mirror* (December, 1869): 113; *Proceedings* (1873), 173; *Trestleboard* (October, 1896): 508. Laine's quotation is from *Proceedings* (1888), 656-657. The National Christian Association is described in George M. Marsden, *Fundamentalism and American Culture: the Shaping of Twentieth-Century Evangelicalism*, 1870- 1925 (New York: Oxford, 1982), 29.

30. The romantic tendencies in earlier evangelicalism are traced in Sidney E. Mead, *The Lively Experiment: the Shaping of Christianity in America* (New York: Harper and Row, 1963), Ch. 7; and in Richard Hofstadter, *Anti-Intellectualism in American Life* (New York: Vintage Books, 1962), Part II.

31. For the liberal period I have relied on Hutchison, *Modernist Impulse*, 5, 44, 52, 80-81, 95-103, 122-132; and Ahlstrom, *Religious History*, II, Chs. 36, 37, 46. Reference to the fraternity's Enlightenment heroes may be found in *Proceedings* (1877), 171-172, *Proceedings* (1883), 306-307, and *Proceedings* (1898), 823.

32. The lack of guaranteed benefits within Masonry is noted in S. Brent Morris, F.P.S., "Trends Affecting American Free Masonry," *The Philalethes* 35 (April 1982): 16.

33. These allegorical themes and their multitude of symbolic expressions pervade the first three (or "Craft") degrees of Masonry. See *Duncan's Manual*, 7-149.

34. For examples, see *Masonic Mirror* (November 4, 1871): 8; *Proceedings* (1877), 149; and *Proceedings* (1895), 214-215.

35. *Proceedings* (1873), 16-17; *Proceedings* (1894), 774; *Proceedings* (1900), 862; Gilbert M. Ostrander, *The Prohibition Movement in California*, 1848-1933 (Berkeley: University of California Press, 1957), 23-26, 34-52, 58-60, 85-91.

36. *Proceedings* (1888), 453; *Proceedings* (1889), 187.

37. *Proceedings* (1875), 15.

38. *Trestleboard* (May, 1895): 234.

39. Sidney Mead advances the general argument about the relationship between Enlightenment and evangelical forces at the time of the Revolution in *The Lively Experiment*, Ch. 3.

40. On Hemphill, see John B. McGloin, S.J., *Eloquent Indian: The Life of James Bourchard, California Jesuit* (Stanford: Stanford University Press, 1949), 154ff; on Brown and the anti-Catholic clergy of the 1890s, see Joseph S. Brusher, "Peter C. Yorke and the A.P.A. in San Francisco," *The Catholic Historical Review* 37 (July, 1951): 129-150.

41. On the religious shift of the Gilded Age, see T. J. Jackson Lears, *No Place of Grace: Antimodernism and the Transformation of American Culture, 1880-1920* (New York: Pantheon Books, 1981), passim, esp. Chs. 4 and 5.

42. The statistical procedure used is mentioned in footnote 16. For exact proportions in the denominational comparison and for an extensive discussion of the data, see my dissertation. Dorothy Ann Lipson reports that the clergymen who joined the Masonic fraternity in Connecticut during the early 1800s came disproportionately from "countervailing" denominations to the Congregationalist establishment, namely, Episcopalianism and Universalism (which was akin to Unitarianism). Lipson, *Freemasonry in Federalist Connecticut*, 128n, 129.

43. On the Genesee Conference, see *Smith, Revivalism and Social Reform*, 129-133; on the California Conference, C. V. Anthony, A.M., D.D., *Fifty Years of Methodism: A History of the Methodist Episcopal Church within the Bounds of the California Annual Conference from 1847 to 1897* (San Francisco: Methodist Book Concern, 1901), 149 and 146-147.

44. Wilna Lucie Edsen, "Early German Churches of San Francisco," MA Thesis (University of California, 1929), 108-

157, esp. 149, 152, 156-157; Ahlstrom, *Religious History*, II, 217-219.

45. The estimate for the proportion of Jews in the San Francisco fraternity is based on a name analysis of a random sample of 1000 Masons taken from the years 1870-1900. The corresponding figure for the Jewish proportion in the city's population is based on an estimate for 1890, but this proportion did not fluctuate greatly over the 1870-1900 period. Details of the name analysis procedure and the method of estimating the Jewish population in the city are presented in my article, "Religious Assimilation in a Fraternal Organization: Jews and Freemasonry in Gilded-Age San Francisco," *American Jewish History* 74 (June, 1985): 369-403.

46. "Freemasonry and Religion: A Concise View of the Origin, Progress and Ultimate Aims of the Masonic Institution," *The Hebrew* (San Francisco, August 25, 1865): 4.

47. These points are argued at greater length in my article, "Religious Assimilation in a Fraternal Organization."

48. *Masonic Mirror* (April, 1870): 267-268; *Proceedings* (1873), 24.

49. For example, *Proceedings* (1880), 553; *Proceedings* (1898), 818, 826-827.

50. *Trestleboard* (August, 1892): 372; Ibid. (January, 1896): 42-43; Ibid. (June, 1896): 319-320; Ibid. (September, 1896): 459; John Higham, *Send These To Me: Jews and Other Immigrants in Urban America* (New York: Atheneum, 1975), 116-173.

51. *Proceedings* (1895), 255.

52. *Trestleboard* (February, 1894): 88-89; Ibid. (January, 1895): 36-37; Ibid. (January, 1896): 40.

53. *Masonic Mirror* (November 11, 1871), 9; *Proceedings*

(1887), 168.

54. Sherman, *Fifty Years*, II, 556.

55. *Proceedings* (1875), 15.

11.
The Mexican American Catholic Community in California, 1850-1980

Jeffrey M. Burns

The Mexican American Catholic community has the unique distinction of being the oldest and newest immigrant group in California, as well as being the largest Catholic immigrant group in the state. Despite this distinction, the history of the Mexican American Catholic community has been largely neglected. Three recent studies by Albert Camarillo, Richard Romo, and Richard Griswold del Castillo have done much to delineate the contours of Mexican American society in southern California, but none adequately describe the religious dimension of Mexican American life.[1] As Leo Grebler's study, *The Mexican American: The Nation's Second Largest Minority*, asserted in 1970, "Despite the importance of this group [Mexican Americans] to the Church (and vice versa), no literature exists on the role of the Church among the Mexican American population." Outside of recent studies by Michael Neri and Antonio Soto, and several articles by Francis Weber, the Grebler assessment remains true as of 1984.[2] In this essay I intend to sketch an historical overview of the relationship of the Church and the Mexican American population in California between the years 1850 and 1980.

California had been a province of Mexico until 1848 when it was ceded to the United States in the Treaty of Guadalupe Hidalgo. As of 1850, when California was admitted to the Union, the remnants of the Franciscan mission system remained highly visible. Though the common perception has been that the California Church had collapsed with the secularization of the missions and the transfer to American rule, regular church life was maintained in California through the careful ministrations of Franciscan Father Gonzalez Rubio, administrator of the California Catholic Church from 1846 to 1850. Fifteen of the twenty one missions still had resident pastors, and the other six were visited frequently by missionary priests. Resident pastors were present at

255

the pueblos of Los Angeles and San Jose.[3] The Hispanic cast of the California Church, however, was on the wane as the Gold Rush brought hordes of non-Mexican immigrants to California. San Francisco was quickly transformed into an American city with the Spanish speaking population assuming a decidedly minority position. In Santa Barbara and Los Angeles the transfer of cultural hegemony from the Mexican community to the American Anglo community was not completed until 1880.

Though California experienced a burst of Mexican immigration in the 1850s as a result of the Gold Rush, Mexican immigration slowed considerably during the last half of the nineteenth century. As of 1900 the foreign-born Mexican population numbered less than 10,000.   The advent of the twentieth century brought increasingly large numbers of Mexican immigrants to California. In 1910 the foreign born Mexican population had risen to 33,444, jumping to 86,610 in 1920, and, amazingly, 199,165 by 1930.[4] The rapid increase was due in large measure to the dislocation created by the Mexican Revolution, but it was also spurred by the expanding economy of southern California which was desperately in need of a cheap labor supply. Immigration declined during the period 1930-1950, and in fact an aggressive drive was launched in the 1930s to "repatriate" the Mexican immigrant. The Depression had made jobs scarce, and the Mexican, who was at best minimally accepted when his labor was needed, was now forcefully driven from the state. Mexican immigration again increased as post-war prosperity came to California. As many as 5,400 Mexicans entered California each month during the 1950s, with about 350,000 entering California legally between 1953-1959. By 1964 over 2,000,000 Spanish speaking people (the vast majority being Mexican American), were in California with over 700,000 residing in the Los Angeles metropolitan area, accounting for about twenty percent of the area's total population.[5] By 1970, fifty percent of all Mexican Americans living in the Southwest United States resided in California, up from thirty percent in 1930.[6] Significant to the Church in California was the fact that nearly ninety percent of these immigrants were at least nominally Catholic, thereby posing enormous pastoral problems for the California Church.

The history of the Catholic Church's care for her Mexican faithful has been termed by one historian "a history of neglect."[7] While this assertion may be true for the period 1880-1980, it was less true for the period 1850-1880. The early Mexican community was made up of two distinct groups--newly arrived immigrants and a group which had resided in California for several generations, the latter referring to themselves as "Californios" to distinguish themselves from the new arrivals. The Californios remained the social and political elite in southern California until the 1880s when the emerging Yankee class stripped them of their land and power. The newly arrived Mexican immigrants clustered from the beginning at the bottom of the socio-economic ladder and were referred to by the Californios as *cholos* (scoundrels) as the Californios wished to keep a separate identity. The Yankee made no such distinction and the Californios soon joined the *cholos* at the bottom of the American society.[8]

Despite their loss of power in San Francisco in the early 1850s, a significant group of Spanish-speaking Catholics continued to reside in the city. The first Archbishop of San Francisco, Joseph Sadoc Alemany, O.P. (archbishop of Monterey-Los Angeles 1850-1853, and archbishop of San Francisco 1853-1884), adopted a conciliatory attitude to the recently displaced Spanish-speaking community and the newly arrived Mexican immigrants. St. Francis of Assisi parish in San Francisco initially provided ministry to the Spanish-speaking, offering a sermon in Spanish at the 8:30 Mass on Sunday mornings. In 1875 Our Lady of Guadalupe Parish (Nuestra Señora de Guadalupe) was established as a Spanish national parish to provide better pastoral care for the Spanish-speaking residents of San Francisco. Further south in the archdiocese large hispanic communities remained around Mission San Jose and Mission San Juan Bautista. In southern San Mateo County, another special parish for the Spanish-speaking, Our Lady of the Pillar (Nuestra Señora del Pilar) was established in 1868. Alemany also provided a Spanish speaking priest for the Mexican gold miners who lived in Sonora in the 1850s. Furthermore, Alemany decreed in the early 1850s that the Mexican population could request a priest of their own nationality to perform their weddings. Historian Michael Neri concludes, "such a decree indicated Alemany's high regard for the Spanish speaking Catholics in California."[9]

However, the institutional church did not enjoy such amicable relations with the larger Mexican communities at Santa Barbara and Los Angeles. From the time of his appointment as Bishop of Monterey and Los Angeles in 1853, Bishop Thaddeus Amat, C.M., a Spaniard like Alemany, demonstrated little sympathy for the Mexican Catholicism he found in his diocese. Amat set out to monitor the religious orthodoxy of his Mexican faithful and to bring them into closer conformity with the American Church. Amat's efforts won him little popularity with his Mexican flock. In one of Amat's earliest pastorals he chastised the people for their careless attitude toward religious observances and the laxity of their moral behavior. To many in the Mexican community used to the easygoing ministrations of the Franciscan padres, the bishop's tone sounded judgemental and threatening rather than paternal. Furthermore, Amat had little patience with Mexican folk Catholicism. Amat prohibited many fiestas as he believed their disorderly quality left the Church open to ridicule from Americans. Nonetheless several fiestas were continued without official approbation. Other folk practices such as the rituals of the *curanderas* or folk-healers, were vigorously discouraged. In Santa Barbara in 1858, Amat suspended the Mexican Franciscans for (among other things) "fomenting superstition."[10] The Franciscan crime was that they tolerated the Mexican folk customs among which was the selling of burial shrouds. Amat contended that such practices amounted to attempts to "purchase heaven." The ancient Indian practices were lost on Amat. Central to his objections was the fear that the "ceremonies, cults and devotions of corrupt Catholicism" (a phrase used by one of Amat's priests in describing Mexican Catholicism),[11] would discredit the Church in the eyes of the increasingly predominant Anglo American society.

At the center of the conflict then, was the difficult switch from a Mexican to an American Catholic Church. The conflict was aggravated by Amat's seeming lack of understanding of the social and historical context of post-Mexican California. His Spanish speaking faithful "saw themselves as victims of American expansionism, who were being disenfranchised socially, culturally, politically, and economically under the new American regime."[12] Amat's policies and attempts to enforce strict discipline seemed like more of the same. One legacy of the conflict would be a continuing chasm between the official and "underground" Church within the Mexican community throughout the twentieth century.

Despite the conflict with Amat, religion continued to permeate the daily life of the Mexican American community throughout the nineteenth century. In the 1850s in Los Angeles, Mexican community life centered around the Plaza Church located in downtown Los Angeles. Little distinction was made between "religious" and "secular" life. As one historian has noted, "it [the Plaza Church] was the place where the community celebrated its traditional secular and religious fiestas, events which had a collective significance unifying the town and reaffirming traditional loyalties."[13]

The numerous fiestas in Los Angeles were legend; central festivals focused on Holy Week, the feast of the Assumption, and numerous feasts in honor of Mary. One major fiesta, the feast of Corpus Christi, was celebrated forty days after Easter, and was described by a contemporary in the following manner:

> On Corpus Christi Day, there was a procession around the Plaza. In front of their homes the wealthier families erected altars, many of which were decorated with satin, lace and even costly jewelry. The procession started from the Church after the four o'clock service and halted at each one of the altars in turn for formal worship, the procedure not requiring less than two hours, one feature being twelve men, who represented the apostles, carrying great candles.[14]

Most fiestas included bull fighting, dancing and general feasting, all of which contributed to the general good spirits of the Mexican community. Despite the active fiestas and ceremonies, however, by the end of the nineteenth century formal religious participation was in serious decline among the Mexican community.

The final two decades of the ninetenth century witnessed the first generation that had to face the reality of being "Mexican in an Anglo society."[15] During this period, the Mexican American community would find itself socially and residentially isolated from the Anglo community, and relegated to the bottom rung of the socio-economic ladder in California in a process termed "barrioization" by historian Albert Camarillo. This barrioization of the Mexican American coincided with increasing neglect and isolation from the mainstream Catholic Church in California. By 1900 few Mexicans were attending the formal worship services of the Church. One historian concluded that for most Mexican Americans, the Church's symbolic and spiritual meanings were more important than its hierarchy and formal services.[16] The most important rites of passage--baptism, marriage, confirmation and burial--continued to be celebrated in the Church but more daily devotions remained detached from parish life. In Los Angeles, the growing sense of religious isolation felt by the Mexican community from the Anglo community was made complete with the opening of St. Vibiana's Cathedral in 1876. The Hispanic community continued celebrating at the Plaza Church in downtown Los Angeles, while the Anglo community moved to the more fashionable Cathedral parish. And in Santa Barbara, "by the 1880s there was little other than tradition that attracted the Chicanos to the Church. Importantly, after 1883, a Spanish surnamed priest was seldom resident at the parish or mission."[17]

As the Church entered the twentieth century in California, the history of ministry to the Mexican American seemed to have become a "history of neglect." Despite their vast numbers, Mexican Americans have often seemed invisible to the American Church. The recurrent neglect of the Mexican American has been attributed to a chronic shortage of Mexican priests. The Chancery Archives of San Francisco, Los Angeles and San Diego are full of requests for Mexican priests from Mexican parishioners.[18] The problem was that few priests were imported from Mexico and priestly vocations from among the Mexican American community were virtually non-existent. A common mistake made in ministry to the Mexican American was the belief that all that was necessary was Spanish-speaking priests. In Los Angeles the Spanish Vincentians and Spanish Augustinians were imported to minister to the Mexican community. However, a wide gap existed between Spanish and Mexican mentalities. One pastor in the 1930s argued that Spanish priests had difficulty in understanding "the psychology, manner, relgious feeling, and educational problems of the Mexican."[19] The Spanish priests were often criticized for remaining too aristocratic and aloof. The simple importation of Spanish priests backfired at times, with the Spanish priest aggravating the isolation of the Mexican American from parish life.

Central to the "Mexican problem," as it was referred to in Chancery circles, was the inability to develop strong ties between the Mexican and his or her parish. The Mexican Catholic was repeatedly accused of making only limited economic sacrifices for the maintenance of the Church. Mexicans seemed content to take over churches built by previous ethnic groups and showed little interest in the American Catholic passion for building the "parish plant." Moreover, pastors from San Diego to San Francisco complained about the infrequency with which Mexicans attended the sacraments. One pastor noted that for most Mexicans "Confession once in a lifetime is sufficient."[20] Estimates suggest that only twenty to thirty-three percent of Mexican Catholics attended Mass regularly. In addition, the Mexican was regarded as uninstructed in his faith and superstitious in his devotional life, and, to the frustration of the American clergy, showed little interest in changing. Parish societies achieved limited success, and what parish life did exist was limited to women. Societies for men were nearly impossible to maintain.

The lack of regular observance on the part of Mexican Catholics was of great concern to pastors who feared the Mexican immigrant would be lost to Protestantism. Although there were over twenty Protestant missions to Mexicans in Los Angeles in 1920, few inroads were made by Protestants as the Mexican immigrant remained staunchly loyal to the Catholic Church.[21] Nonetheless, the presence of several small, evangelical Mexican churches created a fear that the Mexican was lost to the Church.

Strategies for ministry differed in northern and southern California, but neither seemed to make the Mexican a practical Catholic. In the north, a separate ministry to the Mexican American was often discouraged. In mixed parishes pastors tended to concern themselves more with their more regular and financially generous parishioners than they did with their erratic Mexicans. In the south, as many as twenty-four Mexican national parishes were established in Los Angeles and San Diego, but these proved too few to incorporate all the area's Mexicans, and had the untoward effect of creating a less effective ministry to the Mexican community. One observer complained, "some pastors waive responsibility to [sic] the Mexican American because of the national parish."[22] The Mexican Americans were sent to the national parish, despite the fact that not enough such parishes existed to meet their needs.

Central to the failure of ministry to the Mexican American was a continual lack of resources, but racial prejudice seems to be another reason for their neglect, or at least for their isolation. A typical letter found in the Chancery Archives of San Diego reads, "because we are Mexicans [we] are treated as accursed and despised by him [their pastor] who...should defend us."[23]

As had been the case with previous immigrant groups, at the heart of the "Mexican problem" was a conflict over what it meant to be Catholic. Mexican Americans resisted attempts to be regularized and Americanized. The Mexican faith thrived on non-liturgical devotions of a popular nature which have not always been approved by the official Church. Particularly strong among Mexican Americans was their devotion to Mary, particularly to Our Lady of Guadalupe. The majority of Mexican churches are devoted to Our Lady. The passionate devotion to Mary seemed excessive to Anglo Catholics even during "the age of Mary." Appropriately, one of the most active Mexican religious societies at the parish level was the Sociedad Guadalupana, which attempted to utilize Mexican devotion to Mary as a cornerstone for drawing them into more active participation in parish life.

The Marian devotion served as the basis for many fiestas and processions (fiestas and processions remained integral parts of Mexican Catholicism throughout the twentieth century). Particularly popular was the procession and fiesta surrounding the feast of Our Lady of Guadalupe. Another popular Marian ritual was called *mananitas.* In this ritual, the people rose early in the morning, arrived at the Church prior to the first Mass, and proceeded to serenade the Blessed Virgin. The love of procession and ceremonial also informed two traditional Christmas processions, *Las Posadas* and *Los Pastores.* In *Las Posadas,* two parishioners dressed up as Mary and Joseph, rode a burro, and led a procession from house to house in the parish in "search of lodging." The procession ended with a large party. Similarly in *Los Pastores,* twelve parishioners dressed up as shepherds and led a procession from home to home.

The Mexican reluctance to participate in parish life stemmed in part from the strength of the Mexican extended family. The religious socialization of the Mexican child took place largely within the home, as traditional teachings and devotions were passed on within the family. This tradition is called *religion casera.* As one observer explained, "the greater part of one's faith life and devotional life is learned from mothers and grandmothers who make use of novenas, prayers and *imagenes* to communicate the religious sense and to foster a personal and family spirituality. This whole strain of religiosity has been developed without the need for the presence of priests and is generally unrelated to the official liturgical life of the Church."[24] The family nature of religious life is further emphasized by the system of godparents or *compadrazgo* (literally co-parenthood).[25] Godparents are chosen for the child's baptism, first communion, confirmation, and marriage, making it possible for one child to have as many as eight godparents. The role of the godparents is taken as a serious responsibility, which incorporates the godparents into the family in an integral way. Ironically, church functions created an even more extensive Mexican family network, which in turn increased Mexican distance from the parish.

One last element of the popular religiosity of the Mexican

American community is the celebration of and devotion to patron saints. Families celebrated the feast days of their patron saints, but the communal celebration of saint's days could also incorporate the family into the life of the larger community. Towns and villages would hold elaborate celebrations in honor of their patron saints. Celebrations might last as long as a week, consisting of "processions, pilgrimages, novenas, tridua, missions as well as fireworks, fiestas, dances and social gatherings."[26] The celebrations did much to develop the spirit of the community. Ironically, in Montecito, the celebration of the local patron saint's day, which had served to integrate the entire community in the nineteenth century, came to symbolize the Mexican community's isolation from the Anglo community. Anglos viewed the celebration as a "romantic diversion," while to the Mexican community it remained an important communal celebration.[27]

Besides being out of touch religiously with the American Church, the Mexican American found other elements of American culture--elements which the Church actively promoted--difficult to accept. The Mexican sense of alienation increased because of an inability to relate to the American work ethic. For the Mexican, "pleasure is the chief aim of work."[28] Nor was the ambition to succeed highly prized. The Mexican American tended to be more satisfied with his or her existing station in life. Satisfaction was found in one's family and friends. To outsiders, this was often interpreted as sloth. The lack of initiative made many Anglos assume that the Mexican was best suited for menial labor.

Neither did the Mexican family place much stress on formal education. Reports in 1929 and 1963 to the Archdiocese of Los Angeles complained of Mexican American children who came to school or catechism with little previous instruction in the faith. One report reads, "there are hundreds of little children in the parish who don't even know God."[29] The Catholic school and the Confraternity of Christian Doctrine (CCD) were seen as "solutions" to the Mexican problem, but Catholic schooling never really took hold to any significant degree, and education remained rooted in the family.

In the 1920s, the Archdiocese of Los Angeles, under the direction of Bishop John J. Cantwell, began a program designed to Americanize the Mexican immigrant, a task which was seen as "pre-eminently a Catholic undertaking."[30] Supra-parochial organizations such as the National Catholic Welfare Conference and the Knights of Columbus organized citizenship classes for the Mexicans. To draw the Mexican into American life these groups promoted athletic programs (especially baseball), classes for mothers, and picnics and sewing classes for young girls. The Knights published a Spanish language *Civics Catechism* which discussed the rights and duties of U.S. citizens.[31] Cantwell expressed an age-old dictum which had been used for other immigrant groups when he observed, "in making better Catholics we shall be making better citizens."[32]

Despite the intense efforts of church and civic agencies few Mexicans filed for citizenship. As a Los Angeles priest observed in the 1920s, "as long as Americans treat Mexicans as an inferior race, undervalue their work and mistreat them in general, Mexicans would show little interest in becoming American citizens."[33] Americanization of both a religious and civic nature has also been frustrated by the constant influx of Mexican immigrants. In 1970, twenty-four percent of the Mexican population in Los Angeles remained first generation, and the influx of immigrants has increased since 1970.

While the Archdiocese of Los Angeles tried to Americanize the Mexican immigrant, it also devoted considerable resources to their temporal and spiritual care. Archbishop Cantwell has been called by one historian the "Irish born champion of the Mexican Americans."[34] In fact, aside from Archbishop Robert Lucey of San Antonio, Cantwell was one of the few members of the hierarchy who seriously addressed the Mexican problem. Under Cantwell the Archdiocese sponsored several settlement houses and recreation centers for the Mexican Americans. Health clinics which primarily benefitted the Mexican community were set up in the poorer neighborhoods. In the 1920s over fifty percent of the expenditures of the Archdiocese's Catholic Welfare Bureau were devoted to the Mexican community. Despite these efforts the temporal and pastoral needs of the Mexican remained overwhelming and Cantwell's efforts were not enough. To the modern activist, Cantwell's attitude toward the Mexican may seem too paternalistic, and he may have seemed overly concerned with the Americanization of the Mexican immigrant. Despite Cantwell's concern the Mexican remained isolated from the institutional Church.

Another reason for the failure of the Mexican American to be integrated into the American system was that the Mexican American has remained at the bottom of the socioeconomic heap. As late as 1970, seventy-seven percent of the Mexican work force in Los Angeles remained among the laboring classes.[35] Reports from Mexican parishes in San Diego from the 1940s to the 1960s repeatedly refer to the "economic decline" among their parishioners.[36] Social mobility continues to be a problem for the Mexican American community.

If the urban Mexican has suffered from poverty and neglect, the plight of the rural Mexican community has been worse. In 1940, the Mexican was the most rural of the ethnic minorities (though they were still over sixty-five percent urban). Mexican Americans were the "backbone of California agriculture," working as migrant and seasonal laborers.[37] Ministry to this group of migrant Catholics was non-existent at times, and at most consisted of a priest occasionally visiting the workers at their camps. In 1949 the Archdiocese of San Francisco developed a traveling Spanish Mission Band to serve the agricultural community. The Band went from Mexican center to Mexican center, giving missions, saying Mass, and administering the sacraments. Weekly service to the agricultural worker, however, remained irregular.

In 1951, a member of the Spanish Mission Band, Father John Garcia, reported his endeavors to the Archbishop. Garcia noted several semi-stable Mexican communities around Richmond and Berkeley, but observed that Mass attendance and knowledge of the faith were low. He cited as causes lack of personal contact with priests, a situation caused by language difficulties as much as anything, and also the large distances Mexicans were required to travel in order to attend Mass. Garcia began a home visitation program emphasizing the recitation of the rosary in the home. He complained of financial problems and the need for more personnel. Missions organized in these areas were well attended (averaging 300 per mission). Garcia then lamented the difficulty of working with Mexican migrants as they were continually on the move. He reported:

> Lately I have been concentrating more on the camps. Around Brentwood during peak season, lasting about six months, there are about 1,000 men to say nothing of women and children. These are practically all Catholic and there are many more between Brentwood and Stockton, a distance of thirty miles.... I have been going to camp in the evenings, saying the rosary, giving talks, hearing confessions, and saying the Mass in the morning before they go to work.... Perhaps something could be worked out with other dioceses to keep following the migratory worker. They keep moving from one diocese to the other, yet they still remain Catholic and in need of a priest.[38]

In short, personnel, resources and above all planning were needed if the Mexican American farm workers were going to be cared for properly.

The Mission Band's close contact with the farmworker's led to an increasing concern for social justice. Several of the mission priests sympathized with efforts to provide unions for the farm workers, and several priests spoke out against the abuses of the farm owners. In 1962, the Spanish Mission Band was disbanded, ostensibly because Oakland, Santa Rosa, and Stockton were separated from the Archdiocese of San Francisco to form their own separate dioceses. However, there is some evidence to suggest that the mission priests were becoming too strident in their complaints against the growers (who in many cases were well-to-do Catholics), and the reorganization of the Archdiocese presented the Bishop with a chance to avoid this increasingly difficult situation. Not until the late 1960s would the Church hierarchy actively support the Mexican farmworker.

The common perception of the Mexican American Catholic community for the period 1962-1980 is that it has moved increasingly into the social justice arena. Church support of Cesar Chavez and the farmworkers protests of the 1960s and 1970s was a watershed in the relationship of the Church and the Mexican American community. Unlike many of the more radical Chicano movements which saw the Church as irrelevant, Chavez made explicit use of Catholic symbols and rhetoric. Preaching Christian non-violence, Chavez could tell his followers that "to be a man is to suffer for others." Present at all Chavez's protests was a large banner of the Virgin Mother of Guadalupe. Besides its newly found support of the Mexican farmworker, the Church also became active in neighborhood organizing among Mexican Americans. In East Los Angeles, the Church was instrumental in the formation of UNO (United Neighborhood Organization) which is an action group centered in the area's parishes. The Church's support of Chavez and of organizations such as UNO, as well as various episcopal pronouncements indicate an increasing commitment to social justice on the part of institutional Catholicism.

While the Church's more aggressive stance has proved attractive to many Mexican Americans, the primary problems confronting the Mexican American Catholic community remain the same: a lack of priests who can speak Spanish and a lack of funds to provide for the proper pastoral care of the Mexican community. The pastor of a parish in Riverside expressed a common lament in his annual report of 1975: "The parish is badly in need of an associate; great potential is going down the drain, and what could become an alive Catholic community is becoming another neglected Mexican American barrio."[39]

Successful ministry to the Mexican American Catholic community requires more than just money and priests; it also requires a fundamental the restructuring of expectations and a greater acceptance of Mexican culture. Happily, with the appearance of the recent pastoral on Hispanics issued by the U.S.

Bishops entitled "The Hispanic Presence: Challenge and Commitment," a more open attitude to Mexican culture would seem to be in the offing. The pastoral challenges Catholics "to be more 'catholic,' more open to the diversity of religious expression." It also encourages study of Hispanic prayer forms and Hispanic culture, an appreciation of the familial quality of Mexican religiosity, and an appreciation of the "popular Catholicism" manifest in the Hispanic community.[40] In short, the pastoral suggests a greater acceptance and tolerance of Hispanic culture and practices, a policy which represents a sharp break with the Church's century-long policy of Americanization.

The shift in Church policy has resulted in some confusion and contradiction. In a recent forum on Hispanic ministry in the Diocese of Orange the same complaints that have been circulating for over 100 years once again resurfaced. Participants complained that the Mexican American did not attend the sacraments regularly, and that Mexican knowledge of the faith was poor. More fundamentally, one speaker complained, "I note a lack of incentive among Hispanics. There is a need to convince them to strive for a better life."[41] Ironically, not long after the forum, the leading spokesman for the Diocese of Orange on Hispanic matters was quoted as saying, "it is the Church's conviction that Latinos should become critical of the Americanization process," and the Bishops' pastoral warned Hispanic youth of "self-seeking values" and "dreams of success at any price" which seem to be such a fundamental part of the American system.[42] At the heart of the new policy toward the Hispanic community is a new definition of "a better life." It is no longer assumed that the American way is best. It is now conceded that the American community may learn much from the attitudes and values of the Mexican American Catholic community. Though this attitude is a long way from being accepted at a popular level, it marks a switch on the part of the hierarchy away from the aggressive Americanization policies which have characterized Church and Mexican American relations for over a century.

Notes

This article is also being published in a forthcoming collection by Paulist Press entitled *The American Catholic Parish*. It is printed here by permission of Paulist Press.

1. Albert Camarillo, *Chicanos in a Changing Society: From Mexican Pueblos to American Barrios in Santa Barbara and Southern California* (Cambridge, MA: Harvard University Press, 1979); Richard Griswold del Castillo, *The Los Angeles Barrio, 1850-1880: A Social History* (Berkeley and Los Angeles: University of California Press, 1979); Richard Romo, *East Los Angeles: History of a Barrio* (Austin: University of Texas Press, 1983).

2. Leo Grebler et al., *The Mexican American People: The Nation's Second Largest Minority* (New York: Free Press, 1970), 456-7. Michael C. Neri, "Hispanic Catholicism in Transitional California: The Life Of José Gonzalez Rubio, O.F.M. (1804-1875)," (Ph.D. dissertation, Graduate Theological Union, Berkeley, 1974); Antonio R. Soto, "The Chicano and the Church in Northern California, 1848-1978" (Ph.D. dissertation, University of California, 1978); and Francis Weber, "Irish-Born Champion of the Mexican American", *California Historical Society Quarterly* 49 (September, 1970): 233-249.

3. Harry B. Morrison, "Report to the Bishop on the History of the Mexican Americans, 1983", unpublished manuscript, Archives of the Diocese of Oakland, Oakland, California.

4. Warren S. Thompson, *Growth and Changes in California's Population* (Los Angeles: Haynes Foundation, 1955), 70.

5. Castillo, *Los Angeles Barrio*, 40.

6. "Mexican Americans," *Harvard Encyclopedia of American Ethnic Groups* (Cambridge, MA: Harvard University Press, 1980), 699.

7. Castillo, *Los Angeles Barrio*, 169.

8. See Leonard Pitt, *The Decline of the Californios: A Social History Of Spanish Speaking Californians* (Berkeley and Los Angeles: University of California Press, 1971).

9. Neri, "Hispanic Catholicism," 110.

10. Francis Weber, *California's Reluctant Prelate: The Life and Times of Right Reverend Thaddeus Amat, C.M.* (Los Angeles: Dawson Book Shop, 1964), 56.

11. Quoted in Neri, "Hispanic Catholicism," 174.

12. Ibid., 136.

13. Castillo, *Los Angeles Barrio*, 17.

14. Francis Weber, *The Old Plaza Church: A Documentary History* (Hong Kong: Cathay Press Limited, 1980), 182.

15. Camarillo, *Chicanos in a Changing Society*, 78.

16. Castillo, *Los Angeles Barrio*, 168.

17. Camarillo, *Chicanos in a Changing Society*, 63.

18. For example, a letter in the Parish File for Our Lady of Guadalupe, San Francisco, in the Chancery Archives of the Archdiocese of San Francisco, written by a parishioner to the Archbishop in 1956 states, "It is imperative for us Mexicans to have a good Mexican priest in our Church instead of the actual priest now in charge." This letter is quite typical.

19. Parish Files, Archives of the Diocese of San Diego, San Diego, California.

20. Ibid.

21. G. Broxley Oxnam, *The Mexican in Los Angeles* (Los Angeles: Los Angeles City Survey, 1920).

22. Parish Files, Archives of the Diocese of San Diego.

23. Ibid.

24. Rigoberto Calcoa-Rivas, "U.S. Hispanics and the Catholic Church," *The Oakland Catholic Voice*, 26 September 1983, p. 18.

25. George Crispin, "Understanding the Hispanic Family", *The Oakland Catholic Voice,* 3 October 1983, p. 10.

26. Calcoa-Rivas, "U.S. Hispanics", 18.

27. Camarillo, *Chicanos in a Changing Society*, 63.

28. Pitt, *The Decline of the Californios*, 13.

29. Parish Files, Archives of the Diocese of San Diego.

30. Grebler, *The Mexican American,* 457.

31. Romo, *East Los Angeles*, 145.

32. Francis Weber, *John Joseph Cantwell: His Excellency of Los Angeles* (Hong Kong: Cathay Press Limited, 1971), 105.

33. Quoted in Romo, *East Los Angeles*, p. 147.

34. Weber, "Irish-Born Champion of the Mexican American," passim.

35. Castillo, *Los Angeles Barrio*, 175.

36. Parish Files, Archives of the Diocese of San Diego.

37. *Harvard Encyclopedia of American Ethnic Groups*, 697.

38. Parish Files, Archives of the Diocese of Oakland.

39. Parish Files, Archives of the Diocese of San Diego.

40. U.S. Bishops, "The Hispanic Presence: Challenge and Commitment," *Origins* 13 (19 January 1984): 530-541.

41. "Hispanic Leaders Express Concerns for Young Adults," *The Diocese of Orange Bulletin*, July, 1983, p. 7.

42. David Reyes, "In Pursuit of the Latino American Dream," *Southern California's Latino Community* (Los Angeles: Los Angeles *Times*, 1983) 14; U.S. Bishops, "The Hispanic Presence," 536.

12.

A Balm in Gilead: The Black Church and the Thrust for Civil Rights in California, 1850-1880

Larry G. Murphy

The year 1850 marks the numerically significant influx of blacks into the State of California and the beginning of their fight against discrimination. By 1880, *de jure* discrimination had been challenged and, for the most part, eliminated. Black Californians then turned to capitalizing on their gains while yet contending with a persistent discrimination *de facto*. This essay will examine the way in which the black church and the black appropriation of Christianity informed this movement for social and political justice.

Across the nation, the church was a focal institution in black communities. For slaves, among whom it was often a clandestine, unofficial organization, the church gathering served as one of the few oases of respite and relief from the ardors of chatteldom.[1] There in retreat with their fellow sufferers, their burdens could be laid down, if but for a moment, and they could celebrate their common joy in God's acceptance of them, as well as their hope in God's deliverance. For free blacks, the church was one of the few institutions which they wholly owned and administered. This was a particularly attractive feature because it gave opportunity for them to exercise skills and invest creative energies in an agency which was black oriented and could return both personal status and concrete benefits for the black community. Further, the church building was usually the only public facility available to blacks for community meetings and social functions.[2]

The importance of the church in the lives of black Americans was evidenced in the fact that whenever black settlements or communities were established the church followed close behind; often it was the black preacher who led in the founding of a new community and who became its patriarch. California was no exception to this pattern. When "gold fever" spread through the East in the latter 1840s, blacks were among those infected, or sometimes affected. That is to say, many blacks set out to seek their fortunes in the California gold fields, and many others were brought as slaves to assist the masters in the treasure hunt. In 1850, the year California was officially initiated into statehood, its first black church, St. Andrews African Methodist Episcopal (AME) Church, was established. Located in Sacramento, then one of the major cities of the mining region, and organized by the Rev. Bernard "Barney" Fletcher, St. Andrews was admitted to the Indiana Conference of the AME Church in 1851.[3]

The following year two more black churches were organized, this time in San Francisco. August 1, 1852 was the founding date of the First AME Zion Church, under the pastorate of the Rev. John J. Moore. In the same month another group of blacks, led by a Rev. Capon, set up a church organization which initially was named the First Colored Baptist Church of San Francisco. The name was later changed to the Third Baptist Church, indicating its chronological relation to the other, white, Baptist churches of the city. Apparently some of the charter members of Third Baptist were previously members of First Baptist (white). The church records of First Baptist show that a church council was called to consider recognizing the new black fellowship. Recognition was granted and on October 11 a public recognition ceremony was held. The black Baptists had no pastor at this time. They held a prayer meeting among themselves and communion was conducted for them by the white Baptist clergy of the city. By 1858, a black pastor had been secured in the person of Rev. Thomas Howell.[4]

On February 14, 1854, some AME's in San Francisco organized themselves into the St. Cyprian's Bethel AME Church. The Rev. Barney Fletcher left the Sacramento church to another local preacher, the Rev. Darius Stokes, and came to San Francisco as pastor to the newly-formed congregation. Numerous other AME congregations were organized throughout northern California, largely as a result of the work of the Rev. T. M. D. Ward, who came to California in 1854 as the first AME Missionary Elder to the West Coast.[5]

AME Zion churches were to be found in Napa, San Francisco, Stockton, Sacramento, and Marysville. And there were two congregations under the charge of the Rev. P.W. Cassey, a deacon of the Protestant Episcopal Church. The first of Cassey's mission congregations, St. Phillip's, was in San Jose, the other, St. Cyprian's, was in San Francisco.[6]

A spirit of friendly cooperation existed among the various black churches. For instance, during the 1863 Annual Conference of the AME Church, AME preachers conducted services in each of the three San Francisco churches.[7] When the new Bethel Church building was dedicated in 1865, Zion pastor J.J. Moore participated in the ceremony. Moore also joined with Ward and W.H. Hall on a project to establish a literary institute for young men. On another occasion, the Rev. Cassey conducted his Episcopal services in Zion and Bethel churches [8]

Between the black and white churches there was some limited cooperation. Two instances of whites helping in the establishment of black churches have already been mentioned. In addition, the Rev. J.L. Shuck, a white Southerner, organized the black Siloam Baptist Church, Sacramento.[9] And in 1865, T.M.D. Ward sent to the California Annual Conference of the Methodist Church a report of AME progress on the Coast. In the letter Ward tendered thanks to those Methodist clergy who had "...rendered [to AME's] substantial help in prosecuting this great work." Unfortunately, Ward did not specify what aid had been rendered. The Methodist conference issued a statement of congratulations to the AME's on their progress and encouraged their continued advancement.[10] Occasionally, white Methodist clergy visited the sessions of the AME Annual Conference personally to give encouragement and moral support.

The black Baptists of the state were in regular affiliation with their white fellow Baptists. The Sacramento Valley Baptist Association and the San Francisco Baptist Association (merged into one body around 1861) included all Baptist churches in the State--black, white and Chinese. Apparently none of the white churches had programs of evangelism among blacks. The minutes of their annual associational meetings included reports on home missions but the work was only among what were termed the "heathens"--Chinese and Native Americans.

In terms of the movement for citizen's rights and social progress, the cooperation given to blacks by the white churches was scant. The statements of officers and committees of the Baptist associations referred to black Baptist congregations with respect and concern as regards strictly church affairs, but the special problems and needs of blacks as an oppressed class were never noted. The Protestant Episcopal Church gave the Rev. P.W. Cassey no financial aid toward his educational work for blacks. Even the monies he received for his mission work were barely enough to make ends meet.[11] And the Catholic Church seemingly was somewhat hostile to blacks. When black slaves were freed by the Emancipation Proclamation in 1863, the *Monitor*, the Catholic news organ, declared that, "...the Negro on this continent, [sic] is not improved by freedom."[12] The *Monitor* ignored the crucial 1874 Supreme Court decision on black school rights and later asserted that blacks should not attend the public schools with whites.[13]

The record of the white Methodists was somewhat better. In 1862 their Annual Conference adopted a firm stance against slavery; in 1865 a prominent Methodist clergyman, O.M. Briggs, permitted the use of his church building for a session of the Fourth Colored Convention;[14] from 1865 to 1868 the Methodist Conference pronounced in favor of the franchise for blacks. Beyond these supportive public statements there are no indications of corporate Methodist action for the rights of blacks.[15]

The Congregational General Association was very firm in the stand it took in the 1850s and 1860s against slavery, both in California and in the nation at large. In 1859, the Association initiated a boycott of literature from the New York branch of the American Tract Society because of that body's stand that publications attacking slaveholders were unconstitutional. And in 1865, the Association passed a resolution calling on the legislature to grant the franchise to blacks.[16] The General Association thus did more in terms of concrete action than did the other denominational bodies. Yet, what they did was limited.

The Methodist *Advocate* and the Congregationalist *Pacific* carried very widely scattered articles on black rights issues. For the most part black religious and secular activities were ignored. Even such major events as the State Colored Conventions were not reported, though white conventions were noted. This was so even when the events took place in the same city where both papers were published (San Francisco). Further, there was a decided inattention in these papers to issues of racial justice. For instance, in the *Advocate*'s three-part series on the "State of Education" in California, published in January, 1873, there was no mention of the fact that blacks, Chinese, and Native Americans were not allowed into the public schools and thus were growing up without the benefits of learning. The same omission is to be found in the *Pacific's* 1872 article on education entitled "Progress in California."[17]

These religious papers could have been very useful to the black rights movement as one means of exposing and attacking injustice. Yet the only consistent, frequently recurring criticism to be found in them was directed toward Catholics and the alleged antipathy of "Romanism" to American democratic institutions. Rather than social action, these papers, like the denominational associations of the state, focused their concerns on what they conceived to be Christian pietistic issues--temperance, Sabbath observance, prayer, and the cultivation of a "Christian atmosphere" in public institutions and governing bodies.

Thus, as black Californians pursued their religious and civil advancement, they were left largely to their own social and religious resources for the task. It is difficult to determine how many blacks were affiliated with the various churches. Third Baptist Church in 1858 had eighty-four members.[18] Statistics included in the printed minutes of the 1863 AME Conference give the following figures for some of its churches:

Church	Membership
San Francisco	92
Sacramento	32
Stockton	29
Placerville	6
Oakland	8
Marysville	16

The total list included fourteen churches with a total membership of 267.[19] Evaluation of these statistics must take into account two factors. First, they apparently do not reflect those who attended regularly, only official members. Statistics included in the minutes of the Fourth Colored Convention give this accounting of the San Francisco situation: churches, 2; members, 250; attendants, 800.[20] Further, P.A. Bell, referring to only a portion of the black clergy, the AME's, claimed that they "represent a large constituency." Bell also said that the best way to insure an audience (black) for an event was to publicize it in the churches. So it seems that a large portion of the black population had regular, direct contact with the black churches.[21]

Secondly, though the figures given above for official members are small in comparison to the size of the black population, the same apparently held true for the white churches. The minutes of the State Baptist Convention held in 1860 listed the membership figures for all Baptist churches in California. Thirty-three of the fifty-three churches had memberships ranging from fifteen to twenty-five; a church reporting eighty-one members was said to have had a "large congregation."[22] Comparing the membership figures for the largest black and white denominational bodies in the state in 1863 to the number of their potential constituents, the following is revealed:

White Population	Methodist Episcopal
361,353	3,497, or approx. 1%

Black Population	A.M.E.
4,086	240, or approx. 6%

These figures suggest that black churches had a much higher percentage of their potential constitutency in actual membership than did white churches.[23]

In reviewing the available sermons, orations, and journal articles of California's black clergy and laity, one is led to conclude that there were areas of similarity and also areas of fundamental difference between black and white Christians' conception of the faith.

One discovers among blacks what seem to be dogmatic and creedal understandings easily congruent with one or another of the diverse strands of nineteenth-century white American Protestant thought. Hence, the conflict in American Christendom which gave rise to separate black denominations was not related to dogmatic or creedal formulations. The black-white schism was primarily the outgrowth of white racism which denied to black Christians the fellowship and status in the churches accorded to whites. For white American Christians conceived of God's actions in history as primarily in behalf of those who had achieved dominance in the unfolding American drama. And they developed theological constructs which, in their minds, validated their proscriptive, abusive treatment of blacks. Black Christians, on the other hand, were more acutely sensitive to the biblical message of God's commitment to the cause of the oppressed. It was this which informed their theological reflections.

Christianity had been introduced to blacks from the earliest days of their arrival in the colonies as slaves. Mission efforts developed around them; in some cases, special catechisms were written for their instruction. Such notable divines as Cotton Mather, Jonathan Edwards, and John Wesley attended to evangelizing blacks. But white fear of the incendiary potential of the gospel's message of human freedom caused tight restrictions to be placed on the access of blacks to the Bible or to the clerical office. The form in which the faith was presented to them by whites most often supported their servitude and advanced the necessity of acquiescence in their condition. For instance, the biblical text most frequently used for sermons to slaves was

Ephesians 6:5: "Servants, be obedient to them that are your masters...as unto Christ." For this reason many slaves rejected Christianity. But others adopted this new faith as their own because within the biblical literature as they heard it recounted and as they managed secretly to read it for themselves, they perceived the hope for their liberation--in a dual sense. They believed that just as in the Old Testament God's people, the Israelites, were oppressed by their Egyptian overlords and were brought out across Jordan to a Promised Land by God, so, too, would He bring his new people, faithful Christians, across the "deep river" into his promised heavenly kingdom. This was the sense both the missionaries and the planters intended the slaves to receive, and they did. The story of the Hebrew children, however, had another, more mundane signification to the slaves. To them, the saga of the Old Testament Israelites was more than a metaphor of spiritual salvation; it was a paradigm of their own physical deliverance: enslaved blacks were a New Israel, God's oppressed people. And as God once raised up in the midst of His people a Moses to command an exodus, so would he do it again. Indeed, many slave revolt leaders felt themselves to be that Moses. Free blacks, most of whom were ex-slaves, employed the Exodus motif in reference to their own condition; they spoke as persons who, though unbound, were yet abused; they emphasized the sure visitation of God's justice on those who trampled the poor and the weak underfoot.[24]

The writings and speeches of California's black clergy and laity reflect very clearly these conceptions of God as the enforcer of justice and the deliverer of the oppressed. Dr. Ezra Johnson, in an Emancipation Day Oration, drew upon the Scriptures (Ps 12:5) for his description of God as

> ...Him who is thundering in the Heavens for the oppression of the poor: for the sighing of the needy. I [God] will arise. I will set him in safety from him that puffeth at him.[25]

The Civil War and related events elicited from blacks numerous statements of their beliefs about God's action in history. As the fighting raged in the South, the Rev. T.M.D. Ward declared that "...the God of battles is leading on the armies of the free, and breaking, with His strong right hand, the bonds of the oppressed...."[26] In an address before the 1863 AME Annual Conference, Ward reiterated this idea. He chose as his text Jeremiah 10:7, "Who would not fear Thee, O King of Nations?" He said God,

> ...the Dread Avenger, is raining down his wrath on the despot. The death knell of slavery has sounded. At the first shots of the war, the captives shouted "He is coming--our deliverer, he is coming!"

The Conference unanimously adopted a report in which God was credited with emancipation. The war, said the report, was His fearful response of anger, triggered by the cries of the oppressed.[27]

Two years after the war ended, a layperson writing to the *Elevator* over the signature "E.H." used the metaphor of the theater to convey his interpretation of events. In his view,

> The war was ordered by Divine Providence for the delivery of the oppressed. Jeff Davis and Abraham Lincoln (God bless him) were on the stage before the people, but the God of Justice was behind the curtain, and just as sure as God ruleth the destiny of man, just so sure will the oppressed of America be delivered, if they put their trust in him.[28]

In an oration delivered in 1861, the Rev. J.B. Sanderson said that loyal Unionists saw the Emancipation Proclamation as an act of national repentance for the crime of slavery. It was also the coming of the year of jubilee.[29] The slave, said Sanderson, heard in the Proclamation the voice of God saying,

> I have surely seen the afflictions of my people. I have heard their cry by reason of their taskmasters. I have come down to deliver them.... I have surely visited them

and will bring them up out of their afflictions.[30]

Sanderson claimed that Lincoln didn't fully understand the far-reaching significance of the Proclamation; he wrote it hesitantly as a matter of unavoidable state policy. Unbeknownst to him, he was an instrument controlled by the Spirit of God, which controls all the events of life in accordance with His purposes.[31]

The Scripture which Sanderson quoted was part of the narrative of the Exodus. The terminology of this ancient drama was frequently used by blacks in reference to their emancipation. In the 1863 AME Conference, T.M.D. Ward had attested that the pillar of fire which led Israel would also lead blacks through the war's sea of carnage and blood.[32] In an address before a public meeting in San Francisco, in 1865, P.A. Bell dubbed the slain President Lincoln the "Moses of his age." Ezra Johnson, possibly not willing to confer so high an honor on Mr. Lincoln, said that "God has been our leader, and we have passed through the Red Sea, and now rejoice that Canaan is in view."

Black Californians' desire to maintain an unfettered existence was not contingent upon a faith affirmation but rather existed independent of any faith. Blacks expressed the belief that written into the essence of the natural order was the imperative to freedom--both to have it and to permit it. But looking "... through nature up to nature's God," they saw Him as the source of this imperative.[33] That is to say, they felt the inner compulsion to liberty and they witnessed what appeared to be the same force operative in the other entities of the natural order. Combining this observation with the tenets of the Christian faith as they received it, they concluded that the God who created and ruled the universe also instilled and validated in creation the will to freedom. So blacks spoke of the freedoms for which they fought as the "rights of God to Man."[34] The Colored Convention of 1865 published an "Address...to the People of California" which declared that blacks were "free men by creation."[35] P.A. Bell answered a white newspaper editor's attack on the validity of giving blacks full rights by stating that no rights could be granted to blacks which were not already their natural, "God-given" rights. Shameful to say, continued Bell, those rights which had been "restored" by the nation came only under "God-scourging" (the Civil War).[36] And the Rev. J.J. Moore, speaking of the elective franchise for blacks, claimed it was a God-given right; God demanded that it be conceded, he said, and God would reap judgment on the nation until it was given.[37] Thus, the Judeo-Christian tradition was the conceptual framework by which blacks accounted for their instinctive desire for freedom and from which they argued the categorical validity of their claim to civil rights. The rights effort, then, was seen by blacks as a drive to bring human circumstances into line with Divine intention. It was considered to be, at root, a religious enterprise, or, as some blacks termed it, "a holy cause."[38]

Because the rights movement was viewed in this light the black churches as institutions cooperated with it. Minutes of public meetings and articles in the news organs of the period reveal that the churches opened their doors to the public meetings, the strategy sessions, and the lectures connected with the rights movement. They participated in fund-raising drives for the movement. It was in the churches that the Colored Conventions were held, and there that a great many of the colored schools were located. When a long-fought battle of the movement was crowned with victory it was often the church building which housed portions of the victory celebration and the annual commemorations of the victory.

There are very few church records and conference minutes extant today for these black churches. Therefore, it is difficult to assess their involvement in the movement beyond the cooperative type; that is, making their resources available upon request. One can only surmise on the basis of scant evidence. The minutes of the 1863 AME Annual Conference are preserved in full. This body focused its deliberations mainly on matters relating to the state of the church and its progress in membership and evangelism. In terms of subjects not directly related to the church, the Conference resolved to give support and encouragement to the *Pacific Appeal*; this was possibly out of recognition of the role of that news organ as a vital communication channel for black people. The Conference also adopted a report on the state of the country which cheered Emancipation and Union War victories and pledged unreserved assistance in putting down the Rebellion.[39] Beyond this, the Conference embarked upon no social action. Apparently the same was true of each of the Conferences. Their annual meetings were noted in the *Elevator*, the *Advocate* (Methodist organ) and the *Pacific* (Congregational organ), but never is there mention of concrete social action proposed or taken.

Black Baptist churches in the state were usually affiliated with the white state-wide Baptist associations. In the minutes of the associations there is no recorded instance of blacks raising issues of social justice for blacks.[40]

The situation at the congregational level seems to have been the same: there are no indications of public positions taken, confrontations with civil authorities, memorials to legislative bodies, or the like. It appears that the black clergy, when meeting in official church bodies, concerned themselves primarily with strengthening the denominational organization and with the advancement of devotional piety and individual morality.[41]

Yet one sees a different picture when the black clergy are observed outside of the associational structure. They not only cooperated with the black rights movement but were visibly active in it from its inception. This was congruent with the national pattern of black clergy. For instance, among slaves it was the preacher who often acted as liaison between the master and his fellow blacks, securing for them whatever favors and concessions he could obtain from the master. Often it was the preacher who encouraged and led resistance and revolt among slaves. In the community of free blacks, the preachers served much the same functions. Their number included such names as publisher Charles B. Ray, educator Daniel A. Payne, activist/orator Henry H. Garnet, and abolitionist J.B. Sanderson. In the congregational arena, they oversaw the spiritual life and social standards of black people. In the civic arena they fought against slavery, disfranchisement, colonization, proscription in education, and other racial injustices. Following the Civil War, black clergy held a number of seats in the Reconstruction governments; one, the Rev. Hiram R. Revels, served as U.S. Senator.

The California black community saw their black clergy as a locus of power. A delegate to the 1857 Colored Convention, Thomas Duff, said in a *Mirror of the Times* article that there should be preachers in every town, because an intelligent clergy could exert a vast influence.[42] P.A. Bell ascribed much importance to the AME Annual Conference of 1863 and noted that its clergy "...represent a large constituency and wield a powerful influence." Black clergy were conscious of both the power and the responsibility which attached to their pulpits. In a letter to the *Appeal*, The Rev. J.B. Sanderson touched on this point, saying that much of the elevation of black people depended on the pastors; he urged them to redouble their efforts in the rights struggle.[43] A similar sentiment was expressed by the Rev. J.J. Moore. Moore pointed out some of the things necessary for black elevation to independence, such as land and education. Then he said:

> Our clergy must deeply interest themselves on these subjects, if they would be the leaders of our people, which they are. From their position they exert an influence on the young and the old; hence, they must be the guardians of our people's spiritual and temporal interest in a great degree. Let us, under God, be united on this subject, and put forth our mightiest efforts to possess our people of religion, education and land.[44]

The black clergy contributed on every level of the effort for black elevation. From their pulpits they occasionally preached on this theme, as, for instance, the Rev. Hillery's sermon, "The Present Wants of the Colored People," or the Rev. Moore's sermon, "The Common and Particular Duties of the Colored People to Raise Us to the Social Eminence of the Favored Classes."[45] The clergy sometimes stepped from pulpit to podium to lecture on matters affecting blacks, as in AME Bishop J.P. Campbell's address on "The War and Its Issues" and Moore's lecture, "The Rights of the Colored Man in the United States, as a

Man, a Citizen, a Race, and a Christian."[46] Even more frequently, the clergy took to the columns of the black news journals to appeal for black rights, to arouse blacks to action, and to answer the anti-black slanders of whites. [47] Moore even established a paper of his own, the *Lunar Visitor*, which he declared to be devoted to "...the elevation of our race."[48]

The black clergy did not confine their efforts to rhetoric. When the leading black men of the state gathered to formulate plans for concrete action towards attaining black rights, the clergy were there among them; it was the Rev. Sanderson who called to order the first of the Conventions in 1855.[49] They were active in the floor debates, held some Convention offices, and served on the various committees, including the important Business Committee. The Rev. Fielding Smithea was elected one of four vice-presidents at the First Convention; Sanderson was Secretary. Reverends Ward and Moore were appointed to prepare an address to the state's black citizens on the importance of sending their children to school where possible; Sanderson was selected for the State Executive Committee, which was to coordinate the rights activities across the state. At the Second Convention, the Rev. Thomas Detter served on the Business Committee and Sanderson was again appointed to the State Executive Committee. The Fourth Convention delegates made J.J. Moore the chairman of the Business Committee and recording secretary of the State Executive Committee. In addition, the clergy, particularly Moore and Ward, often took the convention floor to make speeches, offer resolutions, and join debates. At the Education Convention of 1871, Sanderson was chosen as vice-president and the Rev. J.H. Hubbard as secretary.

On the local level the clergy were just as active. For example, a meeting of San Francisco blacks appointed the Rev. Fletcher to a committee to draft a public position statement on the Negro suffrage issue. In 1865, the black citizens of Sacramento elected the Rev. Hubbard to the presidency of the Sacramento Executive Committee (the local counterpart of the State Executive Committee). And the Revs. Ward and Flowers were elected to San Francisco's Executive Committee for 1866. The platform which the San Francisco delegation carried to the Fourth Colored Convention was apparently the joint production of San Francisco's clergy. According to P.A. Bell, the clergy came to the delegate-selection meeting with a prepared program which they allegedly forced through.[50]

There was still more variety in the efforts of black clergy on behalf of black rights. J.B. Sanderson and P.W. Cassey secured the release of some blacks in Stockton and San Jose who were being held in slavery contrary to California law.[51] When some California blacks in the late 1850s began to despair of ever attaining justice in the state, J.J. Moore was among the primary proponents of emigration to a place of greater opportunity, and he was among the leaders of those who went.[52] The Revs. Ward and Cassey undertook to be agents for the two black newspapers, recognizing them to be essential organs of communications in the rights struggle.

The area in which black clergy made their most direct, most extensive contribution to the struggle was education. They argued before blacks and whites the urgent necessity for blacks of all ages to secure the benefits of public education. They also initiated and chaired public meetings called to plan agitation for school rights. Often it was the black clergy who shouldered the task of establishing day and night schools in the absence of public school facilities for blacks. They served, too, as the teachers of many of the colored schools, the Revs. Moore, Sanderson, Cassey, Jennifer, and Johnson in particular. Black teachers, especially Cassey and Sanderson, received high praise from public school officials for their classroom competence. (Interestingly, Cassey and Sanderson also received the rebuke of school officials in 1873 for what the officials deemed to be too heavy an inclusion of religion in the class sessions.)[53] Finally, it frequently was the local black clergy who visited the colored schools at examination time and who acted with school officials as examiners.

The anticipated departure from the state of the Revs. Moore and Ward provided the occasion for testimony on how significant in the cause of black people these clergymen had actually become. In

1868, the General Conference of the AME Zion Church elected Moore to the episcopacy and assigned him to a district in the Southeast. As the time of his departure from California approached, a reception was given in his honor by P.A. Bell, W.H. Yates, and other "secular friends," as they termed themselves, men who "...[did] not belong to any sect or church, but claim[ed] a reverence for religion and its consistent votaries...." One of those present, a Mr. N. Cook, made a statement which revealed the degree to which Moore, the ranking Zion clergyman on the Coast, had become deeply immersed in the rights struggle. Cook said he believed that

> ...non-profession has as much claim in the Rev. John J. Moore as had his own church members. He was a public man and belonged to the whole community, and not wholly to any class or denomination.

Moore responded that he

> ...had always felt that while he endeavored to faithfully fulfill his ministerial duties, there were also other duties incumbent upon him as a man and a Christian--the civil and political rights of his people.[54]

The Rev. T.M.D. Ward, too, was preparing to journey eastward to the General Conference of the AME Church. At a reception in his honor, also given by his "secular friends," Ward was similarly acclaimed for his total devotion to the effort "... to raise his downtrodden and oppressed people in this land."[55] This tribute was paid to Moore and Ward on the occasion of their imminent and potentially permanent departure from California.[56] But the same would readily have been rendered to Sanderson, P.W. Cassey, Barney Fletcher, and numerous other clergy and laypersons who were constant in the black rights movement.

As one reviews the struggle of black Californians for the legal and political rights of citizenship, there emerges a picture of the active involvement of the black religious sector. One could not clearly identify this involvement as a church crusade, *per se*. The issue is more complex than that. For example, how does one define "the church"? When are the actions and pronouncements of clergy and of laity to be construed as representing "the church"? How does one identify and/or separate religious motives from other motives in seeking to understand the impetus of an individual's or a group's actions? This essay has not attempted to sort out these questions. Rather, it has sought only to show that in every phase and on every level of the struggle for the civil rights of black Californians, the black clergy were a significant presence, acting as persons whose innate proclivity for freedom was enlightened and elucidated in its encounter with their Christian faith.

The black clergy were men of force and vision. They believed themselves to be rendering highest service to the church which commissioned them by challenging unjust human constructions with the divine imperative to justice. They were men who, in the oppressive conditions of the mid-nineteenth century, when hope for black folk seemed perenially to issue forth stillborn, could yet seize upon the words of the prophet Jeremiah of old and invert the question mark of his plaintive query into the exclamatory assurance that,

> "There is a balm in Gilead
> To make the wounded whole...."

Notes

This essay is a revision and updating of an earlier piece by the author entitled, "The Church and Black Californians," which appeared in *Foundations*, Vol. 18, no. 2 (April-June 1975). It is printed here by permission of the *American Baptist Quarterly*.

1. For a good treatment of slave worship, see Albert Raboteau, *Slave Religion* (New York: Oxford University Press, 1978).

2. Free blacks established their own denominational bodies in response to segregative practices in the white churches. These black churches were completely independent of the white parent organizations, though they retained similar ecclesiastical and liturgical structures.

3. Cf. the San Francisco *Elevator*, March 26, 1869, p. 2. The *Elevator* and the San Francisco *Pacific Appeal* (hereafter *Appeal*) were the main black-owned and-operated news organs in the state during the period of this study.

4. On the founding of Third Baptist, see Sanford Fleming, *God's Gold: The Story of Baptist Beginnings in California, 1849-1860* (Philadelphia: The Judson Press, 1949) 100, 102; Sue Bailey Thurman, *Pioneers of Negro Origin in California* (San Francisco: Acme Publishing Company, 1952) 24.

5. Ward's district included all of California but at this time there were very few blacks in the southern portion of the state. Around 1870, however, he did discover a small congregation of AME's in Los Angeles.

6. Not to be confused with the AME church of the same name. For an account of Cassey's California ministry, see Lionel U. Ridout, "The Church, the Chinese, and the Negroes, 1849-1893," *The Historical Magazine of the Protestant Episcopal Church*, 28 (June 1959): 132-138.

7. *Journal of Proceedings of the Third Annual Convention of the Ministers and Lay Delegates of the African Methodist Episcopal Church* (San Francisco: B.F. Sterett, Printer, 1863), 19ff.

8. *Elevator*, April 7, 1865, p. 2; November 17, 1865, p. 3; January 8, 1869, p. 2.

9. *Minutes of the Organization and First Meeting of the Sacramento Valley Baptist Association* (Sacramento: Crocker & Edwards, 1857), 16.

10. *Minutes of the California Annual Conference of the Methodist Episcopal Church, 1865* (San Francisco: Towne & Bacon, 1865), 26-27.

11. Cf. Ridout, "The Church, the Chinese, and the Negroes," 136ff.

12. Quoted in the *Pacific*, January 8, 1863, p. 2. If there was Catholic hostility toward blacks it may have been related to the fact that a sizeable percentage of California's Catholics apparently were Irish. There was tension, sometimes violent, between Irish and Blacks in many parts of the nation.

13. *Monitor*, August 7, 1875, p. 4.

14. The State Colored Conventions were periodic assemblies of blacks elected by town or area across the state. They were called to address crucial issues affecting black citizens of the state, such as access to public education and the admissibility of black testimony in court cases involving whites.

15. Cf. *Minutes of the Annual Conferences of the Methodist Episcopal Church*, Pacific School of Religion, Berkeley, California.

16. Cf. *Minutes of the Annual Meetings of the General Association of California*, Pacific School of Religion, Berkeley, California.

17. May 2, 1872, p. 3. Another striking example of this inattention to racial justice issues is found in the sermon of the noted Congregational minister Horace Bushnell, delivered at First Congregational Church, San Francisco, July 6, 1856. The topic was "Society and Religion: A Sermon for California." Bushnell asserted that ancient slavery was "abhorrent to the fraternal principles of Christ." But he said nothing about the slavery which was even then being practiced covertly in California and openly in half of the country. The full text is bound with the *Minutes of the Annual Meetings of the General Association of California*.

18.*San Francisco Directory*, 1858 (San Francisco: Commercial Steam Presses, S.D. Valentine & Son, 1858), 373.

19. *Journal of Proceedings*, 19. The California Conference included the entire Pacific Coast. The membership for churches within California itself was 240.

20. *Proceedings of the California State Convention of Colored Citizens* (San Francisco: "Elevator" [sic] Printing Office, 1865), 12. The total black population of the city at this time, according to the *Proceedings*, was 1850. The listing of only two churches for San Francisco is probably a typographical error; there were three and possibly four there by that time. San Francisco was, unfortunately, the only city for which the membership and attendance figures were given.

21. *Elevator*, March 26, 1869, p. 2; April 7, 1865, p. 3.

22. *Minutes of a Baptist Convention* (San Francisco: Towne & Bacon Book, Card, and Fancy Job Printers, 1860), 17. The black Baptist churches listed in the *Minutes* (17) show the following memberships: Second Baptist, Stockto -25; Mt. Olivet, Marysville - 15; Siloam Baptist, Sacramento - 35.

23. Eighth Census of the United States, 1860; *Journal of Proceedings*, 19; *Pacific*, January 1, 1863, p. 2. The *Pacific* gave the state's Baptist membership as 1,620, which included black Baptists.

24. Cf. James Weldon Johnson, *Books of Negro Spirituals* (New York: The Viking Press, 1969); William Styron, *Confessions of Nat Turner* (New York: Random House, 1967).

25. Johnson, *Emancipation Oration* (San Francisco: Elevator Office, 1867), 3.

26. *Appeal*, July 26, 1862, p. 2.

27. *Journal of Proceedings*, 40, 41, 22.

28. *Elevator*, December 13, 1867, p. 3.

29. In the book of Leviticus (25:8-55) the Israelites were commanded to set aside every fiftieth year, to be called the year of jubilee, in which, among other things, all persons held in bondage were to be set free. Afro-Americans, slaves and free, likened Emancipation to the Jubilee. Cf. Lerone Bennett, "Jubilee," *Ebony*, February, 1972, pp. 37-46.

30. Cf. Exodus 3:7.

31. Emancipation Day Oration, printed in the *Elevator*, January 3, 1868.

32. *Journal of Proceedings*, 43; *Elevator*, April 21, 1865, p. 2; Ezra Johnson, *Emancipation Oration*, 4. For some other statements by blacks on the Exodus theme and on God's influence in the War and Emancipation see the *Elevator*, May 5, 1865, p. 2; January 5, 1866, p. 2; January 31, 1868, p. 2; January 29, 1869, p. 2; February 26, 1868, p.1; *Proceedings, Fourth Convention, 8.*

33. *Journal of Proceedings*, 11.

34. *Proceedings of the Second Annual Convention of the Colored Citizens of the State of California* (San Francisco: J.H. Udell and W. Randall, Printers, 1856), 13.

35. *Proceedings, Fourth Convention*, 26.

36. *Elevator*, May 5, 1865, p. 2.

37. Ibid., May 26, 1865, p. 3.

38. *Proceedings, Fourth Convention*, 19; *Elevator*, March 11, 1870, p. 2.

39. *Journal of Proceedings*, 22.

40. *Cf.* Minutes, Sacramento Valley Baptist Association, and San Francisco Baptist Association.

41. This was true of the white clergy also, judging from the fairly complete files of their state Association minutes.

42. December 12, 1857, p. 2.

43. November 18, 1871, p. 2.

44. *Elevator*, November 27, 1868, p. 3.

45. Ibid., April 22, 1870, p. 2; May 5, 1865, p. 3.

46. Ibid., April 7, 1865, p. 2; September 8, 1865, p. 2.

47. See, for example, *Appeal*, November 8, 1862, p. 2; February 28, 1863, p. 2; *Elevator*, December 20, 1867, p. 2; July 1, 1870, p. 1.

48. *Lunar Visitor*, February, 1862, p. 3.

49. Out of approximately fifty delegates at each Convention there were six ministers at the First (1855), eight at the Second (1856), and six at the Fourth (1865). The records of the Third Convention (1857) do not include enrollment figures.

50. Cf. *Proceedings First, Second, Fourth Conventions,* passim; *Appeal*, November 25, 1871, p. 2. *Elevator*, June 2, 1865, pp. 2, 3; January 26, 1866, p. 2; October 6, 1865, pp. 2, 3.

51. Delilah Beasley, *Negro Trailblazers of California* (Los Angeles: n.p., 1919), 92.

52. Peter Cole, "Cole's War with Ignorance and Deceit," a published lecture (San Francisco: J.H. Udell and R.P. Locke, 1857), 13.

53. The Superintendent of Cassey's school district was dissatisfied with Cassey's opening and closing religious exercises. Sanderson was accused of "introducing sectarianism and making too long prayers." The sources do not indicate whether any direct teaching of religion took place. Cf. *Elevator*, December 20, 1873, p. 2; March 1, 1873, p. 3.

54. The account of the reception is found in the *Elevator*, April 17, 1868, p. 2.

55. Ibid.

56. Ward was elected to the episcopacy by the Conference but was reassigned to the Pacific Coast.

13.

Church Life Among Filipinos in Central California:
Social Ties and Ethnic Identity

Edwin B. Almirol

Today there are 774,640 Filipinos in the United States, which is about a 158% increase over the 1970 count. In California, where nearly half of the total Filipino population in the U.S. resides, there are 357,514 Filipinos, making them the largest ethnic group of Asian origin. In spite of their increasing number, our understanding of Filipino-American history and contemporary conditions is rather limited. This essay hopes to alleviate that situation. Specifically, it shows that for many members of the Filipino ethnic community the church provides important social ties and social contacts. Through the extensive network of personal and social ties which the church fosters, economic, social and cultural difficulties are assuaged by mutual assistance and support. This essay will also demonstrate that the Filipino ethnic church provides an important arena for expressing and maintaining cultural identity.

*   *   *

To better understand the role of the church in Filipino immigrant adaptation and settlement, it is important to understand the conditions and history of immigration. It was not until the 1920s that significant numbers of Filipinos started coming to the U.S. mainland. The Filipinos who came to the mainland before the 1920s were mostly students on government scholarships who were being prepared for government service as soon as the Philippines was granted its independence from the United States.[1] Thus in 1920, there were only 5,603 Filipinos in America with 3,360 in California. Between 1920 and 1929, 31,092 Filipinos were admitted to the United States through California, and by 1930 there were some 45,000 Filipinos in the mainland United States.[2] But in 1934, as a result of the Tydings-McDuffie Act which promised Philippine independence, Filipino immigration to the U.S. was reduced to 50 persons per year (later increased to 100). According to the census of 1950, there were 45,563 Filipinos on the U.S. mainland. The dramatic rise in Filipino migration began during the 1960s; during that decade there was a 95% increase of Filipinos in America, partly as a result of the repeal of the "National Origins" immigration laws.

A 1930 report by the California Department of Industrial Relations presenting facts about Filipino immigration into California consistently referred to it as an "invasion."[3] Before Filipinos started to arrive in California in large numbers, opposition to Asian immigration was already strong and concerted. In the late 1880s there was the "Chinese Peril," and at the turn of the century there was the "Japanese Menace." The battle-cry against the "invading Orientals" was "Yellow Peril" and that battle-cry was extended to the Filipinos.

In the early 1900s, Asians were barred from legally entering the United States, but the Filipinos were exempted. Following the defeat of Spain in the Spanish-American War, the Philippines became an American territory and the Filipinos were regarded as "American Nationals" or "Wards." This status, however, did not exempt them from the discriminatory treatment to which other Asians were subjected. In spite of their special entry status, the Filipinos were still considered, like the Chinese and Japanese before them, "unassimilable Orientals." They were also prohibited from owning property, buying and leasing land, joining labor unions, marrying women outside of their own ethnic group or becoming American citizens.

In the 1920s and '30s Filipinos were considered at best a problem and at worst a menace.[4] Political and labor leaders condemned Filipinos as "cheap labor." But at the same time, American-owned steamship agents and farm labor recruiters actively recruited Filipino laborers with guarantees of work and good pay. The departure of the Chinese and Japanese for urban jobs had left a labor vacuum in the West's agribusiness economy, and Filipinos were specifically recruited to fill it. "There is scarcely a Filipino who did not leave the Philippines at the

300

invitation, expressed or implied, of some employer."[5] Their arrival on the U.S. mainland was the direct result of Japanese labor strikes in Hawaii and labor shortages in California. The Gentleman's Agreement of 1908, later followed by the Exclusion Act of 1924, further reduced the Japanese population, thus exacerbating the agricultural labor shortage. It was therefore fortunate for the California landowners and farm growers that the United States had acquired the Philippines as a colony and with it a ready supply of exploitable labor.

These early Filipino arrivals on the mainland were mostly young single males; 93% of the early immigrants were male; 84.3% were under 30 years of age (almost 5% were under 16 years of age).[6] Most were single, but even the few who were married invariably came alone, leaving their families behind. They did not perceive themselves as permanent settlers. They expected to earn a living, save some money, and return to their own homeland. But this was a dream that, for many, would never come true. Some wanted to go to school and improve their chances at making a better living, but as "unassimilable Orientals" they were only allowed in segregated schools.

Unschooled and unfamiliar with America, the Filipino could only work in two types of job: farm labor and domestic work. Those who found domestic work were employed as houseboys, waiters, cooks, elevator boys, and dishwashers. Since farm labor was seasonal, the Filipinos employed in it were kept constantly on the move, following the crops up and down the West Coast. Consequently, stable Filipino communities comparable to the German settlements in the Midwest or the Italian communities of Canada were never established until after the Second World War.

The Filipinos were seen as an economic threat by organized labor. "They represent cheap and irresponsible labor of the type that cannot be assimilated, and as such they threaten American standards of wages and living conditions," declared a resolution by labor spokesmen in the state of Washington.[7] But the truth is that Filipinos were chiefly in domestic work and farm labor, jobs which interested few whites, and so posed no threat to white employment.[8] On the contrary, they contributed to the living standards of whites by undertaking socially necessary tasks which whites tended to shirk. For example, in the Salinas Valley lettuce farms, the Filipinos were restricted to fields doing "stoop labor" and were prohibited from competing with the white workers in the packing sheds.

Low wages were hardly the fault of the Filipinos. They had little power against organized farm growers and farmers. When they tried to organize labor unions to raise their pay and defend themselves against labor abuses, they met vicious condemnation and physical abuse. "I realize it was a crime to be a Filipino in California," complained an early Filipino immigrant.[9] Thus, when a group of Filipino farmworkers in Salinas struck for higher wages, a Filipino farm labor camp was burned to the ground, "many Filipinos were coralled, held incommunicado, beaten and driven out of town."[10] Laments another early Filipino immigrant-farmworker, "we were not allowed to join unions or to have the weapons that organized labor uses."[11] Deprived of bargaining power and unfamiliar with local wage scales and labor conditions, some Filipinos were easy prey to unscrupulous employers. Such was the nature of their "unjust and unfair competition."

But the confusion and panic of the great Depression of the 1930s required scapegoats. Many white Americans vented their anger at losing their jobs on immigrants who were easily singled out--such as Asians. In California, Washington and Oregon, this anger was particularly directed against the Filipinos. Throughout the Depression, Filipinos remained a major target of racist attacks. White vigilante groups attacked Filipinos with impunity in such places as Sacramento, Reedley, Imperial Valley, Sonoma, Turlock, Modesto, Stockton, and Sun Valley in California, Hood River, Oregon and Yakima Valley, in Washington.

The American concept of the "Filipino menace" was not restricted to economic matters. It extended to the very moral fiber of America. A professor of geography and international trade at Stanford University argued that

the influx of Filipinos is a menace in many ways. They
arrived green and simple as babes in the woods and after
a couple of seasons in the canneries and more or less idle
winters in the town, they evolved (by the example of
former arrivals) into big-time gamblers, knife-fighters
and first-rate Apaches. They showed great aptitude in
becoming acquainted with institutions of disorderly
character.[12]

These "institutions of disorderly character" were mostly American-
owned taxi-dance halls and Chinese gambling houses and pool
halls.[13] A former superintendent of the Department of Public
Instruction in the Philippines from 1903-1909, later professor of
political science and president of the University of California at
Berkeley wrote in 1929: "The Filipino's natural weakness is a
moral weakness. He is smart enough. For a small race he has an
unusual endowment, if it can be built up and freed of chronic
disorders. But morally, he is deplorable. The Malay conviction is
that if a man can lie and cheat, oppress and get away with it, he is
smart and something to brag about."[14]

In 1930, the Attorney General of California announced his
support for exclusionary legislation against the Filipinos "to
protect the racial purity and integrity of the United States."[15] The
Executive Secretary of the California Joint Committee on
Immigration testified during a hearing before the U.S. House of
Representatives that "the sex problem presents a special difficulty
in connection with Filipino immigration . . . the Filipino does not
bring his women with him. You can realize his preference for
white women."[16]

What was not mentioned was that a Filipino immigrant could
not "bring his women with him" because American labor recruiters
were interested only in recruiting working-class men. The labor
recruiters carefully inspected the hands of the men who wanted to
come to America. Early Filipino immigrants report that they
roughened their hands by rubbing their palms on rocks on the road
in order to pass this "rough hands inspection." Rough hands
meant that they were hardworking and assured them a free ticket to

the States.[17] Filipino women and wives were discouraged from joining their men and husbands by the lack of facilities for women in the labor camps, by the cost of bringing them to the U.S., and by the general economic uncertainty and social hostility experienced by the Filipinos. The resulting gender imbalance among Filipino immigrants prompted a 1933 legislative amendment banning Filipino-white intermarriage in California. Filipino-white marriages were nonetheless contracted by couples who went to such places as Idaho, Mexico, and Illinois where inter-racial marriages were not banned, then returned to California to live.[18]

Being an "unassimilated alien," the stigmatized Filipino was deprived of basic rights such as owning or leasing property, deciding where he could live, and defending himself in courts.[19] He was refused service in restaurants, hotels, and barber shops, and excluded from public swimming pools, tennis courts, billiard parlors and other recreational facilities.[20]

The Second World War had a significant impact on the Asian population in the United States. Americans of Japanese ancestry were viewed as the "enemy race" and were sent to concentration camps. Many Chinese wore buttons announcing, "I am not Japanese; I am Chinese-American" to avoid harassment. Filipinos signed up to join the U.S. Army. Their homeland was bombed the same day Pearl Harbor was bombed. The Army initially turned them away because of their peculiar status as "American wards." The Draft Act applied only to American citizens and aliens living in the U.S. They were considered neither. Because of their status as "nationals" a special agreement had to be negotiated; it provided that all those who registered for military service would be reclassified as U.S. citizens.

After the War, the U.S. Congress passed the War Brides Act which allowed Filipinos who served in the U.S. military to bring their wives and children from the Philippines. In 1942, the House of Representatives passed a resolution which enabled Filipino residents in the United States to become naturalized citizens. Since 1945, Filipino residents have been able to buy land in California.

The Anti-Miscegenation Law which prohibited interracial marriages was repealed on October 1, 1948.[21] The period between 1945 and 1965 marked the second major wave of Philippine immigration to the U.S. Many of these second wave immigrants were in the military services or families of the first-wave immigrants.

The Immigration and Naturalization Act of 1965, which abolished national quotas and set up a preference system favoring relatives of U.S. citizens, has had a most significant effect on Filipino immigration. Between 1965 and 1976, 279,321 Filipinos immigrated to the U.S., almost 90% over the pre-1965 Amendments. The 1965 Amendments intended to reunite families and the post-1965 Filipino immigration patterns confirms this.

* * *

As the above narrative indicates, a pervading theme in the history and experience of Filipinos in the U.S. has been exclusion. As a response to this widespread exclusion from the larger American society, the Filipino ethnic community actively attempted to provide opportunities for establishing and maintaining contact and ties with members of the ethnic group. Various voluntary associations provided a much-needed social stage for bringing Filipinos together and giving them a sense of belonging and self-esteem. These Filipino organizations often tended to be particularistic and function as an extension of the familistic ties where support, protection and mutual dependence are expected.[22]

Besides the various voluntary associations, churches have provided another important social stage for the Filipinos to establish mutual bonds of support and protection. Not only does the church serve as an arena for establishing social contact and social nurturing, it also functions to preserve and maintain the ethnic members' cultural heritage and traditional links with the home community. These roles can be glimpsed in a case history of Filipino church groups in an important Filipino settlement: the city of Salinas, near California's agricultural Central Valley.

Although a majority of the early Filipino arrivals were Catholics, they were not readily accepted by Salinas's Catholic churches. As a reaction to this form of institutionalized discrimination and exclusion, the Filipinos attempted to establish a Filipino Protestant church. Many pioneers of this church maintained that the momentum for starting their church was a response to the discrimination they experienced in the Roman Catholic churches. "We were ushered into one corner in the last back pews," a 78 year old retired farm worker reported, "so we joined the Protestant church with the hope that we would be treated better. There were many American Protestant missionaries in the Philippines who often preached about all men being brothers. Eventually we decided to organize our own church because what we expected did not actually come true." Another early immigrant explained that "to be accepted then, we thought that being a Protestant would help, but it did not really matter much. We were different and difference was equated with inferiority. We were treated like dirt by the Americans, regardless of whether we professed to be Catholics or Protestants."[23]

The early Filipino church in Salinas was inter-denominational; as an Anglo Protestant observed in 1934, it was "nominally Methodist, but ... really a joint enterprise as it receives considerable support also from the Presbyterians."[24] In 1929, the first Filipino minister, Pedro Royola, concentrated on Bible study and prayer devotions in the labor camps. When Reverend Royola was not preaching in the labor camps he was organizing job referral services for arriving farm workers and writing letters to Philippine relatives of those farm workers who could not write.[25] Royola served the Filipino farm community until 1931 when Vicente Guerrero arrived from the Philippines to replace him, but Guerrero stayed only a year. It was in 1932 that Guerrero conducted the very first Filipino Protestant service in Salinas in a downtown Methodist Church, with 20 Filipino farm workers attending.

From 1932 to 1934, Juan Callao continued the Filipino Protestant ministry. Callao was a college graduate with some training in a theological seminary in the Philippines. "He is a capable, energetic pastor, and is evidently a leading figure in the community," one outsider reported.[26] It was during Reverend Juan Patacsil's time, from 1934 to 1943, that the campaign to build the Filipino church began. Most of the early immigrants agree that Patacsil was a dedicated fund-raiser. "He would go to the numerous pool halls and gambling halls asking donations from those who won," reminisced an elderly respondent. A Catholic Filipino, who still lives on Soledad Street in Salinas around the corner from the old Filipino Protestant church, proudly announced, "We Filipinos, Catholics, Protestants and non-believers alike, built that church." The Filipino church became a symbol of Filipino unity and identity; it had nothing to do with one's religion or denomination. With a piece of land donated by Juan Clemente, a successful Filipino farm contractor, the church was erected downtown, on 21 California Street.

In 1943, Juan Patacsil left to become chaplain of the segregated Filipino unit of the U.S. Army, organized at Fort Ord, California. An Anglo pastor, Rev. L.M. Kemper of the Salinas First Presbyterian Church, served for seven months. During this time the Filipino Protestant Church was reorganized as the Filipino Presbyterian Church. In September, 1943, Reverend Robert Crichton took over the church; his "distinct contribution was the proper and orderly keeping of church records."[27] In 1947, Juan Callao returned and served the Filipino community for the next 16 years. He worked closely with the Filipino community and participated in projects which were for the benefit of both Catholic and Protestant Filipinos. In 1963, Callao retired and was replaced by Reverend Amadeo Zarza, a college graduate with extensive seminary training and church experience. When Zarza arrived, there were approximately 30 active members and by the time he retired in 1977, there were more than 200 active members. The current pastor is Reverend Dick Solis, who was formerly a college teacher, seminary-trained and an active community leader. In 1968, the church was renamed St. Philip's Presbyterian Church and moved from 21 California Street to its present location in a North Salinas suburb, primarily because of the rundown location of the downtown area and the members' fear of being molested when they attend Sunday services and evening meetings. Drunks and hobos seem to abound in the area. As a result of the move, a rift developed among the members on the wisdom of leaving a wholly-owned property and acquiring a new loan to buy a more expensive property. A majority of those who took the former position were also unsure of leaving the downtown area for sentimental reasons. This division has resulted in some members not attending the church.

The move diminished the close association between the Filipino community and the neighboring Chinese community but at the same time improved the Filipinos' social standing with the white community. The North Salinas area is predominantly white and basically a newly developed residential area. California Street is still the location of the Japanese-speaking Buddhist Salinas Temple and the Chinese Confucian Church but many Filipinos argue that it is unattractive and dangerous because it has acquired a "ghetto" status.

Although the Filipino Protestants do not normally celebrate the feast day of saints as the Catholics do, they have an equal number of banquets, potlucks, and socials. The church members hold Easter breakfasts and Christmas dinners together. The luncheons and potlucks usually coincide with Mother's Day, Father's Day, Philippine Independence Day, or Philippine-American Friendship Day. When a member celebrates any of the rites of passage, the rest of the church members are invited, including friends and *compadres* (ritual co-parents) who may even be Catholics. This practice strengthens social ties and friendships within the ethnic community. In addition to these social occasions, the church members have Bible discussion groups and evening devotionals in members' homes. During these devotions and prayer meetings, Tagalog and Ilocano words and phrases are used to explain or clarify certain points and issues dealing with Biblical parables and verses. But in most cases, the discussions and the Sunday services are conducted in English.

The pastor and some members think that the use of a specific Filipino language might exacerbate the differences among the congregation since there are Ilocanos, Tagalogs and Cebuanos who do not necessarily understand each other's language. There are also an increasing number of American-born Filipinos who cannot speak or understand the Philippine languages. There are equally an increasing number of non-Filipino members in the congregation, mostly married to Filipino "oldtimers" (Filipinos who arrived before the Second World War), who also do not speak any of the Philippine languages.

During the time of my field research in Salinas, the pastor of the Filipino Presbyterian Church was Amadeo Zarza, an Ilocano. When he went on his pastoral visits he spoke Ilocano to his Ilocano parishoners and at times would conduct Bible studies and prayers in Ilocano. At many church occasions and events Filipino languages are readily and widely spoken, but for members from different language backgrounds, English is the *lingua franca.*

Of the Filipinos in the Salinas Valley, about 95% are Catholics; a significant number of them, however, might be called nominal Catholics. Regarding this nominal membership, there is a clear discrepancy between the number of Filipinos who attend Sunday masses and the list of members kept in the Catholic church records. One Catholic priest complained, "the problem with the Filipino members is that we only see them during baptisms, weddings and funerals." This phenomenon is not restricted to Filipinos in America since it is also widespread in the Philippines.

A singular complaint of Filipino Catholics is that the Roman Catholic Church is forcing them to be like everybody else. They argue that church leaders would like to treat them like everybody else, that is, primarily and exclusively as Catholics. "But we are not like everybody!" they insist. "We are Catholics but we are also Filipinos. The fact must be recognized that we are Filipino Catholics and it must occur to them that we might have some special needs as Filipino Catholics." The Filipino Catholics in the Salinas area have been campaigning for a Filipino priest and have been talking about a separate Filipino Catholic church, similar to the Filipino Protestant church, but so far only the Filipino-American Catholic Association has been organized.

Opposition to a separate Filipino church comes from the bishop of the diocese in Monterey and from the local church hierarchy. The main argument against an ethnic Filipino Catholic church is the divisiveness that would result in the diocesan ministry, its organization, and its financial commitments. Officers of the Filipino Catholic Association report that the prevailing sentiment among the church hierarchy in Monterey is that the Filipinos do not need a separate church. A separate church would tend to isolate the Filipinos from the other Catholics.

The leaders of the Filipino Catholic Association are nonetheless unrelenting in their petitions for at least a Filipino priest. For several years officials of the Filipino Catholic Association have written letters petitioning the bishop of the diocese to consider appointing a Filipino bilingual priest who might be sympathetic and sensitive to their culture and language. The Association has even suggested names of priests who are from the Philippines. The letters have not been acknowledged and requests for a meeting with the bishop were not granted.

Any Filipino Catholic can become a member of the Filipino-American Catholic Association regardless of parish membership. The Association was organized in 1961 by Dr. Florentino Gonzales, a medical doctor from Cebu, with the assistance of Fernando Guerzon, a Salinas priest of Spanish descent. The Association meetings always provide an opportunity for the members to get together since meetings tend to be scheduled in members' homes. These meetings in members' homes tend to coincide with a birthday party, wedding anniversary or a baptismal reception.

Despite denominational differences, there are no significant differences in the associational activities of the Filipino Protestants and Catholics. In fact, there is a significant overlap in their activities and projects. The Filipino-American Catholic Association also has frequent potluck lunches, picnics, and other socials which provide occasions for Filipinos to meet. These socials more often than not include the Filipino Protestants as well. There is a strong indication that differences in faith or religion are considered relatively unimportant; what is crucial is that they are all Filipinos. Differences in faith are seldom raised in conversation. They are not regarded as important in day-to-day interaction nor are they used in personal evaluations of character. The church and its accompanying activities are considered a forum for expressing a sense of "we-ness," a sense of peoplehood. When the Catholics celebrate religious feast days, Filipino Protestants are invited to attend and participate. When the Protestants have their own celebrations Catholics likewise attend.

The Catholics celebrate the feast of Immaculate Conception, the Filipino Catholic Association's patron saint, and other parish patron saints at various times of the year. St. Joseph's feast day is celebrated in March and the feast day of the Blessed Mother in May during the *Santacruzan* festival. During this particular festival, the Catholic Association sponsors a beauty queen contest and the winner reigns as the May Festival Queen. The contestants are usually young girls between the ages of seven and twelve. The queen and her escort, usually a young boy of similar age, re-enact the drama of Reyna Elena and her escort, Rey Constantine, searching for the cross of Calvary. The re-enactment is followed by a procession of young girls and women waving canopies of flowers over the queen's head. This is also called the *Flores de Mayo* (May Flowers) festival, and is a widely celebrated occasion in the Philippines. During the *Flores de Mayo* and other similar celebrations, Filipino folk dances are performed and folk songs are sung. In June and July, the Association holds rosary prayers to the Mother of Perpetual Help and, in November, to the Lady of Miraculous Medal.

During Christmas, the members organize *aguinaldo* (carol) groups to go to members' and even non-members' homes to sing carols. The homes are expected to give money and, oftentimes, they also offer light snacks and drinks. In an average season, the members would raise about $500 from such an activity. Besides the *aguinaldo*, the Catholic Association raises money by sponsoring raffles, bingo, dances and beauty queen contests, where the contestants give a percentage (about 50%) of their ticket sales to the Association. They also raise funds by organizing trips to Reno, wherein the Association gets a commission for every passenger. From its funds, the Catholic Association awards scholarships worth $400 apiece. It also contributes $150 to the family of a deceased member.

Members and their families also receive from the Association small gifts at their weddings, anniversaries, and baptism. The Association also sends a wreath of flowers to their members' funerals. For Christmas, sick members as well as other Filipinos in the hospitals receive gifts. The Association also gives a variety of awards, from "youth of the year award" to "outstanding member award" to "service award." This award-giving activity is rather widespread within the community indicating its importance for the community members.

The Association not only provides assistance and opportunities for social contact, it also performs the ritual requirements of the Filipino Catholics. A *pamisa* or a mass is sponsored at regular intervals to pray for the souls of departed members. After the death of a member, the Association conducts a *pasiyam* or a nine-evening novena to pray for the repose of the person's soul. *Pasiyam* consists of the recitation of prayers for a period of nine evenings. Usually, a temporary altar is built in the home of the deceased. The altar is frequently adorned with votive candles, flowers and a picture or a statue of a saint.

The leaders of the Association derive considerable prestige from their position, not only within the Association but in the Filipino community as a whole. The leaders are often invited as guests to the homes of members during parties and rites of passage celebrations. Members are honored when the leaders of the Association go to their homes. Generally, those who show great interest and are active in the various Association programs and activities are chosen as leaders. Ideally, Association leaders have good rapport with all the members and with the chaplain, usually an Anglo who is appointed by the bishop of the diocese.

During the past years, the Association donated money to Philippine flood victims through the Filipino Catholic Federation of America, an umbrella organization of Filipino Catholic associations. The Filipino association also donated $500 toward the construction of a Catholic church in Salinas. The Assocation also contributes about $100 to the personal funds of two priests, one of whom functions as a chaplain to the Association. The Association also occasionally sends money to small Catholic churches in the Philippines that request donations. Such churches are usually the former parish churches of the Association members.

Clearly, for many of the members of the Filipino ethnic community in central California, churches and their various activities provide a social life which they would not have otherwise. Church activities provide the members of the ethnic community with an outlet for their energies and an instrument with which to serve their home communities in the Philippines and in the new land. Their social history in this country--characterized by exclusion and stigma--provided an essential impetus in the formation and maintenance of extensive social and personal ties. Through the broad network of personal and social ties which the church and its activities provide, economic, cultural, and social difficulties are assuaged by loyalty, mutual assistance and support.

Notes

1. Carlos P. Romulo, *I Walked with Heroes*, (New York: Rinehart and Winston, 1961), 130-154; Carey McWilliams, *Brothers Under the Skin* (Boston: Little, Brown and Company, 1964), 234.

2. Louis Block, *Facts about Filipino Immigration into California* (San Francisco: California Department of Industrial Relations, California State Printing Office, 1930), 3-15.

3. Ibid., 15.

4. C.M. Goethe, "Filipino Immigration Viewed as Peril," *Current History* 34 (1931): 353-354.

5. McWilliams, *Brothers Under the Skin,* 236.

6. Block, *Facts about Filipino Immigration,* 34.

7. Paul Scharrenberg, "The Philippine Problem," *Pacific Affairs* 2 (1929): 52.

8. H.Brett Melendy, "California's Discrimination Against Filipinos, 1927-1935," in *Racism in California,* eds. R. Daniels and S.C. Olin (New York: Macmillan, 1972), 142.

9. Carlos Bulosan, *America is in the Heart* (New York: Harcourt, Brace and Company, 1966), 120.

10. Carey McWilliams, "Exit the Filipino," *Nation* 141 (September 4, 1935): 265.

11. Manuel Bauken, *I Have Lived with the American People* (Indiana: Caxton, 1948).

12. E.G. Mears, *Resident Orientals on the American Pacific Coast: Their Legal and Economic Status* (New York: American Group Institute of Pacific Relations, 1928), 272.

13. Paul Cressey, *The Taxi-Dance Hall* (Chicago: University of Chicago Press, 1932), 145-174.

14. Quoted in Dorita Clifford, "California's Struggle Against the 'Filipino Invasion' 1929-1934," unpublished manuscript (1975), 9.

15. *The Evening Pajaronian,* January 8, 1930, p. 1.

16. *Hearings before the Committee on Immigration and Naturalization of the House of Representatives,* 43 (1930): 35-36.

17. Edwin B Almirol, *Ethnic Identity and Social Negotiation: A Study of Filipinos in California,* (New York: AMS Press, 1984).

18. Emory Bogardus, "Filipino Immigrant Attitudes," *Sociology and Social Research* 14 (1929): 472-479; Bogardus, "Filipino Americans," *One America,* eds. F.J. Brown and J.S. Roucek (New York: Prentice-Hall, 1954), 67-71; Grayson Kirk, *Philippine Independence* (New York: Farrar and Rinehart, 1936), 99-100; Anne Loftis, *California--Where the Twain did Meet* (New York: MacMillan Publishing Company, 1973), 197-199.

19. Wallace Stegner, *One Nation* (Boston: Houghton Mifflin, 1945), 43; John Burma, *Spanish Speaking Groups in the United States* (Durham, North Carolina: Duke University Press, 1954), 138-155; Carlos Bulosan, *America is in the Heart,* 268-269.

20. Bruno Lasker, *Filipino Immigration* (Chicago: University of Chicago Press, 1931), 129-132, Melendy, "California Discrimination," 141-151; Bauken, *I Have Lived with the American People,* 73-74.

21. Bauken, *I Have Lived with the American People,* 340; Edward C. McDonagh and Eugene S. Richards, *Ethnic Relations in the United States* (New York: Appleton-Century-Crofts, 1953), 392.

22. Edwin B. Almirol, "Filipino Voluntary Associations: Balancing Social Pressures and Ethnic Images," *Ethnic Groups* 2 (Spring 1978): 65-92.

23. These and several quotations that follow are from the author's field interviews in Salinas in the mid-1970s.

24. A.W. Palmer, *Orientals in American Life* (New York: Friendship Press, 1934), 83.

25. Amadeo Zarza, "Emergence of the Filipino Presbyterian Church," unpublished manuscript (1973), 2.

26. Palmer, *American Life*, 83

27. Zarza, "Emergence of the Filipino Presbyterian Church," 3.

V

Education

14.

Public and Private Education in San Francisco: The Early Years, 1851-1876

Catherine Ann Curry

This essay will survey the first twenty-five years of the public and private educational systems in the city of San Francisco. It will trace the change that occurred between 1851 and 1876 in the relationship between public and private schools. At first viewed as partners with public schools in the educational enterprise, private schools enrolled a significant number of the city's schoolchildren. By the end of the period, however, they were seen as competitors and their share of students dropped dramatically. In the early years, educational arrangements in San Francisco were similar to those in many eastern cities where denominational schools were a prominent part of the educational system. By the 1870s the situation was similar to that in most of today's cities, where public education is paramount.

Particular educational systems arise as appropriate for particular societies. National trends in education as well as local conditions influenced the development of San Francisco's educational system. The city reflected national trends because many of its citizens were natives of the eastern states who brought to their new home the concerns and customs of their old. Early San Francisco, however, differed in several ways from the well-established eastern cities such as Boston and New York. The social structure of the city, for example, was somewhat different. Among the financial leaders were a number of Jews and Irish Catholics. Italians founded a college; Irishwomen established a hospital; Germans were prominent in social and business circles and a Spaniard served as bishop. The rapid growth of the city's population and the cosmopolitan nature of that population made for a confused cultural identity, unlike the eastern cities where the old American hegemony was well established.[1] Ironically, such confusion paved the way for the rise of nativist influence in the schools.

In 1852, the year of the first surviving census, foreign-born inhabitants predominated over native-born by a ratio of nine to eight. Although this ratio changed in the next ten years so that the native-born acquired a slight edge, the large number of foreign residents seemed threatening to Americans determined to make their outpost an American city.

The growing city was subject to the strains of economic uncertainty, political corruption, administrative confusion and racial and cultural antagonisms. Nativist fears and concern for public order were central to the rise of such groups as the Vigilance Committees of 1851 and 1856 and the Know Nothing Party, which at its height elected a governor, a mayor of San Francisco and various state and city officials. The Vigilance Committees, with their predilection for direct violent action, were an ominous development since they raised the specter of mob rule.[2]

To those alarmed by the apparent deterioration in the social fabric and by the conspicuous poverty, corruption and crime, the idea of public schools was attractive. Many San Franciscans were influenced by Horace Mann's ideology of the common school. Mann believed that the common school attended by all social classes would encourage social harmony and reduce crime and poverty. It would teach a consensus Christian (Protestant) morality and include Bible reading.[3] Leading citizens wanted such a civilized, homogeneous society to take shape in San Francisco. In 1856, a city publication maintained:

> Perhaps in no city of the world are there children brought together with such diversity of habits, creeds and thoughts and feelings, but with ready adaptation and quick assimilation of childhood these destructive traits gradually pass away, they catch the impress of the prevailing tone and when they enter upon the responsible duties of life will prove themselves Americans in heart and Americans in action. All ranks of society send their children to these schools, hence, if for no other reason,

they should be exalted to the highest place of excellence, that the rich and poor alike draw sustenance from the same fountain.[4]

The shape of San Francisco education was to mirror some of the concerns of this group. The first schools in San Francisco, as in the eastern states, had been established under denominational auspices. Baptists, Episcopalians, Methodists and Catholics sponsored separate schools. In 1851, the city inaugurated a system of free common schools. According to the enabling legislation for this public system, denominational schools would receive public support so long as they taught the subjects offered in the public schools and demonstrated, under examination, that they were well conducted.[5]

With the growing influence of the Know Nothings, public funding for denominational schools in California was temporarily ended by the Soule Act of 1852. This law had been passed at the behest of the State Superintendent of Public Instruction, John G. Marvin. Under the act, common schools could receive public funds only if their teachers were "examined, approved and employed by competent and legal authority" and the schools were "free from all denominational bias, control and influence whatsoever." Sectarian or denominational books were also forbidden in the schools.[6]

San Francisco's Catholic Bishop (later Archbishop) Joseph Alemany had been away when the Soule Act was passed. Upon his return, he wrote the State Superintendent of Public Instruction to request that state aid to Catholic schools not be terminated. Alemany argued:

The will of the people throughout the whole Republic is obviously to give such assurance and stability to education as to have by law its doors thrown open to every child, to guaranty [sic] to all a school-house and a teacher, and to reward through the hands of its most prominent functionaries such as devote their time, labor, and energies to the holy cause of education. The laws are nothing but the expression of the good will of the people, and the main object of the laws of education is to educate. Thus the schools shown in the accompanying report having substantially complied with the law by laboring materially in the cause of education, I would respectfully ask of you the kindness of your influence towards a *pro rata* appropriation of the collected public funds for the number of children taught in the schools....[7]

Attached to the letter was a list of twelve Catholic schools in the state, three of which were in San Francisco.

Marvin responded by sponsoring the Ward School Act of 1853. Amending the Soule Act of 1852, it removed the stipulation that schools receiving public funds should be free of denominational bias and control.[8] In San Francisco, three Catholic schools were designated ward schools and received public support. Other public schools were classified as district schools. Public support for denominational schools, however, was to last only a short time.

In 1855 the state legislature passed the Ashley Act, which terminated the subsidy for schools which taught sectarian doctrine.[9] This law was passed while the Know Nothing Party was at its zenith in California. The Ashley Act was passed even though the ward schools were teaching more than thirty percent of the children enrolled in the public schools of San Francisco during the school year ending in October 1855. In the ward schools religious instruction was usually provided outside regular school hours.[10]

A new Board of Education took office in September 1855 and invited the ward schools to come under its supervision. Of the eight members of the board, four were Democrats and four were Know Nothings. Coming under the board's supervision involved board examination and appointment of teachers, review of textbooks and inspection of classes.

Lay instructors in the Catholic schools sat for examinations.

322

Representatives of the board then visited the two groups of nuns who were teaching in the schools to examine them. One of the Know Nothing members discovered that the sisters could not teach males or take charge of schools other than their own, while the Sisters of Charity could not teach in schools unless supervised by a female. The Know Nothing member concluded that it was improper to employ the nuns as teachers. A Catholic member of the board disagreed and the board adjourned.

The other order, the Sisters of the Presentation, were cloistered and refused to leave their convent for an examination. As a result, their school lost its tax support. In Ireland, from whence they had come, they had received tax money for teaching in state schools. Now they were left without support. They had to turn for their income to rich benefactors, fairs and bazaars, and fees for teaching "extras" such as music and French. Despite the economic pressure, their schools remained free until 1906. The Sisters of Charity also lost support, but they were also able to maintain their free school.

After the loss of public support some Catholic schools remained free while others charged those willing to pay. Some had a free school and a select school for those willing to pay. Public schools in San Francisco never charged tuition, although schools in many other California school districts charged tuition until it was abolished in 1867.

San Francisco public schools, for lack of sufficient space, did not accept children under the age of six. The average child attended school for approximately four years. Privileged children finished the grammar school course which lasted eight or ten years. A high school (now Lowell High) was established in 1857, but very few attended high school. In common with most American cities, San Francisco simply could not accommodate all of its children in its schools. (There was no effective compulsory education law in California until 1907.) In 1856, when there were 3700 children on roll in the city, a report by the State Superintendent of Public Instruction noted:

In the City of San Francisco, where the effort to sustain common schools has deservedly won her a worldwide reputation (and as a natural consequence amid all her disasters put her bonds at a premium), in that city there is a daily average of 2938 out of school.[11]

Although Catholics were probably as interested as other San Franciscans in building up their city and state, they were not able to subscribe wholeheartedly to the theory that all children should attend the common schools. Catholic schools became the largest segment of the private educational sector in the 1850s. No doubt Catholic parents felt some pain, both psychological and economic, from being outside the majority consensus which proclaimed the importance of common schools for the social harmony of the city and the nation. Nevertheless, they considered separate schools a necessity even though they were never able to accommodate in them all Catholic children.

As the decade of the fifties ended, San Franciscans could be proud of their schools, both public and private. In 1860 San Francisco had a population of almost 57,000 of whom 14,000 were children. Approximately 6100 children were enrolled in public schools while 2100 attended private schools. Of the latter, approximately sixty percent were in Catholic schools.[12] Private schools were necessary partners in the educational enterprise even though denominational schools had been excluded from public support by the Ashley Act.

The 1860s would bring many changes to California. Many people came west to avoid the Civil War or to pursue economic opportunity. In 1865 the population of San Francisco was 115,000, almost double what it had been five years earlier and by 1870 the city had 150,000 inhabitants. Expenditures for schools greatly increased during and after the Civil War. As voters passed bond issues handsome brick buildings replaced ramshackle rented quarters. The expensive new facilities symbolized the greater value placed on public education in the sixties. Enrollment in the common schools tripled along with the population. Average attendance increased from approximately forty percent to approximately eighty percent of those on roll, the increase suggesting again the new value attached to education. Private school enrollment, although it had doubled, did not keep pace with the public sector. In 1860 private school enrollment was roughly thirty percent of public school enrollment with Catholic schools still accounting for sixty percent of private enrollment. By 1870 private school enrollment fell to twenty-five percent of the public total.

There are several explanations for the growth in public enrollment which kept pace with the increase in population. Bond issues made possible improved facilities which attracted many to the schools. More significantly, educational authorities implemented two reforms to attract students: cosmopolitan schools and sexually segregated schools.

Cosmopolitan schools were schools in which foreign languages (French, German and Spanish) were taught. These schools were designed to attract the children of immigrants who desired their children to learn their respective mother tongues. The first such school opened in 1865. In a few years several large schools became cosmopolitan schools, suggesting that language instruction was an attractive feature of the public system. Indeed, when the cosmopolitan schools were closed in 1874 the public outcry was so great as to compel the School Department to reopen them.[13]

Near the end of the sixties, City Superintendent James Denman decided that the sexes would be separated in six of the city's eight grammar schools. Previously, some parents had chosen private schools because they preferred separate education for girls. Contemporary accounts from the time of the changes reveal approval of separate education. A letter to the editor of the *Evening Bulletin*, for example, expressed the popular sentiment concerning segregation of the sexes:

> Until a school is furnished which will satisfy the reasonable demands of the parents of about two hundred female children attending the schools of these ladies

[Presentation Sisters], they... will deem it something like an outrage to refuse to recognize as a public school the only one in San Francisco to which they can with due decency send their children.[14]

The School Department clearly tried to accommodate itself to the interests and needs of the populace. Private schools had been teaching languages and separating the sexes for some time. By adopting these attractive measures public schools were better able to compete with private schools. Educational authorities had already made an additional gesture toward Catholic and Jewish parents by discontinuing prayer and Bible reading in the public schools in 1856.

There was also an ideological explanation for the expansion of the public school system. This explanation is illustrated in the attitudes of John Swett. A native of New England, Swett achieved a national reputation as a teacher and administrator in San Francisco and as State Superintendent of Public Instruction. Considered by many the founder of public education in California, he worked tirelessly for public schools which he considered "the great nurseries of patriotism and devotion to constitutional liberty."[15] In 1865 he confidently asserted:

The results of the great rebellion have proved conclusively that but for the public schools in the loyal States the nation could not have been saved, and but for the lack of them in the other States, rebellion could not have existed. More deeply in the future than in the past will statesmen recognize that popular education is the only safeguard of a republic.[16]

John Swett believed that common secular schools were necessary for the welfare of the nation and the support of democratic society.

A final important reason for the greater expenditure and interest in public schools was a desire to preserve the hegemony of old Protestant American values by Americanizing the children of immigrants, of which there were many in San Francisco. Natives of the eastern states, raised in a more homogeneous society, were concerned that newcomers with different ideals and agendas would change the character of America. Thus, they wanted the children of these newcomers to attend the public schools where they would be indoctrinated with traditional American ideals.[17]

In the 1860s the citizens of San Francisco apparently came to share John Swett's faith in public schools. In 1861 a proposal by Zach Montgomery to reestablish public support for denominational schools failed.[18] Although two years later attendance at private schools climbed to almost ninety percent of public school enrollments--during the Civil War the normal operation of public schools was disrupted--they then began a precipitous decline that, by the end of the decade, would reduce private enrollment to less than twenty-five percent of public. Parents were increasingly inclined to send their children to public schools, while the general public was willing to commit public funds to the same schools.

The development of San Francisco's common schools coupled with the denial of state subsidies to denominational schools was not inevitable; indeed, it ran counter to trends in the East. Legislatures in New Jersey, New York and Rhode Island provided subsidies similar to those requested by Montgomery at about the same time that his proposal failed. The famous "Poughkeepsie Plan," in which city school boards approved and paid teachers in parochial schools, went into effect in New York in 1873 and a number of states in the Midwest and elsewhere adopted similar plans.[19] It was not until the late nineteenth century that private schools in many Eastern cities lost their subsidies.

As noted above, after losing public support a number of San Francisco Catholic schools were able to remain free schools. Others charged tuition to those who could afford it. Mother Mary Teresa Comerford, a prominent Catholic educator in the city, commented:

At the period of our first convent [1854] no opposition arose from the public schools, of which there were but few, and our friends urged us to accept payment from those pupils who could afford it. Wishing, however, to keep the spirit of our holy rules, and fearing that such a distinction would alienate the less wealthy in this country, where equality was the watchword of the day, we struggled on through all difficulties, and still maintain our school entirely free, with the exception of a small charge for music lessons.[20]

A member of the Presentation Order, founded in Ireland to teach the poor, Mother Mary Teresa had arrived in San Francisco with four companions in 1854. With the aid of wealthy Catholics and other benefactors she and her companions built the Presentation Convent on Powell Street as a free school for girls. Behind the main building was a small school for Black and Indian girls, which eventually closed after protests from the parents of white children in the free school.

The sisters expanded their first convent in the sixties and built another one, Sacred Heart Presentation Convent, in 1869. By that time Catholic schools were in competition with public schools, and Mother Mary Teresa noted:

The system of the public schools being now matured with a very high standard of education, we were obliged to embrace the same sciences in our teaching, in order to compete with them, and be enabled to save the children from the destructive influence of a godless education. As the attraction of science seems to be a principal weapon in the hands of the enemies of the faith here, we endeavor to have our schools progress so as not to be behind but rather in the advance; and thus we have been enabled to gain youth to God.[21]

Clearly, Catholic religious orders like the Presentation Sisters opposed the "godless" public schools and considered their schools important instruments of evangelization.

Thus during the 1860s officials of San Francisco's public schools attempted to appeal to various groups in the city by means of better school buildings, cosmopolitan schools and sexually segregated schools. Bible reading and prayer continued to be proscribed to avoid offending Catholics and Jews. Of course throughout the period the focus was on the education of white children. Black children were restricted to separate schools or were not accommodated. Chinese children were usually not accommodated at all.

In the 1850s private schools had been considered important partners in the educational process and, as such, deserving of public tax support. By the beginning of the 1870s civic sentiments had changed and private schools were seen as competitors of the well-established public school system. An older pattern of pluralistic sponsorship of schools had given way to a system dominated by schools under public sponsorship. Although denominational and other private schools remained a part of the educational scene, public education had won the day. The modern pattern of American education had been established in the city by the Golden Gate.

Notes

1. Gunther Barth, *Instant Cities* (New York: Oxford University Press, 1975) and Roger Lotchin, *San Francisco, 1846-1856* (New York: Oxford University Press, 1974).

2. Peter R. Decker, *Fortunes and Failures: White Collar Mobility in Nineteenth-Century San Francisco* (Cambridge: Harvard University Press, 1978), 137; William T. Sherman, *The Sherman Letters: Correspondence between General and Senator Sherman from 1837 to 1891*, ed., Rachel Sherman Thorndike (New York: Charles Scribner's Sons, 1894), 59.

3. Lawrence A. Cremin, ed., *The Republic and the School: Horace Mann and the Education of Free Men* (New York: Teachers College, 1957), 8.

4. Samuel Colville, *San Francisco Directory,* (San Francisco: Colville, 1856), I, xlv.

5. Act of May 1, 1851, sec. 10, quoted in John Swett, *History of the Public School System of California* (San Francisco: A. L. Bancroft and Co., 1876), 15.

6. California, *Statutes,* 1852, Chap. 53, art. 6, sec. 1 and 3, 125.

7. Joseph Alemany to John Marvin, 13 February 1853, quoted in California, Superintendent of Public Instruction, *Report,* 1853, Appendix C, 27.

8. California, *Statutes,* 1853, Chap. 166, sec. 8, 232.

9. California, *Statutes,* 1855, Chap. 185, 235.

10. Sister Mary Rose Forest, "With Hearts of Oak: The Story of the Sisters of the Presentation of the Blessed Virgin Mary in California, 1854-1907" (unpublished manuscript in the possession of the author), 165. The account of the struggle for state support is based on the excellent treatment in Chapter VIII of this manuscript.

11. California, Superintendent of Public Instruction, *Report,* 1856, 4.

12. Statistics concerning enrollment at public and private schools are taken from the reports of the city and state superintendents. These reports include average attendance for public schools which is often much less than enrollment. Catholic figures are from the National Catholic Directories and Almanacs. They cover all students in Catholic schools while state and city reports cover only certain age groups. Reports from the Catholic Directories are not very reliable when compared with other sources, but are useful for indicating trends.

13. Cosmopolitan schools demanded special teachers. Perhaps the best known was Kate Kennedy. A native of Ireland, she had been educated in a convent school and knew four languages. She and her family left Ireland after the famine and came to San Francisco by way of New York. In 1867 Miss Kennedy became principal of the North Cosmopolitan School which ranked as a grammar school. All other grammar school principals were men. When Kennedy was paid the lesser salary of a primary school principal she protested and through her efforts the legislature passed what is considered the first equal pay law in the country. Kate Kennedy was also a Knight of Labor, a friend of Henry George and, in 1886, an unsuccessful candidate for State Superintendent of Public Instruction. See Miriam A. DeFord, *They Were San Franciscans* (Caldwell, Idaho: Caxton Printers, 1941); and Alice Clare Lynch, *The Kennedy Clan and Tierra Redonda* (San Francisco: Marnell, 1935).

14. *Evening Bulletin*, 27 November 1855, quoted in Forest, "With Hearts of Oak," 173-4. See also, "The Rincon (Girls') Grammar Schools," *Alta California*, 2 August 1868 and "Important Changes Proposed in the School Department," *Alta California*, 7 June 1868, in Bancroft Scraps, vol. 31, 150, 152, Bancroft Library, University of California, Berkeley, California.

15. John Swett, *Public Education in California* (New York: American Book Co., 1911), 146-7.

16. California, Superintendent of Public Instruction, *Report*, 1865, 77.

17. Some writers have questioned whether there was a perceptible American culture in nineteenth-century San Francisco to which immigrants could assimilate. See Dino Cinel, *From Italy to San Francisco* (Stanford: Stanford University Press, 1982), 7; and Douglas Daniels, *Pioneer Urbanites: A Social and Cultural History of Black San Francisco* (Philadelphia: Temple University Press, 1980), 82.

18. *Monitor*, 20 April 1861, Bancroft Scraps, vol. 31, p.46.

19. James A. Burns, *The Growth and Development of the Catholic School System in the United States* (New York: Benziger Brothers, 1912), 264-72. In Poughkeepsie, New York, Catholic children attended parochial schools where they were taught the regular public school curriculum by a Catholic teacher nominated by the parish priest but approved and paid by the city school board. The teacher was free to give religious instruction before or after regular school hours. Robert D. Cross, *The Emergence of Liberal Catholicism in America* (Chicago: Quadrangle Books, 1968), 140.

20. Quoted in William Hutch, *Nano Nagle: Her Life, Her Labours, and Their Fruits* (Dublin: McGlashan and Gill, 1875), 322-3.

21. Ibid.

15.
Americanization, Conflict and Convergence in Catholic Higher Education in Late Nineteenth Century California

Ronald Eugene Isetti, F.S.C.

During the last half of the nineteenth century, denominational colleges sprouted up throughout California. Several of them were Catholic institutions, established mainly to spread the faith and human knowledge and to form leaders for the Church and civil society.[1] These schools also sought in many instances to propagate in the Far West educational traditions which had been born and bred in Europe. The two male religious orders which operated colleges in California during the late nineteenth century--namely, the Jesuits and the Christian Brothers--had been established long before in the Old World. Within the economy of the Catholic Church, they had come to be identified over the centuries with particular kinds of schools, clienteles, and philosophies of education.

The Jesuits, who opened Santa Clara College in 1851 (and Saint Ignatius College, now the University of San Francisco, four years later) had since their founding in 1534 been providing young men with a humanistic education which blended the classical tradition with the new scientific knowledge acquired during and after the Enlightenment. Although by the nineteenth century they were educating students from all social classes, the Jesuits had been long associated in the popular mind with the wealthier strata of European society. By contrast, the Christian Brothers, who assumed the operation of Saint Mary's College in San Francisco in 1868, followed a different educational philosophy and served different social and economic groups. Since their founding in the late seventeenth century, they had sought to give young men from the working and middle classes a practical, even vocational education in fields such as commerce, banking, and architecture.

Between the two Catholic orders a division of labor had been worked out informally--in French towns of more than 40,000 population, the Jesuits would conduct a classical college and the Brothers a vocational boarding school as well as grammar schools for the poor.[2] Such an arrangement virtually eliminated competition between the two largest teaching orders of the Catholic Church.

In late nineteenth century in California, it proved very difficult and finally impossible for the Jesuits and the Christian Brothers to remain faithful to their European educational traditions while at the same time adapting to life in the Far West and seeking to meet a wide range of educational needs in a frontier society. Attempts by both orders to adjust to new conditions led to sharp disagreements within and between them. This essay examines these disputes and in the process makes some general remarks about the kind of adaptations which took place in California Catholic education in the late nineteenth century. In the American Far West, the European division of labor between the Jesuits and Christian Brothers broke down, and relations between the Church's two most powerful teaching orders erupted into conflict as a result of the convergence of their educational philosophies in a new American synthesis.

In 1868, a small band of Christian Brothers arrived in San Francisco from New York City to take over Saint Mary's, the struggling archdiocesan college which Archbishop Joseph Sadoc Alemany, O.P., had founded some five years earlier.[3] It is significant that the Brothers did not come to California to assume the operation of a charity school or even of a vocational boarding school. Like many of their confreres in the United States, they would be teaching in a true college with schools of classical and scientific studies.[4] In teaching most of their students banking, commerce, and other such practical subjects, the pioneer Brothers would be following faithfully in the footsteps of their European confreres, who had been providing young men from the middle classes with a vocational education for nearly two centuries. However, in teaching a small number of their students Latin and Greek grammar and literature, they would be opening up a new and different educational path for the Institute in the New World. In fact, they were broadening the apostolate of the Christian Brothers to include liberal as well as vocational education and also extending the educational reach of the Institute to the level of higher education, something which had been unknown among the Brothers in the Old World. Indeed, when the Brothers in California instructed students in the classics, they violated the letter of the Rule which had been written for them by their founder, Saint Jean Baptiste de La Salle.[5] He had explicitly forbidden his followers to study or teach Latin for fear that they might aspire to become priests or perhaps abandon the humble work of teaching reading and writing to poor boys. An educational pioneer, De La Salle popularized in Europe the novel method of teaching students simultaneously in their native tongue.[6]

Why, then, did the Brothers who came to California in 1868 bend their Rule and try to compete with the Jesuits? The reasons are very interesting and important. California in the latter part of the nineteenth century was still a mission field, and Archbishop Alemany was desperately short of priests to staff the churches of his far-flung archdiocese. He wanted the faculty of his college in San Francisco to teach Latin and Greek in order to prepare young men for the priesthood. Of course, the Jesuits at Santa Clara College or at Saint Ignatius College could have performed this task. However, like other members of the hierarchy, Archbishop Alemany may have feared that the Jesuits would persuade young men to join their own order rather than enter the archdiocesan major seminary.[7] In fact, Alemany never got along very well with the Jesuits in the archdiocese. In his opinion, Saint Ignatius College failed to live up to expectations; its curriculum was too narrow and its tuition too high for the needs of his frontier see.[8] Archbishop Alemany was also furious with the Jesuits at Saint Ignatius for their refusal to turn over to him the title of their church.[9] Although he had been one of the "founders" of Santa Clara College in 1851, the archbishop became upset with the Jesuits there in the 1860s when they raised the school's fees to get money for an extensive building program at both Jesuit colleges in the archdiocese. Under pressure from Archbishop Alemany, officials at Santa Clara College cut back tuition and room and board in 1861 to $350. Even then, writes Santa Clara University historian Gerald McKevitt, "the archbishop ... believed that the charge was still excessive, and he began to look elsewhere for a solution to his educational problem. Thus it was that Saint Mary's College ... was founded in San Francisco in 1863, after Alemany invited the Christian Brothers into his diocese to establish schools available to a wider spectrum of the Catholic population. The archbishop permitted a few of his seminarians to continue to attend Santa Clara, but he remained convinced that the Jesuits 'keep many away' from their schools 'because they charge too much tuition.'"[10]

McKevitt's remarks are suggestive in many respects--they point to the fact that Saint Mary's was founded as a result of Alemany's disappointment with the Jesuit colleges in his see, that it sought to give a higher education to young men from less affluent families, that it offered by design a broader curriculum than could be found at Santa Clara or Saint Ignatius, and that, by implication, one of its chief purposes was to serve as a kind of minor seminary for candidates for the priesthood. Alemany's successor, Archbishop Patrick W. Riordan, was even more explicit regarding this last reason for founding an archdiocesan college to compete with the Jesuits. In the 1890s, Riordan reproached the local provincial of the Christian Brothers "for not teaching Latin better [at Saint Mary's College], since one of the reasons for securing the Brothers was to foster vocations to the priesthood."[11]

There was another reason why the curriculum of Saint Mary's College included the classics. American higher education in the late nineteenth century still placed heavy emphasis on Latin and Greek for students pursuing a degree in arts and letters. The Harvard elective system and modern science courses did not become popular in many colleges and universities until late in the century. The classics, moreover, provided young men from immigrant stock with access to liberal professions such as law, medicine, and teaching.[12] The student body at Saint Mary's College in the late nineteenth century was composed mainly of the sons of Irish immigrants;[13] the Brothers were able as a result to justify the teaching of Latin and Greek to such students in the name of democracy, equality, and upward mobility. In a republic imbued with democratic sentiments, a class-based educational system, such as that which obtained in France, was out of the question. Here in America, the sons of the rich and the sons of the poor must sit side by side in the same classroom and make their way in the world more by their wits than by their wealth.[14] This at least was the social ideal, although not always the social reality.

In a memorial addressed to Church officials in Rome, asking that the Christian Brothers be permitted to continue teaching their students the classics, Archbishop Riordan stated in 1899 that "the Declaration of Independence implies as a fundamental law that the supreme power lies in the hands of the people; therefore, it was impossible to erect in America for the children of the people, schools called after names and conditions which formerly existed in France under the Bourbons. The name 'Poor School' was not found favorable in America, nor could any limit be placed on the extent of education given to the children of the poor, as by public opinion rich and poor have equal rights to all means tending to educate them provided they are in a financial position to attain them."[15] The phrase "financial position to attain them" seems on first thought to be contradictory; however, it is important to recall that public education in America was free, that most Catholic schools accepted poor children even if they could not pay tuition, and that the level of prosperity in America was higher than that of Europe at the time. On the basis of such an argument, the Brothers and many American bishops who supported them defended the teaching of Latin not only in the colleges of the Institute in America but in its classical academies and high schools as well.

Like many of the students they taught, the Christian Brothers in the United States also began to climb to more prestigious positions in society on the ladder of a classical education. No longer content with looking up to the Jesuits, they were now prepared to compete with them on an equal footing. Teaching the classics gave the Brothers a status which they lacked in the Old World, where they had been commonly called *les frères ignorantins*.[16] Although the European superiors of the Institute warned their confreres in America not to be ambitious for "learned chairs,"[17] the Brothers in this country were jealous of their newly-acquired position in higher education and were determined not to be pushed out of it-- either by the Jesuits or the European superiors of the Institute. However, their attachment to liberal education arose more from conviction than from pride. In defending the teaching of the classics in the Brothers' schools in America, Brother Maurelian Sheel, the President of Christian Brothers College in Memphis, argued in 1885 that "it would be a fatal and a dangerous experiment to lower the standards of our existing Colleges and Academies by Commercializing them in excluding the Latin and Greek classics. . . . [W]e have in America too many Commercial Colleges and Schools and it will never do for us to aid the growing tendency to materialize everything by excluding that which will cultivate and elevate the intellect."[18] In short, not simply the need for vocations or the status aspirations of the Christian Brothers but, as the San Francisco archdiocesan newspaper put it in 1868, "the wants of American society" required modification of the Brothers' traditional role.[19]

As one might expect, the Jesuits were not pleased when the Christian Brothers began to move into the field of classical education. It would be better, the Jesuits apparently thought, if the Brothers remained in parish schools and technical institutes where, given the European scheme of things, they rightly belonged. The number of Catholic young men who could afford to attend a college in the late nineteenth century was not large, and competition for students between schools run by the Jesuits and the Christian Brothers could become quite intense.[20] In 1858, Jesuit officials complained to the Propaganda Fide in Rome that the Christian Brothers in America were being "irregular" in teaching courses in Latin. The American primate was sent to Christian Brothers College in Saint Louis, where the teaching of Latin had been introduced five years earlier, to look into the charges brought by the Society of Jesus. However, he brushed them aside as soon as it became apparent that the local archbishop (who was his blood brother) had himself pressed the Brothers into teaching Latin in order to prepare young men for their studies in the major seminary.[21] Disappointed but not deterred, the Jesuits decided in 1866 to lodge a protest with the Second Plenary Council of Baltimore about the teaching of the classics by the Christian Brothers, which was spreading rapidly in various parts of the country. Handling the complaint informally, the bishops not only rejected the Jesuit overture but told the Christian Brothers that their only regret was that there were not more of them competent to teach the classics. This response was not surprising, of course, because it had been members of the hierarchy who had urged the Brothers all along to teach Latin and Greek in order to foster vocations to the secular priesthood. Officials of the Council must have been reassured when the Brothers who had been summoned to Baltimore told them that the Institute's General Chapter in 1854 had given special permission to the American Brothers to teach the classics.[22]

Circumstantial evidence suggests that the Jesuits, foiled in America, eventually used their influence in Rome to help persuade the Propaganda Fide in 1899 to order the closing of the classical departments in all of the Institute's schools and colleges in the United States.[23] The Brothers complied with this ruling with great bitterness toward their chief competitors whom they blamed, fairly or unfairly, for all their woes. In reality, it was the French superiors of the Institute who were most instrumental in securing the suppression of the classics. In this, they needed little encouragement from outside sources. Ignorant of the democratic nature of American society (or even contemptuous of it), the French superiors felt that the Brothers in the United States were abandoning the main mission of the order to give an elementary or vocational education to young men from the working and middle classes and were seeking, in effect, to become Jesuits without holy orders. Brothers in the Old World argued that offering classes in Latin and Greek in the Institute's schools in the United States constituted a flagrant violation of the spirit and letter of the Rule written by the Founder and created a caste system in the congregation made up of plebian Brothers who worked in grammar schools and patrician Brothers who taught in the classical academies and colleges.[24]

The idea that the European educational traditions of the Institute should be adapted to the special needs of the United States was too ghastly for the European superiors even to contemplate. It smacked of the so-called heresy of "Americanism,"[25] which supposedly held that the age-old Catholic Church should adapt itself to the changed circumstances and democratic mentality of the United States. An article in the *Montreal Star* in 1899 drew a connection between the efforts of European Catholics to stamp out Americanism in the Church and the efforts of the French superiors of the Institute to suppress the teaching of the classics in the Christian Brothers schools in this country. "European Catholics," the article declares, "who have opposed the so-called Americanizing of the Catholic Church in the United States have taken the side of the French Brothers in the conflict [over the classics], and so the case has assumed international importance."[26] Roman suspicions about the orthodoxy of certain American bishops may help to explain why curial officials so readily rejected petitions from the hierarchy in the United States pleading that that the Christian Brothers be permitted to continue teaching Latin and Greek to their students.[27] It probably did not help the cause of the American Brothers that leading Americanists were their most ardent champions in the Latin Question.

Having briefly examined how the Christian Brothers adapted to the needs of California society in the late nineteenth century, let us turn to the Jesuits at Santa Clara College and view them from the same perspective. At Santa Clara, we find almost the opposite story. The Jesuits who founded the school in 1851 were Italians from the Jesuit Province of Turin. McKevitt suggests that these Old World missionaries had certain shortcomings from an American point of view. Their ideas about how to run an institution of higher learning were just too Italian for many of the Irish students who, as in the case of Saint Mary's, made up a good part of the student body. The European Jesuits seemed determined, among other things, to keep the students away from the diversions of neighboring towns and to get them to Mass every day. Even non-Italian Jesuits at Santa Clara bridled under the strict regimen of their Italian superiors. The Jesuits in California argued among themselves not only about religious discipline but, more importantly for our purposes, about the educational philosophy which should guide their college. The Italian Jesuits were in general true believers in the venerable tradition of the liberal arts. They disdained vocational education, especially the study of business, and stressed the teaching of Latin, Greek, philosophy, literature, and theology. The real purpose of a college education, these classicists argued, was to cultivate good moral and intellectual habits rather than to prepare young men for the world of industry and commerce.[28]

In upholding the ideal of educating the whole man, the Italian Jesuits were faithfully following the *Ratio Studiorum* of the Society of Jesus. However, the parents of many of the college's students apparently felt that its classical curriculum was too elegant and effete for the Western frontier. They wanted their sons to master useful subjects which would prepare them well for positions in the world of business, banking, and commerce. Andrew Moulder, California's Superintendent of Public Instruction in the 1850s, probably gave voice to the views of those who favored a more utilitarian course of studies when he declared: "Ours is eminently a practical age. . . . We want no pale and sickly scholars. . . . This may do for old settled communities, but will never do for California. ...For the mere bookworm--for the Latin and Greek antiquarian--this is certainly not the country."[29]

Moving with the place and time, Santa Clara introduced a commercial course of studies in 1854, but not without protests from those Jesuits who still clung to the older tradition of the liberal arts. Four years later, the college was forced to make another concession to circumstance by setting up a science department which did not require students to study Latin and Greek. Again doubts were raised about this departure from European educational traditions and practices. However, the process of adaptation, once initiated, continued to pick up momentum, as was also the case with the Christian Brothers and the teaching of Latin and Greek. In 1877, the president of the college decided not only to expand the commercial department but also to build a special hall to house it. According to McKevitt, this decision

> encountered some faculty opposition. The promotion of
> mere vocational training seemed not only a betrayal of
> hallowed Jesuit educational practice, but an odious
> compromise with American materialism. The commercial
> course may be "greatly suited to the temperament and
> training of Americans, who from their very cradle are
> engaged in the accumulation of money," complained one
> unhappy European, but it is "very foreign to our [Jesuit]
> customs, by which boys are educated in the study of the
> humanities and natural sciences."[30]

The similarity between this condemnation of American
commercialism and materialism and that of the classicists among
the Christian Brothers is remarkable.

The conflict between the traditionalists and the modernizers at
Santa Clara College (or, in other words, between the classicists
and the vocationalists) divided the institution for the remainder of
the nineteenth century. Although there were some exceptions, in
most cases the former were Italian Jesuits and the latter American
Jesuits. It was the European faction which in 1887 was
successful in requiring students who were pursuing a bachelor of
science degree to pass an examination in Latin and Greek. To
reinforce this return to tradition, Jesuit officials sent a Visitor-
General to Santa Clara in 1889 to make certain that officials there
adhered to the prescriptions of the *Ratio Studiorum*. The
investigator they sent was the Reverend Rudolph J. Meyer, S.J.,
Provincial of the Missouri Province of the Society and the former
president of Saint Louis University. A staunch defender of
classical studies, Meyer "had earned a reputation for an
inflexibility that had 'frozen the mid-western Jesuits in a European
educational posture.'" Not surprisingly, he told Santa Clara
officials that they would be expected in the future to put Latin and
Greek in "first place" and to spell out the reasons for continuing
the commerical department to the Father General of the Society.[31]

As the European superiors of both the Christian Brothers and

Jesuits sought to keep their American colleagues true to the educational traditions of the Old World, they apparently explored the possibility of dividing the educational pie between the two orders. In 1885, a prominent American Brother claimed that the Jesuits "had assured . . . [a high official of the Christian Brothers] of their determination to exclude their Commercial Course of Studies from their Colleges, as soon as the Brothers would decide upon ceasing to teach the Latin and Greek classics in the Schools."[32] Efforts of this kind to re-establish the European division of labor in America could not hope to succeed in the long run. The Jesuits at Santa Clara were determined to hold on to their commercial departments, and the Christian Brothers at Saint Mary's were equally determined to continue teaching the classics, despite the edict of the Propaganda Fide.

In 1923, Pope Pius XI finally lifted the ban on the teaching of the classics in the Brothers' schools. Indeed, he virtually ordered the Christian Brothers to teach Latin to young men from all social classies, including even the "well-to-do." His main reason for reversing previous papal edicts was the democratization of education in the modern world.[33] Today the Jesuits and the Christian Brothers compete in the same educational arena. There is very little difference between the curriculums at Saint Mary's and Santa Clara. Indeed, it is arguable that the Great Books Program of the latter school, introduced during World War II, is more faithful to the educational ideals of the *Ratio Studiorum* than any comparable program at Santa Clara. The social and economic backgrounds of the students who attend the two schools are also very much alike.

The evidence cited in this paper suggests that a great deal of educational change and adaptation took place both at Santa Clara and Saint Mary's in the last half of the nineteenth century. Interestingly, the Americanization of the Jesuits and Christian Brothers in California occurred along different if not opposite lines. At Saint Mary's, the modernizers were those Brothers who wanted to teach Latin and Greek; at Santa Clara, they were those Jesuits who wanted to teach business and other vocational courses. In both cases, European superiors opposed any changes in the educational traditions of the two orders. Whether Italians in one instance or Frenchmen in the other, these Old World religious were determined that hallowed European philosophies and practices should take precedence over the special and diverse needs and conditions of a frontier society built on the twin ideals of democracy and social mobility. The California Christian Brothers and the California Jesuits, although alike in demanding change and adaptation, differed in what they considered to be the special educational needs of the time and place. The Brothers responded to the desires of those Irish immigrants who wanted their sons to have the kind of classical education which had been reserved for the rich in Europe or to use such an education to climb to higher and better positions in society. The Jesuits responded to the desires of Irish immigrants who wanted their sons to acquire a more practical education to fit them for positions in an increasingly industrial society. Both sets of needs were valid, and both orders were committed to offering in their colleges a comprehensive curriculum which included courses in business and science along with the humanities. At issue in both cases was not so much the abandonment of an apostolate as its expansion into new areas. Both Santa Clara and Saint Mary's found it expedient to offer a very broad selection of courses because their student bodies were composed of young men from all social and economic classes, although most of them came from the vast middle class which predominated throughout the country.

The fact that modernizers at both Saint Mary's and Santa Clara campaigned for opposite educational changes might suggest that the whole question of "adaptation" was itself at issue. The reforms advocated by American religious at the two schools may have been symptomatic of a deeper desire for independence from European traditions and superiors as such. Correlatively, the opposition of European superiors to "novelties" at Saint Mary's and Santa Clara may have arisen from a deep-seated fear that American religious were subverting the original purposes for which both the Jesuits and the Christian Brothers had been established. For example, the Superior General of the Christian Brothers declared in 1897 that "if contrary to our Rules our Institute were to admit classical teaching in its establishments, it would, in a short time, result in a complete deviation from its spirit and providential end. It would allow itself to be invaded by ideas of pride and ambition, which would be fatal to it; it would rapidly depart from its road, and soon the Institute of Blessed de La Salle could no longer be recognized."[34]

Jesuit superiors at Santa Clara and in Rome also feared that their own Society would no longer be recognizable if it began to offer commercial and technical courses rather than instruction in the classics. It should be noted that the fears of the European factions in both orders were not entirely groundless or without merit. There is much to be said for remaining true to the founding vision of a religious order, just as there is much to be said for adapting institutions to new times and places.

A final reason why the Jesuits and the Christian Brothers in California drifted from their European educational moorings was economic necessity. This was particularly the case at Santa Clara. In the late nineteenth century, the school was not only carrying a heavy debt but also competing for students with other schools, both public and private. From the beginning, the classical department at Santa Clara had been quite small; many more students enrolled in the scientific and commercial curriculums. Consequently, the college simply could not have survived if it had staked its future solely on teaching Latin and Greek. The European superiors apparently found it very difficult to grasp this fact.[35] The Christian Brothers at Saint Mary's College had financial worries of their own late in the century, having incurred heavy debts in moving the institution from San Francisco to Oakland in 1889. A devastating fire in 1894 added to their burdens.[36] In pleading with European superiors to permit the continued teaching of the classics at Saint Mary's and other Christian Brothers colleges throughout the country, the so-called Latinists in America argued that banning Latin and Greek would reduce enrollments, put collegiate charters at risk, and ruin the reputations of the Institute's schools.[37] Clearly, there were sound economic as well as educational reasons for opposing the prohibition of the classics.

Earlier it was noted that native-born Jesuits and Christian Brothers in California justified their respective educational reforms in the name of adapting to time and place. This fact does not mean, however, that Frederick Jackson Turner was correct in suggesting in 1893 (incidentally, at the same time the Latin Question was being debated) that the American frontier had forced European traditions and institutions to become more democratic. It is true that the Brothers wanted to provide educational opportunities for immigrant boys to rise in society on the ladder of a classical education. However, the educational philosophy which the Latinists championed in defending the teaching of the ancient languages was surely very traditional and even European in a certain sense. For their part, the Jesuits at Santa Clara College were attempting to respond to diverse educational needs in teaching business and other vocational courses to their students but without abandoning the *Ratio Studiorum* in the process.

Perhaps Daniel Boorstin can provide us with a better way of understanding what happened to the Jesuits and Christian Brothers in late nineteenth century America. In his provocative study of early American history, Boorstin argued that it proved to be very difficult to maintain European standards of professionalism and specialization in the New World. As he puts it, the learned lost "their monopolies." Professions became fluid; doctors and lawyers became generalists; experience became more important than theory.[38] Something analogous to these developments can be seen in the respective histories of the Jesuits and Christian Brothers in late nineteenth century America. Under the pressure of meeting diverse needs in a frontier society, both orders became more flexible, diffuse, and variegated. Indeed, they ended up looking very much alike, at least from an educational point of view. In the process of placing American experience over European theory, the Jesuits and Christian Brothers relinquished the separate roles which they had played for so long in the Old World and converged upon an eclectic educational practice. Along the way the humble Brothers found themselves defending the classics, while the scholarly Jesuits became the champions of vocational education. In this as in so many other areas, the Americanization of Catholicism was not without its ironies.

346

Notes

1. Santa Clara College was established in 1851; Saint Ignatius College (now the University of San Francisco) in 1855; Saint Mary's College in 1863; Notre Dame College in 1868; Holy Names College in 1880; and Dominican College in 1890.

2. This information was given to the writer by the head of the Jesuit Archives in Rome during a personal conversation in January, 1977.

3. Between 1863 and 1868, Saint Mary's College was administered by secular priests of the Archdiocese of San Francisco. For a history of the school, see Matthew McDevitt, F.S.C., *The First Century of Saint Mary's College, 1863-1963* (Moraga: Saint Mary's College, 1963.)

4. The classics were being taught before 1868 in several Christian Brothers academies and colleges throughout the country, including Manhattan College in New York City and La Salle College in Philadelphia.

5. See Chapter XXVI of the Rule of 1717. This chapter became No. XXVIII when the Rule was reprinted in 1725. It prescribes that

> Those Brothers who have learnt Latin will make no use of it after they have entered the Society, and they will behave as if they did not know it. It will not be permitted to any Brother to teach Latin to anyone either in the house or outside.
>
> Likewise it will not be permitted to read a Latin book or to say a single word in Latin without an absolute necessity and with the order of Brother Director . . . .
>
> There will be no Latin book in any house of the Institute, except the books for the Divine Office. There will be none which might be used to learn Latin.

6. W. J. Battersby, F.S.C., *The Christian Brothers in the United States, 1900-1925* (Winona: St. Mary's College Press), xv, 9-12.

7. See *Récit sommaire de l'introduction du Latin aux Etats-Unis*, (ca. 1894), p. 1, Box EL 612-1, Dossier 14, Doc. No. 11, Archives of the Christian Brothers, Rome, Italy (hereafter cited as ACBR). During a visit to the United States in the spring of 1898, Brother Aimarus Gaussiun, a special Visitor General from France, was told by Bishop John Foley of Detroit that "he wanted the teaching of Latin to be continued because the Brothers alone send top quality men to the [diocesan] seminaries; the others--Jesuits, Lazarists, etc.--garner for themselves the best subjects and send only the leftovers to the [diocesan] seminaries." See *Ephémérides de ses visites canoniques du 6 janvier 1856 au 26 juin 1905*, p. 213, Box EG 312/1, Dossier 15, ACBR.

8. McDevitt, *The First Century of Saint Mary's College,* 26.

9. For a thorough discussion of Archbishop Alemany's jousts with the Jesuits in California, see John B. McGloin, S.J., *California's First Archbishop: The Life of Joseph Sadoc Alemany, O.P., 1814-1888* (New York: Herder and Herder, 1966), 192-226, 253-276.

10. Gerald McKevitt, S.J., *The University of Santa Clara: A History, 1851-1977* (Stanford: Stanford University Press, 1979), 66, 75-77.

11. *Récit sommaire*, 4-5.

12. Frederick Rudolph, *The American College and University: A History* (New York: Knopf, 1962), 302-304.

13. Ronald Eugene Isetti, F.S.C., *Called to the Pacific: A History of the Christian Brothers of the San Francisco District, 1868-1944* (Moraga: Saint Mary's College, 1979), 36-37.

14. A group of Christian Brothers in the Midwest made this point in a manifesto which they issued in 1898. See Doc. 1, *La Question Latine*, pp. 1-3, in Brother Gabriel Marie Brunhes, *Deuxième Réponse du Superieur General des Frères à la Réplique de Mgr. de Nashville* (1899), Folio XXIII, Dossier 415, Doc. No. 34, Archives of the Procurator General of the Christian Brothers, Rome, Italy (hereafter cited as APGR).

15. "Copy of [a] Memorial of His Grace Archbishop Riordan of San Francisco to His Eminence the Cardinal Prefect of the Propaganda [on] 'The Question of the Brothers of the Christian Schools in the United States,'" (December 8, 1899), p. 2, Box NS 503, Dossier 25, ACBR.

16. See W. J. Battersby, F.S.C., *The History of the Institute of the Brothers of the Christian Schools in the Nineteenth Century, 1800-1850* (London: Waldegrave, Ltd., 1961), 18.

17. Brother Gabriel Marie Brunhes, "Circular Letter to Our Dear Brothers of the Districts of the United States," *Instructive and Administrative Circular No. 81* (February 19, 1898), p. 21, LaSallian Research Center, Saint Mary's College Library, Moraga, California (hereafter cited as LRC).

18. Brother Maurelian to Brother Patrick, 28 August 1885, Box EL 612-1, Doc. No. 1, ACBR.

19. "The Christian Brothers in California," *San Francisco Monitor*, 15 August 1868.

20. For a description of the keen competition for students between Jesuit and Christian Brothers colleges in Buffalo and Philadelphia, see Battersby, *The Christian Brothers in the United States*, 46-50, 200.

21. *Récit sommaire*, 1; "Notes of the late dear Brother Justin, Statement, A Few Facts on the Latin Question," n.d., p. 1, Box NS 503 Dossier 35; Brother Facile Rabut to Brother Patrick Murphy, 5 October 1859, in *La Question du Latin aux Etats-Unis:*

Projet de Circulaire aux Frères des Etats-Unis, Travail du F. Assistant Reticius [Gonnet], (ca. 1898), p. 26 (backside), Box EL 612-4, Dossier 4, Doc. 1, ACBR (hereafter cited as *Projet*).

22. "Notes of the late dear Brother Justin," pp. 1-2; "Copy of a Memorial submitted to the [General] Chapter of 1897 and Read in Public Assembly by Brother Justin, April 2, 1897," p. 1, Box NS 503, Dossier 6, ACBR; Brother Facile Rabut to Brother Patrick Murphy, 3 October 1866, *Projet*, p. 60; Brother Facile to Brother Patrick, *Projet*, 18 October 1866, *Projet*; p. 60; Brother Facile to Brother Patrick, 7 April 1868, *Projet*, p. 26 (backside), 74 (back side). See, also in *Projet*, pp. 55-56; *La Question du Latin aux Etats-Unis: Mémoire du F. Assistant Reticius [Gonnet]*, (1907), pp. 36, 54, 136, Box EL 612-6, Dossier 6, ACBR; and *Num. V. Il F. Luigi de Poissy Assistente del Superiore Gen. dei Fratelli delle Scuole Cristiane confuta le ragioni arrecate degli Arcivescovi Americani nella loro petizione*, p. 11, in *Relazione con Sommario circa una proposta delgi Arcivescovi degli Stati Uniti relativa all'insegnamento dei Fratelli delle Scuole Cristiane in America, Acta de Sacra Congregazione de Propaganda Fide*, A 1895, N. 34, Prot. N. 13464, Vol. 265, Archives of the Sacred Congregation for the Evangelization of the Peoples, Rome, Italy.

23. See Battersby, *The Christian Brothers in the United States,* 46-50, 53, 141-143, 177, 181, 198-200, 281, whose evidence, however, is not conclusive. Battersby himself says on p. 50 that whether the Jesuits "exercised their influence in Rome against the Brothers to the extent suggested by the press is an open question." This author has found additional evidence concerning the Jesuit role in securing the ban on the classics in the Archives of the Christian Brothers, the Archives of the Procurator General of the Christian Brothers, and the Archives of the Sacred Congregation for the Evangelization of the Peoples, all in Rome. These discoveries will be detailed in a forthcoming article on the Jesuits and the Latin Question.

24. For the position of the European Brothers on the Latin Question, see *La Question du Latin aux Etats-Unis: Mémoire du*

F. Assistant Reticius [Gonnet]. Remarkable for its bias against the American Brothers and hierarchy, this manuscript of a few hundred handwritten pages contains just about all of the crucial documents on the controversy over the classics.

25. Battersby, *The Christian Brothers in the United States*, xvi, 65-66, 103-104, 149.

26. "The Christian Brothers Lose, Papal Authorities Decide Against Allowing Them to Teach the Classics," *Montreal Star*, 27 December 1889, clipping, Box 612-3, Dossier 11, Doc. No. 4, ACBR.

27. Four American Metropolitan Archbishops sent an appeal to the Propaganda Fide in 1895; Bishop Thomas Sebastian Byrne of Nashville travelled to Rome in 1898 to present voluminous briefs to the Propaganda Fide on behalf of the American hierarchy, along with a second appeal; and a year later Archbishop Riordan of San Francisco presented another memorial to the Holy See--all of these appeals pleading for the continued teaching of the classics by the Christian Brothers were rejected by curial officials and Pope Leo XIII.

28. McKevitt, *The University of Santa Clara*, 3, 5, 53, 117-120.

29. Ibid., 57. Moulder is quoted in William Warren Ferrier, *Origin and Development of the University of California* (Berkeley: University of California Press, 1930), 34.

30. McKevitt, 55-58, 107-110.

31. Ibid., pp. 120-124.

32. Brother Maurelian to Brother Patrick, 28 August 1885.

33. Cardinal Gasparri to Brother Imier of Jesus Lafabregue, 17 April 1923, Box EL 612, Dossier 27, Doc. No. 1, ACBR. See also, *Acta Apostolicae Sedis*, 16 (February, 1924), 67-68.

34. Brother Gabriel Marie Brunhes, "The General Chapter," *Instructive and Administrative Circular No. 75* (April 1897): 67-68, LRC.

35. McKevitt, *The University of Santa Clara*, chaps. VIII, IX, X.

36. Isetti, *Called To the Pacific*, 101-109, 122-124.

37. Battersby, *The Christian Brothers in the United States,* 7, 56.

38. Daniel Boorstin, *The Americans: The Colonial Experience* (New York: Random House, 1958), especially 149-168, 171-265. I am grateful to Professor Philip Gleason of the University of Notre Dame for suggesting the relevance of Boorstin's thesis.

VI

Social Christianity
in the City

16.
In Quest of a "City on a Hill": Seattle Minister Mark Matthews and the Moral Leadership of the Middle Class

Dale E. Soden

The relationship of religion to the process of urbanization has intrigued historians for a number of decades. Recently, increasing attention has been given to the emerging middle class culture that was inextricably connected to the rise of the city. In general, historians have stressed the influence of the late nineteenth century Social Gospel movement on the Progressive urban reforms in the first two decades of the twentieth century. In particular, Paul Boyer has detailed the efforts on the part of ministers to create righteous communities by legislating elements of social control. Most American social and religious historians argue that with the end of World War I this civic influence on the part of the clergy significantly declined. American Protestantism was fragmented over the issue of fundamentalism, and the middle class, historians such as Martin Marty argue, "privatized" its religious experience. More specifically this meant that the middle class increasingly turned to the secular university; the social sciences rather than theology were thought to be more important to the life of the city. The expertise of the trained professional in urban planning or political science was given greater authority. In the end, this meant that ministers should be confined to "issues of faith" and should stay out of public affairs. Ferenc Szasz and Sidney Mead have argued that by 1930, the nation had witnessed "the demise of Protestant hegemony in America." By then, secularism and pluralism were clearly dominant values in the United States.[1]

Historians have examined the civic involvement of a large number of urban ministers in the late nineteenth and early twentieth century. However, few studies have centered on west coast clergy and their relation to urban politics and middle class culture. One of the most prominent clergymen in the country during the early twentieth century, who remains relatively unexamined, was Seattle minister Mark Allison Matthews. Pastor of the largest Presbyterian church in the country, Matthews was extraordinarily active in Seattle politics during the first three decades of the twentieth century. Indeed, what makes Matthews a compelling subject for analyzing the larger patterns of religion, urbanization and middle class culture is the fact the he was strongly identified as the most influential pastor in the city.[2]

The study of Matthews' career reveals that in the early twentieth century the influence of Social Christianity was significant in Seattle. He typifies the widespread desire among many clergy and social reformers to make cities righteous entities. Matthews longed to establish a "city on a hill", as he liked to call it. He wooed, cajoled and exhorted the middle class to allow him to lead them in their shaping of the city. Everything from the style of city government to the availability of kindergartens absorbed his attention. Above all, he sought to establish a moral order and a broad middle class consensus about what the urban environment should be. Where Matthews' career deviates from the normal pattern is in the years after the First World War. One would expect the rise of professionalism fostered by the university, and the decline of reforming zeal associated with the end of Progressivism, to make it more difficult for a minister like Matthews to exercise civic influence. One would expect to see substantial evidence of the impact of privatization on Matthews' ability to act outside of the pulpit. In fact, however, he continued to maintain an active political role in addition to his pastoral duties. Seattle residents seemed unwilling to relegate him strictly to matters of faith and were not immediately ready to embrace the university-trained expert as their only civic guide.

The reasons are complex but a principal one is Matthews' early success at establishing himself as an urban spokesman for the middle class. He so thoroughly appropriated middle class values that it seemed natural for him, in the post-war years, to continue in that role. A second reason rests in the nature of Seattle's sense of identity in the years between the wars. Economic stagnation helped perpetuate an intimate feeling for the city among its residents, and Matthews seemed to be an important symbol of a moral order the middle class wanted to maintain. A close look at this important minister indicates that in many ways the west coast was not immune from the religious forces occurring throughout the United States in the early twentieth century. However, Matthews' career also suggests that no general pattern can fully account for an individual city's unique acceptance or rejection of religious leadership.

The roots of Matthews' political and social involvement can be found somewhat unexpectedly in his native Georgia. Born in Calhoun in 1867, he was the son of a carriage maker who experienced great hardships after the Civil War. Matthews' childhood poverty encouraged an ethical outlook that relied on hard work and traditional moral values. His moral orientation and piety were further influenced by the environment of Southern revivalism with its standard fare of itinerant preachers, tent meetings, and fiery sermons. Crucial to Matthews' social outlook was the fact that he grew up in the state's politically most radical region. From an early age he experienced the politics of farmers' groups protesting against corruption in Atlanta and exploitation by big business. Shortly after his entrance into the ministry at age twenty, Matthews could be found in the Georgia countryside speaking before farmers and supporting Populists like Tom Watson.[3]

For Matthews, Populism represented a political attempt to restore the virtues of Jeffersonian America in which he believed small farmers cooperated with small businessmen and lived together in communities that embraced Protestant values. The issues raised by the Populists increased Matthews' awareness of the potential threats to traditional values and the harmony of the community. He became convinced that the best way to prevent evil politicians and greedy businessmen from destroying the fabric of society was for people to become involved in local politics and to take pride in their town. "I am tired of the ignorant spirit that abuses our beloved town. You simpleton you, the town is what you make it," Matthews told his first congregation in Calhoun. "He is the basest of base who does not love and work for his own home, his native town."[4]

In addition to being influenced by Populism, Matthews felt the effects of the Social Gospel movement in his early years. During his ministries in Dalton, Georgia, between 1893 and 1896, and most particularly in his years in Jackson, Tennessee, between 1896 and 1902, Matthews directly involved his church with the political and social problems of the day in an attempt to develop an urban environment that reflected a moral order consisting of Christian values. In Jackson, for example, he developed a Presbyterian hospital, a night school, and an unemployment bureau; he founded the Humane Society, led the drive for the Y. M. C. A., and secured funds from Andrew Carnegie for the town library.[5] "Rev. M. A. Matthews never misses an opportunity to do something for the moral and material advancement of Jackson," noted the local newspaper.[6] For Matthews, the urban menace was best fought by nurturing the social conscience of urban dwellers such that the pride in their city would naturally allow good to overcome evil.

What triggered Matthews' imagination concerning Seattle is not altogether clear. His scrapbooks reveal an intense interest in the Orient even when he was in Tennessee, and once he was in Seattle in 1902, he did not abandon it; in fact he believed he was on the cutting edge of the westward march of history. He quickly came to believe that he could become the spiritual leader of a city that would be the gateway to the Orient. "We are the descendents of Japheth who moved northward and westward until we arrived at Seattle," Matthews told his congregation, "and our feet touched the shores of the Pacific in our tramp of the ages back to Asia . . . ."[7] But very quickly Matthews began to pursue the task of shaping Seattle's moral order rather than missionizing the Orient.

Matthews' sense of history, which was crucial to his belief that he could establish a holy city, was based on a loose form of post-millennialism. Adherents to the post-millennial view maintained that Christ would come only after a thousand years of progress and peace had been established. Almost universally, advocates assumed that America would be the place where the millennium would occur and thus be the seat of Christ's kingdom. The millennium would include a great revival of Christianity and a conversion of all the nations of the world. Matthews' early sermons depict this process in the form of a constant battle between the forces of good and evil; Christians must be very willing to be politically involved, believed Matthews, if the righteous world were to be established. Like many of his fellow clergymen, Matthews understood that the city would be the key battleground in this war.

Within three months of his arrival in Seattle, Matthews was receiving substantial publicity for his vision of social Christianity. Described by one reporter as "without question the best orator in the city," Matthews would later be depicted as "a master of smashing similes that stick and scald and burn." Matthews preached on topics ranging form the "gospel of soup, soap, salve, and salvation," to "Christian Socialism."[8] He berated the church for not paying taxes and chastised women for being more interested in displaying their hats than in strengthening their Christian faith. On a typical Sunday, one could expect to hear the six foot five inch minister deliver a sermon that emphasized three things: first, one's spiritual condition and therefore one's salvation; second, one's duty to foster an appropriate moral environment within the home and to act in a "Christian" manner which meant avoiding the traditional vices; and finally, one's responsibility for community concerns.

It was this last area that gained the attention of a great many people, and from the beginning Matthews' bold social initiatives separated him from other evangelical preachers. For example, he urged the construction of a medical school in conjunction with the University of Washington; he called for the building of an emergency hospital that would offer free care to the needy; he wanted additional parks and a great civic auditorium that would attract national conventions. He also reminded Seattle residents of their obligations to Christian principles and exhorted them to obey Biblical injunctions. "If Christianity continues to dominate, grow and prosper," Matthews preached, "[Seattle] will, when it reaches a population of two or three millions, be, from a religious standpoint, the greatest city in the world."[9]

What Matthews had in mind as the basis for the greatest city in the world was distinctly middle class. There were countless sermons on the importance of law, organization, and the family. In a sermon entitled, "A Recipe for a Beautiful City and Happy Homes," Matthews emphasized one of the cornerstones of his urban vision. "The happiness of the domestic circle is absolutely essential to the success and beauty of the city, and the stability of the government," Matthews preached. "The saddest thing confronting this republic today is the unhappiness of its homes. The nagging wife, the quarrelsome husband and disobedient children all make the filthy, unattractive and unhealthy home."[10]

In another sermon, "The Practical Church," urged his congregation to recognize how functional the church could be for the problems facing the city.

> The Protestant church is the friend and sympathizer of the oppressed, the needy and the friendless. The trouble is, men do not appeal to the church, use the church, and appreciate the church as they should. However, they are rapidly learning that the church has a remedy for their every condition.... The church is preaching a practical gospel, a gospel that meets the everyday condition of men. The church is using its influence for the enforcement of law, the betterment of society and the elevation of the submerged class.[11]

The phrases "practical gospel," "everyday condition of men," "enforcement of law," and "elevation of the submerged class," all reveal how deeply Matthews was influenced by a middle class ethic.

Many of the specifics for Matthews' "city on a hill," and much of his early appeal to the middle class was due to his involvement in the Progressive reform movement. Historians have suggested that no single set of beliefs could be used to identify Progressives from non-Progressives but some scholars have argued that three clusters of ideas attracted the vast bulk of the middle class reformers. One historian, Daniel Rodgers, has persuasively argued that these ideas were expressed in three different languages of reform.[12] The first was one of anti-monopolism. Matthews utilized this language frequently. "In the field of business these ubiquitous parasites rob you by the power of the oily tongue, a hypnotic pen or a rose covered threat," Matthews preached. "The eighth commandment prohibits oppression, and every form of injustice . . . When wood yards combine to extort money from the common people; when coal mines enter into a league to rob the hearth stone of warmth and comfort; . . . . you have monumental graft."[13]

The second cluster of ideas that had particular appeal to middle class reformers was one broadly based on the goal of social harmony. This concern centered on improving the social and physical environment, ending the oppression of various groups, and promoting a type of social cohesion based on a moral order. It was in this arena that Matthews felt most comfortable because the language and concepts could be integrated so nicely into his vision of a righteous community. He fully believed the middle class would accept his leadership. Frequently Matthews preached about the necessity of developing a healthy environment by constructing parks and public facilities that would break down the alienation endemic to a large city. "It is cheaper to establish schools, parks, amusement halls, art galleries, libraries, and places of refinement, culture and morality," Matthews said, "than it is to support a standing army of hundreds of policemen, jails, penitentiaries, and asylums for inebriates."[14]

Matthews' concern for social harmony pushed him into a variety of areas. He was very interested in the criminal justice system and as a result pushed for the establishment of the juvenile court in Washington state.[15] On one occasion, Matthews suggested that the city purchase twenty to twenty-five acres close to the city and build cottages, erect workshops, establish forges, shoe shops, and small manufacturing plants. "To this farm every vagrant, every petit criminal and worthless, indolent person in the community should be forced to go," in order to learn good work habits and middle class values.[16]

Not surprisingly, Matthews became involved in the attempt to eliminate urban vice. During the Progressive period these efforts received a wide degree of middle class support. Active in the Prohibition movement throughout his career, Matthews described the saloon as "the most fiendish, corrupt and hell-soaked institution that ever crawled out of the slime of the eternal pit."[17] The tall preacher was well known in Seattle for his attacks on brothels; frequently he sent investigating committees from the church into the red-light district in order to discover illegal operations.

Seattle's middle class responded favorably to the fact that Matthews addressed the issue of consumer protection, a key element for the middle class in the Progressive movement. Matthews capitalized on the outrage generated by Upton Sinclair's *The Jungle*, and argued that a righteous city must rid itself of health hazards from chemically impure catsups to adulterated candy.[18] Seattle residents and city leaders respected Matthews enough that in 1911 he was named to the Seattle Milk Commission, responsible for establishing and enforcing health standards for the production and distribution of milk.[19]

The language of social cohesion was very much in evidence when Matthews addressed the conflict between labor and capital. Sympathetic to labor in his early years, Matthews frequently chastised big business for its treatment of labor, and he openly supported labor organizations. But Matthews clearly believed that in the end labor and capital should come together and agree on a common vision of society--a vision strongly determined by middle class values. "When the common people own their own homes," Matthews preached, "and have the privilege of owning small manufacturing establishments, prosperity and peace will abide in every hamlet and city."[20]

The third language used by Progressive reformers and certainly one of the hallmarks of a middle class ethos was the language of efficiency and expertise. Matthews did not seem to realize that the implication of this language would be the reduction of influence for people like himself. Instead he was caught in the seductiveness of the notion of expertise and believed that a holy city would be a model of efficiency. Matthews frequently spoke about the need for greater efficiency in city government. He believed the commission form of government would provide the necessary expertise and eliminate the graft and corruption of the ward system. He even proposed that the Washington state legislature create a committee of seven lawyers that would draft every bill for the state.[21]

Matthews' involvement in the Progressive movement solidified his identity as a civic leader. He strengthened that identity and increased his notoriety by using the local press most effectively to express his views. *The Seattle Times, Post Intelligencer, Argus, Town Crier, Mail and Herald,* and *Patriarch* all carried abridged versions of his sermons. There were few weeks between 1902 and World War I when Matthews was not pushing or promoting elements of his vision of a righteous city. He constantly reminded Seattle residents that civic leadership was a key to the future development of the city. "The building of a city cannot be left to men of mediocre brains or determination. In other words, a city cannot be built by parasites who simply live because they have commercial or clerical positions," Matthews wrote. "It must be built by men who have broad views, whose perspectives are those of giants."[22] No one in Seattle during the early years of the twentieth century could have doubted that the giant Matthews was referring to was himself.

To a great extent Matthews was justified in thinking that he could exercise leadership and influence over the public affairs of the city. After ten years of ministry in Seattle, he had built a congregation that ranked as the largest church in his denomination with almost ten thousand members. Often he tried to influence how those ten thousand voted. From 1910 until 1914, he led the Seattle Ministerial Federation to endorse candidates for public office. Although his influence on political elections is difficult to gauge, many Seattle residents believed that Matthews exercised significant control over the mayor's office. In the most famous incident, Matthews was involved in the recall of Mayor Hiram Gill because of the inability of Gill to control his police chief Charles

Wappenstein. Hiring the William Burns Detective Agency in hopes of uncovering major corruption, Matthews was seen by most Seattle residents as responsible for the eventual imprisonment of the police chief. In addition, George Dilling, who succeeded Gill after the recall election in 1911, reputedly took his orders from Matthews. George Cotterill's election in 1912 was also widely credited to Matthews' support.[23]

During the teens Matthews developed a fairly close relationship with President Woodrow Wilson. Matthews had gained the attention of Wilson when the Seattle minister was elected moderator of the General Assembly of the Presbyterian Church United States of America in 1912. A frequent visitor to the White House, Matthews was sought by Seattle politicians to make specific requests of Wilson. Indeed, Matthews had some success in a few areas including appointments to bodies like the Federal Trade Commission. The end result was to enhance Matthews' standing as a civic leader.[24]

On the surface all seemed to be going well for Matthews, but between 1913 and 1915, the strain of maintaining religious influence over the city began to tell. Increasingly it was clear to him that one key dimension of his urban vision was not being fulfilled. Matthews believed in a basic homogeneity of thought and life-style. The precondition for righteousness was agreement on the basic questions. The combination of religious dissent, labor troubles, and World War I made Matthews more anxious about the prospects of achieving a holy city. The result was that theologically he became outspoken in defense of fundamentalism. He abandoned his vague post-millennialism in 1917 and over the next few years openly advocated premillennialism. The immediate result was greater interest in Biblical prophesy and specifically the time of Christ's Second Coming. Matthews was more self-conscious about distancing himself from liberal theologians. Politically he argued for repression of dissenting voices, particularly during the First World War.[25]

At first glance, his gravitation toward fundamentalism seems curious. This would appear to drive him farther away from the middle class, but it is quite plausible that Matthews believed fundamentalism might be the only way to maintain Christianity as a force that would revolutionize not just the city but the world. In retrospect, fundamentalism was a divisive force, but from the perspective of the teens it seemed to Matthews that what Christianity needed was consensus on its theology, and what the middle class needed was a unified religious vision.

Matthews' acceptance of premillennial fundamentalism came at a time when the zeal for urban reform began to decline across the nation. Scholars have also suggested that in the post-war years the middle class became increasingly professionali::d; this professionalism led to wider acceptance of the notion that urban planning must be done by university-trained experts and specific moral codes should not be imposed on pluralistic communities. All of this would lead one to expect that Matthews' involvement in civic affairs was at an end. Such was not the case, however, for the Seattle preacher continued to be active in city affairs in addition to his pastoral duties. While many Protestant clergymen wielded civic influence during the pre-war years, few, if any, fundamentalists were as active in public affairs as Matthews in the postwar years.

In February, 1919, a general strike was called in Seattle which attracted national attention. Matthews was notably visible as one of three civic leaders appointed to the Industrial Relations Committee which attempted to negotiate a solution to the strike.[26] When the strike remained peaceful, Matthews received recognition from the local press for his civic role: "Dr. Matthews is . . . credited with having control of one of the greatest political machines is the West, and perhaps without that machine the city would not have been cleaned up.[27]

Beginning in 1922, Matthews reached unprecedented numbers with his sermons when he established KTW radio--the first church-owned radio station in the country. It was this continued public presence that helped make it possible for Matthews in 1926 to play a significant part in three separate civic events. The first was a serious labor dispute in February, 1926, when laundry unions and laundry owners were at a stalemate in contract negotiations. Matthews was called in to assist the process, and on the occasion of the settlement, William Short, President of the Washington State Federation of Labor, acknowledged the minister for throwing himself "whole-heartedly into the threatening situation for several months, devoting the major portion of his time to it and never letting up until both sides had put their feet under the table in joint conference...."[28] According to Dave Beck, nationally known teamster leader, this was the first of several situations in which he or business leaders would ask Matthews to help bridge the gap between management and labor in the twenties and thirties.[29]

A second event in 1926 revealed Matthews' continued interest in affecting public policy, and also the willingness of the public to let him do so. This was Matthews' election to the position of freeholder on March 9, 1926, for the task of revising the city charter. Receiving the second highest vote total in a field of forty-six, Matthews advocated the city-manager system of government. Though this proposed revision by the freeholders was voted down in a general election, Matthews' participation in the process underscores how religious figures had not been relegated solely to the pulpit.[30]

A final event that involved Matthews as a civic leader was the attempt to save the job of the president of the University of Washington, Henry Suzzallo. Engaged in a bitter dispute with Governor Roland Hartley, Suzzallo had been asked to step down. Much of the Seattle community came to Suzzallo's defense, including Mark Matthews. Local headlines read, "Rhodes, Dr. Matthews and Eckstein in closed parley with Governor," as the three tried to convince Hartley to rescind his decision to terminate Suzzallo. Matthews and company were not successful, but clearly the Seattle pastor was regarded by the public as a civic leader who had sufficient standing to visit with the governor about more than just religious concerns.[31]

The precise degree of Matthews' influence on public policy in the twenties and thirties is difficult to gauge. In 1924 he was cited in a national poll of 25,000 Protestant clergymen as the only pastor west of Chicago to be among the twenty-five most influential ministers in America.[32] But at a deeper level Matthews' ability to maintain influence and visibility as a civic leader might have depended as much on Seattle's general economic condition after World War I as it did on the specifics of his vision. In the years between the wars, Seattle stagnated and remained reasonably homogeneous in population. Roger Sale, in his history of Seattle, observed that economically the area never quite recovered from the recession following the First World War. "Battered, withdrawn, greatly reduced in optimism and vigor, blessed and cursed with a simple and generally honest inactive city government," Sale wrote, "Seattle settled in as a provincial commercial city, content to live off its past achievements . . . ."[33] Town fathers began to justify the absence of growth by arguing that Seattle was either better off because it was not larger or that the city had simply reached its natural growth potential.

Matthews certainly did not envision his holy city to be "provincial" or "withdrawn" but it is certainly plausible that city residents were willing to let a person like Matthews symbolize the traditional moral order that was a rationalization for the provincialism. "In this jazz-mad age--this day of mental, moral, and religious chaos," reported one weekly newspaper in the twenties, "a church such as the First Presbyterian Church of Seattle is a mighty comforting sort of fortress to contemplate ...."[34]

Sale emphasized one other element about Seattle life between the wars that would have made it easier for Matthews to retain visibility as a civic spokesman. Sale argued that by the late twenties and thirties, Seattle residents identified with a strong sense of community and neighborhood. The city's geography is punctuated by lakes and hills in a manner that promoted distinct neighborhoods; churches and local high schools were important institutions for inculcating not only traditional values but pride in one's city. Leaders like Matthews helped personify this small-town feeling in a city of 350,000 people. The comments of the *Seattle Times* on the occasion of Matthews' twenty-fifth anniversary at First Presbyterian both reflected this sense of intimacy and acknowledged his civic role:

> It is likely that Dr. Matthews is known to more persons in Seattle than any other man. We have grown to regard him as an institution--certainly as an interesting and magnetic personality. His shrewd common sense, his business acumen and his civic wisdom have helped Seattle upon many an occasion. While he has ministered to his growing flock as spiritual adviser, he also has served this growing city as elder counselor and civic guide.[35]

In his own congregation and in the city at large, Matthews symbolized the quest for a civic moral order. "It is hardly an exaggeration to say that Dr. Matthews has been the greatest single influence for good that this city has known," another editorial asserted in 1929. "Dr. Matthews is a Seattle institution. He is an essential part of Seattle, an indispensable factor in its community life, indefatigable worker for its welfare and progress. We look up to him, we follow him, we are proud of him and we love him-- even when he chastens us, as sometimes he deservedly does. "[36]

In 1931, Seattle voters preparing for the upcoming mayor's race encountered an editorial from the leading middle class weekly newspaper proposing Matthews as "the best candidate."[37] Matthews did not run for mayor but retained a fairly prominent public profile. Throughout the thirties, Matthews continued to meet regularly with mayors and urge his Congressmen to pass specific pieces of legislation. Most notably he spearheaded the drive to build a major new hospital for the city in 1931, and actively fought drug abuse in the city. On February 5, 1940, Matthews died at the age of seventy-two from complications arising from pneumonia. City residents and politicians from around the state paid him tribute, and two years later civic leaders helped dedicate a statue of Matthews in a city park.

As has been suggested, Matthews' career through the First World War bears striking similarity to the careers of many clergymen in other parts of the country. Active in politics and devoted to the establishment of righteous environments, Matthews and others like him strove to involve the church at every level of urban life. Seemingly more unique was Matthews' later career. Remarkably, even as an outspoken fundamentalist Matthews participated in a number of civic issues. The reasons for this continued involvement center on his strong identity with the middle class as a spokesman for their values. Even though the middle class acceptance of professionalism tended to undermine Matthews' base of authority, he had established himself by World War I as a key civic leader. Perhaps more importantly, in the post-war period, Matthews had become identified by a significant number of Seattle residents as "their pastor" even if they did not belong to his church. He was more than simply a grand patriarch but functioned until he died as participant and counselor. Matthews seemed to symbolize a moral code that the middle class was reluctant to abandon in places like Seattle. His "city on a hill" never reached fulfillment, and perhaps most of the middle class would have found it too repressive in its entirety. Yet when the toll of the twentieth century psychological strain began to tell on Seattle residents, they seemed to seek Matthews out in an attempt to reassure themselves that traditional values were still viable.

It should not be concluded that Matthews did not have enemies or that he had not alienated a number of people throughout the years. He had a penchant for secrecy, covert investigations, and power politics that offended many people. At the same time this essay should not imply that the culture of professionalism was not having any impact on Seattle. Increasingly the lawyers and urban planners from the University of Washington would come to exercise influence. But the career of this important west coast minister indicates that the notion of a decline of religious influence on urban policy in the twentieth century needs to be re-examined.

Notes

1. The impact of religion on Progressivism is discussed in the following: Robert Crunden, *Ministers of Reform: The Progressives' Achievement in American Civilization* (New York:

Basic Books, Inc., 1982); Clyde Griffen, "The Progressive Ethos," in *The Development of an American Culture*, eds. Stanley Coben and Lorman Ratner (New York: St. Martin's Press, 1983), 144-180; Henry F. May, *Protestant Churches and Industrial America* (New York: Octagon Books, 1949); Paul Boyer, *Urban Masses and Moral Order in America* (Cambridge: Harvard University Press, 1978). The impact of professionalism on middle class culture is discussed in Burton Bledstein, *The Culture of Professionalism: The Middle Class and the Development of Higher Education in America* (New York: W.W. Norton, 1976); Thomas Haskell, *The Emergence of Professional Social Science* (Urbana: University of Illinois Press, 1977); Martin Marty, *The Modern Schism* (New York: Harper and Row, 1969); Ferenc Szasz, *The Divided Mind of Protestant America 1880-1930* (Tuscaloosa: The University of Alabama Press,1982), xi.

2. A brief panegyrical account of Matthews' life is Ezra Giboney and Agnes Potter, *The Life of Mark A. Matthews* (Grand Rapids, Michigan: Wm. B. Eerdmans Pub. Co., 1948). Some colorful anecdotes concerning Matthews are recorded in Murray Morgan, *Skid Road* (New York, 1951). Matthews' connection with the Progressive movement has been identified but not analyzed in Mansel Blackford, "Reform Politics in Seattle During the Progressive Era, 1902-1916," *Pacific Northwest Quarterly* 59 (1968): 177-89; and Ferenc Szasz, "Progressive Clergy and the Kingdom of God," *Mid-America*, 55 (1973): 3-20. Matthews' civic interests and his fundamentalism are cited in C. Allyn Russell, "Mark Allison Matthews: Seattle Fundamentalist and Civic Reformer," *Journal of Presbyterian History,* 57 (1979): 446-66; the author's more complete views on Matthews can be found in Dale E. Soden, "Mark Allison Matthews: Seattle's Southern Preacher" (unpublished Ph. D. dissertation, University of Washington, 1980), and Dale E. Soden, "Mark Allison Matthews: Seattle's Minister Rediscovered," *Pacific Northwest Quarterly*, 74 (1983): 50-58.

3. Matthews' Scrapbooks 9 and 4 are in the Mark Matthews Papers at the University of Washington Libraries, Seattle,

Washington, hereafter cited as the Matthews Papers.

4. Matthews quoted in Jewell Reeve, *Climb the Hills of Gordon* (Atlanta, 1962), 74.

5. For a more complete view of Matthews' ministry in Tennessee, see Dale Soden, "The Social Gospel in Tennessee: Mark Allison Matthews," *Tennessee Historical Quarterly*, 41 (1982): 159-170.

6. Matthews, Scrapbook 5, Matthews Papers.

7. Matthews, "Tramp of the Ages," *Sermonettes*, January-July, 1908, p. 7, Matthews Papers.

8. *Seattle Argus*, May 31, 1902, p. 4, col. 2; *Seattle Post-Intelligencer*, February 3, 1902, p. 5, col. 1; Peter Clark MacFarlane, "The Black-Maned Lion of Seattle," *Collier's*, 50 (December 28, 1912): 22; Matthews, "Christian Socialism," *Sermonettes*, September 1906-January 1907, Matthews Papers.

9. Matthews, "The New City--Newly Discovered Seattle," *Sermonettes*, January-June, 1911, Matthews Papers.

10. Matthews, "A Recipe for a Beautiful City and Happy Homes," *Sermonettes*, January-June, 1911, Matthews Papers.

11. Matthews, "The Practical Church," *Seattle Mail and Herald,* March 11, 1905, p. 6, col. 1.

12. Daniel T. Rodgers, "In Search of Progressivism," in *The Promise of American History: Progress and Prospects,* ed. Stanley Kutler and Stanley Katz (Baltimore: The Johns Hopkins University Press, 1982), 113-132.

13. Matthews, "He Talks to Grafters," Scrapbook 7, Matthews Papers.

14. Matthews, "Society's Crimes Due to a Diseased Nervous System," *Sermonettes*, 1907, Matthews Papers.

15. Matthews, Scrapbook 9, Matthews Papers.

16. Matthews, "Coffee or Coffin Houses-Which?" *Sermonettes*, 1907, Matthews Papers.

17. Matthews quoted in Norman Clark, *Dry Years: Prohibition and Social Change in Washington* (Seattle: University of Washington Press, 1965), 66.

18. Matthews, "The False Label and its Consequences," *Sermonettes*, 1906, Matthews Papers.

19. Report, "History of Milk Commission," June, 1911, Matthews Papers, 97-4, folder 1-8.

20. Matthews, "Song of the Saw," *Sermonettes*, September 1906-January 1907, Matthews Papers.

21. Matthews, "The Spirit of the Hour is Responsible for Statutory Lawlessness," Scrapbook 7, Matthews Papers.

22. *Seattle Post-Intelligencer*, Sept. 18, 1911, p. 3, col. 3.

23. *Seattle Argus*, August 12, 1911, p. 2, col. 1, and March 9, 1912, p. 3, col. 2.

24. See correspondence between Matthews and Woodrow Wilson between 1913 and 1921, Matthews Papers, 97-2, folders 3-24 to 5-10.

25. Matthews, *The Second Coming of Christ* (Grand Rapids, Michigan: Zondervan Publishing House, 1918).

26. Robert Friedheim, *The Seattle General Strike* (Seattle: University of Washington Press, 1964), 95-96.

27. *Seattle Argus*, February 22, 1919.

28. *Seattle Times*, February 20, 1926, p. 2, col. 4.

29. Interview with Dave Beck, January 7, 1980.

30. *Seattle Post-Intelligencer,* March 10, 1926, p. 3, col. 1.

31. *Seattle Post-Intelligencer,* October 6, 1926, p. 1.

32. *New York Times*, December 22, 1924, p. 1, col. 3.

33. Roger Sale, *Seattle Past to Present* (Seattle: University of Washington Press, 1976), 136.

34. Matthews, Scrapbook 17, Matthews Papers.

35. *Seattle Times*, February 6, 1927, p. 6, col. 1.

36. *Town-Crier*, April 20, 1929, p. 4, col. 3.

37. *Seattle Argus*, December 26, 1931, p. 1, col. 2.

17.

The Reverend J. Stitt Wilson
and Christian Socialism in California

Douglas Firth Anderson

The last decade of the nineteenth century was a time of "social awakening" among America's Anglo-Protestant middling classes. Jane Addams, herself a key leader in the awakening, recalled some of the colorful figures who promoted economic discussion in Chicago: "Professor Herron filled to overflowing a downtown hall every noon with a series of talks entitled 'Between Caesar and Jesus'--an attempt to apply the teachings of the Gospel to the situations of modern commerce."[1]

George D. Herron (1862-1925), Professor of Applied Christianity at Congregationalist Iowa College in Grinnell from 1893 through 1899, was a leading revivalist of the Social Gospel. He was the principal prophet and lightning rod of the upper Midwest's Anglo-Protestant social conscience in the 1890s. As an itinerant and a charismatic inspirer of others, he also helped spread the reborn social passion to other regions of the United States.[2]

In addition, there was

> a young Methodist minister who, in order to free his denomination from any entanglement in his discussion of the economic and social situation, moved from his church building into a neighboring hall. The congregation and many other people followed him there, and he later took to the street corners because he found that the shabbiest men liked that the best.[3]

The "young Methodist minister" Addams mentioned in the same breath as Herron is in all likelihood J. Stitt Wilson. He was an outspoken Chicago Herronite at the time, and he engaged in social gospel street meetings. He is also a figure worth more than cursory attention. Wilson is an intriguing example of an individual galvanized by a well-known social revivalist such as

Herron into spreading and adapting the social gospel to other times and places. Wilson's juxtaposition of modernistic Christian theology and progressivist economic socialism was remarkable. This, together with his activities in the Socialist Party of America from 1901 through 1915, make him a significant but historically slighted leader of the Christian Socialist wing of the American social gospel movement.

Further, Wilson's residence in California after 1901 points to the need to include the region of California in any consideration of the social gospel movement in the United States. The standard accounts of the social gospel movement have been revised recently to include the South.[4] California and the Pacific Coast region remain to be seriously explored in social gospel historiography.

J. Stitt Wilson is a particularly helpful figure with whom to open up this historiographical frontier. Historians C. Howard Hopkins and Robert T. Handy acknowledge Wilson's early record among the Christian Socialists of the Midwest who looked to Herron for their inspiration. California historians note Wilson as a leader of the state's Socialist Party of America and a prominent political radical of the early decades of the twentieth century. Wilson the Herronite Christian Socialist and Wilson the California radical are overdue for an analysis as one indivisible personage of regional religious history.[5]

Jackson Stitt Wilson was born in 1868 in Auburn, Ontario, Canada.[6] His Scotch-Irish parents were devout Methodists; the Wilson home was often used as a meeting place for worship and prayer. His parents taught him to read the Bible before he could pronounce all the words. "The New Testament," Wilson recalled, "was opened to my young mind not as a book full of strange and fantastic doctrines, but as containing the records of the wonderful life of a great lover of men."[7]

At age thirteen Wilson had his first experience of what he with hindsight described as the "Socialization of Personality." His recollections of it and later similar experiences are brief and imprecise, but they apparently contained elements he interpreted through his Methodist evangelical heritage and elements he felt were congruent with theological modernism. His turn toward wider horizons involved renouncing his private interests and realizing that "I was in some way 'not my own,' but the servant of my brother men."[8]

The Wilson family eventually moved to Huron County, Michigan and Stitt became a U.S. citizen in 1893. After various jobs during his teens in Canada and the United States, he married in 1889 and attended Garrett Biblical Institute (1890-1891) to prepare for ordained ministry in the Methodist denomination. He did not receive full ordination until 1897. In the meantime, he filled various pastorates in the Chicago area and prepared to enter Northwestern University. From 1893 through 1897 he worked on his B.A. in English at Northwestern, pastored the Erie Street Methodist Episcopal Church near the Chicago slums, and also worked at Northwestern's social settlement. He demitted his ordination almost as soon as he received it. He resumed his formal education at Northwestern from 1897 through 1901, receiving an M.A. for his thesis on "The Social Value of the Religious Work of a Section of the City of Chicago."

It was during these Chicago years that Wilson turned to the Christian Socialism expressed by George D. Herron. Herron's gospel of social righteousness, social sacrifice, and social reconstruction articulated Wilson's own vision. "The question before me," recalled Wilson, "was how totally and utterly life might be made the organ and instrument and agent of Universal Good, of the Kingdom of God in the Earth."[9] He ultimately embraced Socialism as the political and economic program that incarnated his new moral and spiritual passion.

Wilson's social awakening eventually led him out of the pastoral ministry. The reaction of some of his parishioners and denominational superiors to his radical concerns was decidedly unappreciative:

When it was reported . . . that I was preaching one sermon on the Labour Question each month, and holding a mass-meeting of working men to discuss the problems of Labour on Friday nights in the church, my bishop... wrote me a letter of severe chastisement .... One of the officials...expressed fear that my soul was lost ."[10]

When he left the ordained ministry, Wilson founded and led a group called the Social Crusade (1898-1901). Its avowed purpose was to foster a Christianity of social redemption. The group published a journal called *The Social Crusader* (1899-1901), engaged in social gospel street preaching, and traveled the Midwest and beyond on speaking tours and in organizing social gospel conferences.[11]

Wilson made trips to England in 1899 and again in 1900 on behalf of the Crusade. He studied British socialism, particularly the Independent Labour Party, the Fabians, and the Mansfield Social Settlement. The Crusaders were outspokenly Herronite; Herron was "the natural leader of the spiritual forces making for economic righteousness," "the Isaiah of our times." Wilson and his Crusaders eventually espoused the Socialist Labor Party (SLP) as the "one party that fills the requirements of labor today."[12] In January of 1901 Herron himself joined Wilson's Crusade and linked the Kingdom to the political program of the SLP. Ironically, the Crusaders' hero wrecked the group within a few months through the scandal of his divorce, remarriage, deposition from the Congregationalist ministry, and his final renunciation of the churches.[13]

In 1901, the year of the Herron scandal and the dissolution of the Social Crusade, Wilson was on a lecture tour of California. Attracted to the state university, Wilson and his family decided to move to Berkeley.[14]

When Wilson took up residence in California he was an active member of the Socialist Party of America (SPA). Formed in 1901, the SPA brought together breakaway members of the more strictly Marxian SLP with a group of radical Midwestern Populists and railroad workers, the latter headed by Eugene Debs. The SPA rapidly became the dominant Socialist political group in the United

States.[15] It was also the party with which most Christian Socialists associated after 1901.

Christian Socialism in the United States was a diffuse movement.[16] The indefatigable Episcopalian W.D.P. Bliss (1856-1926) was representative of those Christian Socialists who, out of a concern for Christian orthodoxy, were wary of associating with any particular Socialist political program. To Bliss,

> Christian Socialism is the application to society of the way of Christ ...Christian Socialists do not deny the necessity of individual Christianity. Christian Socialism is no salvation by the wholesale, by machinery, by power of environment... It is, rather, the carrying out of the full gospel.... Its starting point is the Incarnation.[17]

Baptist Walter Rauschenbusch (1861-1918) was less theologically orthodox but, like Bliss, also theologically critical in his Christian Socialism. Rauschenbusch argued that while

> Christian Socialism [is] the effort to combine the fundamental aims of Socialism with the religious and ethical convictions of Christianity . . . Christian Socialism is not a mere echo of orthodox Socialism. Its Christian spirit creates a distinctive consciousness. . . . The religious belief in the fatherhood of God, in in the fraternal solidarity of men, and in the ultimate social redemption of the race through Christ lends religious qualities to the Socialist ideals.[18]

Methodist J. Stitt Wilson represented a decidedly partisan and theologically heterodox strand of Christian Socialism. Wilson was instrumental with others in organizing the Christian Socialist Fellowship (CSF) in 1906. The CSF was the outgrowth of a journal, *The Christian Socialist*, edited by another ex-Methodist clergyman, Edward Ellis Carr (Wilson was an associate editor). The group was a self-conscious heir of Wilson's Social Crusade. Openly aligning itself with the SPA, the organizing convention of the Fellowship invited the membership of all those "who thoroughly believe in the Christianity of Socialism and the Socialism of Christianity--who are loyal to the Socialist party and believe that socialism should also have a distinctly religious expression."[19]

The doctrine of the Kingdom of God "is itself the social gospel," argued Rauschenbusch.[20] This was true for the social gospel movement in general, but especially so for Christian Socialists. Robert T. Handy has noted that "the key" to understanding Christian Socialism after 1900 "is the identification that was made between the coming Kingdom of God and the socialist state to be inaugurated by the Socialist Party."[21] Wilson, while he did not equate the Socialist utopia with the Kingdom, came close to it in his identification of the Socialist vision as the major necessary step to the Kingdom. He once summarized his social and religious vision:

> There is but one meaning of life and action to me, and that is the establishment of the Kingdom of God on the earth--the Kingdom or condition of Social Justice, brotherly love and spiritual inspiration and fellowship among men, and it has been my abiding and all-compelling conviction for nearly twenty years that the next supreme step in that coming Kingdom is the abolition of the present capitalist system and the establishment of the Socialist co-operative commonwealth.[22]

Wilson was able to make such an identification of the Kingdom with the Socialist commonwealth because of his modernistic reinterpretation of the Christian faith. In 1901 he made what amounted to a modernist confession of faith:

> God is no longer a great monarch on a distant throne who holds "formal receptions once a week," but the immanent presence in all energy and life, co-extensive with all orders of existing and possible phenomena. Christ is not a dying mediator paying debts to offended deity, but the living revelation of the divine possibilities of every

man. Sin is social as well as individual, and evil is the pain of life unadapted to environment and in violation of the common good. . . . Salvation is character here and now and everywhere. Heaven is not a distant abode of a ransomed few, but a state of the free and harmonious here and everywhere . . . .

The Bible, though unparalleled, is not the only source of moral teaching. We have other books and all history. We have our own minds as privileged in the Spirit of Truth as those of Isaiah or Paul, and likewise as responsible. The gospel is no longer a message to sinking, dying mutineers or pirates in a foundering ship. It is the whole message of the ideal life, to a race being schooled from ignorance and limitation to divinity and completeness.[23]

Despite such a radical reinterpretation of Christianity, Wilson did not follow Herron in ultimately rejecting all semblance of the faith. Rather, he continued to uphold the earlier tension Herron dropped. Wilson leapt to the defense of "the Christianity of Jesus" when another Socialist argued for rejecting it entirely in favor of what Wilson called "the dead hand of pagan ethics."[24] Wilson never cut himself off from the institutional church. The lines between church and world, however, were very blurred. The "Messianic Movement," came from "outside the temple." It was the church which was materialist, he argued, corrupted by "money-gods" and needing to be "spiritualized" by the idea of Socialism. [25]

The enemy of humanity for Wilson was capitalism, "private ownership of that which is socially operated." Capitalism was unjust in its basis, inhuman in its operation, and tyrannous in its outcome. The way to bring about social justice was by the simple principle, "what the people socially need the people must socially own."[26] Yet despite his rhetoric about "the impending Social Revolution," Wilson downplayed a Marxian interpretation of class conflict. His Socialism was gradualist, democratic, and trade-union oriented. In company with the members of the Christian Socialist Fellowship, he was on the "right wing" of the SPA.

The right wing, while generally loyal to the party, was often indistinguishable from its progressivist political contemporaries. They concurred in the era's secularized millennialism and general optimism over modernity. Wilson and the CSF were but extreme examples of the period's paradigmatic evangelical Protestant cultural ethos. It was an ethos that saturated the general politics of the day, that even enabled many non-churchgoers to feel at home with a public moral millennialism of repentance for social sin, conversion to social righteousness, and sanctification of the social order through a moralistic modernity.[27]

For Wilson, the way to the Kingdom was through socialist education of the working and middle classes, who would then, through the ballot box, bring in public ownership of public resources. "As Socialists we don't want to take your private property," Wilson told the Berkeley electorate in 1913; "we don't want to divide your wealth among the needy. We don't want to invade your private affairs. We only want to make it impossible for the few to exploit and rob the many." If history progressively realized God's kingdom on earth, the Socialist co-operative commonwealth was surely coming--and without violence.[28]

Wilson's religio-social utopianism found a receptive environment in California. California was as much a mythic state of mind as it was a geographic or political entity. The Gold Rush of 1848-1849 made California the land of material success. Coupled with its westward remoteness, Asian and Hispanic influences, and varied natural beauty and climate, California had become symbolic of the American Dream, a place where material or spiritual utopias seemed especially possible. Mormons in San Bernardino, Indiana Protestants in Pasadena, Swedenborgians near Santa Rosa, Oneida communalists in Orange County, and Theosophists at Point Loma; these were some of the major religious communitarian and semi-communitarian endeavors in California in the nineteenth and early twentieth centuries. Berkeley itself had spawned a social gospel community, named after William Dean Howells's literary utopia, "Altruria." The colony, near Santa Rosa, was founded by Edward Biron Payne, pastor of Berkeley's Unitarian congregation and an admirer of Herron and

Bliss. Many of the colonists were from Payne's congregation, including at least one professor from the state's university.[29]

California was also the opposite of utopia. It was a frontier--not of plains or forest so much as of urbanism and social modernization. It was a region of "instant" modern social problems from the Gold Rush onward. It was a region of fluctuating employment, of abused Asian and Hispanic migrants, of monopolistic wheat farms and cattle ranches, of ruthless Southern Pacific railroad influence on the economy and politics. It was as a Californian who had known what it was to be out of work and begging on the streets of San Francisco that Henry George developed his single tax ideas to discourage monopolistic land holdings, propounded in his controversial *Progress and Poverty* (1879). Edward Bellamy's utopian vision of a socialist America--*Looking Backward* (1888)--spawned "Nationalist clubs" across the country; the greatest number of these short-lived groups sprang up in California.[30]

George D. Herron himself had toured the state in the depression year of 1895. His visit culminated in an address to an enthusiastic San Francisco audience of over 3,000 people. Controversy over his visit was initiated by C.O. Brown, pastor of San Francisco's First Congregational Church. The stir in California brought forth a defense of Herron by California supporters in a national forum.[31]

Immediately following Herron's tumultuous visit, Presbyterian minister Joseph E. Scott, with the aid of a fellow cleric, launched a San Francisco weekly baldly named *The Socialist*. To readers who might be shocked, Scott replied that "Socialism is essentially a scheme of right and justice for all," the practical application of the journal's masthead motto: "Thou shalt love thy neighbor as thyself." Scott's paper led a shaky existence from July 1895 through 1897, gathering local clergy contributors and regularly printing news of Socialist locals until infighting in the state began to undermine the journal. When W.D.P. Bliss came for an extended stay in the Bay area in 1897, Scott eagerly brought the paper into line with Bliss' Urban Reform League movement.[32] The League soon faded, as did the paper, but the undaunted Scott launched a monthly magazine, *The Pulpit and Social Problems*, in 1898. With a group of associate editors that included local Protestant and university figures as well as more distant correspondents such as George D. Herron, editor Scott preached classless, Fabian, Golden Rule socialism until his magazine met its demise in 1900.[33]

With such a regional and local background, J. Stitt Wilson's 1901 move to Berkeley was in no way a removal to the fringes of social gospel activity in the United States. He was not even the only outspoken Christian Socialist to move into California in the first decade of the twentieth century. In 1902, black Baptist minister George Washington Woodbey arrived in San Diego from Nebraska. In Nebraska, Woodbey had converted from Populism to Socialism through reading Bellamy and through contact with Eugene V. Debs. Like Wilson, Woodbey was a contributor to *The Christian Socialist.* He was also an active SPA lecturer, both in rented halls and on the streets. He was arrested in company with I.W.W. agitators more than once. At the same time, he was pastor of the San Diego Mt. Zion Baptist Church, maintaining that "Socialism is but the carrying out of the economic teachings of the Bible." Socialism was "a scheme for bettering things here first" before the hereafter, for "mankind is entitled to the best of everything in both this world and the next."[34]

When Wilson came to California, the state SPA was small, and it grew only slowly. Organized in 1901, by 1903 its total membership was around 1,300, spread among some 74 locals, the largest ones being in San Francisco (c. 350), Los Angeles (c. 200), and Oakland (c. 100). Externally, the party put its energy into educating the public through lectures, debates, classes, street soapbox oratory, literature, and the Socialist press. Internally, the party was continually divided over ideology and strategy. The "right wing" was usually in the majority, and it was led by the Los Angeles Socialist Job Harriman. Of the major figures in the state SPA, several were either clergy, former clergy, or had had some significant religious training: Wilson, Harriman, Woodbey, Edward Adams Cantrell, James T. Van Rensselaer, and T. W. Williams.[35]

Wilson aligned himself with the California SPA and quickly became one of its leading public speakers. Fellow Berkeley Socialist Herbert Coggins recalled,

> [Wilson] would have been a great actor. He had dramatic power. He was the best campaigner for the Party that I ever knew. . . . In a way he was trained for the work. He was a minister. He could sway people and also raise money from them. [Norman Thomas] was a good debater. A little like Stitt Wilson, too. But he could not close a sale like Stitt Wilson could.[36]

Wilson preached his brand of Christian Socialism up and down the state. In 1904 he was a particularly prominent speaker in California on behalf of the national SPA's presidential candidate, Debs. He also gained the hearing of significant Christian audiences in California. For example, in 1904 Wilson addressed the Bay Area Association of Congregational Churches and Ministers on the topic of "The Message of Socialism to the Church." He delivered an impassioned speech in 1911 on "The Message of Jesus to Our Time" to the annual Northern California Congregational Conference meeting in Berkeley; its impact was such that prayer rather than discussion followed his remarks. At the Federal Council of Churches' World Social Progress Congress at the 1915 Panama-Pacific International Exposition, Wilson was a featured speaker. He also frequently preached on Sundays, renting halls and addressing his audiences on religious themes.[37]

The end of the first decade of the twentieth century saw political tumult on the national level: William Howard Taft versus Theodore Roosevelt versus Woodrow Wilson, and the SPA making its best showing ever in the 1910 elections. Historians have long noted how California was a prime example of progressivist politics at a regional level.[38] What has not been as consistently recognized is California's role as an exemplar of regional Socialism and the significant religious ethos underlying both political movements of the period. The 1910 California gubernatorial race is a case in point. The major party candidates were progressive Democrat Theodore Bell, a Catholic, and Republican Hiram Johnson, an evangelist for Rooseveltian progressivism. Johnson's running mate for lieutenant governor, A.J. Wallace, was a Methodist minister. The SPA candidate was Christian Socialist J. Stitt Wilson.

The year was one of public outcry against the political and economic power of the Southern Pacific Railroad Company. It was also a year of labor unrest, particularly in Los Angeles. The right wing was in control of the SPA, and it deliberately pitched its campaign to attract the trade union vote. State labor unions were won over. As Wilson stumped the state, he toned down the Socialists' radical image by adding a blue stripe to his Socialist red-and-white car. Although he received little media coverage except in the SPA and labor papers, Wilson covered the state, doggedly emphasizing public control of monopolies and utilities, universal suffrage, initiative, referendum, and recall, state insurance for labor and farmers, and factory inspections. The final result was a victory for Hiram Johnson, but Wilson received 12.9% (47,819) of the votes cast, significantly outpolling the rest of the Socialist ticket through his personal charisma.[39]

By 1911, the SPA was riding high. Its membership in California was around 6,000, the largest of any state, and the momentum of the time seemed something solid to build on. That year, Wilson was touring the San Joaquin Valley with Job Harriman, speaking on behalf of some labor bills pending before the new progressive legislature. He received a telegram from the Berkeley Socialists asking him to accept their nomination for the pending mayoral campaign. Harriman doubted that the Socialists could get many votes in Berkeley. But Wilson returned to his city and, following a sleepless night, accepted the nomination.[40]

Berkeley was nearing the end of a decade of growth in 1911. The aftermath of the 1906 San Francisco earthquake and fire had directly and indirectly benefited it. From a 1900 population of 13,000 the town had become a city of 40,000 by 1910, with convenient water and rail connections to San Francisco and Oakland. Except for the laboring-class West Berkeley, the university city was decidedly Protestant and "highly Anglo-Saxon". It was the only city in the Bay area at that period whose Protestant church membership kept pace with the population growth. The city was noted for its middle-class native Protestant ethos; it outlawed alcoholic beverages some twelve years before the state did, it was a center of support for women's suffrage, and its 1909 charter was regarded as model for modern cities.[41]

Wilson was at home in this environment. He was able to build on the 1910 campaign. He was securely established as a Berkeley resident. Most important, Wilson was the beneficiary of a political falling out between Friend W. Richardson, editor of the *Berkeley Gazette* and later California governor, and Berkeley's incumbent mayor, Beverly L. Hodghead, who was seeking reelection but who had ousted some of Richardson's friends. Richardson threw his paper's support to Wilson.[42]

Wilson moderated his Socialist rhetoric even more than he had in 1910. In addition to appealing to the working class, he sought the support of the progressive middle class, "the people". His platform included municipal ownership of utilities, lower street car fares, public improvements under city supervision at union wages, progressive school reform, and the single tax. He argued that "the stirring of the people all over the world and all over America--and all over Berkeley--is the effort of the people to deliver themselves from privilege and monopoly of every form and to come into their own." Besides implementing the public ownership of public utilities that was already in the 1909 city charter, Wilson said he would "stand for all other elements of progressive civic administration--for economy; for all needed public improve-ments...; for the 'City Beautiful,' and for all those civic attain-ments that a patriotic people desire to realize." But, he cautioned, "I hold before the voters no rosy hopes. I am too familiar with the powerful and relentless hostility of the public service corps to think that this [program] can be accomplished in a day."[43]

Wilson won the election, 2,749 to 2,468. The center of his electoral strength was in the university community and in the working-class districts.[44] However, Wilson's own general appeal was not enough to lead a Socialist sweep; only one other Socialist was elected to the five member city council.

Wilson tried to put the best face on this situation. To a reporter from the San Francisco *Call*, he said that his election "was simply the beginning of a new era in the politics of this and other nations. The sleepers have awakened, the giant has realized his strength." In his inaugural address, Socialist class distinctions were heavily filtered through urban and scientific progressivism. "The one supreme issue," Wilson argued, "is the People versus the Plutocracy." He acknowledged that "a small city like ours can do little to solve this great question." There were nonetheless some things which Berkeley could do:

> We are entering upon the era of scientific civic and municipal administration. Why should Berkeley not be in the van? It is replied that Berkeley is too small a city for a civic laboratory[;] perhaps the very opposite is the case. A scientific method of taxation, scientific methods and processes in administering our public utilities, and the most ideal plans for civic art and civic betterment--all of these and other developments might be more easily initiated in smaller cities than in larger. Let us at least dream of the day when Science and the Passion for Humanity shall determine civic policies.[45]

Since the Socialists were a minority in the government, Wilson decided that the best policy was to be efficient and non-controversial. "I vowed," he later wrote, "that while I was in that office every act and word and plan would be such that the whole city would be compelled to honor and approve--not Stitt Wilson--but the Socialist official." He pressed for municipal ownership of public utilities but was unsuccessful with most of his proposals. The most significant accomplishment of his two year term (1911-1913) was the establishment of a municipal employment bureau.[46]

The general electorate seemed satisfied. The "left wing" of the local SPA, however, maintained their criticism of Wilson. They saw his progressivist Christian Socialism as, in practice, gutting true Socialist distinctions.[47]

Wilson himself tired of his office. Herbert Coggins remembers that he was not very interested in day-to-day administration. "He was interested in speaking and moving people and being before the people. He wasn't interested in the details. He was not very closely related to business and a mayor's job was a business job. His interest was in promoting Socialism." Wilson ran as the SPA candidate for representative from the Sixth Congressional district in 1912. His showing against the incumbent, Oakland Republican Joseph R. Knowland, was very strong: 26,000 to 35,000. But he declined renomination for mayor, and the Socialists lost the next mayoral race. It was probably against his better judgment that he was drafted into an unsuccessful try at regaining the office in 1915.[48]

Both nationally and in California, the SPA crested in its strength and appeal from 1910 through 1912. The two mainstream parties successfully co-opted much of the SPA program and spirit, and World War I and the Bolshevik revolution radically reshaped the party. Wilson took up lecturing once again. Initially he opposed the European war as a capitalist fight. By 1915, though, he and other Socialists such as his mentor Herron, Upton Sinclair, and Jack London, formally left the SPA to follow the progressivist moral idealism of Woodrow Wilson.[49] Stitt Wilson spoke on behalf of prohibition in California in 1915-1916, and in 1917-1918 he sold war bonds. In 1917 he ran again, unsuccessfully, for the Berkeley mayor's office, but this time as an independent "peoples'" candidate.[50]

In January of 1919, not long after his son was killed in a military airplane accident, Wilson came full circle and rejoined the Methodist denomination. "The church has begun to change," he noted to the congregation of Trinity Methodist Church in Berkeley. "I have lived to see some of the ablest men in Methodism, as well as in other bodies, take in these later years identical ground with myself on the social application of Christ's teaching."[51]

In the 1920s, Wilson lectured on college campuses on post-war world reconstruction. Although he had left the SPA and rejoined the institutional church, his religio-social utopianism remained. He ran as a Democrat for the Sixth Congressional District seat in 1932 and 1936; he was a state delegate to the 1936 and 1940 National Democratic Conventions. He was an active supporter of his fellow ex-Socialist Upton Sinclair when the latter threatened to win the California governorship in the depression year of 1934 with his "End Poverty in California" program. Wilson died in Berkeley at age seventy-four in 1942.[52]

J. Stitt Wilson's unique and anomalous blend of a Methodist evangelical ethos with modernistic Christianity and evolutionary Socialism made him "an itinerant herald and apostle of the Social Revolution." His lecture tours were like a Methodist pastor's circuit, only he preached a religio-Socialist awakening:

> The greatest need of the world--and of our own California. . . is a spiritual and ethical revival, an awakening and education of the social conscience, and a mighty outpouring of the Spirit of Christ, culminating in the spiritual illumination of the individual and the reconstruction of the Social Order.

What was needed went beyond a "new birth" of individuals:

> Except this civilisation be born again we cannot enter the next phase of the Kingdom of God. That which is born of the flesh of Capitalism is Capitalism. That which is born of the new spirit is of the kingdom of the free. Marvel not that I say unto you, Ye must be socially born again.[53]

He embodied the ambiguities of radical Christian Socialism in a striking way. He virtually identified the Kingdom of God with the Socialist commonwealth, but in so doing he had neither a full Christianity nor a full Socialism. When "the Golden Age of American Socialism" passed, Wilson's religio-social vision passed as well. George D. Herron had quickly given up the attempt to maintain the tension of Christianity with the specific political-social movement of Socialism. He opted for Socialism as the key instrument of history's movement--until Woodrow Wilson captivated him. W.D.P. Bliss and Walter Rauschenbusch each kept the Kingdom separate from the Socialist utopia. They believed that the Kingdom, including the church, was the larger and more fundamental movement of God in history. Neither of them fully made the "great identification".[54] Wilson more faithfully represented the earlier Herronite view of a fully mixed Christianity and Socialism. But in so doing, he made plain not only the perils of his particular radicalism, but also the ambiguities inherent in any attempt to absolutize a political-economic position as the Christian program.

Finally, as a Californian for most of his adult life, Wilson embodied a significant thread of the region's religious and social history. His Christian Socialism was shaped in the Midwest, yet it found receptive soil in California. Wilson was more than a colorful precursor of post-1960 Berkeley radicalism. He is a major indicator that California has a religious history waiting to be told. Indeed, the reception of Wilson's blend of religiosity and politics raises the question of regional nuances in the overall story of American religion. American culture has undergone some significant intensification and reshaping in California. And religion has had a key role in this California culture-making. Wilson's modernistic Christian Socialism and its favorable reception by many churches and voters may constitute not only a local example of broader national trends in theology and politics, but also one clue among others to the historical experience of Protestantism in the urban frontier of the San Francisco Bay.[55] Besides Wilson, other people with Protestant connections in Chicago came to the Bay area, including the far more famous Dwight L. Moody. Wilson came to the Bay region in the early twentieth century to live and to evangelize for a religious Socialism; Moody came a couple of decades earlier, not to live, but nevertheless to transform the region through intensive mass revivalism for conservative evangelicalism. Wilson and Moody each had a significant constituency and success in Chicago. Yet in the Bay area, Wilson and the Protestant religious and political stream he represented found more of a resonance than did Moody and the Protestant religious and political stream he represented. The far western religious scene thus featured regional continuities juxtaposed to regional discontinuities; only the further work of religious historians on the West and other regions can solidify the tantalizing hints made by the story of Christian Socialist J. Stitt Wilson and California.

Notes

1. Jane Addams, *Twenty Years at Hull-House, with Autobiographical Notes* (New York: Macmillan, 1910; reprint ed., with a foreword by Henry Steele Commager, New York: New American Library, 1960), 141. For a stimulating application of the concept of "awakening" to the period 1890-1920, see William G. McLoughlin, *Revivals, Awakenings, and Reform: an Essay on Religion and Social Change in America, 1607-1977* (Chicago: University of Chicago Press, 1978), 1-23, 141-178.

2. On Herron, see Charles Howard Hopkins, *The Rise of the Social Gospel in American Protestantism, 1865-1915,* (New Haven: Yale University Press, 1940), 184-200; James Dombrowski, *The Early Days of Christian Socialism in America* (New York: Columbia University Press, 1936), 171-193; Robert T. Handy, "George D. Herron and the Kingdom Movement," *Church History* 19 (1950): 97-115; and Robert M. Crunden, "George D. Herron in the 1890s: a New Frame of Reference for the Study of the Progressive Era," *Annals of Iowa* 3d ser. 42 (1973): 81-113.

3. Addams, *Hull-House*, 141.

4. Hopkins, *Rise of the Social Gospel*; Henry F. May, *Protestant Churches and Industrial America* (New York: Harper & Row, 1949); and Aaron Ignatius Abell, *The Urban Impact on American Protestantism, 1865-1900* (Cambridge: Harvard University Press, 1943) are the major older histories; the most

comprehensive revision of these is Ronald C. White, Jr. and C. Howard Hopkins, *The Social Gospel: Religion and Reform in Changing America* (Philadelphia: Temple University Press, 1976).

5. Hopkins, *Rise of the Social Gospel,* 196, 199, 236-237; Robert T. Handy, "Christianity and Socialism in America, 1900-1920," *Church History* 21 (1952): 46, 48. Ralph Edward Shaffer, "Radicalism in California, 1869-1929" (Ph.D. dissertation, University of California, 1962), 165-167, 179-180; Royce D. Delmatier, Clarence F. McIntosh, and Earl G. Waters, eds., *The Rumble of California Politics, 1848-1970* (New York: John Wiley, 1970), 179; Walton Bean, "Ideas of Reform in California," *California Historical Quarterly* 51 (1972): 216, 217.

6. The single most helpful source for biographical data on Wilson is Michael Hanika, "J. Stitt Wilson: California Socialist" (M.A. thesis, California State University, Hayward, 1972). Other sources include Joseph E. Baker, ed., *Past and Present of Alameda County California,* 2 vols. (Chicago: S. J. Clarke, 1914) 2:275-277; *Oakland World,* 8 April 1911, p. 1; *San Francisco Call,* 3 April 1911, pp. 1, 2; *Berkeley Gazette,* 29 August 1942, n.p; and Wilson's own writings, especially his *How I Became a Socialist and Other Papers* (Berkeley: published by the author, 1912).

7. Wilson, "How I Became a Socialist [Pt. I]," p. 1, in *How I Became a Socialist.* This volume contains several different tracts (originally speeches), including the title tract in two parts. Each tract has separate pagination. For simplification, further references to these tracts will be by tract title, tract page number, and the abbreviation *HIBS.*

8. Wilson, "How I Became a Socialist [Pt. II]," pp. 6-8, *HIBS.* For the relation of theological modernism to the social gospel movement, see William McGuire King, "The Emergence of Social Gospel Radicalism: the Methodist Case," *Church History* 50 (1981): 436-449. On theological modernism in American Protestantism, see William R. Hutchison, *The Modernist Impulse*

in American Protestantism (Cambridge: Harvard University Press, 1976).

9. Ibid. [Pt. II], 8.

10. Ibid. [Pt. II], 3-4.

11. Hopkins, *Rise of the Social Gospel,* 199, gives the "five fundamental truths" which the Crusade propounded: 1) the eternal social ideal of the Kingdom of Heaven on earth, 2) the fundamental social law of the principle of sacrifice (this point was a particular theme of Herron's), 3) the teachings of Jesus as the eternal laws of social health, 4) the immediate social hope of co-operative industry, and 5) the divine spirit as the dynamic of faith. See also Handy, "Christianity and Socialism," 46.

12. The quotations on Herron are cited in Hopkins, *Rise of the Social Gospel,* 199; the remark on the SLP is cited in Handy, "Christianity and Socialism," 46.

13. Handy, "Christianity and Socialism," 47-48. Crunden, "Herron in the 1890s," 98-99, 107-111, perceptively analyzes Herron's unstable character. On Herron's break with organized Christianity, see his "Letter to Grinnell Church Committee," *International Socialist Review* 2 (1901): 21-28, his 1901 column "Socialism and Religion" in the same journal, and his "The Recovery of Jesus from Christianity," *Arena* 26 (1901): 225-243.

14. Wilson supported his family with income from his lecturing. Whether his wife also earned income is unclear; in any case, the family was well enough situated by 1911 to own a home on the upper end of Ridge Road with a view of San Francisco Bay. See *San Francisco Call,* 3 April 1911, p. 2. From 1906 into 1909 Wilson and his brother Ben lived in England, working with the British Labour Party. Also during this time, Wilson began a Ph.D. at Oxford which he never completed.

15. On late nineteenth and early twentieth-century Socialism in the United States, see Howard H. Quint, *The Forging of*

American Socialism: Origins of the Modern Movement (Indianapolis: Bobbs-Merrill, 1964) for the period 1865-1901; David A. Shannon, *The Socialist Party of America: A History* (New York: Macmillan, 1955) for 1901-1940; and Daniel Bell, *Marxian Socialism in the United States* (Princeton: Princeton University Press, 1967).

16. On Christian Socialism in the United States, see Handy, "Christianity and Socialism"; Dombrowski, *Christian Socialism;* Hopkins, *Rise of the Social Gospel*; Robert James O'Brien, "Theological and Economic Doctrines: A Study of Christian Socialism in America" (M.A. thesis, University of California, Berkeley, 1951); Richard B. Dressner, "William Dwight Porter Bliss's Christian Socialism," *Church History* 47 (1978): 66-82; and Peter J. Frederick, *Knights of the Golden Rule: the Intellectual as Christian Social Reformer in the 1890s* (Lexington: University Press of Kentucky, 1976).

17. Bliss, "Christian Socialism," in *The New Encyclopedia of Social Reform*, ed. Bliss (New York: Funk & Wagnalls, 1908), 204.

18. Rauschenbusch, "Christian Socialism," in *A Dictionary of Religion and Ethics*, eds. Shailer Mathews and Gerald Birney Smith (London: Waverly, 1921), 90-91. On Rauschenbusch, see Frederick, *Knights of the Golden Rule*, 143-161 and Robert D. Cross, "Introduction," in *Christianity and the Social Crisis*, Walter Rauschenbusch (1907; reprint ed., New York: Harper Torchbooks, 1964), viii-xx.

19. O'Brien, "Christian Socialism in America," 89-90, 92; Hopkins, *Rise of the Social Gospel*, 235-244. Bliss moved in this partisan direction himself, at least temporarily, for he soon joined the CSF; Rauschenbusch, while friendly to the CSF, kept his distance.

20. Rauschenbusch, *A Theology for the Social Gospel* (1918; reprint ed., Nashville: Abingdon Press, 1945), 131.

21. Handy, "Christianity and Socialism," 45.

22. Wilson, "Letter to Berkeley Socialists: Declining the Nomination for the Mayorality of Berkeley (Second Term)," in *The Harlots and Pharisees: or, the Barbary Coast in a Barbarous Land*, (Berkeley: published by the author, 1913), 32.

23. Wilson, "The Present Moral Conflict," *International Socialist Review* 1 (1901): 389.

24. Wilson, "Christianity and Paganism (A Reply)," *International Socialist Review* 2 (1901): 12, 13.

25. Wilson, "The Messiah Cometh: Riding Upon the Ass of Economics," pp. 9, 10, 15, *HIBS*.

26. Wilson, *The Impending Social Revolution, or the Labor Problem Solved* (Berkeley: published by the author, n.d.), 20, 21; cf. 34-35.

27. On the SPA right wing, see Shafer, "Radicalism in California" 203-204. On secularized postmillennialism and modernity, see Jean B. Quandt, "Religion and Social Thought: the Secularization of Postmillennialism," *American Quarterly* 25 (1973): 390-409; and James H. Moorhead, "The Erosion of Postmillennialism in American Religious Thought, 1865-1925," *Church History* 53 (1984): 61-77. On the Protestant ethos of the Progressive era, see Robert M. Cruden, *Ministers of Reform: the Progressives' Achievement in American Civilization, 1889-1920* (New York: Basic Books, 1982); Henry F. May, "The Religion of the Republic," in *Ideas, Faiths, and Feelings: Essays on American Intellectual and Religious History, 1952-1982* (New York: Oxford University Press, 1983), 163-186.

28. *Berkeley City for the People*, 3 April 1913, p. 1; Wilson, "The Kingdom of God and Socialism," p. 1, *HIBS*.

29. Kevin Starr, *Americans and the California Dream, 1850-1915* (New York: Oxford University Press, 1973) is a brilliant

and eloquent exploration of California cultural regionalism. On California utopias, see Robert V. Hine, *California's Utopian Colonies* (1953; reprint ed., New York: Norton, 1973). The Altruria colony's story (1894-1895) is detailed on pp. 101-113.

30. On Henry George's California connection, see Starr, *Americans and the California Dream,* 110-141. Dombrowski, *Christian Socialism,* 35-49 especially highlights the religious impulse and ethos of George's social ideas. For Bellamy's impact in California, see Bean, "Ideas of Reform," 216-217; Dombrowski, *Christian Socialism,* 84-95; Quint, *Forging of American Socialism,* 72-102. Dombrowski points out the significant proportion of ministers who supported the Nationalist movement. Quint argues that Bellamy's Socialism, only one step removed from formal Christian Socialism, was a far profounder influence on American Socialism of the Victorian and Progressive eras than was Marx's.

31. May, *Protestant Churches and Industrial America,* 255; Hopkins, *Rise of the Social Gospel,* 184; Dombrowski, *Christian Socialism,* 179-181.

32. *San Francisco Socialist,* 13 July 1895, p.1. Scott's *Socialism: What Is It? Is It Christian? Should the Church Take Any Interest in It?* (San Francisco: n.p., 1895), is an address in which he explained his theologically based socialism to the San Francisco presbytery. On Bliss and the Urban Reform League, see *San Francisco Social Economist,* 11 September 1897; and Quint, *Forging of American Socialism,* 257-260.

33. The magazine featured articles by Herron, Mayor Samuel ("Golden Rule") Jones of Toledo, A.M. Dewey, R. Heber Newton, and evangelist B. Fay Mills on aspects of the co-operative commonwealth and municipal socialism.

34. Philip S. Foner, ed., *Black Socialist Preacher: the Teachings of Reverend George Washington Woodbey and his Disciple Reverend George W. Slater, Jr.* (San Francisco: Synthesis Publications, 1983), 1-35.

35. Shaffer, "Socialist Party of California," 36, 25-30, 45-59.

36. Herbert Coggins, "Herbert Coggins: From Horatio Alger to Eugene Debs," transcript of oral interview conducted by Corine L. Gilb, Regional Oral History Office, Bancroft Library, University of California, Berkeley, 1957, pp. 88, 125. Quoted by permission of the Bancroft Library.

37. Shaffer, "Socialist Party of California," 39; Wilson, *The Message of Socialism to the Church* (Berkeley: published by the author, 1904), inside cover; William Warren Ferrier, *Our Church in Social Thinking and Action* (Berkeley: n.p., 1936), 14; Wilson, "The Minimum Social Program of a Militant Christianity," in *Addresses, World's Social Progress Congress, San Francisco, California, April One to Eleven, Nineteen Hundred and Fifteen,* ed. William M. Bell (Dayton: World's Social Progress Council, 1915), 22-34.

38. George E. Mowry, *The California Progressives* (Berkeley: University of California, 1951); and Spencer C. Olin, Jr., *California's Prodigal Sons: Hiram Johnson and the Progressives, 1911-1917* (Berkeley: University of California Press, 1968).

39. Bean, "Ideas of Reform," 217; Bean, *California*, 324-325; Shaffer, "Socialist Party of California," 85; Hanika, "J. Stitt Wilson," 76-84.

40. Shaffer, "Socialist Party of California," 83-85; Wilson, "The Story of a Socialist Mayor," in *Harlots and Pharisees,* 24-25.

41. For Berkeley's population, see U.S. Department of Commerce, Bureau of the Census, *Fifteenth Census of the United States, 1930: Population,* 1:22. The Protestant strength is assessed in [Gilchrist, Hugh W.,] *A Survey of Evangelical Churches in San Francisco, Oakland, Berkeley and Alameda* (San Francisco: published by the author, 1916), 5-6. On Berkeley's general history, see George A. Pettitt, *Berkeley: the Town and Gown of It*

(Berkeley: Howell-North Books, 1973) and Phil McArdle, ed., *Exactly Opposite the Golden Gate: Essays on Berkeley's History, 1845-1945* (Berkeley: Berkeley Historical Society, 1983).

42. James T. Burnett, "J. Stitt Wilson," in *Exactly Opposite the Golden Gate*, 279-282.

43. *Berkeley City for the People*, 28 March 1911, n.p.; Wilson, mimeographed letter, 30 March 1911, in Berkeley Politics, 3 boxes, miscellaneous pamphlets and leaflets, Bancroft Library.

44. *San Francisco Call* 3 April 1911, pp. 1-2. Stanford University Professor Ira B. Cross, in his "Socialism in California Municipalities," *National Municipal Review* 1 (1912): 616, noted that there was no evidence of unusual class division in the Berkeley election.

45. *San Francisco Call*, 3 April 1911, p. 2; *Oakland World*, 8 July 1911, n.p.

46. Wilson, "Socialist Mayor," *Harlots and Pharisees,* 26. Hanika, "J. Stitt Wilson," 100-121 is the most detailed account of Wilson's administration.

47. Shaffer, "Socialist Party of California," 144-145. One particular sore point was Wilson's appointment of a non-Socialist city attorney.

48. Coggins, "From Alger to Debs," 89; Shaffer, "Socialist Party of California," 125, 146; Wilson, "Letter to Berkeley Socialists," *Harlots and Pharisees*, 32-36.

49. Shaffer, "Socialist Party of California," 164-175; Bell, *Marxian Socialism*, 100-101.

50. Campaign material in Berkeley Politics, 3 boxes, miscellaneous pamphlets and leaflets, Bancroft Library.

51. *San Francisco Call and Post*, 28 January 1919, p. 51.

52. Hanika, "J. Stitt Wilson," 126-127.

53. Wilson, "Letter to Berkeley Socialists," *Harlots and Pharisees*, 34,35; Wilson, "Impending Social Revolution," p. 3, *HIBS*.

54. "The Golden Age of American Socialism" is Bell's appellation in *Marxian Socialism*; Crunden, "Herron in the 1890s," 111; Dressner, "Bliss's Christian Socialism," 68-70, 81-82; Handy, "Christianity and Socialism," 51.

55. For further discussion of these issues, see Douglas Firth Anderson, "California Protestantism, 1848-1935: Historiographical Explorations and Regional Method for a Nascent Field" (Unpublished paper, Graduate Theological Union, 1983); also Anderson, "San Francisco Evangelicalism, Regional Religious Identity, and the Revivalism of D.L. Moody," *Fides et Historia* 15 (Spring-Summer 1983): 44-66.

18.
Peter C. Yorke:
Advocate of the Irish from the Pulpit
to the Podium

Mary E. Lyons

On the 16th of March 1935 the *San Francisco Call-Bulletin* announced the schedule for that California city's forthcoming St. Patrick's Day celebration. DeValera was to be the keynote speaker at the festivities, but, as the newspaper explained, he and the assembled crowds of San Francisco's Irish would, during one minute of silence, pause to remember a friend on the tenth anniversary of his death, the Reverend Peter Christopher Yorke. The paper further reminded its readers to attend the Palm Sunday graveside memorial to Yorke, an Irish immigrant priest who was born in Galway in 1864 and died in 1925 after a thirty-seven year ministry to the Catholic community of San Francisco. The annual event commemorating Yorke attracted between ten and fifteen thousand people to Holy Cross cemetery.[1] In fact, these annual pilgrimages by the city's Irish Catholics to Father Yorke's grave continued until several years ago. Despite the cessation of this public ceremony, Yorke's legend survives in the memories and through the oral histories of many Bay Area Irish Catholics whose parents were Yorke's contemporaries. This generation, now mostly in their seventies and eighties, will easily relate anecdotes from their family history which feature Peter Yorke.[2] Until very recently this local folklore about Yorke has been complemented by the academics who studied him. His epithets included "Consecrated Thunderbolt," "Father of the organized labor movement in San Francisco," and this tribute in the 1931 volume of the *Moraga Quarterly:* "Those of us who grew up in the community which he adorned can never be persuaded that the age of our youth was not a golden age indeed."[3]

The public character of Peter Yorke has received quite contrasting reviews in recent years. He has been described as a kind of "Peck's bad boy," as a single-minded Irish nationalist, and as a militant leader who misled his people in order to sustain their ghetto mentality.[4] The mixture of laudatory and critical comment about Yorke chronicles well his activity in and around San Francisco and accurately portrays him as a public advocate for the Church and the Irish. Thus, the focus of this essay is less on how Yorke represented himself publicly *for* the Church or the Irish, than on how he represented himself *to* the Irish community.

Yorke arrived in San Francisco during the episcopate of Archbishop Patrick Riordan, at a time when the number of the faithful greatly exceeded the capacity of the archbishop's institutions and clergy. Between 1890 and 1900, the Irish community alone increased from ten to thirty percent of the city's population.[5] In short, at the turn of the century Catholics in San Francisco were in the midst of their own "brick and mortar age." This was a time when above all the archbishop needed priests; he needed churches and schools; he needed money.[6] But in 1894, just three years after Yorke had returned to San Francisco as one of the first graduates of the Catholic University in Washington, D.C., Archbishop Riordan needed something else: an articulate apologist for Catholicism. Increasing public criticism of Catholicism by members and sympathizers of the American Protective Association provoked a public response from the archbishop.[7] Although he did not choose to enter personally the arena of relogous polemic, he sought and found one who had become an oratorical "heavyweight," Peter Yorke.

Yorke had excelled as a scholar at the Catholic University and, during his brief tenure as a curate at San Francisco's St. Mary's Cathedral, he had earned a reputation as a forceful and popular preacher. This made him the archbishop's choice to spearhead the offensive against the APA, to engage in what was called the "Great Controversy."[8] In 1894 Yorke's credentials as his church's spokesman were affirmed by his appointment as chancellor of the archdiocese. He was then provided with an official vehicle for his offensive by his assignment as the first priest-editor of the archdiocesan weekly newspaper, the *Monitor*. With his editorial pen and public voice Yorke led a successful campaign which, by 1896, seriously undermined the credibility of anti-Catholic attacks.[9] In the city elections of 1896 even the mere suggestion that a candidate shared some allegiance with the APA could and did sway the large Catholic vote. Yorke exploited this opportunity just before the elections. Armed with allegations connecting the Republican candidate for mayor, John D. Spreckles, with the APA, Yorke waged a successful battle against him in the press and the lecture hall.[10] The electoral victory of mayor James D. Phelan was, then, a triumph of sorts for the young priest. By the end of the century, Peter Yorke had found that his voice carried power and influence, a formidable force for his church's enemies and a growing source of concern to the very person responsible for encouraging his public stance, the archbishop.

This period in Yorke's career marked, at once, the forging of the bond between him and the dominant Irish-Catholic community, and the deterioration of the bond between him and his church's dominant authority, Archbishop Riordan.[11] In his biography of the archbishop, James Gaffey summarized this development:

> The political victory of 1896 signaled a new stage in the life of Peter Yorke. During the Great Controversy, he had displayed exceptional promise. Only thirty-one years of age and already chancellor of a large archdiocese and editor of a formidable Catholic weekly, his reputation had spread along the Pacific Coast. Yet an individual whose temperment flourished in a conflict or crusade, he found it impossible to divest the martial spirit which had sustained him for three years. And it was equally unfortunate that his archbishop neglected to adjust this young, robust priest to a more conventional ministry at a time when he was approaching the height of his energies and mental prowess.[12]

From the perspective of his clerical colleagues, Yorke's "martial spirit" certainly needed adjusting. Yorke invited upon himself harsh criticism from all directions when, in the months before the 1898 city and gubernatorial election, he repeatedly attacked candidates James Phelan and James Maguire, whose politics Yorke considered anti-Catholic or anti-Irish. When the archbishop finally reprimanded the outspoken priest for his inflammatory written and spoken commentaries, Yorke submitted his resignation as chancellor of the archdiocese, editor of the *Monitor*, and director of the Catholic Truth Society. Although it took the archbishop several months to accept the resignations, accept them he did.[13]

Despite Yorke's troubles with the archbishop, that "martial spirit," as it was read or heard by the city's Irish, earned him an allegiance few clerics in San Francisco could claim, an allegiance which provided him more real influence among the faithful than if he confined himself to preaching, teaching, and sanctifying within his parish boundaries. It would seem, in fact, that the more Yorke alienated himself from the hierarchies of the church and city hall, the more he endeared himself to the masses. For many of the city's Irish-Americans during the first quarter of this century, Yorke was both their "Pope" and their "President."[14]

One of the moments in the history of San Francisco during which this bond beween priest and people became most public was during the city's Teamsters-waterfront strike of 1901. In the summer of that year Yorke accepted a request from the Irish-Catholic labor leaders to speak for them and help rally public support for their cause. Several factors prompted Michael Casey, then business agent for the Brotherhood of Teamsters, to approach Yorke. The meteoric rise of labor organizations in San Francisco beween 1899 and 1900 put employers on the defensive. In response they formed the Employers' Association in April 1901, a secret organization whose members sought to turn San Francisco back into an "open shop" city. Between April and July, the Association had successfully forced out of existence several newer and weaker unions. The July lockout of the teamsters and subsequent sympathy strike by waterfront workers, however, precipitated a two-month strike which brought San Francisco to an economic standstill.[15]

Shortly after the strike began and, later, during the tension-filled days before it ended, Yorke delivered two major speeches for the strikers which were transcribed and then published in *The Examiner*. It is these speeches which reveal Yorke's own presumptions about himself as priest-advocate, about his primary audience of Irish workers, and about the effect he intended to produce on his auditors.

On the evening of August 8th, two weeks after the teamsters declared their strike, Yorke faced a multitude that filled the seats and aisles of Metropolitan Temple.[16] In the opening moments of his address he made explicit why he stood before them and what he intended to say:

> I want to put before you, and I want to put before the larger audience of this city and of this State, as clearly as I know how to, how this question stands. What is the present condition of labor in this city, and, in order that that end [sic] I will speak to you... first on the question of the rights and duties of labor in general, secondly on the nature of the present crisis, and thirdly on your duty in the premises.

Yorke took the next hour to fulfill this oral contract with his audience. First he laid down the "principles of labor" taught by Pope Leo XIII in the encyclical *Rerum Novarum*. He quoted liberally from the Pope, whom he called "the greatest moral authority in the world," and, by the end of this section of his speech, he confidently asserted:

> That it is the dictate of common sense, that it is the universal consent of philosophers, that it is the word of the Pope himself, that such matters dealing with the rights of the workingman, come properly within the sphere of the law: and in this country it depends upon the workingman entirely and altogether how soon the law will take cognizance of those rights. [Applause]

Yorke continued the speech by addressing his second question: the nature of the present crisis. His strategy in this section was to characterize the stance of the employers and to refute them. He attributed to the employers both the demand that they "have the right to run their business absolutely as they please" and the assertion that they would "not recognize unions." To these alleged claims Yorke merely offered counter-claims: "it is perfectly plain that a man has not a right to run his business as he pleases" and "If the men cannot form a corporate body and appoint their deputies to speak for them to any employer whatsoever, then they might as well give up and bury their unions." Yorke knew, of course, that against the background of the Pope's justification of unions (especially as Yorke presented it), the employers' stance (again as Yorke presented it) might be effectively dismissed as blatantly absurd.

After first proclaiming his church's teachings, then exposing the labor crisis as an effort to undermine those teachings, Yorke proceeded with the third section of his discourse, the application. He asked, "What is your duty in the present circumstances?" He answered, "it is your duty to stick together . . . be law abiding . . . be more temperate now than ever." Briefly and succinctly, Yorke told his listeners what was to be done and how it was to be done. As in the second section he offered little explanation or elaboration. He presumed that none was required for this audience of mostly Irish-Catholic laborers.

In his conclusion Yorke made explicit for his audience the common ground upon which he and they stood and which supported their cause: religion. Having moved his auditors through text, exposition and application, the classical tripartite sermon structure, he concluded with a prayer.[17] He voiced a credo, a litany intended to inspire within his listeners not only commitment to the strike action but also commitment to the "higher purpose" for which he had been "preaching" during the previous hour.

> I believe in the cause of the workingman. I believe in a fair wage. I believe in fair hours. I believe in one rest day in seven. I believe in enforcing those things by unionism. I believe in putting them into the law whenever you can. I believe that those things are at stake

today in this city: that it is not a question of wages or hours, that it is not a question of of teamsters or longshoremen, that it is not a question whether you will haul this freight, or whether that steamer shall go to sea; but it is the question, Shall men for whom Christ died to teach them that they were free men, with free men's rights, be crushed beneath the foot of the least bright of all the angels that fell from heaven, Mammon, the spirit of Greed? [Prolonged applause]

Yorke's decision to imitate the sounds and structures of that profession of faith which every Catholic learned from childhood was indeed strategic. As both a leader in prayer and in labor, Yorke could presume that in these closing moments of his speech, most of his listeners would intuit and assent to his thesis that to deny the efficacy of this strike would be to deny the efficacy of Christ's salvific act.

While the sermonic structure of this labor speech and its unabashedly Catholic character signifies the suasive influence which Yorke enjoyed from both the pulpit and the podium, the distinctive character of his intention on the August evening begs attention.

This speech is synecdochic for all of Yorke's discourse, for its inventor brought consistently to the pulpit, to the writing desk, and to the rostrum an understanding of himself as the guardian and expositor of moral truth and authority; an understanding of his discourse as a vehicle for instilling and preserving that truth and authority; and an understanding of his auditors as in want of his mediation.

The particular hermeneutics which Yorke applied to *Rerum Novarum* on this occasion illustrate a significant presumption he held about his audience: the suasive effect upon them of the Pope's word as explained and mediated by himself as their priest. If Yorke had rested his case for labor solely upon the principles of the encyclical, he would have stood upon firmer--if not fairer-- ground with his critics, for this priest-advocate ameliorated, at best, the intention of the papal letter. For example, he excised from one passage the papal *caveat* that wages should be sufficient for a frugal and *well-behaved* wage earner.[18] Given the public accusations of disruption and violence attributed to strikers by some local papers, Yorke's motive for omitting "well-behaved" seemed deliberate.

A more subtle but effective strategy used by Yorke to move his listeners was the extrapolation he devised from the encyclical. Yorke quoted from that section of the letter which defends the rights of "private societies" to exist without the interference of public authority. The passage itself actually prefaces Leo's defense of religious associations.[19] Yorke, however, suggested a different context for this by offering the following: "Unions exist of their own right, and no State has any right to prohibit them." After he underscored the Pope's defense of "unions," he continued to opine that "In the next place, unions are absolutely necessary in the present condition of affairs to get any modicum of the demands which I have said the laboring man has a right to make." This masterful move, of course, would leave the auditor unaware that the speaker had moved beyond the regions of the papal text into his own. Also the uncritical or too trusting listener might not have noticed how, in a single sentence, Yorke aligned himself with the "greatest moral authority of the world" in order to "get any modicum of the demands which I have said the laboring man has a right to make."

The Pope's words, he implied, would be taken as "dogma" not merely as *docens*, describing Leo's words as a "rule which is laid down . . . by one who speaks with the authority of his great office." At the same time, Yorke signalled to his listeners that he and the Pope spoke with similar authority, an authority invested in them at ordination by God, the church and, not insignificantly, by the people. The homiletic structure of his speech combined with its dogmatic content suggest strongly that as labor's advocate Yorke was a mediator--certainly not a conciliator--between his people and the powerful Employers' Association. He found justification for this role in his own understanding of priestly mediation.[20] What he implied from the podium he made explicit from the pulpit. Among the Yorke papers, for example, is the following excerpt from a sermon he preached to a priests' retreat.

It is hard for any grown man to put on the mentality of a child. It is hardest of all for a priest. He is by his office a ruler and his rule over his own is so unquestioned. Sometimes the difficulty arises from plain ordinary pride. Sometimes from just animal obstinancy--sometimes from mere routine. We have been sitting so long at the wheel that it is hard for us to get down and march with the machineless mob.[21]

As the strike dragged on through August and into September, Yorke responded to the growing desperation of the "machineless mob" by confronting them again from the podium. The Sunday morning issue of *The Examiner* on September 22 featured the entire text of Yorke's second major speech, a two hour address given the previous evening at Metropolitan Temple.[22] To a capacity crowd Yorke offered essentially the same outline as he had done in August. He defined the principle at issue during the strike as the survival of unionism; he amplified this with a history and defense of unions; and, again, he called the strikers to action: to contribute to the strike fund, to boycott the city's merchants, to avoid violence, to beware of politicians. The audible emotion of Yorke's speech was far louder than before and more bellicose. More prominent too were his personal attacks on such important city figures as John Spreckles, Michael de Young, Benjamin Wheeler, John Irish, James Phelan and various employers and merchants in San Francisco.

On one level this speech might be examined as typical propaganda. The speaker did his best to villify the opposition and to dignify his audience and their cause. Indeed, Yorke proved himself a master of invective, of ridicule and of verbal abuse as he wove into the fabric of the part-sermon, part-diatribe endless attacks on the employers and their political supporters. But while his jabs might have effectively rallied his auditors, they were part of a larger strategy. On this occasion Yorke intended to produce in the audience more than applause, even more than the actions he proposed at the end of his speech. He expanded and made more explicit the intention of his August speech.

As in the August address, Yorke's method of argument reveals as much, if not more, about his attitudes as does the content of the discourse.[23] His method of argument for unionism here, as elsewhere, was to posit a series of "definitions," "principles" or "questions." Thus, he assured his audience, "You are fighting for a principle, and it is a principle that makes life worth living, and it is a principle that gives dignity to everything that men do." Yorke framed his speech with first principles, but upon it he draped one lengthy digression after another: a brief report on the church's support for poor workers, a short history of the development of unionism, an apologia for foreign-born citizens, an encomium for *The Examiner* and the governor and a diatribe against party politics. Yorke would have known that these hungry and desperate strikers needed little "proof" of the Employers' Association's desire to crush their unions, and little evidence that their cause was just. Thus onto a speech outlined with the "principles" of unionism, the priest hung a series of specific arguments intended for his listeners' immediate response.

Yorke's habit of framing his discourse by references to how things *should* be, to the *principles* which ought to direct events or guide men's choices, suggests that he was an idealist, a believer in and an advocate of a principle "that makes life worth living." This kind of argument gave even Yorke's adversaries the impression that he was, above all, the champion of liberalism. For example, an intentionally critical editorial which appeared shortly after this labor speech compared Yorke to Edward McGlynn, a New York priest who, in the late nineteenth century, supported Henry George's single-tax campaign, opposed public funding of parochial schools, and attacked the primacy of private property.[24] Had the editor known how stridently opposed Yorke was to these and other progressive views of liberals like McGlynn he might not have written that Yorke "parades himself as the Western Successor of Father McGlynn of New York City."[25]

Yorke's persistent arguments from principle or definition that mark not only his labor speeches but all of his oratory characterize him as a believer in a world of static, unchanging essences, in a world which cannot and should not change. In this respect he stood far to the right of those liberal clergy with whom both his supporters and critics often associated him.[26] Despite the liberal nature of the union cause, Yorke's appeal in his speech of September 22, as a review of his arguments shows, was not motivated by a desire for change or for social and economic reform. Rather, it was prompted by his consistent desire to preserve the values and beliefs of "his people": in short, to make the real conform to the ideal.[27]

On that night in September, Yorke again called his listeners to "Stand together and have courage." This imperative implied more than cohesion for the sake of unionism. It sprang from Yorke's determination to preserve the identity of Irish-Catholic laborers. His battle that evening was only a skirmish in his persistent war to keep the Irish working-class community intact, pristine and protected from outside social, economic and religious influences.[28] He advanced this case in three ways: first, he reminded the listeners of their identity as Catholics; second, he reminded them of their identity as members of the working class; third, he reminded them of their identity as immigrants. Through all of this, Yorke advocated the appropriateness of this, their "state in life."

Yorke spent the first fifteen minutes of his speech ostensibly justifying his presence at the podium. He introduced his listeners to a major theme in this speech: his "proper sphere" as their priest was to speak for them as Catholics and the victims of the rich. He argued:

> It would appear that there has been a sentiment growing in the free State of San Francisco within the last five or six years. . . . I have seen the germ of it appear, and I have noted its noxious growth, and in days past I have warned those who wished to hear me about it--that such a sentiment should grow and should become prevalent, that the city of San Francisco was founded by rich men, is

preserved by rich men, and should be occupied only by
rich men.

Any speaker knows that *where* something is placed in a
discourse is often as important as the content itself. What Yorke
chose to say first was not accidental; it was strategic. He told his
audience quite plainly that he, their priest and prophet--"I have
warned"--had come to stop the "noxious growth" of a "germ" that
was spreading among them. At this point the listeners might have
thought the priest intended to castigate those who invested their
trust only in rich, powerful men. As he continued, however, the
caveat expanded. Yorke included in his condemnation those who
pursued prosperity itself, those who sought to live beyond the
level of "frugal comfort." He developed this argument by
inventing an elaborate antithesis which aligned, on one side, the
rich, the employers, the politicians, the "upper classes," the
native-born and the non-Catholics against, on the other side, the
poor, the laborers, the immigrants and the Catholics. In short,
Yorke sought to build an argumentative corral for his people to
keep them in as much as to keep out the others. He began
construction in his introduction.

> Therefore, when now they ask why any man should
> come and put himself upon the side of those who have
> not; on the side of those who much labor; on the side of
> those who do not belong to any such clubs; on the side of
> those who should not be able to tell one brand of claret
> from another to save their lives; on the side of those who
> think champagne is a sweetened kind of soda water; on
> the side of those who care little about French etiquette;
> when they ask this they ask it with the thought back in
> their mind, that they have made this city, that they have
> bought this city, and that no man in this city should raise
> up a voice for anything except theirs [sic] because they
> are our lords and masters.

The real worth of San Francisco, he explained, rested in the
people, "the poorer the better." From that point, which suggested
that labor and poverty were synonymous, Yorke added a third

concept: Catholic. He noted, ". . . I am here to say what good word I can on behalf of those who do not possess these world's [sic] goods; on behalf of those who have to labor for their daily bread, because I am a priest of the Catholic Church." He followed with a description of the Church.

> So, when I look at what the Catholic Church has done, when she stood against the hucksters of Front Street; when she stood up against kings; when she stood up against emperors; when she stood up against the money powers of all the world, and threw a charmed circle around the workingmen, and said to the money powers of the world, "Thus far shall you go, and no further," why should not I, a humble priest of that church, do my best for the working people?

In this passage Yorke presented another version of "Thus far shall you go, and no further." For, besides defending his and his church's right to stand up for the poor, he declared that the church--a humane society which has stood up against nearly every other--was the only refuge for these oppressed working people. For the worker, the church provided a truly "charmed circle."

Once Yorke established the grounds of his argument, making clear who was and who was not of this "circle," he did his best to tighten the knot that bound them all by stressing the impossibility of reconciliation between the two sides. He insisted that "the principles on which each are acting are absolutely irreconcilable." Thus, Yorke emphasized that the laborer was, and should remain, separated from those outside the "circle." Those who opposed unionism he condemned as "devils" and "purblind idiots" who wanted the workers to be "their chattels, their slaves, to be treated far worse than chattels or slaves were treated in the days of old."

If the purpose of this speech was to defend unionism, strengthen the resolve of the strikers and urge specific actions which would hasten labor's victory, Yorke might have ended his address after ninety minutes. Instead, he introduced, in the final thirty minutes, other arguments.

Another point. We have been lectured for the last week
or so on the foreign-born people. We have been told that
foreign-born people are the scum of creation. . . . And
we have been told (I am ashamed to say it) that the
foreign-born people have no right here except to keep
their mouths shut; that is they do not like their country,
why don't they go back to where they came from? I do
not know how many of you are foreign-born, and I do
not know how many of you are native-born. Moreover I
don't care. I am foreign-born myself. . . .   The man
who tries to make division between the native-born and
the foreign-born citizen is a traitor to America.

By using "we" in this passage Yorke acknowledged the
identification he shared with his audience. Earlier Yorke had
stressed his and their common ground of poverty and religion;
now he emphasized their common status as immigrants. He
highlighted this at this particular place in the speech by design for,
in the remaining minutes of the discourse, he capitalized on the
point when he advanced an argument concerning political
involvement.[29] He told his audience that their concern in this
"fight" should be only the "principle of unionism." Yorke
warned, "Put not your trust in politicians. Put not your trust in
political parties."

Having stressed the prejudice against immigrants, Yorke
proceeded to recount the betrayal of the strikers by the city's
elected officials, especially Mayor Phelan whom the fiery priest
had once supported. Politicians were worse than opportunistic
businessmen. They were "the incarnation of all that is selfish." To
meet and defeat that diabolic incarnation, Yorke advocated a plan.

What can you do? . . . The politician is a fierce man, but
he is afraid of things, and above all things, he is afraid of
the men who are not tied down to a party, he is afraid of
the men who know what their interests are and who are
determined to vote according to their interests. Your
power does not consist in electing people; your power

consists in defeating people, in keeping out of office bad men.

He concluded by telling them to trust in God's guidance when they cast their votes, disregard thoughts of advancement, friends and favors and think only of their "great struggle."

In this final argument Yorke accomplished two ends. He had "picked off the enemy one by one": the employers, the merchants, the upper classes and politicians. He had also eliminated for his audience all possible social and political allegiances save one, that to the only "humane society," the church. This well-crafted *expeditio* threw a "charmed circle" around those whom he had elevated throughout the address: the poor, the working class, the foreign-born, "God's people," in short, the Irish-Catholic laborers in his audience.[30]

Besides defending unions and strikers and instilling in his listeners a resolve to continue their struggle, Yorke called on his people to remember always who they were, where they had come from and to whom they owed their allegiance. He warned that to wander from the circle was to wander from the fold, and to stray was to perish.

At one point in his September address Yorke reminded his audience, "We are behind the whole country in everything." Considering Yorke's position, it might be argued that in some ways, he too was "behind the country" in which he found himself. The western experience provided opportunities unknown to immigrant communities along the eastern seaboard. Indeed, by the time Yorke reached San Francisco, the Irish had already stamped their signature upon the city's character. In his recent study of the Irish community at the turn of the century, R. A. Burchell explained the relatively rapid mobility of these immigrants.

A relatively friendly environment thus gave the Irish the chances they took. The cosmopolitanism of the city was a reflection of its youth, the lack of what an English upper-class visitor described as "settled society" with the unchallenged, pre-eminent right to dictate the tone and style of the city, order its affairs and exclude those who were, in its view, undesireable. The massive growth of the city gave opportunity for the Irish to build into its central structure, which took form and character from their own efforts.[31]

A telling fact that emerges from this story of Yorke's involvement in the labor strike and which underscores Burchell's thesis is that immediately after the strike those very Irishmen who had heard Yorke's arguments on politics established their own Union Labor Party.[32]

A study of these labor discourses reveals how frail, slippery and useless are labels like "conservative" and "liberal" when applied to Peter Yorke. During the Teamsters-Waterfront strike of 1901 we see Yorke using an apparently liberal cause--workers rights, unionism, etc.--to promote an apparently conservative argument--the importance and superiority of the ecclesial authority of pope and priest.

Yorke encouraged his audience to identify themselves as Irish-Catholic workers and to isolate themselves from the rest of the community. By denigrating every other social, economic and political association that might attract them, he left his listeners no other option save that of the Irish-Catholic working class community. By encouraging "frugality" and adherence to the mandates of *Rerum Novarum*, Yorke sought for that community economic and social stability sufficient for its continued independence. Too much prosperity or mobility, he inferred, simply invited upon the community "infection" and fragmentation. Finally, Yorke warned the community against traditional partisan politics. To step into the established political arena was to step outside that "charmed circle" which enclosed Irish-Catholic workers. Yet is clear that during the strike of 1901 Yorke helped both to organize and politicize Irish labor. In a Labor Day address one year after the strike, he claimed that "the labor movement is as truly a moral movement as the Church movement."[33] That "moral movement," however, owed much of its victory and survival to party politics.

The paradox of Yorke's arguments is striking. The success of San Francisco's Union Labor Party was, as labor historians have noted, a direct response to events of the 1901 strike.[34] The party depended heavily upon the leadership and votes of Irish labor. How does one account for this behavior on the part of the Irish community? Were they ignoring their priest's warning against partisan politics? On the contrary, Yorke was partly responsible for that involvement. He provided the justification for such involvement and he nurtured the power base of the Union Labor Party. Yorke intended to isolate his people from politicians, "the incarnation of all that is selfish." Instead, he inadvertently promoted the creation of a cadre of Irish labor politicians.

By throwing a "charmed circle" around his people, by insisting that the church provided everything for the needs of the community, including the moral criteria for decision-making and behavior, and by insisting that the church had no place in politics, Yorke promoted compartmentalization among his listeners. If religion had no place in politics and its dictates did not apply, then one who became political did so with religious impunity.

Yorke's labor speeches during the 1901 strike emphasized that religion was on one side and everything else, especially politics, was on the other. These arguments promoted among the Irish a bifurcated view: one could live separately at once in the church and in the state and apply in each realm separate, non-competing moral criteria. Ironically, the priest's repeated appeals for Irish cohesiveness strengthened the influence of the Catholic community and empowered the Irish as a political force. Thus, Abraham Ruef's political machine, the Union Labor Party, owed much of its success to a power base among Irish voters, a base which Yorke's arguments helped to foster.

While Yorke's speeches tended to elevate labor as a moral movement, they implicitly argued that labor was on its own once it descended into the political arena. By marking the boundaries so distinctly between the sacred and the secular, Yorke implied that the Irish workers who participated actively in politics could no longer depend on the favored position of those who were part of the "charmed circle." He suggested that, since it had no place in politics, religion had nothing to do with what, in fact, was a very real part of life. As a result, the vision of the church as the preserver and protector of the Irish laboring community faded as that community moved further into the social, economic and political mainstream of American life.

Yorke deserved the honor granted him by the San Francisco Labor Council as one of the "founders and leaders of the San Francisco Labor Movement."[35] Unfortunately, where he might have fostered social and economic progress and promoted political leadership within the Irish community, Yorke offered isolation rather than assimilation, frugality rather than prosperity, and political timidity rather than leadership. He brought to the pulpit and the podium a mentality and a rhetoric which lagged behind the process of Americanization that had already begun among the Irish of San Francisco.

Notes

1. *The San Francisco Call-Bulletin*, 16 March 1935, p. 5:2.

2. Personal interviews with Vera Ryan, 1 February 1984; Ethel Wood, 18 February 1984; John Butler, 25 February 1984; Msgr. Bernard Cronin, 26 January 1984.

3. Bernard C. Cronin, *Father Yorke and the Labor Movement in San Francisco, 1900-1910* (Washington: Catholic University Press, 1943), 229; Joseph Brusher, *Consecrated Thunderbolt* (Hawthorne, N.J.: Joseph F. Wagner, Inc., 1973); Brother Leo Mahan, "Father Yorke in the Pulpit," *Moraga Quarterly* 2 (Fall 1931): 31.

4. James P. Gaffey, *Citizen of No Mean City* (Wilmington, N.C.: Consortium Books, 1976); James P. Walsh, "Peter C. Yorke: San Francisco's Irishman Reconsidered," in *The San Francisco Irish, 1850-1976*, James P. Walsh, ed. (San Francisco: Irish Literary and Historical Society, 1978), 54; Timothy Sarbaugh, "Father Yorke and the San Francisco Waterfront, 1901-1916," *The Pacific Historian* 25 (Fall 1981): 29.

5. 1890 census in Gaffey, *Citizen*, 438, n. 3; 1900 census in Walsh, "Peter C. Yorke," 55, n. 13.

6. Gaffey, *Citizen*, 73-74.

7. Recent scholarship suggests that the so-called Great Controversy might have withered away without any intervention by Catholics given their demographic and religious dominance in San Francisco. See R. A. Burchell, *The San Francisco Irish, 1848-1880* (Berkeley: University of California Press, 1980), 190; Walsh, "Peter C. Yorke," 55, n. 14.

8. Gaffey, *Citizen*, 152.

9. Ibid., 150-162. For a rhetorical analysis of this campaign see Robert C. Maguire, "The Analysis and Criticism of the Persuasive Discourse of the Rev. Peter C. Yorke, 1894-1898" (unpublished Ph.D. dissertation, UCLA, 1967).

10. Brusher, *Consecrated Thunderbolt,* 33-35.

11. Gaffey, *Citizen*, 137.

12. Ibid., 162; Walsh, "Peter C. Yorke," 46.

13. Gaffey, *Citizen*, 163-175. In later years some of Yorke's disgruntled colleagues were so eager to restrain him that they hired private detectives to shadow him, hoping to convince the archbishop to silence Yorke. Yorke withstood this undercover investigation. See "Detective Report," T. S., Peter C. Yorke

Papers, Archives of the Archdiocese of San Francisco, Colma, California; Brusher, *Consecrated Thunderbolt*, 143-147.

14. That Irish immigrants would invest their local priest with full authoritative leadership in matters beyond those specifically religious has been established elsewhere. See, for example, Jay Dolan, *The Immigrant Church* (Baltimore: John Hopkins University Press, 1975). A study of contemporary Irish cultural life concluded, ". . . Irish social life revolves about the institution of the parish, and the central figure in the parish is the local priest. He is by office, by education, and by tradition, the leader of his people." Francis Bruce Biever, *Religion, Culture, and Values: A Cross-Cultural Analysis of Motivational Factors in Native Irish and American Irish Catholicism* (New York: Arno Press, 1976), 501.

15. Ira B. Cross, *A History of the Labor Movement in California* (Berkeley: University of California Press, 1935), 236-245.

16. This account and the transcript of Yorke's speech are taken from "Father Yorke's Notable Address on Unions," *San Francisco Examiner*, 9 August 1901, pp. 2 and 6.

17. The following texts offer examples of late nineteenth and early twentieth century homiletic theory in which Yorke would have been trained: Bernard Feeney, *Manual of Sacred Rhetoric* (St. Louis: B. Herder, 1901): Thomas McNamara, *Sacred Rhetoric* (Dublin: Browne and Nolan, 1881). For a discussion of homiletic theory in this era see Joseph M. Connors, "Catholic Homiletic Theory in Historical Perspective" (unpublished Ph.D. dissertation, Northwestern University, 1962), 191-288.

18. I have limited my remarks only to those blatant deletions or extrapolations which would be evident in any English translation of the encyclical since I have found no evidence of the actual translation used by Yorke. The following translation matches Yorke's quotations exactly except for those passages which appear to be deliberately altered: Etiene Gilson, ed., *The*

Church Speaks to the Modern World: The Social Teachings of Leo XIII (Garden City, N.Y.: Image Books, 1954), 230.

19. Ibid., 233.

20. One insightful note from a homiletic textbook of that time suggests where Yorke and other clergy of his generation developed their presumptions about the "flock:" "A Catholic preacher needs no 'credentials to his flock,' except the authorization or mission of his ecclesiastical superior." Feeney, *Manual*, 109.

21. Peter C. Yorke, "The Particular Examen," n.d., Peter C. Yorke Papers, Archives of the University of San Francisco, San Francisco, California.

22. "'Stand Together!' is Father Yorke's Advice to Men of Labor Unions. 'Fight Like Men,'" *San Francisco Examiner*, 22 September 1901, pp. 19-21. References to this text are taken from this source.

23. For evidence as to how a speaker's method can provide a better index to his/her belief than any explicit statement of principles, see Richard M. Weaver, *The Ethics of Rhetoric* (Chicago: Henry Regnery Co., 1953), 55-114.

24. James Hennesey, S.J., *American Catholics* (New York: Oxford University Press, 1981), 189-190.

25. *San Francisco Call,* 24 September 1901, p. 6.

26. For a discussion of the characteristics of the argument from definition in the discourse of Abraham Lincoln, see Weaver, *Ethics of Rhetoric*, 85-114.

27. In his analysis of Yorke's arguments against the APA, Robert Maguire described Yorke's argumentative method as "a didactic rhetorical theory" rooted in Thomistic philosophy. Maguire, "Analysis," 347-353.

28. "Basically in all his lectures Father Yorke followed one line of thought. . . . The Catholic Church was the custodian of revealed truth." Ibid., 297.

29. Elsewhere in this speech Yorke supported Governor Gage. On October 2, the governor discussed with Yorke a request from the city's merchants for intervention by the state militia. Yorke objected, the militia was not mobilized and the strike was declared over the next day. Cronin, *Father Yorke*, 84-85.

30. The editorial columns of Spreckles' paper, *The Call*, accused Yorke of parading himself as "the western successor of Father McGlynn of New York City," and denounced him for "putting out his nets in the open season for converts to Catholicism." *San Francisco Call*, 24 & 26 September 1901, p. 6.

31. Burchell, *San Francisco Irish*, 182.

32. Jules Tygiel, "Where Unionism Holds Undisputed Sway," *California History* 3 (Fall 1983): 197-215.

33. "Address by Rev. Yorke to the Workingmen of San Francisco on Labor Day," *The Leader*, 6 September 1902, pp 6-7.

34. Cross, *Labor Movement*, 245-247; Tygiel, "Unionism," 197.

35. Memorium for Yorke issued upon his death in 1925 by the San Francisco Labor Council, Yorke Papers, Archives of the Archdiocese of San Francisco.

VII

Communal Sects
and New Religions

19.
William Keil and the Aurora Colony: A Communal Society Crosses the Oregon Trail

Patrick J. Harris

In 1853 William Keil sent ten trusted scouts from Bethel, Missouri with instructions to locate a new site in the Pacific Northwest for his religious communal society. Established in 1844, Bethel had become a secure and self-sufficient German enclave in the West, but Keil was convinced that his followers were losing their spiritual focus as they participated in Missouri's rapid growth before the Civil War. The scouts traveled to Willapa, in Washington Territory, and sent word that they had located a "Second Eden." Keil had requested an isolated environment, and the scouts had apparently found one with great potential. Members of the Bethel Colony immediately began preparations for a migration across the Oregon Trail to resettle on the Pacific coast. Soon 175 of the estimated 600 Bethelites embarked upon the overland journey.

Keil's charismatic leadership was reestablished and reasserted during the 1855 crossing. His letters from the trail demonstrate the techniques he employed to help the migrants survive the arduous trip and to maintain influence over the colony members remaining in Missouri. Undoubtedly Keil's leadership on the trail was similar to the methods he applied in Missouri, but away from home the members' extreme dependence upon him heightened his power.

Upon arrival in the west, however, Keil found that he had not anticipated the sheer magnitude of the problems created by the frontier environment and climate. In response, Keil chose adaptation rather than isolation by moving his colony to Aurora in the Willamette Valley near Portland. His decision assured the continuity of the communal experiment, but it also exposed the colonists to increased external influences. Keil had declared that he left Missouri because of outside temptations to his people, yet he

425

settled the new colony in a region guaranteed to attract thousands of people. His decision to migrate meant that he never regained his former influence over those left behind in Missouri, while in Aurora the frontier's promise of individual opportunity gradually eroded those traditional community values Keil had come west to revive.

The histories of Bethel and Aurora have been recorded elsewhere in some detail, but there has been no adequate analysis of the process by which the colony was transplanted to the American West.[1] This account, based primarily on the unpublished letters and diaries of the colonists, interprets the overland migration of the Bethelites as a communal experience and assesses the impact of the frontier upon their ideals and practices after they arrived in Oregon. Recently Robert Hine has reminded us that episodes of cooperative behavior on the overland trail helped ensure the migrants' survival and relieved their longings for sociability.[2] But in contrast to the temporary and superficial communities of most overland emigrants, the Bethelites, like the Mormons before them, began and ended their journey as a community. The success of their westward journey testified to the charisma and practical ability of William Keil in maintaining communal solidarity under extremely difficult conditions. At the same time, Keil's interpretation of the ordeal provides a vivid example of how pious emigrants, unlike most gold seekers, imbued the overland journey with meanings and symbols drawn from the Judeo-Christian drama of sin and salvation, exodus and search for the promised land. But religious colonization on the frontier proved as problematic as the crossing itself. The history of Aurora demonstrated how conditions on the booming frontier created pressures to assimilate which proved irresistible even to the leader who intended to preserve the colonists' distinctive religious and communal orientation.

William Keil was born on March 6, 1812 in Erfurt, Prussia. He learned the tailor's trade as a young man, but also studied natural healing and botany, and came under the influence of post-Reformation mysticism. In 1831 Keil married Louisa Ritter and emigrated with her to America; by 1837 he had moved to Pittsburg and opened an apothecary. There he attended Methodist revivals and eventually became an itinerant minister himself, though without official sanction because Keil insisted that ministers, following the example of Christ, should give their services freely.[3] Keil's intense enthusiasm and sincere purpose impressed many, and within a few years he attracted a band of German ministers who traveled throughout western Pennsylvania, Indiana, and Ohio with Keil's message of simple Christianity. Pittsburg was only a few miles from the site of George Rapp's Harmony Society, a German communal sect founded in 1804, which had recently suffered divisions because of Rapp's insistence that members practice celibacy. Some researchers have surmised that former Rappites may have suggested the idea of a communal society to Keil.[4] In any case, at some point in the early 1840s Keil began to preach about the formation of a communal society featuring shared property and labor but not requiring celibacy. German farmers and craftsmen contacted during the ministry and the ex-Rappites were asked to pool their earnings into a common fund established to purchase land for such a society. Bethel, Missouri, located forty miles northwest of Hannibal, was selected by Keil on the advice of three scouts. This site was close to markets via the Mississippi River, but still isolated. The first members arrived at Bethel in 1844, and most were present by 1847. Population figures have been exaggerated, but it seems that about 600 active members were living at Bethel in 1850.

The members of the Bethel Colony purchased over four thousand acres of land in two adjacent Missouri counties. The first years were difficult, but Keil had made few promises. Colonists built their own homes and provided shelter for newcomers. The ex-Harmonists provided needed craft skills and counseled Keil about ways to organize the society. Their advice and Keil's insistence on brotherly love meant that Bethel was based on practical economic foundations and sustained by high spiritual ideals. Workers performed specific tasks geared to benefit the economy of the whole community, and were expected to consider the welfare of the community over personal ambitions. Members shared labor and property. Keil's followers tilled their own fields and supplied crafts for other members of their community, and they provided surplus goods to neighbors at a profit for the communal treasury. While agriculture was the chief industry, the Bethelites also built a flour mill, a saw mill, a woolen mill, a distillery, a tannery, a lime and brick kiln, and a glue plant. Items such as boots, shoes, hats, gloves, wagons, plows, woolen and linen goods, liquors and linseed oil were made and sold for community profit. By 1850 the Bethel Colony was established and successful. German professors were teaching some of the children, and a music teacher prepared the colony band for performances given throughout the region. Colonists attended regular services in their church, and the Bethel hotel served fine meals to travelers.[5]

Why then did William Keil decide to leave Missouri? Keil explained in a letter written from Willapa, Washington to his followers in Bethel. "It was not the fault of the country," he wrote, "that we undertook the journey to Oregon, but the people themselves. If the people had submitted to discipline and given heed to the voice of God it would not have been necessary to leave Bethel."[6] Scholars have suggested that Keil was caught up in the spirit of the westward migration, or that he saw the west as a broader arena for his communal dream.[7] In addition, antebellum Missouri was a state in uproar, bitterly divided by the question of slavery, and apparently some Bethelites found it difficult to remain neutral. But Keil's reference to his people's sins has been overlooked. Though lacking specifics, this indictment seemed to refer to the attraction of outside influences which Keil felt threatened the continuity of the Bethel colony. A prosperous economy, the opportunity to educate their children beyond the community's borders, and the tumult of Missouri politics were luring Keil's followers into the ways of the outside world. Keil's solution was to seek a refuge on the frontier where his followers' godly ideals could be preserved in relative isolation.

The ten scouts selected by Keil to survey the West for a new site were some of the colony's best members. They included George Link, a veteran ox-driver, Adam Schuele, one of the scouts who selected Bethel, and other experienced hunters and trappers.[8] The scouts arrived at Fort Vancouver in the Fall of

1853 and were directed to the southwest coast of Washington. After wintering at Fort Steilicoom, four of the scouts took out Donation Land Claims at Willapa, while the others returned to Bethel with the news. Keil immediately began preparations for his people to leave Missouri.

175 people were ready to depart from Bethel in the Spring of 1855 when Keil's nineteen year old son Willi contracted malaria. While Keil hoped for his son to improve, a smaller wagon train led by Peter Klein left Bethel.[9] Willi died, however, and Keil, fulfilling a promise to his son, brought the boy's body along the trail to be buried in Washington. Under Keil's direction a metal coffin was hastily constructed, then a heavier one was purchased in St. Louis. Alcohol was poured inside to act as a preservative, the boy's body placed within, and the coffin was sealed.

The eerie story of Willi's dead body leading the Keil caravan across the Oregon Trail has attracted much attention, but Keil actually wrote very little about it. One member of the Aurora Colony described his response to Keil's directive in the following manner: "It was not a pleasant task," wrote Moses Miller, "to escort his boy's remains 2,000 miles, the distance from Missouri to Oregon, and to have with him amid that wild and lonely country the depressing influence of the boy's dead body; but it made people think; it made a lasting impression; the purpose of it was plain; a colonist dared not lie."[10] Miller's reaction helps to explain the colonists' willingness to see a father's grief expressed in such a bizarre way. For the colonists, it was another of Keil's lessons, and they were familiar with lessons. Keil may have had additional motives. He was not about to bury his son in a state that he disliked. Perhaps he blamed the Missouri swamps for Willi's death. Keil may also have seen rich symbolism in the act: with Willi's coffin in the lead the caravan became simultaneously a funeral procession for Bethel and a promise of the rebirth of Keil's communal dream in a new land. In any case, the story illustrates Keil's strong resolution and his determination to carry out extraordinary policies despite severe odds. "When I blow the trumpet," he wrote, "there is a tumult like an earthquake. Willi goes ahead and we follow him."[11] Willi led the wagons as his father had promised.

Keil's caravan left Bethel on May 25th, 1855. The record of the crossing comes primarily from letters written by Keil to the members remaining at Bethel. (Keil planned to settle in Washington and to send for the other members who meanwhile would arrange for the sale of colony property.) Keil's letters dwell upon his followers' unity despite physical separation; they detail the day-to-day log of the crossing; and perhaps most important, they offer insight into the way it reinforced Keil's leadership. Because of these letters, three facets of the crossing experience can be studied in greater detail: 1) Keil's extraordinary relationship with the Indians, 2) Keil's use of dreams or visions as sources of spiritual insight and practical guidance, and 3) Keil's portrayal of the environment as a devilish enemy to be conquered by a godly people.

Accounts of Indian attacks on covered wagons have been exaggerated, but Keil's letters indicate that 1855 was thought to be a particularly dangerous year to cross the Oregon Trail.[12] Keil describes an atmosphere full of rumors and fears at Fort Laramie and Fort Dalles. Indians had specific grievances with soldiers at Laramie, and a few wagon trains had already been attacked. The fears expressed offered Keil a first opportunity to assert his leadership. "All the anxiety and fear that was in the hearts of men," wrote Keil, "gather about me. Strangers and respectable men warned me and plead with me that I should not cross the plains with my people at such terrible times." Keil reported that a rumor about the capture of Laramie was circulating throughout the area. In the face of this concern Keil retreated to a high hill overlooking camp and began to pray:

> I could find no point of contact that satisfied me. I paused for a little while and the spirit came to me and said: "If what you have done during your lifetime in defeating your enemies does not suffice, then no other atonement will be found for you." Then there arose in me a melancholy feeling for all my brothers and sisters, and I

swore three times to myself that the first hostile force that might approach my people should fall, though it gathered by thousands. When I came back to the camp all fear had vanished from me and from those who belonged to me.[13]

Fortified by this mystical experience, Keil expressed renewed confidence in his mission. He suggested that his followers shared this fortification experience, thanks to the deep relationship that Keil had established with them. In matters of divine inspiration most followers believed that Keil was especially blessed.

By the time it reached western Nebraska Keil's caravan had passed through several larger ones whose leaders asked to join Keil. Keil turned down their requests, believing that their fear of Indian attack could affect his followers. The rumors about Indians continued to Fort Kearney, but the colonists had not seen one Indian along the way. "It seems," wrote Keil, "as if a peculiar feeling has come over them, so that they do not tarry on the way at all."[14] He apparently felt that his mystical experience had somehow affected the Indians and kept them at a distance. A fearless group holding implicit trust in God could not be threatened.

The colonists' first encounter with Indians raised their confidence. Indians at Ash Hollow left their camp and crossed the river, leaving the area to the emigrants. Several times Indians gathered on the hills but watched the caravan pass in silence. At Hams Forks seven Indians ventured into the camp. Keil gave them dinner and sent food home with them. In the morning about twenty-five Indians returned in full dress as if in special ceremony. Keil remarked that he could "read the love and gratitude in their faces." Soldiers at Fort Laramie warned the emigrants that Indians had been attacking scout parties without warning, but Keil's confidence grew to such an extent after passing hundreds of Indians without incident that he boldly declared: "I had power over the Indians and could do with them what I wanted." Keil's strategy was to avoid contact if possible, but to be very friendly when the Indians made the first gesture. In the Grand Round Valley some Cajuses Indians were camped near

Keil's resting point for the evening. "The principal chief," wrote Keil, "was an old, honest man. His name is Camapallo Ullman. Because we all spoke German, they thought we were Frenchmen. I made them understand that we were Germans.... They said Cajuses good, Frenchmen good, Dutchmen good, Americans no good . . . shoot." Keil's children exchanged gifts with the Indian children, and several meals were shared. Keil recorded that Camapallo cried when it was time for the train to continue.[15] This incident almost landed Keil in jail at The Dalles. A soldier traveling with Keil from Laramie reported the Indians' comment to the fort commander, and Keil was detained for defaming Americans. Keil, however, had a good rapport with other men in positions of command, and he was able to convince the officer of his innocence.

Some writers have suggested that the Indians were afraid of Willi's dead body, others that the singing of the colonists awed the Indians. Keil never mentioned these factors. His letters do note that he discouraged soldiers from travelling with his group, fearing that their presence would provoke Indian attacks. But Keil believed that God had blessed the crossing, and his mystical experience was all the proof he needed of his colony's safety. Keil pursued a friendly yet fearless policy, and it worked. His followers were impressed. They left apparent security for the unknown, and had a triumphantly successful crossing. Despite their personal fears, the emigrants felt greater confidence in their leader.

Keil's mystical experience at the beginning of the trail is reminiscent of Moses at Mt. Sinai, and the similarity was not lost on him. Keil styled himself on the trail as the mediator between God and his followers, alternately scolding and fearlessly leading them to their promised land. Along these same lines, Keil reported a dream that he had while detained at The Dalles. "I dreamt that I was sounding a trumpet for the start," he wrote, "suddenly someone whispered into my ear that I should not sound it, that the enemy were near. At the same time I saw myself surrounded by the enemies and my people scattering in every direction in flight. The instrument which I held in my hand would not give forth a sound; on the contrary I heard a great battle cry."[16] While other interpretations are certainly possible, Keil considered the dream a prophetic warning that his people would be helpless without his leadership. Almost immediately, an incident seemed to confirm his interpretation: while he was detained, the main group had traveled to the cascades, and Keil later learned that they had nearly capsized in a flatboat accident. Keil wrote to Bethel about this dream, and he must have told the emigrants also. The colonists expected such experiences from their leader, and they were a key source of his influence.

The crossing was difficult in other ways. Many oxen and cattle died, and the dry, dusty land and poisoned grass plagued animals and humans alike. Keil declared that such conditions were the curse of the devil. Told at Laramie that "we were starting on our way to hell," Keil warned those remaining at Bethel: "You have your earthly home which the Lord has given you. Do not dispose of it until you get further news of me." Keil described one section after they had missed the correct trail: "We drove the whole night. Some of our oxen collapsed before we reached the ford and died. Some cows perished from weakness. No grass, no water, was to be found anywhere...." As supplies dwindled Keil expressed more concern. He described Salmon Falls on the Snake River as "a horrible world..., everywhere in nature the signs of death and destruction...the roads actually marked out by graves and bleaching bones." "The desert cried out," he wrote, "that we should perish there." But Keil thrived in situations which forced his people's dependence upon him. After the train reached a safe camp he gloated that "the devil had been put to shame."[17] When colony members John Stauffer and Michael Schafer, coming from Willapa, met the caravan near Boise, the colonists were cheered. The reestablished contact with other members confirmed their hopes that the end to the trip was near. Soon all arrived safely in Oregon.

After a journey of four and a half months, Keil wrote his first letter from Willapa on October 13, 1855. Most of the colonists had remained in Portland while Keil and families of the scouts traveled to Willapa. A few nights before reaching Willapa Keil had a vision in which many Bethelites were standing before him; they "expressed the wish that I might come back into their midst. My love for them became so fervent that if I had wings I would have flown to them on the spot."[18] This experience offers insight into how Keil was able to maintain influence over two communities separated by 2000 miles. His letters implied that he was very much with the Bethelites, lest they forget.

To the distress of his scouts, Keil reacted negatively to Willapa. Weary from six months on the trail, Keil had little patience with a site that he considered unsuitable. "On the first day of our stay," he wrote, "I climbed to the top of one of the prairie hills... and saw at first glance that the purpose of Bethel Society could not be accomplished here...." He claimed that he felt greater danger in Willapa than on the trail. After a tour of the farm settlements Keil summarized the site's deficiencies: "Our clothes and shoes actually rot on our bodies because of the mud and wetness. We are imprisoned worse than prisoners in jail. In Oregon a barrel of flour costs $3.50, while in Bruceville [nearest supply for Willapa] it costs from $15.00 to $20.00 and at present it is impossible to get there by boat." Keil now realized that an isolated spot like Willapa could not meet the economic needs of a communal society. "In the first place," he wrote, "there is no market for the things produced; in the second place there is no prospect for the development of such a market; in the third place everything that one needs is too far away and too expensive, and there is no way by which one can earn his livelihood."[19]

Keil cautioned the Bethelites to hold their lands, as he could not promise the continuity of the society under such conditions. He expressed anger with the judgment of his scouts. "Their valley," he wrote, "is very much enclosed but the minds of the three men who own the prairie, which can scarcely be reached by man, and who nevertheless invited thousands of people to come hither, those minds are still more closed in." Nevertheless, the apparently hopeless situation energized Keil. Declaring that he was a man who "possesses the key to unlock all hidden places and publicly proclaims what he has seen," he announced his intention to look for a new site in Oregon.[20]

At Willapa in December of 1855 Keil buried Willi. What should have been the end of a journey was now only the beginning. It appeared that Keil had erred in his judgment. He had not anticipated the difficult conditions, and he started to blame the ones who had followed his instructions. This alienation of some of the colony's finest members had lasting implications, and created doubts about Keil's overall leadership. While the trail experience demonstrated Keil's charismatic qualities, the trail's end showed that external factors could not be overcome. Just as important, Keil's rejection of Willapa signalled a fundamental change in direction for the colony. Short of supplies and exhausted, Keil looked for a site close to markets, abandoning his call for an isolated environment. Eventually he chose a site in the Willamette Valley, an area of rapid growth. The Aurora Colony was located in Oregon's populated interior valley, and its members soon learned to adapt to the conditions created by such proximity to neighbors and markets. But the move to Aurora radically altered Keil's communal dream and probably hastened the colony's breakup.

During the winter of 1856 Keil's colonists were scattered across the country. Perhaps as many as four hundred remained at Bethel, more hesitant than ever to leave their secure homes. About a hundred wintered in Portland, while the rest lived at Willapa in established houses and hastily built shelters. Keil was in Portland working as a physician, and other colony members performed their crafts as well. In this way funds for the community were replenished. It was in Portland that Keil met J.W. Grimm, who told him about available land in the Willamette Valley. Twenty-five miles south of Portland, this land had saw and grist mills from French Prairie days. Keil investigated the situation, purchased two quarter sections of land for $1000, and named the site Aurora after his daughter. Aurora was not isolated. Steamers had penetrated the upper Willamette River close to Aurora, and by the mid-1850s farmers in the Willamette Valley were supplying markets throughout the west. Keil knew that Aurora's products could be marketed, and this apparently was his primary motivation for selecting such a crossroads site.

Former colony member Michael Rapps later recalled that only twenty-five people moved to Aurora in early 1857. By September Keil had applied for postal service; the request form indicated a population of sixty.[21] The scouts at Willapa were reluctant to abandon their claims, and were required to live on them for a period of time because they were Donation Land Claims.[22] Most of Keil's followers in Portland waited for the site to be cleared. Keil organized the initial workers at Aurora by insisting that a work gang either fell a tree or or kill a deer before breakfast. He had chosen a heavily timbered site believing that great economic advantages could be derived from cutting and selling the local fir. The land was cleared, the lumber sold, and extensive orchards were planted. Keil's house was built first--he was the leader and also had his entire family with him--and the others followed. As Keil explained to Charles Nordhoff, "though we had hard work at first, and got ahead slowly, we were soon able to buy out the prairie farmers, who had got into debt and were shiftless, while we were prudent Germans building our place."[23] Once Aurora had been settled, Keil renewed his call for the Bethelites to come from Missouri.

In the early 1860s transportation improvements brought the outside world even closer to the Willamette Valley. The stage coach began a regular north-south route through Aurora in 1862, and the telegraph lines connecting the Pacific Northwest with San Francisco were completed shortly thereafter. Keil let the stages stay at one of his barns, and entertained passengers overnight at his family home while colony members tended the animals.[24] The stage coach brought a greater cross-section of people through the valley. The telegraph brought something equally important: the news informing the colonists about the Civil War. Almost immediately Aurora formed a Union Club, and Keil affirmed his allegiance to the Northern cause at a town meeting. Nevertheless, Keil repeatedly advised the young men back in Missouri to migrate rather than fight. At Bethel a number of young men had joined the militia, and were confused about their options should they be required for service. "I like the active participation of our young men in the war," Keil wrote his deputy at Bethel, "as little as you seem to like it. The impending immigration will then furnish sufficient reason to decline the service." Fear of the Union draft in Missouri and the dangerous internal civil war there became the impetus for the next great migration from Bethel.[25]

The crossing came in 1863, eight years after the first wave. Two hundred fifty-two colonists, including many young men and their families, moved to Aurora. This huge influx of people greatly altered the internal structure of the Aurora community. Keil hoped that the increased manpower would forge Aurora into a stable and cohesive community. But conditions had changed. Some of the emigrants, having been without Keil's direct leadership for eight years, were not willing to be passive followers; indeed, a significant number had not wanted to leave Missouri. Keil himself was not as active in the community because four of his children had died of smallpox within a month in late 1862, and he had not recovered from the shock. At a period when his strong leadership might have helped to heal some of the differences, the leader was withdrawn. Perhaps most important, the new emigration ushered in an era of expansion and prosperity for Aurora. Many of the newcomers were impatient to strike out on their own in the quest for frontier opportunity. Invigorated by their energy and by Keil's own promotionalism, Aurora evolved further from the communal village ideal into a bustling, market-oriented settlement bent on assimilation into American life.

The 1863 crossing was also casualty free for the colonists, but as recorded in diaries, it had a different flavor than that of 1855. Christopher Wolff, a German professor, led the crossing. Wolff followed Keil's example of friendly treatment of the Indians, on one occasion expressing anger when a group of girls found Indian beads and brought them to camp. "He scolded us," wrote one girl later, "for robbing Indian burial places of these tokens of deep regard of their loved ones."[26]

In other respects, however, the crossing contrasted with 1855. Without Keil's charismatic leadership, the colonists resorted to a formal style of organization similar to other caravans along the trail. George Wolfer described the procedure:

The migrating group were divided up into companies. A company was made up of three wagons: two heavy wagons and a light wagon. Two cows were allowed for each company. . . . Eighteen people to each company were formed largely of families. . . . Our 1863 wagon train was composed of 42 wagons and 252 souls, making fourteen companies. . . . each day found a different group at the head as leaders of the day, who brought up the rear the next day and fourteen days later again kicked up the dust for benefit of company No.2. One fire was made for each company when the camp circle was made.[27]

A second contrast with 1855 was the unmistakable presence of dissent. Some of the colonists clearly would have preferred to stay in Missouri. "The plains is nothing but sandy soil and covered with bones," wrote Walter Bauer. "I and Boehringer think of Bethel every day. [We've allowed] one year and if we don't like it we come home in June.... I think I won't find no place like Bethel." The crossing made Bauer homesick: "I wish I could be at home yet and help to work in the shop which I rather do than be on this journey. Some days we haven't got no water hardly fit to drink." Bauer was relieved when the trip was completed, but he vowed to "never cross that way anymore."[28] Christina Wolfer also doubted the wisdom of the trip, but grudgingly acceded to the "orders" to migrate.[29]

George Wolfer's diary provides mundane details of the trip. Colony marksmen shot antelope and other animals while the wheelwrights and blacksmiths kept busy repairing the wagons. Although they had left Bethel partly to avoid the war, the colonists showed their patriotism with a celebration on the 4th of July. Wolfer recorded that "we hoisted the Stars and Stripes and fired two rounds and cheered for the Union."[30]

The wagon train arrived in Aurora in early October. Weary from the trail and remembering the prosperous community they had left behind, the Bethelites were disappointed by the sight of

Aurora. "Toward noon," Wolfer noted, "we arrived at the old bridge over the Pudding River [and] began the long, winding climb over a narrow timber road to Ziegler's barn. Here I met Henry Fry, whom I knew well, and asked him, 'How far is it to Aurora?' 'You are right in Aurora,' answered Henry. . . this so took the wind out of my sails that I was speechless. . . . We had given little thought as to what Aurora might look like and we were rather loathe to accept the truth so disrupting was the effect.[31]

Still, families who had been separated for eight years held celebrations which lasted several days. Then they moved to land recently purchased by Keil in anticipation of the new arrivals. The great wagon train arrival found the leader listless and uninspired. Life had changed at Aurora since the death of Keil's children. "We have had some sorry times since we are here in Oregon," wrote Jonathan Wagner, "when the Dockt Keil lost his four grown children at the awful sickness of smallpox. Dockt Keil takes it very hard up to the present time. . . . Indeed, such a time I have never witnessed and never want to witness again."[32] Some members later suggested that Keil started to lose control of the colony at this time. They recalled that when other members' children died he showed little concern, but in speaking of his own sacrifice he referred to it as "an offering for the sins of others."[33] This kind of judgment could have soured Keil's relationship with his followers. Others needed no dissatisfaction with Keil to be disappointed with Aurora. Walter Bauer expressed a fundamental problem that the Missouri craftsmen felt with the western part of America. "This country is not fit," he wrote his brother in Missouri, "no how for our trade. The timber is nothing but fur wood [sic].... I wish I could be with you for to learn my trade. I think it would do me more good than to pass my time in this mud hole. I hope we will soon see each other for we don't like it in Oregon."[34]

But William Keil always had vocal supporters, and they came to his defense. John Wagner wrote that no one had been forced to come to Oregon. "Them that don't like it can return to Missouri again or another Country as this is a free country and so I can't help it if some don't like it. I didn't tell any of them to come.

They all came from their own free will." Wagner was disturbed that many of his old friends who arrived in the 1863 train stayed in their own groups. He attributed this problem to a growing division within the colony specifically focusing on William Keil's leadership. "I am still a lover of Old Dockt Keil," he wrote, "and will always be & now I will tell you the boys mostly stays at Scheulys & the Scheulys are down on old Dockt and his ways of doing business in this country."[35] It is perhaps significant that Adam Schuele had been one of Keil's scouts, and was specifically mentioned by Keil in his letter to Bethel expressing anger about the Willapa site.

What emerges from this correspondence is that Keil's lack of direct control over the Bethelites had made them more independent. His alienation of the scouts had made some of them angry, and there were a significant number in both groups to create a stir in Aurora. The younger members were more objective than their elders in assessing Keil. Henry T. Finck is an example of such younger members who had been exposed to a variety of experiences which Keil's philosophy did not seem to cover. He had been privately tutored by Christopher Wolff, and his father purchased many current books for his children. "Dr. Keil," wrote Finck, "though personally rather unprepossessing, short and heavy, had a pleasant manner and an undoubted gift of leadership, and he managed to blind his followers to his own selfishness. The colonists gladly gave him the lion's share of their best without questioning his right to it, and he died the rich man of Aurora."[36] Finck did not mean to attack Keil's followers or his religious beliefs: the ideals established by Keil were strongly believed even during the times of difficulty, and Finck noted that most colonists were "extremely kind, good-natured, sensible, and mutually helpful." But Finck implied that Keil had duped his simple-minded followers, and that both had too "little knowledge" of the world to compel the obedience of their more ambitious and sophisticated children.[37]

Keil himself reflected on the situation in a song he wrote in 1864. The song, referring to a dream or vision, portrayed Keil as the leader, up before sunrise to watch over his sleeping flock. "In the spirit of friendship" he called them to "the work of God," but his message had not been heeded, and he berated his followers for their "poor attention."[38]   Keil continued to project a mystical image of leadership by speaking of a communion with God. But some colonists, especially those at Bethel independent of his influence for a number of years, sensed a contradiction between some of his actions and his proclamations.

This is not to suggest that an open revolt raged. By 1864 Keil had recovered and was organizing the building projects which occupied most of the colonists' time. New migrations brought over two-thirds of the Bethelites to Aurora by 1867. A colony church and hotel were completed that year, and these buildings served as focal points for community achievement. The church was built after members of the 1863 crossing complained about a lack of services in town. The hotel allowed the colonists to capitalize on the growing traffic in the valley. A restaurant at the Oregon State Fair had brought respect for the colony's food to many outsiders, and the hotel provided an obvious vehicle to feed travelers at a profit to the community. Until 1870 the hotel catered mainly to stage riders, but in that year the Oregon and California Railroad came through Aurora, and the hotel's reputation grew apace. Henry Finck noted that the engineers stopped in Aurora for their meals rather than go to Portland.[39]   Keil himself often entertained railroad magnate Ben Holladay or Federal Judge Matthew Deady. "I wish," Deady wrote in his diary, "there was a Dutch Town [Aurora] at every station in Oregon."[40]   There is irony in the fact that Keil, who originally came west hoping for an isolated paradise, now let his colonists serve meals to passengers of the railroad, the greatest vehicle of change in nineteenth century America. By moving to Aurora, Keil had assured that his people would be living in a faster paced environment. More than that, through correspondence and visits with railroad promoter Holladay, Keil had enthusiastically sought construction of the railroad through Aurora. The razing of buildings for a railroad "right through the middle of town" might have caused a stir in Bethel, but Henry Finck noted with tremendous enthusiasm that Holladay had "changed the whole country! Our town looks quite unlike what it was last year."[41]

441

Finck had summed up life in Aurora in 1870: little remained from the early days. While the Aurora colonists continued to share property and labor, the people knew that the town was caught in the rush to progress which so typified life in America at the time. As early as 1866 documents were signed at Aurora which transferred some of Keil's property to the trustees. These documents defined some of the colony's ground rules for the members who had not been with Keil for years; the very fact that such "Articles of Agreement" had to be drawn reflected the changing situation. At the same time, there was some concern that Aurora could not always remain a communal society and legal procedures were initiated to ease the process of property division.[42] This attempt to divide some of Keil's authority met with some resistance among Keil's loyalists. They did not want Keil to relinquish his position, and, in actual fact, he did not. But written documents were now in the hands of the trustees which legally changed ownership of some lands, and also laid out specific requirements for membership in the colony. Christopher Wolff favored these moves, fearing that the colony could not survive Keil's death if ground rules were not available for reference.

In 1872 a larger division of property occurred. Most colonists had at least partial ownership of their land after this year. A document in the United States Court for the District of Oregon indicates that Keil intended a complete division of property at a later date. Recently discovered evidence suggests that some colony members were contemplating the end of the colony as early as 1869. Phillip Snyder wrote a letter that year to relatives in Bethel detailing this attitude: "I have no more the high opinion of Colony life which I had three years ago: to say the least, if I should advise you from the foundation of an honest and loving heart; I would say make not a step to leave your old situation for I look for gradual dissolution here, annoyance, & trouble, till separation succeeds at last."[43]

Keil died without warning on December 30, 1877. His death created tremendous confusion at Aurora, but his appointed trustees were able to manage the situation. Still the people were stunned.

"This will make a nice mess," wrote Henry Finck, "I am sure that if I still lived at Aurora I would have a house full of people asking me what to do. But I haven't the least intention to mix myself up in this affair. I had not seen Keil for four or five years. Dissatisfaction had been rife for a long time...the Doctor's old adherents had died lately and the more recent members of the colony would have gone away were they not held by their houses, barns, and gardens."[44]

With Keil's death steps were taken to end the communal experiment. Christopher Wolff wanted the socialistic dream to continue, but most members at Aurora had long since realized that such a lifestyle was impractical in their location. By 1883 the Aurora question had been settled in Federal courts under the jurisdiction of Matthew Deady, and the people were on their own. "All the noise in Aurora's streets," wrote Wolff in 1888, "is for making money plenty to live, and to clothe."[45]

William Keil had left the Methodist church in Pennsylvania claiming that its leaders were not following the example of Christ. He took his followers from Pennsylvania to Missouri and later to the west coast, declaring that at every location they had succumbed to the world's temptations, and needed to find renewal in another setting. But in the west Keil reached the end of his frontier; he had no place else to lead his people. The 1855 migration had reestablished his people's sense of mission and solidarity, but also had divided them into two geographic camps. After the advance group's arrival at the frontier, the Northwest's truly isolated environment overwhelmed Keil and led him to compromise his dream of an independent communal society by settling in the growing Willamette Valley. Attempting to be *in* the world but not *of* it, Keil and his followers had yielded at each settlement to the pressures of frontier survival and, later, to the temptations of frontier opportunity. In 1879 the legal divisions of property were concluded when representatives from Aurora returned to meet with the colony members at Bethel who had never left. Ironically, the members of Keil's colonies arranged a peaceful end to their communal experiment by coming together as one at their old home far from the thriving frontier town of Aurora.

Notes

1. For histories of Bethel and Aurora see Charles Nordhoff, *The Communistic Societies of the United States* (1875; rpt. New York: Schocken, 1965), pp. 305-330; Robert J. Hendricks, *Bethel and Aurora* (New York: Press of the Pioneers, 1933); and William Bek, "The Community at Bethel Missouri and its Offspring at Aurora, Oregon," *German American Annals*, 7 (1909): 257-276, 306-328; 8 (1910): 15-44, 76-81.

2. Robert V. Hine, *Community on the American Frontier: Separate But Not Alone* (Norman: Univ. of Oklahoma Press, 1980), 49-69.

3. Carl Koch, *Lebenserfahrungen* (Cleveland: The German Press, 1871), Ch. 5, p. 5. (translated by Ann Rudolf, Canby, Oregon, 1981).

4. Bek, "Bethel," 266.

5. Henry Will, Letter to Editor, *Shelby County Herald*, January 15, 1930, reprinted in *Shelby County Herald*, October 1, 1980.

6. William Keil to Henry Conrad Finck, October 13, 1855, translated by William Bek. English copies on file at Ox Barn Museum, Aurora, Oregon.

7. See Hendricks, *Bethel and Aurora*, 19; Nordhoff, *Communistic Societies*, 306,308; and Bek, "Bethel," 314.

8. Clark Moor Will, The Oregon Trail Crossing File, Ox Barn Museum Collection. Mr. Will did much original research into the history of the Aurora Colony. The University of Oregon Manuscript Library and the Ox Barn Museum Library contain a mass of research materials, largely unpublished.

9. Will, Oregon Trail Crossing File.

10. Quoted in Edgar White, "The German Pilgrims," *Missouri Life*, September-October 1978, p. 19.

11. William Keil to Henry Conrad Finck, June 24, 1855, Ox Barn Museum Collection.

12. In the most reliable account of the overland migration, John Unruh notes that 1855 was especially full of sensational rumors and hoaxes about Indian attacks. The actual number of incidents and casualties was quite low. See John D. Unruh, Jr., *The Plains Across: The Overland Emigrants and the Trans-Mississippi West, 1840-1860* (Urbana: Univ. of Illinois Press, 1979), 176, 185.

13. William Keil to Henry Conrad Finck, June 24, 1855, Ox Barn Museum Collection.

14. Ibid.; see also William Keil to Henry Conrad Finck, July 12, 1855, Ox Barn Museum Collection.

15. William Keil to Henry Conrad Finck, October 13, 1855, Ox Barn Museum Collection.

16. Ibid.

17. Ibid.

18. Ibid.

19. Ibid.

20. Ibid.

21. William Keil, Request Form for Postal Service, September 24, 1857, Ox Barn Collection.

22. William Keil to Henry Conrad Finck, October 13, 1855, Ox Barn Museum Collection.

23. Nordhoff, *Communistic Societies*, 308.

24. *The Oregonian*, April 9, 1863, p. 3, col. 1.

25. William Keil to Henry Conrad Finck, March 18, 1862, Ox Barn Museum Collection.

26. Will Family Records, Ox Barn Museum Collection.

27. George Wolfer Records, Oregon Trail Crossing File, Ox Barn Museum Collection.

28. Walter Bauer to Theodore Bauer, 1863, copy in Ox Barn Museum Collection.

29. Frederick Woodward Skiff, *Adventures in Americana* (Portland, Ore.: Metropolitan Press, 1935), 216.

30. Diary of George Wolfer, Typescript copy by Velma Scholl, Ox Barn Museum Collection. Original in possession of Velma Scholl.

31. Clark Moor Will, notes from conversations with George Wolfer, Oregon Trail 1863 Crossing File, Ox Barn Museum.

32. Johnathan Wagner to Theodore Bauer, May 14, 1863, Ox Barn Museum Collection.

33. Skiff, *Adventures*, 218.

34. Walter Bauer to Theodore Bauer, February 11, 1866, Ox Barn Museum Collection.

35. Johnathan Wagner to Theodore Bauer, January, 7, 1864, Ox Barn Museum Collection.

36. Henry T. Finck, *My Adventures in the Golden Age of Music* (New York: Charles Scribner's Sons, 1925), 38.

37. Ibid., 39. Nordhoff, *Communistic Societies*, 320-323, also stresses the lack of sophistication and ambition among Keil's peasant followers.

38. Martha Miller to Catherine Kocher, June 6, 1864, Ox Barn Museum Collection. Translations by Clark Moor Will and Garfield Voget. Keil's song was enclosed in this mailing.

39. Finck, *Golden Age*, 39.

40. Malcolm Clark, ed., *Pharisee Among Philistines: The Diary of Judge Matthew P. Deady 1871-1892* (Portland, Ore.: Oregon Historical Society, 1975), I, 24.

41. Finck, *Golden Age*, 24.

42. Hendricks, *Bethel and Aurora*, 209. See 215-217 for the Articles of Agreement.

43. Philip Snyder to Michael Snyder, October 31, 1869, Ox Barn Museum Collection. Copy from original in possession of James Miley, Sr.

44. Finck, *Golden Age*, 40

45. Christopher Wolff to Andy Fry, January 2, 1888, Ox Barn Museum Collection. Original lost, copy made by Clark Moor Will at Fry home in 1955.

20.
The Far East, the Far West, and the Second Coming: The Unification Church in America

James McBride

Founded by the Reverend Sun Myung Moon in his native Korea in 1954, the Holy Spirit Association for the Unification of World Christianity--better known as the Unification Church--has grown from its humble origins as an obscure Asian sect into a powerful world-wide religio-political organization. Although the dramatic rise of the Unification Church bears witness to the intensity of its members' faith and the organizational prowess of its leaders, this new religious movement has frequently been perceived as an alien authoritarian ideology, foreign to traditional American religious and political values. The controversies surrounding the Church's conversion practices, ("brainwashing" *versus* "deprogramming"), its business activities as a religiously-protected "financial empire," and its attempts to gain political influence ("Koreagate") have made the Church subject to close government scrutiny.

The notoriety achieved by the Unification Church in the United States has raised certain basic questions: What are the beliefs and ultimate purposes of the Church? Why did the Reverend Moon bring the Unification Church to America? How did this little-known heterodox Christian movement attract so many adherents in a modern technological society and evolve into such a powerful religio-political institution? And finally, what will be its future course of development? This essay addresses these questions by outlining the origins, doctrine, and development of the Unification Church, with particular reference to its history in the San Francisco Bay Area.

Early History and Doctrine of the Church

Although institutionally established in South Korea in 1954, the Unification faith is based on a series of divine revelations made to

449

the Reverend Sun Myung Moon some twenty years earlier. Moon reported that the first of these revelations occurred on Easter morning in 1936 when Jesus appeared to him and announced that he had been chosen by God to effect the physical restoration of the cosmos. Although raised in a family of Pentacostal Christians (many of whom were persecuted by the Japanese, who encouraged emperor worship), Sun Myung Moon was educated in Imperial Japan. Returning to Korea, Reverend Moon began preaching during the post-war era in his native village of Pyongyang in the north and developed a small following. His was one among many of the new religions (*Sin Jonggyo*) which proliferated during this period in Japan and Korea. Imprisoned in a labor camp in 1946 and again in 1948 ostensibly for anti-communist activity, he fled south to Pusan during the Korean War and later moved with his disciples in 1953 to Seoul, where he incorporated the Church as the *Tong Il-Kyo*.[1]

With its emphasis on premillennial expectation and anti-communist ideology, the Church grew rapidly in South Korea during the late 1950s and early 1960s, exhibiting a notable emphasis on recruiting youth and building a highly centralized hierarchical bureaucracy. The *Tong Il-Kyo* flourished largely due to its benign relationship with the Korean government under Presidents Rhee and Park, fostered by Colonel Bo Hi Pak, a graduate of the Korean Military Academy and aide to the Korean Vice Minister of Defense, who converted to the Unification faith in 1957.[2] Another Korean convert, Reverend Sang Ik Choi, brought the Church to Japan in 1958 (where he remained until 1964 when he was deported by the Japanese immigration authorities) and quickly established a student-based movement which emphasized a communal lifestyle.

The evangelical message of the Unification movement is based upon the teachings of the Reverend Sun Myung Moon and his disciples, most notably Mr. Hyo Won Eu, President of the Korean Unification Church during its early years, who lectured on the "Principles" derived from the new revelations granted the Reverend Moon. At the behest of an Australian Apostolic missionary, the Reverend Joseph McCabe, these teachings were translated into English by Ms. Young Oon Kim, a former Methodist seminarian and Professor of New Testament studies at Korea's Ewha University. As elaborated in the movement's scripture, Unificationist theology is a hybrid of Asiatic religious concepts (drawn from Taoism, Confucianism and Buddhism) and Protestant premillennial Christianity. Although the *Divine Principle* claims to expound "the basic Biblical viewpoint," there can be little doubt that the text also claims to be a "new revelation" which seeks to reinterpret traditional Christian theology in a heterodox fashion.[3]

As argued by Young Oon Kim, the Church's only widely recognized theologian, Unificationism "is not primarily interested in defending the trinitarian doctrine of the fourth century creeds."[4] Defined in terms of female and male principles, the *Divine Principle's* conception of the Godhead has more in common with the Taoist notions of *yin* and *yang* than with traditional Judeo-Christian cosmogonies.[5] Citing the *I Ching* (the ancient Chinese *Book of Changes*), the *Divine Principle* identifies the Godhead with the *Tao* or "the Way" which is manifest in forces of "negativity" and "positivity."[6] This venerated text does not reveal "the Way" as a God of personality; but Unificationism couples the Taoist cosmology with the Hebrew God YHWH (Exodus 3:14) as the divine subject of being, described in the scientist language of the *Divine Principle* as the "Universal Prime Energy."[7]

Unification metaphysics is further complicated by the "Four Position Foundation," termed "O-D-U action"-- origin, division, union.[8] The division of the One into subject and object (1st and 2nd positions) anticipates both their union (3rd position) and their relation to the origin (4th position). The "Four Position Foundation" embodies both the perfect state of human existence and the physical restoration of the cosmos; however, the primal division of creation, manifest in the First Man and First Woman, was not properly centered on origin, due to Eve's intercourse with Satan, and hence the "Four Position Foundation" was corrupted by the Fall, i.e. the perversion of the "God-centered family." The fate of creation therefore lies in the success of the messianic task to restore the "God-centered family" to humanity. In this respect,

Kim acknowledges the "syncretistic [albeit unconscious] combination of Confucianism and Christianity" in Unificationism, whose patriarchal social organization is marked by attitudes of paternalism and filial piety and by the spectacle of mass marriages performed by "Father" (Reverend Moon).[9] Taoist and Confucian principles are thereby harnessed to a premillennial Christian belief in the Second Coming in which the Lord will bring the Kingdom of Heaven on earth.

Although Unificationism recognizes the messianic claim of Jesus and acknowledges the spiritual redemption of humanity through his crucifixion and resurrection, the *Divine Principle* argues that Jesus failed to bring about the redemption of the body, that is, the physical restoration of the "Four Position Foundation." According to Reverend Moon, the inability of Christian churches to recognize Jesus's failings results from the inadequacy of their Scriptural hermeneutic. They do not recognize the true character of the Bible as a "coded message" which requires "special revelation" to decipher its true meaning.[10] Rejected by the Jews and crucified by the Roman state, Jesus never fulfilled his messianic task, which was not only to ensure the spiritual redemption of humanity but also to marry and establish the perfect "God-centered family."[11] Since the death of Jesus, humanity has awaited the Lord of the Second Advent and his *sanctorum communio*, the reincarnated spirits of the Heavenly Kingdom [a Buddhist influence], who will succeed where Jesus had failed.[12] The Lord of the Second Coming is therefore not merely the Christ but the consummation of all religions: *Miruk-Bul* (the Buddha expected by Korean Buddhists), *Jin-In* (the "True Man" expected by Confucianists) and *Chung Do Ryung* (the "Man with True Words" expected by adherents of Korean folk religion).[13] Yet, the determination of who shall be this Lord of the Second Advent and from which country he should arise is based upon a traditional source of premillennial Protestant Christianity--the Book of Revelations.

Between the opening of the sixth and seventh seals of the Apocalypse, Revelations 7:2-4 records the appearance of an angel who "ascend[s] from the rising of the sun" and seals the servants of God, 144,000 strong, upon the forehead. By coupling Revelations 7:2-4 with Revelations 14:1 in which the Lord appears with the 144,000, the *Divine Principle* identifies Revelations 7 with the Lord of the Second Coming. Interpreting the "rising of the sun" to mean the Far East, Unification theology suggests that the birth of this new messiah must come from one of three nations: Japan, China or Korea. Since China is characterized by a materialist atheism and Japan by Shinto nature worship, the *Divine Principle* deduces that the Lord of the Second Advent must arise from Korea, the "Third Israel," and has already been born.[14] Just as John the Baptist foretold the coming of Jesus, so too did Jesus prophesy the Lord of the Second Advent whom, according to the teachings of Sun Myung Moon, Jesus calls "Father."[15] Although Unification scripture does not identify Reverend Moon specifically as the Lord of the Second Advent, the "secret teaching" of Unificationism (according to the testimony of ex-members) is Moon's messianic role in the redemption of the modern world.[16]

As the "center of the providence of restoration," Korea embodies the microcosm of the cosmic struggle between God-centered and Satanic forces. The 38th parallel, which divides North and South Korea, symbolizes to Unification theology the opposition of "God-ism" and atheistic communism: the former devoted to the rectification of the "Four Position Foundation"; the latter dedicated to its destruction. According to the Unificationist scheme, the "True Parents" of humanity--the Reverend Sun Myung Moon and his second wife Hak-Ja Han--have restored the perfect relationship of man and God through their marriage and the patriarchal blessing of their offspring, the communion of saints (members of the Church). It is the obligation of Unificationists to bring this promise of physical redemption to the world under the auspices of a Unificationist theocracy--a goal which was expected to be fulfilled by 1967 but now has been postponed until sometime after the year 2000.[17] Although Unificationists are committed to this cosmic struggle with international communism, the outcome of this conflict is not predestined. The Lord of the Second Advent may be betrayed or let down by his followers. The physical restoration of the cosmos is contingent on the acceptance by humanity of this new messiah who, like Jesus, must walk the path of tribulation and suffer rejection by his religious contemporaries.[18] Hence, Unificationism is predicated on an "inner-worldly asceticism" which seeks to win over the world for the Lord of the Second Advent and (in the long run) will tolerate no other competitors. For only by converting the globe can the Church fulfill its mission to aid in the restoration of the cosmic primal unity.

The Unification theory of salvation therefore promotes the development of a "Pacific culture"--the anti-communist ideology of the Pacific basin "democracies" (Korea, Japan, and the United States)--which will serve as a bulwark against the spread of "satanic" international Marxism. The choice of the United States as a centerpiece in the religio-political vision of the Unification Church is not incidental. On the contrary, just as Jesus's followers were drawn to Rome as the "hub of the world" in the 1st century A.D., so too must Unificationism migrate to the contemporary "hub of the world"--America--if the Church is to achieve its "dispensational purpose."[19] Accordingly, the Reverend Moon acknowledges the chief claim of American civil religion: that the United States is ordained by God for a divine purpose. Indeed, his Bicentennial speech at Yankee Stadium in 1976 adopted the familiar rhetoric of American missionary nationalism:

> Why has the Reverend Moon come to America where he has encountered such tribulation? Am I pursuing my own honor? Is money my goal? or power? No! Never! I came to America because I know the heart of God. I know that in spite of America's rebellion against him, God will not abandon this country . . . . I know God's will to save the world, and to do this America must lead the way.[20]

American culture during the post-World War Two era was characterized by a process of secularization, in which the benevolent relationship of faith and democratic ideals became increasingly estranged. Unificationism was brought to this country to revitalize the theocratic elements of American cultural and political institutions, and in so doing to resurrect aggressive anti-communism under the umbrella of religion.[21] Unificationism was therefore conceived by the Church as the means to resolve the American cultural crisis of the 1960s by introducing the "Pacific Culture" of "God-ism," born and nurtured in Korea.

Unificationism and America's Fourth Great Awakening

As argued by Max Weber, the institutions of any social order receive validity by means of a social ethic which mediates between principles of socially-sanctioned activities and human experience.[22] Whenever experience and principles are (in the words of the German sociologist Jurgen Habermas) "dysfunctional," that is, whenever everyday life does not live up to the promises of the social ethic, the authority of the whole social system is placed into question.[23]

According to the most influential American sociologists of the postwar period (Mills, Riesman, and Whyte), the twentieth-century transition from entrepreneurial to corporate social structure and the metamorphosis of the "inner-directed" individual into "organization man" displaced the Protestant work ethic with the success ethic. Lives formerly governed by an essentially ascetic drive to be productive and respectable now became focused on upward mobility and the acquisition of status and wealth.[24] The 1960s witnessed a rebellion against this development. Induced by the experience of the Vietnam war, inflation, unemployment, and intensified competition for lucrative positions, the disillusionment of American middle-class youth with the success ethic prompted the exploration of alternative lifestyles and faiths which might infuse a new sense of meaning and purpose into their lives. Moreover, in light of the increased mobility of the population, the apparent demise of the extended family as a viable social unit, and the decline of neighborhood and ethnic communities of support, the individual increasingly faced large bureaucracies and corporations where once there had been communal personal bonds. The abyss between the individual and large organizations announced the need for new "mediating structures."[25] The rise of new religious movements (including the resurgence of evangelical fundamentalism and its political expressions, as well as "cults"[26]) in the 1960s and 1970s can be attributed, at least in part, to this need to fill the vacuum caused by the decline of meaning in the existing social order and the absence of adequate "mediating structures."

Since 1960 American culture has been undergoing what William McLoughlin has called America's "Fourth Great Awakening."[27] The latest study of Middletown, undertaken as a point of comparison with the Lynd sociological studies of the 1920s and 1930s, indicates that more Americans hold religious views today than 50 years ago and that twice the number attend religious services regularly. In the most recent Gallup surveys, 9 out of 10 Americans state a religious preference, and 7 of 10 claim membership in a religious group. Although just 20% of the general populace fit the evangelical profile developed by the Princeton Religion Research Group, 38% declare themselves "born-again Christians." Conducting polls in the "middle-American" city of Dayton, Ohio during the early 1970s, the Gallup Organization discovered that 31% of the young adults interviewed had been involved in a new religious movement, that is, a "cult," charismatic Christian sect or meditation group--a remarkable figure for a sampling in which only 75% recognized Jesus as the Son of God. Other studies in Montreal and San Francisco indicate that between 20% and 25% of the American population has participated in some way in these new religious movements.[28]

Despite these statistics, this religious revival does not suggest that the American cultural crisis has been resolved. It is estimated that between 60 and 80 million people in the United States remain "unchurched"--a figure that indicates the persistence of contemporary secularization.[29] And the secularization of the public domain by the government--on issues such as school prayer and the legalization of abortion--points to the increasing likelihood of conflict along the church-state boundary.[30]

America's "Fourth Great Awakening" has taken shape in basically four types of religious movements: 1) mystical and devotional faiths from the East, such as ISKCON, Transcendental

Meditation, the Divine Light Mission, Sufism, and the Bhagwan Shree Rajneesh movement, 2) human potential movements based on popular psychology with metaphysical, if not explicitly religious, undertones; for example, est, scientology, Esalen-type psychotherapies, 3) the revival of Evangelical and Fundamentalist Christianity, spearheaded by the "Jesus movement" (often absorbed by established conservative Christian churches[31]) and the "electronic church," and 4) highly structured, tightly controlled communal religious organizations, such as Synanon, Children of God, People's Temple, and the Unification Church.[32] The last of these four types is probably the most controversial, since social organization of this type suggests to some critics that these groups are "authoritarian cults." (I place the word "cult" in quotation marks since it has little value in terms of social-scientific description. It is most often employed to designate any religious group deemed by the observer to be socially deviant.) These groups tend to be perceived by the public-at-large as foreign, sinister, deceptive and violent largely due to the tragedy of Jonestown and the charismatic fanaticism of the Reverend Jim Jones. Of those that remain in this fourth category, the Unification Church is probably the best known.

Although the Unification Church has been popularly regarded as a foreign, "destructive cult," dedicated to the subversion of American values and institutions, Unificationism sees itself as the answer to the moral crisis--the "internal test"[33]--of American society which will advance both its own interests and what it perceives to be the true interests of the United States and the anti-communist world. Hence, the turbulence of the 1960s and 1970s appeared to be particularly propitious for the divinely-ordained evangelical task of Moon's adherents. From a more analytical perspective, Unificationism may be categorized as a regressive religio-political movement which attempts to resolve the American cultural crisis by offering a messianic faith based on "inner-worldly asceticism" (similar to the vestigial American "Protestant work ethic") and a Unification ideology reminiscent of American civil religion.[34] It is what scholars have called a "world-transforming movement" which foresees "total, imminent and cataclysmic structural change placed in the context of an interpretation of history that demonstrates its necessity and inevitability."[35]

Aware of the power and influence of the United States as the leading anti-communist country in the world, the Reverend Moon recognized the necessity of evangelizing in America if Unificationism were to achieve its goals as a world-transforming movement. Since the arrival of its first missionaries on the West Coast in the late 1950s, the Unification Church has undergone a slow process of development, influenced by the internal needs of the organization and the socio-political response of the host culture.[36] The three stages in the growth of the Unification Church in the United States may be conceptualized as mission, institutionalization and legitimation.

The Unification Mission to America

The transplantation of the Unification Church from Korea to the United States was largely due to the efforts of Young Oon Kim.[37] Born in Korea but educated during World War Two at Kwansei Gakuin University in Japan, Ms. Kim taught religious studies at Ewha University during the tense postwar era. Assigned by the President of Ewha University to investigate the controversial *Tong Il-Kyo* sect, Ms. Kim met the Reverend Moon in December 1954. She was profoundly moved by lectures on the "Principle" by Hyo Won Eu, one of the Reverend Moon's most articulate spokesmen, and converted to the movement. Dismissed from her position at the University (along with four other faculty members and six students), Ms. Kim spent the next four years working for her new faith, teaching the "Principle" and translating Mr. Eu's lectures into English. In 1959 Reverend Moon chose her to head the Unification mission to the West. Although the Church was highly organized and closely supervised in Korea, Ms. Kim was given free rein by Moon to direct its development in America as she saw fit.

Emigrating to Oregon in January of 1959, the Church's first missionary managed to recruit a handful of converts; however, her work was impeded by the failure to have an adequate English translation of the *Divine Principle*--a project which would consume much of her time over the next few years. In September 1960 a second Unification missionary, David C. Kim, formed a separate Northwest group, and two months later Ms. Kim moved her small community to San Francisco. Despite being hindered by the lack of a scripture in English, the community grew to 20 by 1962 and to 50 by 1964. Although growth was slow, Ms. Kim did discover valuable insights into missionary work which were to have a lasting influence on Unification proselytization in America.

The Unification group in San Francisco found that recruitment based upon indirect contacts, such as leafletting, public lectures, mailings and radio broadcasts, was generally unsuccessful in attracting converts. However, direct contacts with recruits in which the missionary first established a relationship on a human level tended to have a much higher rate of success.[38] Still, recruits were bored by the community's attempt to foist on them week-long study courses or hours-long tapes on the *Divine Principle*. It was accidentally discovered that a two-day group study session, designed originally to train Unification missionaries, was far more effective in securing the conversion of recruits. These seminars became the model for the weekend sessions at the Unification property in Boonville, California which were to gain such notoriety in the "brainwashing" and "deprogramming" controversies of the 1970s. Seeking direct contacts with potential converts, members of the San Francisco organization dispersed throughout the United States in 1964-65 as Unification missionaries.

During the late 1960s three Unification groups developed in the Bay Area: 1) the remnant of Ms. Kim's group, which was now centered in Berkeley; 2) a group headed by David Kim in Oakland, the nucleus for the missionaries sent to the Northwest, and 3) the so-called "Japanese family," led by the Reverend Choi, a former Pentacostal minister and head of the Unification Church in Japan from 1958-64, assigned to the Bay Area by the Reverend Moon himself. Of these groups, the last was the most successful for several reasons. Reverend Choi brought with him half a dozen of the best youth missionaries that the Church had in Japan. This group brought with it the "Japanese model" of the Church, which emphasized a communal lifestyle in which members ate, prayed, proselytized and worked together. (For example, the "Japanese family" bought and ran a highly profitable printing business.) Based upon the experience of proselytization in Japan, Reverend Choi's student-age missionaries targetted young, unattached recruits rather than the older, well-established adults who had formerly been subjected to evangelization. Furthermore, the age difference between Reverend and Mrs. Choi and their youthful recruits established something akin to a parent-child relationship in the "family." Finally, the "Japanese family" emphasized building a utopian community rather than the theological message of the Unification movement. Pursuant to that end, the group held large public meetings with entertainment for young people in the Bay Area and invited them for weekends to the site of the future "International Ideal City," situated on 600 acres of land which the Church had purchased near Boonville in Mendecino County. The ultimate purpose of the "International Ideal City," however, was not the construction of a utopian living experiment but rather the development of a conversion setting, as was evidenced by the Boonville project's later assimilation by the Church's International Re-Education Foundation. By 1970, the "Japanese family" numbered nearly 200, whereas the Berkeley group remained at about 40.

Despite the success of the "Japanese family," the growth of the Unification Church in the United States remained slow, with perhaps only 500 members nationwide by 1971. Competition and even veiled hostility between local semi-autonomous groups, as in the Bay Area, damaged the movement in spite of the establishment of a national headquarters, organized by Ms. Kim in Washington, D.C. in 1966. And whereas the national headquarters, under the supervision of the Reverend Moon's chief aide, Colonel Bo Hi Pak, stressed the Church's anti-communist rhetoric, the West Coast continued to portray the movement as an alternative lifestyle to the dominant culture of American society.

The Institutionalization of the Unification Church in America

The problems of the Unification Church in the United States during its earliest period were organizational, but were to a large extent resolved by the institutionalization of the Church in the 1970s. Although Reverend Moon gave no explicit instructions to either Ms. Kim or Reverend Choi for the organization of the Church, the disarray of the movement was a cause for deep concern, and Moon decided to intervene personally. The fragmented religious movement was galvanized by Moon's second visit to the United States in 1971-72, signalling the birth of his public ministry. Arriving in late 1971, Reverend Moon planned to crisscross the country in five tours, speaking in some 75 major cities including San Francisco, Berkeley and Oakland. The tours had two aims: to raise funds for the expansion of the American Church and to generate masses of new converts.

In order to finance the tours and to purchase two properties in New York (including a former Christian Brothers seminary) for over $1 million, the Church established Mobile Fund-raising Teams by impressing members from Unification Centers across the United States. These teams sold candles and tickets to the tour throughout the country on a seven days-a-week basis. This tactic proved to be highly successful, raising the Church's national income from $10,000 in 1969 to $250,000 in 1971 and over $500,000 in 1972. In light of these phenomenal results, the Church decided to make the Mobile Fund-raising Teams a permanent fixture of the organization. The Reverend Moon also established a new missionary effort, called the "One World Crusade," based on flying squads of Unification missionaries in "Witno-busses" which stopped at shopping centers, college campuses and other public places in an attempt to expand the Church's membership base. Both mass fund-raising and mass evangelism contributed to a new feeling that the Unification Church was a growing national movement, and infused Church members with enthusiasm.

Assigning Directors of the Church, who were responsible for income and membership in the 48 continental states, the Reverend Moon ended the disorganization of the American Church caused by the jealousy of semi-autonomous local centers by requiring the rotation of Church members among the various U.S. centers. The conflict among the Oakland, Berkeley and San Francisco groups was resolved by his personal intervention. By 1974, the reorganization of the Church began to show encouraging results with the establishment of the Unification Seminary in New York, a national membership of over 3000 and an income topping $8 million.

Although the Reverend Choi had been reassigned outside the Bay Area, the "Oakland family" shared in the new growth of the national movement. With the "family" now headed by Dr. Mose Durst, a social psychologist on the faculty of Laney College and the husband of Yeon Soo Im (an original member of the Choi "Japanese family"), membership continued to grow in the Bay Area to over 250 by 1974. Although the East Coast national headquarters persisted in its theological and political orientation, the "Oakland family" continued the "alternative lifestyle" approach initiated by Reverend Choi.[39] Under the auspices of different Unification auxiliary organizations, such as the New Educational Development Systems, Inc. and the Creative Community Project (both directed by Dr. Durst), the Church focused fund-raising and proselytization by selectively targeting single, unattached youths (usually between the ages of 18 and 24) and inviting them to the "Ideal City" for Booneville weekends. By establishing close emotional ties through "lovebombing," de-emphasizing the religious aspect until the very end of the weekend training session, and using shils to stimulate group affirmation and personal testimonies, the "Oakland family" managed to maintain a slow but steady growth.

Despite these successes, the Church's new posture of high visibility had certain disadvantages. The tactics employed particularly by the "Oakland family" led to allegations in late 1973 and early 1974 that the Church was a "cult" and that its members were victims of "brainwashing." Perhaps America's most controversial "deprogrammer," Ted Patrick, drew a chilling portrait of the alleged "cult conversion" process in an interview in 1979:

> [T]hey can create a kind of on-the-spot hypnosis. . . . They come up to you, stand inches away and talk to you or touch you on the shoulder. Then they stare straight into your eye. If they can make eye contact and get the person's trust, then they can put him in a brief hypnotic trance.[40]

Although other critics of new religious movements describe the techniques of "cults" in less hyperbolic fashion, they nonetheless regard "Moonie converts" as victims of "trance induction," "dissociative states," or "snapping," in which brain wave patterns suddenly change.[41] As a result, these and other critics affiliated with the "anti-cult movement"[42] call for state intervention through conservatorships of parents and guardians over adult converts (those over the age of 18) in order to subject them to "deprogramming."

These allegations of somnambulist "mind control" fall under the category of what has been called the "Invasion of the Body Snatchers" model of conversion, where ostensibly "normal" children become "zombies" overnight and are stolen from their parents.[43] However, there is little sound evidence to support these charges. Testimony from most ex-Moonies is tainted since they are under social pressure from deprogrammers, parents and the anti-cult movement to account for their apparent deviant behavior, which can only be effaced (and the convert exonerated) if the individual were the passive "victim" of "brainwashing."[44] And whereas a case may be made for the effectiveness of systematic social influence used by new religious movements, neuropsychologists give no credence to the "snapping" myth of "sudden personality change."[45]

Although members of the psychological profession reject the "brainwashing" model as either too crude or inadequate to explain the process of conversion, other psychological models, such as religious totalism, authoritarianism or coercive persuasion, have been employed to describe this process of religious conversion to "cults"--a development which Robbins and Anthony have called the "medicalization of deviant religious groups."[46] However, these descriptive models, like "snapping," prove to be highly problematic. Robert Lifton's model of religious totalism is frequently invoked to support allegations of "cultist mind control." Lifton suggests that the only legitimate conversion is based upon rational conviction or a private peak experience, but no room is made for nonrational evangelization, commonly recognized as a legitimate technique of mainline churches, as well as clearly lying within the constitutional right to freedom of religion.[47] The Loyola sociologist Edward Levine has argued that "cults" are "strongholds of authoritarian personalities"--a model of psychological aberration used to explain the attraction of followers for a fascist leader. However, in a 1981 study conducted by the Center for the Study of New Religious Movements in Berkeley, converts to the Unification Church were found to be no more "authoritarian" than those of a local mainstream Lutheran congregation.[48]

Other critics have suggested that since "cultic conversion" techniques resemble the coercive persuasion model described by Edgar Schein in his study of Chinese Communist "brainwashing" of American prisoners, it is incumbent upon the state to "rescue" converts from their new religious faiths through court-ordered conservatorships and "deprogramming."[49] However, since coercive persuasion may be used for good ends--witness Alcoholics Anonymous--as well as bad, these techniques are not inherently evil. And although private citizens may make judgments on the use of such persuasion, the state is constitutionally proscribed from doing so: it cannot decide what is good and what is bad religion.[50] Even if one could prove (using one of these psychological models) that a convert has become mentally incompetent, those designated incompetent or insane have a constitutional right to practice their religious faith.[51] Finally, empirical studies belie the claim of "cultic mind control." In a London study which surveyed 1000 persons who attended two-day Unification training sessions in 1979, only 8% joined the

Church, and two years later only 3.5% remained.[52] In spite of the myths surrounding "brainwashing," Church membership seems to be one of the major problems of the Church, which currently has perhaps only 5000 members in the United States.[53]

Hindered in its attempt to build a mass movement in the United States by the failure of its evangelical mission and the controversies surrounding "brainwashing" and "deprogramming," the Church attempted to gain political influence during the early 1970s. However, the Church's strategy backfired in the "Koreagate" scandal of 1974-75, in which Korean businessman Tongsun Park (whose alleged influence-buying resulted in a Congressional investigation) implicated Reverend Moon and Colonel Bo Hi Pak. The conclusions of the Fraser subcommittee hearings suggested that the Unification Church was a front for the Korean government and the KCIA and that Reverend Moon, Colonel Pak and Church missionaries had violated the Foreign Registry Act.[54]

Despite the success of Reverend Moon in reorganizing the Unification Church in America, these developments in the 1970s presented the movement with two sets of powerful enemies: on the one hand, irate parents, psychological professionals, politicians and other members of a growing anti-cult movement who saw "Moonie" converts as victims of "brainwashing" by an authoritarian and fraudulent religious sect; on the other, government officials who regarded the Church and its members as primarily political agents of a foreign power. As a result, the Church faced four lines of attack. First, anti-cult critics urged state intervention against the Church on the grounds of "brainwashing," violations of federal labor laws (failure to pay minimum wage, social security and unemployment compensation taxes) and violation of the 13th Amendment (through cultic "slavery"[55]). Second, the Immigration and Naturalization Service sought to stop the immigration of Unification missionaries into this country. On this front, the Church won a victory in September 1982 when a D.C. District Court ruled that Unification Church members are legitimate missionaries of a *bona fide* religion and therefore could not be barred from the country. Third, the New

York State Tax Commission argued that the Unification Church was primarily a political rather than religious organization and therefore owed substantial property taxes on its New York real estate. The New York Appellate Court overturned a lower court decision (which had agreed with the Tax Commission) and held the Unification Church to be primarily religious. Fourth, prompted by Senator Robert Dole in the aftermath of the Koregate scandal, the Internal Revenue Service investigated and successfully prosecuted the Reverend Moon for evading payment of taxes on $165,000 in Church funds placed in his personal bank accounts. The Reverend Moon then served an eighteen-month sentence at the federal prison in Danbury, Connecticut.

The Legitimation of the Unification Church in America

"World transforming movements" like the Unification Church "are highly dependent on gaining both visibility and legitimacy from the society they seek to transform in order to maximize support and minimize opposition."[56] Although the Reverend Moon was incarcerated for tax evasion (thereby enhancing his standing as a "martyr" of the "true faith"), the institutionalization of the Church resulted in modest numerical and substantial financial growth of the movement, which has now entered a period of stabilization and consolidation. Accordingly, Unification leaders are attempting to gain legitimacy for the Church in the eyes of several significant sectors in American society. These sectors include the academic and scientific communities, the mass media and the American religious community.

As outlined in the introduction to the *Divine Principle*, Unificationism is predicated on the *rapprochement* of religion and science:

> The day must come when religion and science advance in one united way, so that man may enjoy eternal happiness, completely liberated from ignorance and directed toward goodness, which is what the original mind desires. Then, mutual understanding will occur

between the two aspects of truth, the internal and the external.[57]

Pursuant to that goal, the Church has placed an increasing emphasis since the early 1970s on its relationship to scientists and academicians, establishing in 1972 the International Conference on the Unity of the Sciences. These annual meetings, held in exotic locations around the world, host leading scientists, philosophers, sociologists, theologians and other academics in order to legitimate Unificationism as a respectable viewpoint.

To dispel its poor public image, as well as to prosletize, the Church has also started two major newspapers, the *New York News World* and the *Washington Times*--neither of which has been financially successful. Although the Church pledged to give the conservative non-Church editors free rein in editorial decisions, the dismissal of James Whelan as editor of the *Washington Times* in the summer of 1984 revived allegations that the Church wants to manipulate the mass media in order to benefit its own ends.

Although the Unification Church wants to be accepted as a respected member of the American religious community, particularly by Christian churches, its attempts to join ecumenical consortia and the National Council of Churches have been rebuffed, largely because of its Eastern cosmogony and views on the Second Advent. Whereas the Church may be called Christian, its dogma falls beyond the pale of the Christian tradition that American Protestant churches adhere to.[58] Ironically, despite its doctrinal differences with both mainstream and evangelical Christians, the Unification Church has found support from the National Council of Churches, whose Office of Religious Liberties closely allied itself with the Church on the "deprogramming" issue and filed an *amicus* brief in defense of Reverend Moon in his recent tax evasion case.

Despite the minimum support and limited instructions given to its first missionaries in the United States, the arrival of the

Unification Church on the West Coast twenty-five years ago was not purely happenstance but a result of the premillennial logic of Unification theology. The apocalyptic confrontation between "God-ism" and atheism, Unificationism and communism made necessary the evangelical mission to America. Its religious and political message was strident, but the Unification movement took hold and grew largely because it arrived in the United States during the turbulence of the 1960s, when American society was undergoing a cultural crisis, and because the Church proved flexible enough (through such experiments as the "Japanese family" and the "Oakland family") to adopt a countercultural posture and aggressive recruiting techniques. Although beset by controversy over the past decade, the recent consolidation of the Church's gains and its attempts to gain legitimacy suggest that debate over the movement in the future will focus increasingly on the Church's economic and political activities rather than on the psychological issues of "brainwashing" and "deprogramming."

Notes

1. Although the official Church history attributes Moon's imprisonment to communist persecution, evidence exists that at least the second period of incarceration (1948) was due to complaints from large groups of Christian ministers. During the 1950s Moon and four other male Church members were arrested and tried for sexual impropriety, once again at the behest of scandalized mainline clerics. The ritual practice called *pikarume* required that female converts have intercourse with Reverend Moon in order to "cleanse their blood" and restore the so-called "Four Position Foundation"--a ritual now symbolically enacted through Reverend Moon's blessing at Unification mass marriage ceremonies. Imprisoned for three months during the trial, Moon and his associates were found not guilty. The Church regards this episode as an attempt to discredit the Church's founder by its "satanic" enemies. See D. Syn-duk, "Korea's Tong-Il Movement," 43 *The New Religions of Korea*, 167-80; Frederick Sontag, *Sun Myung Moon and the Unification Church* (Nashville:

Abingdon Press, 1977), 199-200; Young Oon Kim, *Unification Theology* (New York: The Holy Spirit Association for the Unification of World Christianity, 1980), 22.

2. In part due to the friendly relations between the Church and South Korean regimes, the Church has prospered in its native land, amassing a financial empire worth over $100 million including paint factories, a tool machine company (which makes spare parts for the Korean armed forces), a drug manufacturer and a handicrafts company.

3. Kim, *Theology*, 49.

4. Kim, *Theology*, 53.

5. Although the Unification cosmogony is drawn from Taoist sources, Kim argues that the recognition of male and female aspects of the Godhead are not as alien to the Judeo-Christian tradition as it might seem, citing, for example, the Hebrew worship of Astarte, the feminine aspect of the Kabbalistic Sefirah Shekhinah, and the contemporary popularity of radical feminist theology. However, the similarity of the latter, particularly the work of Mary Daly, with Unification theology, is tenuous at best since both official Church dogma and its code of social behavior are emphatically patriarchal. Kim, *Theology*, 57.

6. *Divine Principle* (New York: The Holy Spirit Association for the Unification of World Christianity, 1973), Pt. I, Chap. I, Sec. I, 2.

7. *Principle*, Pt. I, Chap. 1, Sec. II, 1.

8. *Principle*, Pt. I, Chap. I, Sec. II, 3 (2).

9. Kim, *Theology*, 77.

10. Reverend Sun Myung Moon, *The New Future of Christianity* (Washington, D.C.: Unification Church International, 1974), 83.

11. "In this manner, due to the faithlessness of the Jewish people, the foundation of substance for the second course of the worldwide restoration of Canaan resulted in failure; accordingly, the foundation to receive the Messiah for this providence was a failure. Naturally, the second course of the worldwide restoration of Canaan also failed." *Principle*, Pt. II, Chap. II, Sec. III, 2 (3). Rabbi James A. Rudin, Director of the Interreligious Affairs Department of the American Jewish Committee, believes that anti-semitism lies at the heart of Unification theology. See his report, *Jews and Judaism in Rev. Moon's Divine Principle* (New York: The American Jewish Committee, 1976).

12. *Principle*, Pt. I, Chap. V, Sec. II, 4.

13. *Principle*, Pt. I, Chap. V, Sec. III, 2: Pt. II, Chap. VI, Sec. III, 3 (4).

14. *Principle*, Pt. II, Chap. VI, Sec. III, 2 (4).

15. *Master Speaks* (Washington, D.C.: Unification Church, 1965), Part I.

16. David G. Bromley and Anson D. Shupe, Jr., *Moonies in America: Cult, Church and Crusade* (Beverly Hills, CA: Sage Publications, 1979), 40-41.

17. John Lofland, *Doomsday Cult* (Englewood Cliffs, NJ: Prentice-Hall, 1966), 267.

18. *Principle*, Pt. II, Chap. VI, Sec. IV.

19. Interview with Colonel Bo Hi Pak on tape for radio broadcast on KPFA, "Who is the Reverend Sun Myung Moon and What is He Up To Anyway?" (Berkeley, CA: Pacific Tape Library, n.d.).

20. Sun Myung Moon, "'God's Hope for America,' Keynote Speech at Yankee Stadium, June 1, 1976," in Irving Louis Horowitz (ed.), *Science, Sin and Scholarship: The Politics of*

Reverend Moon and the Unification Church (Cambridge, MA: The MIT Press, 1978), 8.

21. See, for example, Bryan Wilson, *Religion in a Secular Society* (Baltimore: Penguin Books, 1969) and Bryan Wilson, "The Secularization Debate," 45 *Encounter* 4 (1975), 77-83; see also Thomas Robbins, Dick Anthony, Madeline Doucas and Thomas Curtis, "The Last Civil Religion: Reverend Moon and the Unification Church" in Horowitz, *Science*, 46-73.

22. Max Weber, "Politics as Vocation" (1919) in H.H. Gerth and C. Wright Mills (ed.), *From Max Weber: Essays in Sociology* (New York: Oxford University Press, 1969), 77-128.

23. Jurgen Habermas, *Legitimation Crisis* (Boston: Beacon Press, 1973), 49.

24. C. Wright Mills, *White Collar* (New York: Oxford University Press, 1951), David Riesman, *The Lonely Crowd* (New Haven: Yale University Press, 1950); William H. Whyte, *The Organization Man* (New York: Simon & Shuster, 1956).

25. Peter Berger and Richard Neuhaus, *To Empower People: The Role of Mediating Structures in Public Policy* (Washington, D.C.: American Enterprise Institute, 1977).

26. See James McBride and Paul Anthony Schwartz, "The Moral Majority in the U.S.A. as a New Religious Movement," in Eileen Barker (ed.), *Of Gods and Men: New Religious Movements in the West* (Macon, GA: Mercer University Press, 1983), 127-146.

27. William G. McLoughlin, *Revivals, Awakenings and Reform* (Chicago: The University of Chicago Press, 1978).

28. Theodore Caplow, Howard M. Bahr and Bruce Chadwick, "Piety in Middletown," *Society/Transaction*, January/February 1981, 34-37; *Religion in America, 1982 and 1984* (Princeton: Princeton Research Center, 1982-84); George Gallup,

Jr. and David Polling, *The Search for America's Faith* (Nashville: Abingdon Press, 1980), 25; Frederick Bird and William Reimer "Participation Rates in New Religious and Parareligious Movements," in Barker (ed.), *Gods*, 215-38.

29. J. Russell Hale, *The Unchurched: Who They Are and Why They Stay Away* (San Francisco: Harper & Row, 1980), 40.

30. See Peter Berger, "From the Crisis of Religion to the Crisis of Secularity," in Mary Douglas and Steve M. Tipton (eds.), *Religion and America: Spirituality in a Secular Age* (Boston: Beacon Press, 1983), 14-24. For a discussion of the Constitutional issues raised by the legal battles between the secular bureaucratic state and religious institutions over governmental regulation of mediating structures, see James McBride "'There is No Separation of Church and State': The Christian New Right Perspective on Religion and the First Amendment," in William Shepherd, Thomas Robbins, and James McBride (eds.), *New Religions and the Law* (Chico, CA: Scholars Press, forthcoming).

31. See James T. Richardson, "Experimental Fundamentalism: Revisions of Orthodoxy in the Jesus Movement," Paper presented before the Annual Meeting of the British Sociological Society, Lincoln, England, Fall, 1981.

32. For these categories, see Dick Anthony, Thomas Robbins and Paul Anthony Schwartz, "Les Mouvements Religieux Contemporaines et le Postulat de la Sécularization," in John Coleman & Gregory Baum (eds.), *Concilium* 181 (1983): 15-27.

33. Moon, "Keynote Speech," 9.

34. Although Unification Church members believe that Reverend Moon offers the best hope for America to resolve its cultural crisis, the American public-at-large strenuously disagrees. In a poll conducted by the Gallup organization after Reverend Moon's 1976 Bicentennial tour of America, the public was asked to rank Rev.Moon in terms of approval on a scale from +5 to -5. Of the total sampling 29% were not acquainted with him;

however, of the remainder over two-thirds (50% of the total) ranked him as -5. (Only 1% ranked him +5.) *Religion in America 1977-78* (Princeton: Princeton Research Center, 1978).

35. Bromley and Shupe, "Moonies", 27.

36. See James T. Richardson, "The 'Deformation' of New Religions: Impacts of Societal and Organizational Factors," in McBride (ed.), *Religions and Law*.

37. Much of the material concerning the early history of the Unification Church in the United States is gathered from Michael L. Mickler, "A History of the Unification Church in the Bay Area: 1960-74" (M.A. Thesis, Graduate Theological Union, 1980).

38. This conversion technique which placed a priority on initial bonding became the basis for charges by anti-cult critics that the Unification Church practiced unethical deception. Richard Delgado of the UCLA Law School has argued that "Moonie heavenly deception" is based upon a reversal of two elements-- knowledge and capacity--necessary for informed consent. Whereas recruits initially have the capacity to make an informed judgment about the group, they are intentionally denied knowledge of or misinformed about the name and nature of the group. After their capacity for objective judgment has been impaired by coercive persuasion, they are finally given information about the true identity of the Church. See Richard Delgado, "Religious Totalism: Gentle and Ungentle Persuasion under the First Amendment," *Southern California Law Review* 51 (November 1977); and "Cults and Conversion: The Case for Informed Consent" in McBride (ed.), *Religions and Law*.

39. In fact, the anti-communist line of the Church was so well hidden that members of many years standing in the "Oakland family" were shocked to discover Reverend Moon's support for the American war effort in Vietnam and for Richard Nixon during the Watergate scandal of 1973.

40. Interview with Ted Patrick, *Playboy*, March 1979, 62.

41. Louis J. West and Margaret Thuler Singer, "Cults, Quacks and Nonprofessional Psychotherapies" in *Comprehensive Textbook of Psychiatry III,* ed. H.I. Kaplan, A.M. Freedman and B.J. Sadock (Baltimore: Williams and Wilkins Publishers, 1980); John Clark, Michael Lagone, Robert Schecter and Roger Daly, *Destructive Cult Conversion: Theory, Research and Treatment* (Weston, MA: American Family Foundation, 1981); Flo Conway and Jim Siegelman, *Snapping: America's Epidemic of Sudden Personality Change* (Philadelphia: J.B.Lippincott Co., 1978).

42. Anson Shupe, Jr. and David Bromley, *The New Vigilantes: Deprogrammers, Anti-Cultists and the New Religions* (Beverly Hills, CA: Sage Publications, 1980).

43. See Robert Shapiro, "'Brainwashing,' Personhood and Religious Beliefs," in McBride (ed.), *Religions and Law.*

44. Trudy Solomon, "Integrating the 'Moonie' Experience: A Survey of Ex-Members of the Unification Church," in Dick Anthony and Thomas Robbins (eds.), *In Gods We Trust: New Patterns of Religious Pluralism in America* (New Brunswick, NJ: Transaction Books, 1981), 275-94.

45. Richard Ofshe, "The Role of Out-of-Awareness Influence in the Creation of Dependence on a Group: An Alternative to Brainwashing Theories," Paper presented at the "Conversion, Coercion and Commitment" Conference, Berkeley, CA, June 1981. See also Stephen Chorover, "Organizational Recruitment in 'Open' and 'Closed' Social Systems: A Neuropsychological Perspective," Paper presented at the same Conference.

46. Thomas Robbins and Dick Anthony, "Deprogramming, Brainwashing and the Medicalization of Deviant Religious Groups," *Social Problems* 29 (February 1982): 283-294. See also James McBride and Paul Anthony Schwartz, "On the Application of Religious Totalism and Authoritarian Personality Models to the New Religious Movements," Paper presented at the Annual Meeting of the Western Psychological Association, Sacramento, CA, April 1982.

47. Robert Lifton, *Thought Reform and the Psychology of Totalism: A Study of "Brainwashing" in China* (New York: W.W. Norton & Co., 1961).

48. Edward Levine, "Religious Cults: Refuges for the Emotionally-Distressed, Idealists and Intellectuals and Strongholds of Authoritarian Personalities," paper presented at the "Conversion, Coercion and Commitment" Conference, Berkeley, CA, June 1981. James McBride, Paul Anthony Schwartz, and Connie Jones, "Authority and Authoritarianism in the New Religious Movements: Empirical Considerations," paper presented at the same conference.

49. Edgar Schein with Inge Schneier and Curtis H. Barker, *Coercive Persuasion: A Socio-Psychological Analysis of the "Brainwashing" of American Civilian Prisoners by the Chinese Communists* (New York: W.W. Norton & Co., 1961).

50. See James McBride, "Regulating the Cults: An Analysis of Mandatory Informed Consent," paper presented before the Yale faculty, New Haven, CT, March 1983.

51. Shapiro, "'Brainwashing,'" in McBride (ed.), *Religions and Law*.

52. Eileen Barker, "From Sects to Society: A Methodological Programme," in Eileen Barker (ed.), *New Religious Movements: A Perspective for Understanding Society* (New York: Edward Mellen Press, 1982), 3-14. See also Eileen Barker, "The Ones Who Got Away: People Who Attend Unification Church Workshops and Do Not Become Members" in Barker (ed.), *Gods*, 309-34.

53. According to Unification ideology, the demise of mass evangelism does not impair the Church's ultimate goal of dominating the anti-communist world, since the "Lord of the Second Advent" needs only 144,000 "saints" worldwide in order to usher in the apocalyptic judgment. Although membership remains a problem, the financial basis of the Church is secure. In

an effort to keep a lower profile and cause less controversy, the Church has deemphasized street solicitation, relying largely on its investments in real estate and small local enterprises in the United States, such as the Gloucester, Massachusetts fishing fleet and processing plant, whose purchase is made possible through the transfer of funds from Korea.

54. "Investigation of Korean-American Relations," Report of the Subcommittee on International Organizations of the Committee on International Relations, U.S. House of Representatives, October 31, 1978. Although the Church continues to retain some influence in Washington through Unification-affiliated organizations such as the Freedom Leadership Foundation (an arm of the Reverend Moon's International Federation For Victory Over Communism), the Korean Cultural Foundation and Radio Free Asia, the Church has invested much more time in developing its relationships with right-wing Latin American regimes. Organized by Colonel Bo Hi Pak and directed by Warren Richardson (a former Washington lobbyist for the extreme right Liberty Lobby), CAUSA has been associated with ultra-conseratives and the right wing in El Salvador, Guatemala, Hondorus, Chile, Paraguay, Brazil and Uruguay where, according to the *New York Times*, the Church has invested over $70 million. See "God-ism Promoted Against Communism," *New York Times*, August 28, 1983 and "Uruguay is Fertile Soil for Moon Church Money," *New York Times*, February 16, 1984.

55. Richard Delgado, "Religious Totalism as Slavery," IX *New York University Studies in Law and Social Change*, 1.

56. Bromley and Shupe, "Moonies", 81.

57. *Principle*, 4.

58. Agnes Cunningham, J. Robert Nelson, William L. Hendricks, Jorge Lara-Braud, "Critique of the Theology of the Unification Church as Set Forth in *Divine Principle*" [Official Study Document of the Commission on Faith and Order of the National Council of Churches] in Horowitz(ed.),*Science*, 103-17.

Contributors

Edwin B. Almirol received his Ph.D. from the University of Illinois and is currently Assistant Professor of Anthropology at the University of California at Davis. He is the author of *Ethnic Identity and Social Negotiation: A Study of a Filipino Community in California,* as well as articles in numerous anthologies and professional journals.

David Alvarez holds a doctorate from the University of Connecticut. Professor of Government at Saint Mary's College of California, he has edited *An American Church: Essays on the Americanization of the Catholic Church* and has contributed articles to such journals as the *Catholic Historical Review, The Historian, North American Review* and *Polity.*

Douglas Firth Anderson, currently on the faculty at New College in Berkeley, is a doctoral candidate at the Graduate Theological Union. His article on nineteenth-century San Francisco evangelicals appeared in *Fides et Historia.*

Mark T. Banker is a doctoral candidate at the University of New Mexico. He has contributed articles on Presbyterianism in the Southwest to the *Journal of the West* and the *Journal of Presbyterian History.*

Maureen Ursenbach Beecher studied at Brigham Young University and the University of Utah. An Associate Professor of English at Brigham Young University, she has published articles in numerous journals including *Dialogue, Utah Historical Quarterly* and the *Journal of Mormon History.*

M. Guy Bishop received a doctorate from Southern Illinois University. He is Assistant Curator of Social History at the Los

Angeles County Museum of Natural History. His articles have appeared in *Mid-America, Utah Historical Quarterly,* and other journals.

Jeffrey M. Burns has a Ph.D in history from the University of Notre Dame, where he worked for the Cushwa Center for the Study of American Catholicism. Currently the archivist for the Archdiocese of San Francisco, he is the author of several articles on American Catholicism.

Frances M. Campbell received her doctorate in American religious history from the Graduate Theological Union.

Catherine Ann Curry, P.B.V.M. holds an M.A. in American History from the University of Santa Clara and an M.A. in Theology from the University of San Francisco. Currently a doctoral candidate at the Graduate Theological Union, she is the author of *Mother Theresa Comerford: Foundress of the Sisters of Presentation, San Francisco.*

Eldon G. Ernst is the author of *Moment of Truth for Protestant America: Interchurch Campaigns Following World War I* and *Without Help or Hindrance: Religious Identity in American Culture.* Professor of American Religious History, Archives, and Theological Bibliography at the Graduate Theological Union and the Franciscan School of Theology, he holds a doctorate from Yale University. His most recent writings have examined the place of the West in American religious historiography.

Tony Fels is a doctoral candidate at Stanford University. His article on Jews and Freemasonry appeared in *American Jewish History.*

Contributors

Lawrence Foster received his Ph.D. from the University of Chicago. He is Associate Professor of History at the Georgia Institute of Technology, and the author of *Religion and Sexuality: The Shakers, the Mormons and the Oneida Community*. He has also published articles in such journals as *Dialogue, Journal of Mormon History, Journal of the Early Republic* and the *Utah Historical Quarterly*.

Carl Guarneri is Associate Professor of History at Saint Mary's College of California. He holds a doctorate from Johns Hopkins University, and has contributed articles to such journals as *Church History, Reviews in American History*, and *Journal of the History of Ideas*.

Patrick J. Harris holds undergraduate and graduate degrees from Portland State University. He is the director of the Ox Barn Museum in Aurora, Oregon.

Ronald Eugene Isetti, F.S.C. has a doctorate from the University of California at Berkeley. He is the author of *Called to the Pacific*, a history of the western province of the Christian Brothers, as well as articles in *Cithara* and *The Pacific Historian*. He is Professor of History at Saint Mary's College of California.

Mary E. Lyons received a Ph.D. from the University of California at Berkeley. She is Assistant Professor of Rhetoric and Homiletics at the Franciscan School of Theology in Berkeley.

James McBride received his Ph.D. from the Graduate Theological Union and the University of California, Berkeley. Currently Assistant Professor of Religion at the College of Wooster, he co-edited *Cults, Culture and the Law,* and has published articles on contemporary religious movements in several anthologies.

479

Salvatore Mondello has published articles on Baptists in the West in *Foundations* and *American Heritage*. He is the author of *The Italian Immigrant in Urban America, 1880-1920* and the coauthor of *The Italian-Americans*. He received the doctorate from New York University and is Professor of History at the Rochester Institute of Technology.

Larry G. Murphy is an Associate Professor at the Garret-Evangelical Theological Seminary. He has a doctorate from the Graduate Theological Union, and is the author of an article on the Black church in California in *Foundations*.

Frederick A. Norwood, now retired, was Research Professor of History of Christianity at the Garrett-Evangelical Theological Seminary, where he taught since 1952. Holder of a Ph.D. from Yale, he is the author of *Story of American Methodism, Strangers and Exiles: A History of Religious Refugees*, and numerous other books and articles.

Dale E. Soden received his doctorate from the University of Washington and currently teaches at North Idaho College. His articles have appeared in *Pacific Northwest Quarterly, American Presbyterians* and other historical journals.

William Toll is the author of *The Making of an Ethnic Middle Class: Portland Jewry Over Four Generations*, as well as two dozen articles on American Black and Jewish history. Holding the doctorate from the University of California, Berkeley, he has taught at the University of Michigan and the University of Oregon.

Index

Index

Index

Southern Methodist Univ.

3 2177 02082 2845